D0786284

Workers, Managers, and Technological Change

Emerging Patterns of Labor Relations

PLENUM STUDIES IN WORK AND INDUSTRY

Series Editors:
Ivar Berg, *University of Pennsylvania, Philadelphia, Pennsylvania*
and Arne L. Kalleberg, *University of North Carolina, Chapel Hill, North Carolina*

WORK AND INDUSTRY
Structures, Markets, and Processes
Arne L. Kalleberg and Ivar Berg

WORKERS, MANAGERS, AND TECHNOLOGICAL CHANGE
Emerging Patterns of Labor Relations
Edited by Daniel B. Cornfield

A Continuation Order Plan is available for this series. A continuation order will bring delivery of each new volume immediately upon publication. Volumes are billed only upon actual shipment. For further information please contact the publisher.

Workers, Managers, and Technological Change

Emerging Patterns of Labor Relations

Edited by
Daniel B. Cornfield
Vanderbilt University
Nashville, Tennessee

With a Foreword by
Ray Marshall
University of Texas at Austin
Austin, Texas

PLENUM PRESS • NEW YORK AND LONDON

Library of Congress Cataloging in Publication Data

Workers, managers, and technological change.

(Plenum studies in work and industry)
Includes bibliographies and index.
1. Labor supply—United States—Effect of technological innovations on. 2. In-
dustrial relations—United States. I. Cornfield, Daniel B. II. Series.
HD6331.2.U5W67   1987   331′.0973   87-2327
ISBN 0-306-42450-9

© 1987 Plenum Press, New York
A Division of Plenum Publishing Corporation
233 Spring Street, New York, N.Y. 10013

Printed in the United States of America

Contributors

James D. Abrams, Institute of Industrial and Labor Relations, University of Michigan, Ann Arbor, Michigan

Dennis A. Ahlburg, Industrial Relations Center, University of Minnesota, Minneapolis, Minnesota

Lawrence D. Anderson, Industrial Relations Center, University of Minnesota, Minneapolis, Minnesota

Adria M. Anuzis, Institute of Industrial and Labor Relations, University of Michigan, Ann Arbor, Michigan

Sandra L. Barrett, Industrial Relations Center, University of Minnesota, Minneapolis, Minnesota

Diane P. Bates, Department of Sociology, Vanderbilt University, Nashville, Tennessee

Dick Batten, Department of Sociology, Boston College, Chestnut Hill, Massachusetts

Vern Baxter, Department of Sociology, University of New Orleans, New Orleans, Louisiana

Gordon Betcherman, Institute of Industrial Relations, University of California, Los Angeles, California, and Economic Council of Canada, Ottawa, Ontario, Canada

John P. Byrne, Institute of Industrial and Labor Relations, University of Michigan, Ann Arbor, Michigan

Ann E. Carey, Industrial Relations Center, University of Minnesota, Minneapolis, Minnesota

Deborah K. Carter, Department of Sociology, Vanderbilt University, Nashville, Tennessee

Trudie W. Coker, Department of Sociology, Vanderbilt University, Nashville, Tennessee

Daniel B. Cornfield, Department of Sociology, Vanderbilt University, Nashville, Tennessee

Richard A. Couto, Center for Health Services, Vanderbilt University, Nashville, Tennessee

Michael Cushion, Department of Sociology, Michigan State University, East Lansing, Michigan

Hans-Helmut Ehm, University of Trier, Postfach 2710 Trier 5500

Tracy Elsperman, Institute of Industrial and Labor Relations, University of Michigan, Ann Arbor, Michigan

John Francis, Center for Technology and Policy and Department of Sociology, Boston University, Boston, Massachusetts

Gerald Gordon, Center for Technology and Policy and Department of Sociology, Boston University, Boston, Massachusetts

Allison Haines, Institute of Industrial and Labor Relations, University of Michigan, Ann Arbor, Michigan

Michael Indergaard, Department of Sociology, Michigan State University, East Lansing, Michigan

Arne L. Kalleberg, Department of Sociology, University of North Carolina, Chapel Hill, North Carolina

Katheleen E. Kitzmiller, Department of Sociology, Vanderbilt University, Nashville, Tennessee

Kevin T. Leicht, Department of Sociology, Indiana University, Bloomington, Indiana

David Lewin, Graduate School of Business, Columbia University, New York, New York

Christopher D. Liguori, Institute of Industrial and Labor Relations, University of Michigan, Ann Arbor, Michigan

Karyn A. Loscocco, Department of Sociology, State University of New York, Albany, New York

Bruce A. Lundgren, Industrial Relations Center, University of Minnesota, Minneapolis, Minnesota

Sally Moulton, Center for Technology and Policy and Department of Sociology, Boston University, Chestnut Hill, Massachusetts

Kent D. Peterson, George Peabody College, Vanderbilt University, Nashville, Tennessee

Polly A. Phipps, Department of Sociology, University of Michigan, Ann Arbor, Michigan

Douglas Rebne, Institute of Industrial Relations, University of California, Los Angeles, California

Sara Schoonmaker, Department of Sociology, Boston College, Chestnut Hill, Massachusetts

Arthur B. Schwartz, Institute of Industrial and Labor Relations, University of Michigan, Ann Arbor, Michigan

Arthur B. Shostak, Department of Psychology and Sociology, Drexel University, Philadelphia, Pennsylvania

Robert J. Thomas, Sloan School of Management, Massachusetts Institute of Technology, Cambridge, Massachusetts

Tom Wachtell, Center for Technology and Policy and Department of Sociology, Boston University, Boston, Massachusetts

Michael Wallace, Department of Sociology, Ohio State University, Columbus, Ohio

Peter B. Wood, Department of Sociology, Vanderbilt University, Nashville, Tennessee

Ashraf Zahedi, Center for Technology and Policy and Department of Sociology, Boston University, Boston, Massachusetts

Foreword

Workers, Managers, and Technological Change: Emerging Patterns of Labor Relations contributes significantly to an important subject. Technological change is one of the most powerful forces transforming the American industrial relations system. In fact, the synergistic relationships between technology and industrial relations are so complex that they are not well or completely understood. We know that the impact of technology, while not independent of social forces, already has been profound: it has transformed occupations, creating new skills and destroying others; altered the power relationships between workers and managers; and changed the way workers learn and work. Technology also has made it possible to decentralize some economic activities out of large metropolitan areas and into small towns, rural areas, and other countries. Most important, information technology makes it possible for international corporations to operate on a global basis. Indeed, some international corporations, especially those based in the United States, are losing their national identities, detaching the welfare of corporations from that of particular workers and communities.

Internationalization, facilitated by information technology, has transformed industrial relations systems. A major objective of the traditional American industrial relations system was to take labor out of competition. Internationalization makes it impossible for unions to restrict labor market competition through *national* regulation and collective bargaining alone. International competition and dynamic change also require much greater attention to productivity, flexibility, and international competitiveness. These economic imperatives require that traditional adversarial labor–management relations be complemented by more cooperative arrangements whereby managers pay more attention to worker security, welfare, and development and workers and their leaders are more concerned with the economic viability of firms. In order to survive and grow in an internationalized information world, labor movements must develop policies and procedures to deal with international corporations and global competition.

Workers, Managers, and Technological Change strengthens our understanding of these complex relationships. It is precisely the kind of industry- and craft-specific work required to provide the knowledge base needed by those involved in the industrial relations system as well as those who seek to understand it. This volume does not answer all of the questions raised by technological change, but it makes an important contribution to our understanding and provides an analytical and factual basis for other work on this subject.

RAY MARSHALL

University of Texas at Austin

Preface

Throughout the course of U.S. industrialization, workers and managers have attempted to control the implementation and outcomes of technological change. In an effort to realize enterprise efficiency and profitability, management has endeavored to retain flexibility and control over the adoption of new production technologies; fearing displacement and loss of income, workers have sought control of technological innovation in order to maintain their job security.

The current era of U.S. labor relations is no exception—however, workers and managers in different industries have developed diverse arrangements for controlling technological change and promoting their respective interests. With technological change during the post-World War II period, two patterns of labor relations have emerged. First, in industries such as newspaper printing, insurance, and air traffic control, management has gained more control of the labor process at the point of production in the shop or office. Increased unilateral managerial control has taken a variety of forms, including job deskilling; the wresting of discretion from workers over the determination of work pace and methods; and computerized supervision and monitoring of workers, worker productivity, and quality control.

Second, in other industries such as coal mining, steel, and autos, workers and managers have developed joint labor–management forums for cooperative decision making on company- and, in some cases, industry-wide issues, such as controlling technological change. These cooperative forums, or formal labor–management cooperation, include joint labor–management committees that address productivity, job security, technical, finance, and marketing problems; joint efforts at lobbying the government for legislation which would buffer the industry from market adversity; and worker representation on company boards of directors.

Although both labor relations patterns have occurred simultaneously in some industries, the difference between them is in the extent of labor participation in managerial decision making—especially in decisions about controlling the implementation and outcomes of technological change.

The recent divergence in labor relations trends among U.S. industries has resulted from differences in the legacy of unionization and collective bargaining among industries and in product market conditions. Increased unilateral managerial control has tended to occur in less unionized, high-growth industries; formal labor-management cooperation has been established in the highly concentrated and unionized, mass production industries, whose stable positions in world product markets have been recently jeopardized by increased foreign competition and government deregulation. How workers and managers attempt to control the implementation and outcomes of technological change, then, is associated with the legacy of labor relations and the product market conditions in their industries.

Workers, Managers, and Technological Change is an interdisciplinary effort at exploring this thesis. The book covers the post-World War II changes in technology, employment, industrial organization, market and political conditions and labor relations in 14 U.S. industries. As such, it carries forth the tradition of institutional economics which was fathered by John Commons, elaborated by John Dunlop and Clark Kerr, and, most recently, expanded by Ray Marshall, Peter Doeringer, and Michael Piore. These writers have sought to explain the ongoing changes in the "web of rules" that define the employment relationship and thereby affect the capacity of labor and management to control the outcomes of economic production.

As an interdisciplinary work, the book also extends the so-called "new structuralism" of industrial and organizational sociology to the sphere of labor relations. The new structuralism is a growing body of theory and research which examines the impact of diverse economic institutions and work roles on socioeconomic inequality. Critically building on sociological theory that had emphasized the effect of individual traits, such as education, on inequality, practitioners of the new structuralism have analyzed the influence of unevenness in the growth of firms, capital intensification, industry concentration, and unionization, on inequality among workers in different work settings. *Workers, Managers, and Technological Change* infuses labor–management action into the new structuralism by examining how industrial institutions and market conditions constrain the process and measures by which workers and managers attempt to control technological change.

The 14 industries covered in the book represent a broad array of economic sectors—manufacturing, extractive industries, services, and the public sector. Furthermore, the industries covered by the chapters in Part II have experienced increased unilateral managerial control of the labor process, while those covered in Part III have experienced increased labor participation in company- and/or industry-wide managerial decision making. Each of the chapters in Parts II and III addresses one industry. The introductory and concluding chapters address general changes in the efforts taken by U.S. workers and managers to control technological change, including a comparative analysis of the 14 industries in the concluding chapter.

The collection of articles in this book evolved out of the 1983 General Motors Business Understanding Program, an interuniversity research competition entitled "The Impact of Technology on the Roles and Responsibilities of Labor and Management." We are gratefully indebted to Mary Elliott of the General Motors Corporation for conceiving and coordinating the program, bringing together scholars from diverse disciplines, and for promoting a genuine, scholarly spirit of inquiry. Half of the 16 chapters in this book (Chapters 3, 4, 6, 10–13, 15) are revisions of papers that were submitted to the General Motors competition; the others were commissioned specifically for this book.

Ivar Berg, Arne Kalleberg, and Ray Marshall made helpful comments on the entire manuscript. All of the contributors to this book acknowledge the assistance of many people who are mentioned at the end of each chapter.

DANIEL B. CORNFIELD

Nashville, Tennessee

Contents

Chapter 3

The Eclipse of Craft: The Changing Face of Labor in the Newspaper Industry **47**

Arne L. Kalleberg, Michael Wallace, Karyn A. Loscocco, Kevin T. Leicht, and Hans-Helmut Ehm

Chapter 4

Technology and Control of the Labor Process: Fifty Years of Longshoring on the U.S. West Coast **73**

Gordon Betcherman and Douglas Rebne

Chapter 5

**Technological Change and Labor Relations in the United States Postal
Service** **91**

   Vern Baxter

Chapter 6

**Office Automation, Clerical Workers, and Labor Relations in the
Insurance Industry** **111**

   Daniel B. Cornfield, Polly A. Phipps, Diane P. Bates, Deborah K.
   Carter, Trudie W. Coker, Kathleen E. Kitzmiller, and Peter B.
   Wood

Chapter 7

Computerized Instruction, Information Systems, and School Teachers: Labor Relations in Education **135**

   Kent D. Peterson

Chapter 8

Technology, Air Traffic Control, and Labor–Management Relations   **153**

   Arthur B. Shostak

PART III. TOWARD LABOR–MANAGEMENT COOPERATION?

Chapter 9

Chapter 10

Chapter 11

Technological Change, Market Decline, and Industrial Relations in the U.S. Steel Industry 229

Dennis A. Ahlburg, Ann E. Carey, Bruce A. Lundgren, Sandra L. Barrett, and Lawrence D. Anderson

Chapter 12

Computer-Based Automation and Labor Relations in the Construction Equipment Industry 247

Gerald Gordon, Sally Moulton, Tom Wachtell, John Francis, and Ashraf Zahedi

Chapter 13

The Impact of Technological Change on Labor Relations in the Commercial Aircraft Industry 263

Arthur R. Schwartz, James D. Abrams, Adria M. Anuzis, John P. Byrne, Tracy Elsperman, Allison Haines, and Christopher D. Liguori

Chapter 14

Technological Change in the Public Sector: The Case of Sanitation Service 281

David Lewin

Chapter 15

Deregulation, Technological Change, and Labor Relations in Telecommunications 311

Dick Batten and Sara Schoonmaker

PART IV. CONCLUSION

Chapter 16

Labor–Management Cooperation or Managerial Control: Emerging Patterns of Labor Relations in the United States 331

Daniel B. Cornfield

I
INTRODUCTION

1

Workers, Managers, and Technological Change

Daniel B. Cornfield

I. INTRODUCTION

Robots, office automation and computer-aided design and manufacturing are among the many new technologies challenging traditional labor–management relations. Labor and management in diverse sectors of the U.S. economy are rethinking and rearranging the relationships which bound them throughout most of the post-World War II era. Along with technological change, the globalization of markets, government deregulation, the conglomeration of businesses, and other factors have affected profitability, job security, skill requirements, and the balance of power between labor and management. These changes have raised divergent issues for labor and management, compelling them to reexamine the issue of workplace control and to establish new arrangements for governing the workplace.

The present volume is an interdisciplinary examination of the diverse changes in labor relations arrangements that have accompanied technological change in 14 U.S. industries during the post-World War II era. Despite their theoretical and methodological differences, the sociologists, labor economists, and labor relations experts who contributed chapters to this book address a common problem: the effect of changes in technology, industrial and firm organization, and macroeconomic and political conditions on changing labor relations arrangements—that is, the rules governing not only the allocation and compensation of labor, but also the degree of labor participation in managerial decision making in an industry. Each chapter analyzes this problem in a manufacturing, extractive, service, or public sector industry, taking

Daniel B. Cornfield • Department of Sociology, Vanderbilt University, Nashville, TN 37235.

into account extra-industry factors which have been transmitted to the focal industry via mergers, acquisitions, and conglomeration. This common problem is predicated on the assumptions that technological change is only one of a set of factors—albeit an important and perennial one—which are reshaping labor relations arrangements; and that these changing arrangements simultaneously reflect and in part determine the redistribution of workplace control between labor and management. The concluding chapter derives, from a comparison of the industries covered in this book, an explanation of the inter-industry differences in changing labor relations arrangements, especially regarding the extent of labor participation in managerial decision making.

Termed the "new industrial sociology" by Hill,[1] recent social science research on work and industry has shown a growing concern with the consequences of market and political conditions and the formal features of industries, firms, production processes, and jobs, for the life chances of workers and the viability of business enterprises. Researchers in this vein have variously descended from the insights of institutional economics, Marxian political economy, sociological theory on stratification and class conflict, and industrial and organizational sociology. Their purpose has been to assess the impact of changing extra-industry and formal workplace features upon the capacities of labor and management to pursue and reconcile their competing interests in controlling the conditions and outcomes of economic production, mainly at the shop or office level of decision making.

The research in this book is similarly characterized by this growing concern with workplace control. What distinguishes this book from the new industrial sociology, however, is its emphasis on changing labor relations arrangements. Indeed, Berg and Kuhn have shown how workers and managers develop work rules, informally or through collective bargaining, that constitute a mutually beneficial adjustment to technological change and other workplace changes.[2] Much research in the new industrial sociology has bypassed these arrangements through the use of cross-sectional analyses showing how industry, firm and worker characteristics influence such labor market outcomes as income, unemployment chances, and career mobility. Missing in this research is the dynamic process by which labor and management establish and reestablish rules for controlling and governing the workplace, especially at the company- and industry-wide decision making levels. Yet these rules address numerous issues of contemporary public concern, including issues pertaining to industrial policy and reindustrialization, such as plant shutdown and plant location decisions; to civil rights, such as the controversy over the criteria—affirmative action, seniority and merit—for hiring, laying

---

[1]Stephen Hill, *Competition and Control at Work: The New Industrial Sociology* (Cambridge: MIT Press, 1981).

[2]Ivar Berg and James Kuhn, "The Assumptions of Featherbedding," *Labor Law Journal* 13 (April 1962), pp. 277–283; James Kuhn and Ivar Berg, "Bargaining and Work-Rule Disputes, *Social Research* 31 (Winter 1964), pp. 466–481. For a review of the new industrial sociology, see Randy Hodson and Robert Kaufman, "Economic Dualism: A Critical Review," *American Sociological Review* 47 (December 1982), pp. 727–739.

off, promoting, and transferring employees; and the adequacy of welfare arrangements, such as employer-provided retirement pensions and life and health insurance, to name only a few. In sum, changes in labor relations arrangements reflect and contribute to the continuous redistribution of authority in the employment relationship and, therefore, to the capacities of labor and management to guide their fortunes.

The effect of technological and other changes on labor relations is an old problem and the new industrial sociology constitutes a renascence of interest in the redistribution of workplace control. In order to place this book in the context of an intellectual and empirical legacy, I review the chief developments in labor relations which have spawned the recent and growing interest in labor relations arrangements and workplace control. Then, I turn to the major shifts in U.S. labor's responses to technological change during the twentieth century. I conclude this chapter with a rationale for the plan of the book.

II. THE GROWING CONCERN WITH CONTROL

Beginning in the 1970s, social scientists revived an interest in examining the nature of workplace control through formal labor relations arrangements and the structural features and behavior of firms, unions, and government.[3] This new industrial sociology is "new" in comparison to the industrial sociology of the 1950s and 1960s which addressed the shop-floor behavior of informal work groups.[4] However, the new industrial sociology also constitutes a rejuvenation and modification mainly of the institutional economics fathered by John Commons. Writing in the pre-World War II era of labor unrest and wide swings in the unemployment rate, when a growing labor movement and emerging corporate employers sought to "regularize" employment by establishing formal workplace rules, Commons promoted institutional economics especially for understanding the formal relations between labor and management. He discarded the assumption of "hedonic," maximizing rational actors in classical economics, arguing instead for the assumption of "futurity." Futurity signified a desire for a certain future which

[3]See, for example, Ivar Berg, Marcia Freedman and Michael Freeman, *Managers and Work Reform* (New York: The Free Press, 1978); Richard Edwards, *Contested Terrain* (New York: Basic Books, 1979); Harry Braverman, *Labor and Monopoly Capital* (New York: Monthly Review Press, 1974); Peter Doeringer and Michael Piore, *Internal Labor Markets and Manpower Analysis* (Lexington, MA: D.C. Heath, 1970); David Gordon, *Theories of Poverty and Underemployment* (Lexington, MA: D.C. Heath, 1972). For discussion of control of technological change, see Donald Kennedy, Charles Craypo and Mary Lehman, ed., *Labor and Technology: Union Response to Changing Environments* (Department of Labor Studies, The Pennsylvania State University, 1982).

[4]For a review of the industrial sociology of the 1950s and 1960s, see Delbert Miller and William Form, *Industrial Sociology*, 3rd ed. (New York: Harper & Row, 1980); on behavioral labor relations research, see David Lewin and Peter Feuille, "Behavioral Research in Industrial Relations," *Industrial and Labor Relations Review* 36 (April 1983), pp. 341–360.

labor and management attempted to achieve by transacting formal rules that reconciled their differences.[5]

Like John Commons' institutional economics, the new industrial sociology has emerged in an era of uncertainty in which once accepted arrangements are in a state of flux. However, unlike Commons' era of institution-building, when unrest and economic catastrophe increased popular control of the workplace through unionization, the era of the new industrial sociology is one in which unraveling arrangements are being modified and unionization is declining. Unlike the industrial sociology which was spawned in the 1950's era of stability, the new industrial sociology is beginning to address labor–management competition and control of the workplace by examining the changing arrangements themselves.

The new industrial sociology, with its emphasis on the formal features of work and industry, emerged alongside of the research on informal work groups during the 1970s, when the stable labor relations arrangements of the Cold War era were jeopardized. The jeopardization of the Cold War arrangements is partly reflected in the changing pattern of strike activity after the 1946 strike wave. Between 1946 and 1963, the annual number of strikes declined by 33% from 4,985 to 3,362; between 1963 and 1974, the number of strikes increased by 81% from 3,362 to 6,074. The number of strikes remained roughly at the level of the 1946 strike wave throughout most of the late 1970s and then declined to 2,568 by 1981.[6] Instability in recent labor relations is captured by such new collective bargaining phrases as "two-tier wage structures," "wage freezes," "codetermination," "quality circles," "concession bargaining," "take backs," "give backs," "union avoidance" and "union busting" that are commonly heard today. Also, vivid, scholarly visions of labor relations in the 1970s and 1980s signify uncertainty in labor relations. For example, Freeman and Medoff announce the "slow strangulation of private-sector unions"; Bluestone and Harrison refer to the "break-up of the social contract"; for Kochan and Piore, labor–management relations are "in transition"; the employment relationship exists on "contested terrain" for Edwards, while Burawoy characterizes employer control of the work force as "hegemonic despotism"; and Garbarino questions the development of "unionism without unions."[7]

· Perhaps the most important proximate cause of instability in current

[5]John Commons, *Institutional Economics* (New York: Macmillan, 1934), pp. 1–9, 52–58.

[6]U.S. Bureau of Labor Statistics, *Handbook of Labor Statistics*, Bulletin no. 2175 (Washington, DC: GPO, 1983), p. 380.

[7]Richard Freeman and James Medoff, *What Do Unions Do?* (New York: Basic Books, 1984), p. 221; Barry Bluestone and Bennett Harrison, *The Deindustrialization of America* (New York: Basic Books, 1982), p. 164; Thomas Kochan and Michael Piore, "U.S. Industrial Relations in Transition," in *Challenges and Choices Facing American Labor*, ed. Thomas Kochan (Cambridge: MIT Press, 1985), pp. 1–12; Edwards, *Contested Terrain*; Michael Burawoy, "Between the Labor Process and the State: The Changing Face of Factory Regimes Under Advanced Capitalism," *American Sociological Review* 48 (October 1983), pp. 587–605; Joseph Garbarino, "Unionism without Unions: The New Industrial Relations?" *Industrial Relations* 23 (Winter 1984), pp. 40–51.

labor relations is post-World War II union decline. A variety of indicators imply that the union has been a declining institution since the end of the Second World War. The percentage unionized in the non-agricultural work force declined from 32.5% in 1953 to 19% by 1984; in the manufacturing work force, the percentage unionized declined from 42% to 26% between 1953 and 1984; and, the union victory rate in representation elections declined while decertification activity increased during the post-World War II era.[8]

Researchers have identified several causes of post-World War II union decline. Factors which reduce extant union membership include the automation of manufacturing, government deregulation of unionized industries, capital flight out of the highly unionized Great Lakes and Middle Atlantic regions to the less unionized "right-to-work" South and Third World, increasing foreign imports that jeopardize unionized, U.S. manufacturers, and increased union decertification. Also, unions have encountered increased employer resistance to union organizing campaigns, in the form of anti-union management consultants and the provision of union-scale wages and benefits by large, non-union employers.[9]

The increasing participation of women in the labor force and the growth of white-collar employment that accompanied the rise of the service sector, technological change and business enterprise bureaucratization were expected by many analysts to reduce unionization. Traditionally outside the sphere of unionism, white-collar and women workers were thought to be averse to unionization because, in the case of white-collar workers, they identified with management and, in the case of women, they lacked a long-term career commitment.[10] Nonetheless, the percentage unionized among white-collar workers increased from 8% to 15% between 1958 and 1980; in the public sector, especially after President Kennedy's Executive Orders and the passage of state public employee collective bargaining laws in the 1960s and 1970s, the percentage increased from 12% to 34% between 1953 and 1983; and the percentage unionized among women workers increased from 11% to 16% between 1954 and 1980.[11] Moreover, non-union women workers are at least as likely as their male counterparts to favor unionization.[12] These data suggest, however, that the unexpected but modest gains in unionization among

[8]Leo Troy and Neil Sheflin, *Union Sourcebook* (West Orange, NJ: Industrial Relations Data and Information Services, 1985), chapter 3, p. 15; Daniel Cornfield, "Declining Union Membership in the Post-World War II Era: The United Furniture Workers of America, 1939–1983," *American Journal of Sociology* 91 (March 1986), pp. 1112–1153.

[9]Cornfield, "Declining Union Membership."

[10]Everett Kassalow, "White-Collar Unionism in the United States," in *White-Collar Trade Unions,* ed. Adolf Sturmthal (Urbana, IL: University of Illinois Press, 1966), pp. 305–364.

[11]Troy and Sheflin, chapter 3, p. 15; U.S. Bureau of Labor Statistics, *Directory of National and International Labor Unions in the United States, 1955,* Bulletin no. 1185 (Washington, DC: GPO, 1955), p. 12; U.S. Bureau of Labor Statistics, *Directory of National and International Labor Unions, 1959,* Bulletin no. 1267 (Washington, DC: GPO, 1959), p. 11; U.S. Bureau of Labor Statistics, Bulletin no. 2175, pp. 37, 44; Courtney Gifford, ed., *Directory of U.S. Labor Organizations* (Washington, DC: Bureau of National Affairs, 1982), p. 3.

[12]Freeman and Medoff, p. 28.

white-collar and women workers have yet to offset the large declines in blue-collar unionization.

Union decline and the jeopardization of basic industry profits by such factors as increasing foreign competition and recent pro-competition government deregulation have caused labor and management to reformulate the relationship which had crystallized during the Cold War. Technological change has emerged as a salient issue of workplace control for labor and management. While managements in basic industry demand greater flexibility in implementing production technologies in order to improve business profitability, unions demand job security and retraining opportunities for their memberships. In the traditionally non-union, rapidly growing, white-collar service sector, managements, by automating offices, are compelling the increasingly career- and rights-oriented work force of women office workers to begin, with the stimulus of the women's movement, to challenge unilateral managerial authority through unionization.

In sum, recent technological changes have raised divergent issues for labor and management in controlling the implementation and outcomes of technological change. Moreover, this divergence in control issues has occurred in an era of uncertainty in labor relations arrangements, adding to the impetus for reformulating labor–management relations.

The arrangements emerging from this conflict over control of technological change are also being shaped by changes in the employment relationship and in the role of the labor union. Indeed, the issues raised by technological change, have always been divergent for labor and for management—but the arrangements for controlling technological innovations have undergone considerable change during the twentieth century. I turn now to developments in U.S. labor's responses to technological change.

III. LABOR'S CHANGING RESPONSES TO TECHNOLOGICAL CHANGE

Nothing could be more untypical of U.S. labor's responses to technological change than the English Luddite rebellion of 1811–1816. Hundreds of workers in the hosiery and lace trades and cotton and woolen industries of Nottingham, Lancashire, Cheshire, and the West Riding of Yorkshire smashed over 1000 stocking and shearing frames, gig mills, steam looms, and other machines. Despite the popular depiction of Luddite motives as opposition to technology, historians claim that the Luddites actually opposed wage reductions, high food prices, unemployment, the hiring of "colts" or apprentices instead of skilled tradesmen, and the decline in status of the trades which accompanied the progressive use of inferior materials and the supplanting of domestic industry by the factory system.[13] According to historians, adverse

13Frank Peel, *The Luddites* (Cheapside: Heckmondwike, 1880), pp. 8–12; Frank Darvall, *Popular Disturbances and Public Order in Regency England* (London: Oxford University Press, 1934), pp. 5–6, 167, 203, 204; Malcolm Thomis, *The Luddites* (Hamden, CT: Archon, 1970), pp. 11, 76.

macroeconomic conditions which derived from bad harvests, the loss of the 13 North American colonies and the closing of that market, the 1807–1810 collapse of the South American market and the Napoleonic Wars account for the occasion and wide prevalence of the Luddite rebellion.[14] Moreover, with the addition of anti-combination laws in 1799 and 1800 to similar Elizabethan-era laws that inhibited unionization, machine-breaking had become a "time-honored tradition among certain occupational groups"[15] and a commonly used bargaining tactic in negotiations on such nontechnology issues as wage adjustments.[16]

Indeed, in their authoritative history of British labor, Sidney and Beatrice Webb claim that by the end of the nineteenth century, after unions had been legalized, the cotton trade unions encouraged mechanization in order to maintain the financial viability of employers and, hence, the job security of workers. As the Webbs put it:

> it is not the individual capitalist, but the Trade Union, which most strenuously insists on having the very latest improvements in machinery. . . In Lancashire it quickly becomes a grievance in the Cotton Trade Unions, if any one employer or any one district falls behind the rest . . . [T]o the Trade Union . . . , the sluggishness of the poor . . . employers is a serious danger. . . Thus, the Amalgamated Association of Operative Cotton-spinners, instead of obstructing new machinery, actually penalizes the employer who fails to introduce it![17]

The irony of the British case presaged the changing posture of U.S. labor toward technological change in the twentieth century. Notwithstanding instances of industrial sabotage in the U.S. and "whistle-blowers" who have revealed dangerous technologies, organized labor has mainly adopted a "willing acceptance" of technological change, according to the surveys done by Barnett in 1926, Slichter in 1941 and 1960 and by McLaughlin in 1979.[18] In his 1941 work, Slichter identified three union policies toward technological change—the policies of obstruction, competition, and control.[19] The latter, the most common of the three, entailed union acceptance of technological change coupled with collective bargaining over protection from such adversity as worker displacement and wage reduction. By 1960, however, Slichter had added the policy of encouragement to his list of union policies. Like that

[14]Peel, pp. 6–7; Thomis, pp. 46, 70; Darvall, pp. 7–8; E. P. Thompson, *The Making of the English Working Class* (New York: Vintage, 1963), p. 543.

[15]Thomis, p. 12.

[16]Thompson, pp. 503–507.

[17]Sidney Webb and Beatrice Webb, *Industrial Democracy* (London: Longmans, Green and Co., 1920), p. 413.

[18]George Barnett, *Chapters on Machinery and Labor* (Cambridge: Harvard University Press, 1926); Slichter, *Union Policies;* Sumner Slichter, James Healy and E. Robert Livernash, *The Impact of Collective Bargaining on Management* (Washington, DC: The Brookings Institution, 1960); Doris McLaughlin, *The Impact of Labor Unions on the Rate and Direction of Technological Innovation* (Washington DC: National Technical Information Service, 1979). The expression "willing acceptance" is from Slichter, Healy and Livernash, p. 344. On whistle-blowing about dangerous technologies, see Alan Westin, *Whistle-Blowing! Loyalty and Dissent in the Corporation* (New York: McGraw Hill, 1981).

[19]Slichter, *Union Policies*, p. 241.

of the late nineteenth-century British cotton unions, the policy of encouragement was pursued when unions were "worried about the ability of an industry . . . to hold its own in competition."[20]

A. From Provider to Advocate: The Changing Role of the Union in Responding to Technological Change

Notwithstanding its continuous "willing acceptance" of technological change, organized labor has shifted from serving as a provider toward becoming a worker advocate in the prevention and relief of technological unemployment since the late nineteenth century. Prior to the Great Depression of the 1930s, unions espoused few employer- and government-provided measures for preventing and relieving unemployment. Unions financed and administered their own unemployment benefits and served as employment exchanges for their unemployed members and prospective employers. The union's role as advocate emerged and crystallized in the Cold War era after World War II, when the labor movement had achieved employer-provided and government-assisted training in the prevention of unemployment as well as employer- and government-provided relief for displaced workers.

The union's shift from provider to advocate was stimulated by at least two events. First, the Depression of the 1930s led to mass unemployment which could not easily be relieved by union benefits. Second, the anticipation during World War II of mass unemployment in the post-War reconversion furthered organized labor's advocacy of non-union-provided relief for displaced workers.

However, the union's changing role from provider to advocate is also symptomatic of two secular changes in the employment relationship. The first is the rise of the internal labor market which accompanied the decline of casual or irregular employment and the growth of mass production and continuous employment. By internalizing their work forces through the provision of seniority-based rules for allocating and compensating labor, large corporations in mass production industries gained a full-time, year-round work force whose livelihood increasingly depended on continuous employment with one employer. In advocating seniority-based rules, the labor movement played no small role in this process of labor internalization. By the 1950s, many workers could not afford to have their non-portable seniority rights jeopardized by quitting or permanent layoffs, which would lower their wages, health and life insurance and retirement pensions and weaken their promotion chances and job security.[21]

The second change is what I have referred to as "union captivity."[22] The existence of a local union has increasingly come to depend on that of a single employer or establishment with the transformation from craft to industrial

---

[20]Slichter, Healy and Livernash, p. 355.
[21]Cornfield, "Declining Union Membership."
[22]Ibid.

unionism. In the era of craft unionism before the rise of mass production by the 1930s, local craft unions recruited their members at-large from the pool of casually employed craft workers in a local labor market area. With closed shop contracts, employment was often conditional on union membership and the union supplied local employers with workers.[23]

In contrast, the industrial local union, which became the most common type of union after World War II, recruits its members in mass production industries by conducting a representation election in a specific shop under the supervision of the National Labor Relations Board (NLRB). The NLRB-representation election system was established by the Wagner Act in 1935 in order to promote unionization. In the era of Cold War conservatism, the Taft-Hartley Act of 1947 prohibited closed shop contracts, undermining the contractual basis of the union's labor supply function. By the 1950s, then, the membership jurisdiction of the local union was partly defined by the representation election and had become shop-specific. Union membership had effectively become conditional on employment in a specific shop.[24] Moreover, the entire local union could be jeopardized by employer bankruptcy, plant relocations and plant shutdowns, what Burawoy alluded to as constituting "hegemonic despotism."[25] With growing worker and union dependence on single employers, mass unemployment in the 1930s, and post-World War II automation, the union shifted from provider to advocate in the prevention and relief of technological unemployment. Furthermore, with the declining position of U.S. basic industry in the world market, organized labor has increasingly adopted a "policy of encouragement," in order to modernize U.S. production processes, restore U.S. competitiveness in the world market and, thereby, maintain the livelihoods of workers.

Generally, U.S. labor's response to technological change has become somewhat more pro-active than its defensive posture of willing acceptance in the late nineteenth century. Compare, for example, the pronouncements of Terence Powderly, Samuel Gompers and the Industrial Workers of the World (IWW) to those of the AFL-CIO in 1984. Head of the late nineteenth century Knights of Labor for many years, Powderly decried the dissolution of the skilled crafts, the loss of worker ownership and control and the displacement of workers which accompanied mechanization and the rise of the factory system. Article XIV of the 1878 Knights' Constitution called for a reduction in working hours—the eight-hour day—so that workers could "reap the advantages conferred by the labor-saving machinery which their brains have created."[26] After "seventy years of life and labor," AFL President Samuel Gompers declared in his 1925 autobiography "the futility of opposing progress," arguing instead for worker and union control of new machinery.[27] In the

---

[23]Ibid.
[24]Ibid.
[25]Burawoy, "Between the Labor Process and the State."
[26]Terence Powderly, *Thirty Years of Labor* (Columbus, OH: Excelsior, 1889), pp. 22–34, 245.
[27]Samuel Gompers, *Seventy Years of Life and Labor* (New York: E. P. Dutton, 1925), pp. 47, 373.

Manifesto read at its first convention in 1905, the IWW stated that "[t]he *great facts* of present industry are the displacement of human skill by machines and the increase of capitalist power through concentration in the possession of the tools with which wealth is produced and distributed" (their italics).[28] IWW leader Bill Haywood convened the delegates in order "to confederate the workers of this country into a working class movement that shall have for its purpose the emancipation of the working class from the slave bondage of capitalism. (Applause)."[29] For the Knights, AFL and IWW, then, technological change was a foregone conclusion—controlling its adverse effects on workers was their agenda.

For the AFL-CIO in 1984, controlling the adverse effects of technological change was more of a foregone conclusion than technological change itself. Claiming that high interest rates, inflation and foreign competition had lowered investment in plant and equipment and U.S. economic productivity, the AFL-CIO called for the establishment of a National Industrial Policy Board and a National Industrial Development Bank. Consisting of representatives of labor, business, academia, the public and government, the Board would identify industries for capital investment and oversee the Bank which would finance the investment.[30] Leading its list of factors that increase productivity was "investment for expansion and modernization of plant and equipment."[31] This comparison implies an increasingly pro-active posture of organized labor toward technological change, especially as recent macroeconomic conditions jeopardize U.S. basic industry and union worker livelihoods.

However, the portrayal of labor's posture as willing acceptance fails to identify continuity and change in organized labor's *issues* about technological change, proposed *measures* for combatting adversity associated with technological change and proposals for who will be the *providers* of these measures. Since the late nineteenth century, organized labor has been concerned mainly with one issue and perceived consequence of technological change: unemployment. In the late nineteenth century, when the term "unemployment" was first coined to connote involuntary joblessness, and supplanted such voluntaristic notions as "idleness" and "pauperism,"[32] organized labor began to adhere to an "underconsumptionist" theory of technological unemployment. Technological change would displace some workers and lower the wages of the employed through job deskilling. Unemployment would continue with the subsequent decline in consumer purchasing power that derived directly from worker displacement and declining wages. Organized labor's fear of unemployment was reinforced in the early twentieth century

[28]*Proceedings of the First Convention of the Industrial Workers of the World,* Chicago, 1905, published as *The Founding Convention of the IWW* (New York: Merit, 1969), p. 3.

[29]Ibid., p. 1.

[30]Bill Cunningham, "Productivity—Policies and Problems," *AFL-CIO American Federationist* 91 (December 8, 1984) in *AFL-CIO News,* December 8, 1984, pp. 5–8.

[31]Ibid., p. 5. Also, see Donald Kennedy, ed., *Labor and Reindustrialization: Workers and Corporate Change* (Department of Labor Studies, Pennsylvania State University, 1984).

[32]John Garraty, *Unemployment in History* (New York: Harper, 1978), p. 121.

by its job-consciousness and job-centered collective bargaining, both products of a managerial, mass production strategy that narrowed jobs and increased worker dispensability.[33]

Labor's theory was controversial, especially during the era of intense mechanization in the 1920's and the Great Depression of the 1930's. Academic economists and pro-business groups who admitted the virtual impossibility of empirically distinguishing between the separate effects of technological change and seasonal and cyclical factors on unemployment, often denied through deduction any permanence in or prevalence of technological unemployment. In their view, technological change increased the scale of enterprise, lowered the prices of goods for the consumer and, thereby, increased labor demand and employment.[34] Notwithstanding its controversial nature, labor's theory partly informed the role of the labor movement: to prevent technologically induced unemployment and wage reductions and to provide relief for the displaced worker.

B. Labor's Measures for Preventing Technological Unemployment

Since the late nineteenth century, organized labor has changed its tactics for the prevention of technological unemployment, shifting the emphasis from shorter hours of work toward worker training and retraining. This new emphasis has resulted mainly from changes in the nature of technological change itself—i.e. the shift from mechanization to automation—in the occupational structure, and in the occupational and industrial composition of union membership.

Before World War II, labor's chief measure for preventing technological unemployment was reduction in the hours of work. By reducing the hours of work through collective bargaining, labor hoped to minimize technological unemployment by sharing more work with more workers.

According to Gompers and other labor leaders of his era, the movement for shortening hours and establishing the 8-hour day was one of the most significant collective bargaining issues of the late nineteenth century.[35] Furthermore, with increased mechanization during the 1920s, the American Federation of Labor focused on technological change as one of the leading causes of unemployment. As AFL President William Green put it in 1929:

---

[33]On labor's theory, see Powderly, pp. 21–34; John Commons, David Saposs, Helen Sumner, E. B. Mittelman, H. E. Hoagland, John Andrews and Selig Perlman, *History of Labour in the United States*, vol. 2 (New York: Macmillan, 1926), p. 479. For discussion of job consciousness, see Robert Cole, *Work, Mobility and Participation* (Berkeley: University of California Press, 1979), pp. 103–106.

[34]National Industrial Conference Board, *Machinery, Employment and Purchasing Power* (New York: National Industrial Conference Board, 1935); Emil Lederer, *Technical Progress and Unemployment* (Geneva: International Labour Office, 1938); Paul Douglas and Aaron Director, *The Problem of Unemployment* (New York: Macmillan, 1934).

[35]John Commons et al., *History of Labour*, p. 479.

the machine came to replace the skilled craftsman and workers were laid off regardless of the effect on their standard of living . . . ; the extraordinary development of machinery in the last ten years has made . . . technological unemployment . . . an outstanding problem.[36]

Technological unemployment, according to Green, could be prevented by
reducing the hours of work.[37]

The hours of work declined in the early twentieth century. In its report to
the 1927 AFL convention, the AFL Executive Council showed that the percentage of U.S. wage earners working 54 or more hours per week declined
from 85% to 32% between 1909 and 1923, especially during World War I with
the support of a War Labor Board that favored shorter hours.[38] In such
industries as steel, electric power, gas works, chemicals, railroads, and telecommunications, what the Executive Council referred to as "continuous industries," employers had begun to change from two 12-hour shifts to three 8-
hour shifts before World War I and were predominantly on the three-shift
system by 1927.[39] In its 1928 report, the AFL Executive Council claimed that
20 international unions had 514 locals with 164,479 members who worked the
five-day, forty-hour week.[40] By 1930, over 500,000 AFL members worked a
five-day week.[41]

Organized labor continued to advocate reduction in hours through the
Great Depression of the 1930s. Leading the list of the AFL's 1930 10–point
program for preventing and relieving unemployment was "reduction in the
hours of work."[42] The AFL Executive Council explained:

> Where work hours . . . are not progressively reduced to keep pace with scientific
> progress, practically the full cost of this progress falls upon wage earners in the
> form of unemployment. Instead of laying off employees as productivity increases,
> the work day should be reduced, the work week shortened and provisions for
> annual vacations with pay should reduce the work year.[43]

The CIO also championed shortened hours in order to prevent technological unemployment. In their testimony at hearings on technological unemployment conducted by the Temporary National Economic Committee in
1940, leaders of eight CIO unions representing steel, coal, textiles, automobile, electrical manufacturing, rubber, office and professional, and communications workers argued that "only through the organization of labor and
the consequent raising of hourly rates and the reduction of hours worked

---

[36]American Federation of Labor, *Trade Unions Study Unemployment* (Washington, DC: American
Federation of Labor, 1929), pp. 5–7.

[37]Ibid., p. 8.

[38]*Report of Proceedings of the Forty-Seventh Annual Convention of the American Federation of Labor* (Los
Angeles, 1927), pp. 60–62.

[39]Ibid.

[40]*Report of Proceedings of the Forty-Eighth Annual Convention of the American Federation of Labor* (New
Orleans, 1928), p. 44.

[41]*Report of the Proceedings of the Fiftieth Annual Convention of the American Federation of Labor* (Boston,
1930), p. 64.

[42]Ibid., p. 60.

[43]Ibid.

have the present effects of machines been substantially mitigated."[44] With the beginning of post-World War II automation, the CIO continued to advocate shortened hours. For example, at the National Conference on Automation sponsored by the CIO in 1955, CIO President Walter Reuther called for a shorter work week.[45]

Organized labor has continued to espouse reduction in hours throughout the post-World War II era. A perusal of the *Proceedings* of all AFL-CIO conventions held during the 1955–83 period shows that at least one resolution favoring shorter hours was passed at almost every convention. Typical of these resolutions is resolution no. 67 which was passed at the 1979 convention:

> . . . . WHEREAS, there has been an alarming growth in the number of long-term unemployed, . . . and
> WHEREAS, the continued introduction of new processes . . . ha[s] contributed to astronomical increases in productivity . . . , and
> WHEREAS, this trend toward job elimination will continue, thus boosting corporate profits to ever more obscene heights while the living standard of American workers declines, and
> WHEREAS, The U.S. labor movement has historically fought for shorter hours as the best solution to creating jobs and reducing unemployment, . . . Therefore be it
> RESOLVED: That the 13th Constitutional Convention of the AFL-CIO go on record calling upon the Congress of the United States to enact . . . a bill . . . to:
> 1- Increase the penalty for overtime from the present time and one-half to double time.
> 2- Provide for payment of this penalty after 35 hours in a given week instead of the 40 hours as provided by present law. . .[46]

The hours of work have declined over the post-World War II era. The average weekly hours worked by production or non-supervisory workers on private non-agricultural payrolls declined from approximately 40 hours in the 1950s to 35 hours in the 1980–83 period.[47]

Its continuous espousal of shortened hours notwithstanding, organized labor has increasingly advocated employer- and government-provided training and retraining in order to prevent technological unemployment during the post-World War II era. Although the AFL had begun to advocate training in the late 1920s, organized labor's call for training greatly escalated in the 1950s with the beginning of automation.

Unlike its theoretical rationale for shortened hours, which assumed that mechanization would eliminate or deskill the skilled crafts, labor's rationale for training assumed that automation would eliminate less skilled jobs but generate new higher-skill jobs. For example, a 1955 CIO pamphlet entitled "Automation" claimed that:

---

[44]See the CIO publication, *The Economic Outlook* 1 (May 1940), p. 4.

[45]CIO Committee on Economic Policy, *The Challenge of Automation* (Washington, DC: Public Affairs Press, 1955), pp. 52–53.

[46]*Proceedings of the Thirteenth Constitutional Convention of the AFL-CIO*, (Washington, DC, 1979), vol. 1 p. 481.

[47]U.S. Bureau of Labor Statistics, *Handbook of Labor Statistics*, Bulletin no. 2217 (Washington, DC: GPO, 1985), p. 186.

the introduction of automated machines and electronic computers will likely result
in lay-offs and in the upgrading of the level of skills required in the work force. . .
The prospect of labor displacement can be eased, in part, by joint consultation
between companies and unions and by management planning—to schedule the
introduction of automation in periods of high employment, to permit attrition of
reduce the size of the labor force, and to allow time for the retraining of employees.[48]

Labor's new recognition of job upgrading, rather than job deskilling, is
consistent with changes in the occupational structure of U.S. manufacturing
that accompanied the shift from pre-World War II mechanization to post-war
automation. The 1910 and 1930 U.S. Census data on occupational employment which were compiled by Alba Edwards are among the best available for describing pre-World War II changes in the blue-collar occupational
structure of "manufacturing and mechanical industries."[49] Between 1910 and
1930, the number of semi-skilled factory operatives increased by 43%, unskilled manufacturing laborers increased by 33%, and skilled craft workers
grew by 29%.[50] The dissolution of skilled crafts during this pre-World War II
period, as reflected in the changing occupational structure, occurred with the
relatively rapid growth in the number of semi-skilled factory operatives and
unskilled laborers in comparison to the slower growth in the number of
skilled craft workers.

Job upgrading is implied by the changing occupational structure of U.S.
manufacturing between 1950 and 1982. The percentage employed as white-
collar workers in manufacturing increased from 24% to 36% while the percentage of blue-collar workers declined from 74% to 62%. Among blue-collar
workers in manufacturing, the percentage of craft workers increased from
26% to 31%, operatives remained at 62%, and laborers declined from 12% to
7% between 1950 and 1982.[51] Although these data do not reflect job content
changes, they suggest that some job upgrading has occurred through the
relatively large increases in the shares of white-collar and craft workers in
manufacturing.

Organized labor's increasing emphasis on training reflected not only the
occupational employment changes accompanying the shift from mechanization to automation, but also the changing occupational and industrial composition of union membership. Before the 1930s and the rise of the CIO, the
AFL's philosophy of craft unionism had generated a union membership comprised mainly of skilled craft workers in the building and printing trades,
transportation, communication, and mining.[52] In 1930, less than 8% of the

[48]CIO Committee on Economic Policy, *Automation* (Washington, DC: Congress of Industrial
Organizations, 1955), pp. 21–22.

[49]Alba Edwards, *Comparative Occupation Statistics for the United States 1870 to 1940, Sixteenth Census
of the United States: 1940* (Washington, DC: GPO, 1943).

[50]Ibid., pp. 63–67.

[51]U.S. Bureau of the Census, *U.S. Census of the Population: 1950*, vol. 4, Special Reports, Part I,
Chapter C, *Occupation by Industry* (Washington, DC: GPO, 1954), p. 11; U.S. Bureau of Labor
Statistics, *Employment and Earnings* 30 (January 1983), p. 160.

[52]James Morris, *Conflict within the AFL* (Ithaca, NY: Cornell University, 1958), p. 10.

manufacturing work force was unionized while almost two-thirds of construction workers were unionized.[53] Hence, the AFL's early concern with the dissolution of the skilled crafts partly derived from this condition which jeopardized the job security and status of many AFL members. With mechanization, mass production and the spearheading of industrial unionism by the CIO in the mid-1930s, both the CIO and the AFL began to organize semi-skilled factory operatives. Indeed, organizing both skilled and less skilled workers, who had been neglected by the AFL, was the chief mandate of the CIO's call for industrial unionism, according to the 1936 CIO pamphlet, "The Case for Industrial Organization."[54] By the early 1950s, union membership included many factory operatives. Unfortunately, adequate data on the occupational characteristics of union membership for this era are nonexistent. However, industry data suggest that many semi-skilled workers in manufacturing had been organized by the 1950s. By 1953, 42% of the manufacturing work force was unionized and in 1956, 49% of union members were employed in manufacturing.[55] Organized labor's shift in emphasis toward training in this period was partly based on a recognition that automation would eliminate less skilled jobs. According to the CIO pamphlet "Automation": "Automation promises the elimination of routine, repetitive jobs."[56]

By the end of the 1950's, organized labor decried technological unemployment in mass-production industries. According to resolution no. 178, which was passed at the 1961 AFL-CIO convention, "[t]he Fifties taught America some automation lessons: As the vast new technology swept through basic industries, millions of workers in mining, railroads and manufacturing found their jobs destroyed and no new jobs in sight."[57] This resolution, along with others passed at the AFL-CIO conventions during the 1960s, called for training in order to prevent technological unemployment.[58]

Employer-provided training became an increasingly common provision in collective bargaining agreements, as indicated by the U.S. Bureau of Labor Statistics' surveys of agreements covering 1000 or more workers. The percentage of agreements providing for on-the-job training increased from 12%, for agreements in effect in 1966–67, to 40% in 1980.[59] These provisions typically established company-sponsored, on-site training programs for displaced workers and the currently employed. Workers were trained to qualify for

---

[53]Troy and Sheflin, Chapter 3, p. 15.

[54]Committee for Industrial Organization, *The Case for Industrial Organization* (Washington, DC: Committee for Industrial Organization, 1936), pp. 8–12.

[55]Troy and Sheflin, chapter 3, p. 15; U.S. Bureau of Labor Statistics, *Directory of National and International Labor Unions, 1957*, Bulletin no. 1222 (Washington, DC: GPO, 1957), p. 13.

[56]CIO Committee on Economic Policy, *Automation*, p. 21.

[57]*Proceedings of the Fourth Constitutional Convention of the AFL-CIO*, Miami Beach, 1961, vol. 1, p. 434.

[58]Ibid.

[59]U.S. Bureau of Labor Statistics, *Major Collective Bargaining Agreements-Training and Retraining Provisions*, Bulletin no. 1425–7 (Washington, D.C.: GPO, 1969), p. 4; U.S. Bureau of Labor Statistics, *Characteristics of Major Collective Bargaining Agreements, January 1, 1980*, Bulletin no. 2095 (Washington, DC: GPO, 1981), p. 105.

other production jobs or for administrative, executive, and supervisory positions. Approximately 46% of the agreements in effect in 1966–67 called for union participation in the training program.[60]

Organized labor extended its support of training beyond collective bargaining and union members by rallying behind the 1962 Manpower Development and Training Act which was designed to provide training and retraining for workers who were displaced by automation.[61] Moreover, by the mid-1960s, the AFL-CIO called for greater government–labor collaboration in the provision of training to unemployed, inner city black workers, many of whom had recently migrated from the South to Northern ghettoes and possessed skills which were being rendered obsolete by automation. As the AFL-CIO Executive Council put it in 1967:

> The Negro migrants to the cities of the past quarter of a century have brought with them a history of slavery, segregation, [and] lack of education . . . On coming to the cities of the North and West, the new migrants have faced the discriminatory practices of those areas . . . and the impact of automation on job opportunities for uneducated, unskilled workers.[62]

In 1968, the AFL-CIO established the Human Resources Development Institute (HRDI) to develop training programs especially for unemployed black workers which would be jointly sponsored primarily by labor and government. With a $1.5 million contract from the U.S. Department of Labor, HRDI began training programs through local central labor councils in 47 major metropolitan areas. It expanded its coverage to about sixty areas through the 1970s as well as its activities to include job development, placement and apprenticeship programs, technical assistance to local unions which wish to receive federal training funds, and other activities.[63]

While organized labor continued to promote training for blue-collar workers and economically disadvantaged minority workers, it began to examine the effects of office automation (i.e. computerized office and business machines and word-processing) on white-collar workers in the 1970's. With the growing prevalence of unionization among white-collar workers in the 1970s, the percentage of union members who were white-collar workers increased from 23% to 35% between 1970 and 1980.[64] By 1980, half of the white-collar union members were employed in service industries or the finance sector where office automation was first introduced during the 1950s.[65]

Given the recency of office automation and its proliferation in high-growth, white-collar service industries, the AFL-CIO has anticipated rather than documented technological unemployment among white-collar workers.

---

[60]U.S. Bureau of Labor Statistics, Bulletin no. 1425–7, pp. 6, 13.

[61]*Proceedings of the Seventh Constitutional Convention of the AFL-CIO*, Bal Harbor, 1967, vol. 2, p. 210.

[62]Ibid., p. 76.

[63]*Proceedings of the Thirteenth Convention*, vol. 2. pp. 56–60.

[64]Gifford, p. 50; U.S. Bureau of Labor Statistics, *Selected Earnings and Demographic Characteristics of Union Members, 1970*, Report 417 (Washington, DC: GPO, 1972), p. 9.

[65]Gifford, p. 50.

For example, in 1979 AFL-CIO Secretary-Treasurer Thomas Donahue claimed that accelerated technological change in the service sector was likely "in the near future" and "the service sector, even with its omnipresent computer, is largely untouched by technological change."[66] Similarly, in 1984 Dennis Chamot of the AFL-CIO Department for Professional Employees predicted declining demand for clerical labor; claimed that the future, net change in the employment of professional workers was uncertain; and stated that the "AFL-CIO believes that we may be entering a period of permanent labor surplus."[67]

Some unions have developed through collective bargaining retraining provisions in order to prevent the displacement of white-collar workers by office automation. For example, the 1978 contract between the Office and Professional Employees International Union and the New York Stock Exchange established training and transfer rights for employees who are displaced by "data processing equipment, computers or automated devices or systems."[68]

In sum, organized labor has shifted the emphasis of its measures for preventing technological unemployment from shortened hours toward training and retraining since the late nineteenth century. The growing emphasis on training accompanied pre-World War II-to-Post-War shifts from mechanization to automation; from downgrading to upgrading in the occupational structure, especially in manufacturing; and from craft unionism to industrial unionism, which increased the proportion of semi-skilled, operative union members whose jobs were threatened by automation.

C. Relief for the Displaced Worker

Labor unions have continuously sought to relieve the displaced worker through reemployment measures and by providing the worker with unemployment benefits. Since the late nineteenth century, the role of the union in providing these measures and benefits subsided as organized labor increasingly sought relief from employers and the government.

1. Reemployment Measures

The major change in the union's role in reemployment is from serving as an employment exchange and performing the job referral function toward securing inter-plant transfer rights through collective bargaining for displaced workers. This change accompanied the decline of seasonal, casual and irreg-

---

[66]Dennis Chamot and Joan Baggeth, ed., *Silicon, Satellites and Robots* (Washington, DC: Department for Professional Employees, AFL-CIO, 1979), p. 28.

[67]Dennis Chamot, "Electronic Work and the White Collar Employee," presented at the Technology and the Transformation of White Collar Work conference, New Brunswick, New Jersey, 1984, pp. 4–5.

[68]Kevin Murphy, *Technological Change Clauses in Collective Bargaining Agreements*, publication no. 81–2 (Washington, DC: Department for Professional Employees, AFL-CIO, 1981), pp. 31–32.

ular employment and the advent of continuous employment in multi-plant corporations. Also, the change was catalyzed by the Great Depression of the 1930s and post-World War II plant relocation and modernization.

Prior to the 1930s, when craft unions often confronted cyclical and seasonal unemployment and employers sought to regularize or stabilize employment and production, most local unions attempted to find work for their members who were unemployed from a variety of causes including technological change. Indeed, it was commonly the duty of local union officers to do so.[69] Although the union reemployment function was largely informal, some international and local unions maintained employment bureaus which received applications from both employers and unemployed union members. According to a 1927 AFL survey of its member unions, thirteen international unions maintained bureaus for inter-region reemployment and 33 international unions reported that at least one local union maintained a bureau for local reemployment.[70]

Moreover, the union was the most persistent provider of reemployment services before the 1930s. Since the nineteenth century, private charities had established temporary employment bureaus, but they bore "the stigma of charity" and were often not patronized; commercial bureaus were often guilty of malpractices and deceit and in violation of government statutes; and public bureaus (municipal and state) were often established temporarily during crises and vulnerable to political mismanagement.[71] Also, the federal government was only minimally involved in the provision of employment bureaus before the 1930s. In 1918, the United States Employment Service (USES) was established to address labor needs in production during World War I but Congress greatly reduced USES funding after the War.[72]

One of the earliest collective bargaining agreements establishing inter-plant transfer provisions was the 1936 Washington Job Protection Agreement between 21 railroad unions and 141 carriers. Railroad consolidations and mergers were a chief strategy for maintaining railroad viability during the Depression. The agreement, which was designed to protect workers from displacement by the mergers, provided the workers with advance notice of closings, transfers to new jobs with income protection, separation pay and relocation allowances.[73]

Inter-plant transfer provisions became more prevalent after World War II as companies relocated plants, closed obsolete plants and opened plants with new technology. These provisions were most prevalent in mass production,

[69]American Federation of Labor, *Unions Provide Against Unemployment* (Washington, DC: American Federation of Labor, 1929), pp. 1–2, 16.

[70]Ibid., pp. 12–16.

[71]Bryce Stewart, *Unemployment Benefits in the United States* (New York: Industrial Relations Counselors, 1930), pp. 31–37.

[72]Ibid., pp. 9–10, 38–39.

[73]U.S. Bureau of Labor Statistics, *Major Collective Bargaining Agreements—Plant Movement, Transfer, and Relocation Allowances,* Bulletin no. 1425-10 (Washington, DC: GPO, 1969), p. 1; Everett Hawkins, *Dismissal Compensation and the War Economy,* Pamphlet Series no. 7 (Washington, D.C.: Social Science Research Council, 1942), pp. 32–33.

continuous-employment industries with multi-plant employers, such as food products, primary metals and transportation equipment; they were uncommon in construction where workers tended to work for more than one employer during the year and where the concept of physical plant was unapplicable.[74] Approximately one-third of collective bargaining agreements covering 1000 or more workers had interplant transfer provisions in 1967 and 1980. Most agreements are with multiplant employers rather than with multiple employers.[75]

Transfer provisions commonly apply to workers who are permanently displaced by technological change and other factors which generate plant shutdowns. Displaced workers are given the right to transfer to another plant and more senior workers are often given this right over less senior workers.[76] Relocation allowances paid by the company have become increasingly common. Between 1966 and 1980, the percentage of inter-plant transfer provisions requiring relocation allowances in contracts covering 1000 or more workers increased from 34% to 41%.[77]

2. Unemployment Benefits

The union's role in the provision of unemployment benefits changed in much the same fashion as its reemployment role. Beginning as a direct provider of cash relief to its unemployed members, the union increasingly sought employer-provided relief through collective bargaining after World War II. In addition, organized labor abandoned its "voluntaristic" antipathy toward government-provided unemployment insurance when it first aligned with the Democratic Party during the Depression and supported the New Deal plan for unemployment insurance.

Prior to the 1930s, unions, along with charities and state-run almshouses which relieved the destitute, were the main source of cash relief for the unemployed. Unemployed union members received cash payments which were financed through union dues and administered mainly by local unions during emergencies.[78] Less common were formal, union unemployment benefit programs. The AFL survey mentioned above showed that 60 locals in 12 internationals and the AFL had benefit plans in 1927.[79] Stewart estimated that fewer than 1% of union members were covered by unemployment insurance plans in 1928.[80]

Far fewer were company unemployment benefit plans. Stewart identified

---

[74]U.S. Bureau of Labor Statistics, Bulletin no. 1425-10, pp. 1–2, 22.

[75]Ibid., pp. 22, 72; U.S. Bureau of Labor Statistics, *Major Collective Bargaining Agreements: Plant Movement, Interplant Transfer, and Relocation Allowances*, Bulletin no. 1425-20 (Washington, DC: GPO, 1981), p. 70.

[76]U.S. Bureau of Labor Statistics, Bulletin no 1425-20, p. 21.

[77]Ibid., p. 4.

[78]American Federation of Labor, *Unions Provide*.

[79]Ibid., p. 16.

[80]Stewart, p. 90.

13 company plans in 1928 which either guaranteed employment or paid unemployment compensation.[81] According to a U.S. Bureau of Labor Statistics
survey, 15 companies had unemployment benefit plans in 1931.[82] The
amount of the benefit in these plans was related to the duration of unemployment. Company-provided dismissal pay (or severance pay) became increasingly common in the 1920s era of mechanization and was a definite sum
paid to the displaced worker. Over 500 companies paid dismissal compensation in the 1920s and 1930s.[83]

Organized labor became an advocate of government unemployment insurance during the Depression of the 1930s. Earlier, the AFL under Gompers'
leadership maintained a voluntaristic philosophy, eschewing not only government unemployment benefits but also the alignment of organized labor
with political parties. The AFL adhered to voluntarism in part, according to
historian Daniel Nelson, because "Labor unions were seldom able to rely on
government, and the courts remained generally antagonistic to their purposes and methods."[84] By 1932, many AFL members, including skilled craftsmen, were unemployed, union membership was declining, and numerous
unions including the powerful United Mine Workers supported state unemployment insurance, causing an internal split between old-guard voluntarists
and the pro-unemployment insurance faction. The delegates to the 1932 AFL
Convention approved government unemployment insurance by a large majority and, thereby, "ended a long history of opposition to social insurance
legislation."[85] Organized labor supported the Social Security Act of 1935
which established state unemployment insurance. Moreover, the AFL and
the CIO became increasingly wedded to the Democratic Party, especially after
the passage of the pro-labor Wagner Act in 1935. As Greenstone put it, "By
the end of World War II, voluntarism as a laissez-faire political doctrine was
entirely dead."[86]

A handful of unions had already established joint union–employer unemployment benefit plans through collective bargaining during the 1920s.
Most prevalent in the highly seasonal and bankruptcy-prone apparel industries of New York City, Chicago and Philadelphia, these multi-employer
plans called for payments, to the unemployed borne either solely by employers or jointly by employers and union members. Also, local unions in the
clothing industry, which was faced with technological change in the 1920s,
won company-provided dismissal pay for displaced workers.[87] By the early

[81]Ibid., p. 97.

[82]U.S. Bureau of Labor Statistics, *Unemployment-Benefit Plans in the United States and Unemployment Insurance in Foreign Countries*, Bulletin no. 544 (Washington, DC: GPO, 1931), p. 6.

[83]Hawkins, p. 26.

[84]Daniel Nelson, *Unemployment Insurance, the American Experience 1915–1935* (Madison, WI: University of Wisconsin Press, 1969), p. 67. Also, see J. David Greenstone, *Labor in American Politics* (New York: Vintage, 1969), pp. 25–36.

[85]Nelson, *Unemployment Insurance*, p. 161.

[86]Greenstone, p. 54.

[87]U.S. Bureau of Labor Statistics, Bulletin no. 544, pp. 14–19; Hawkins, p. 32.

1940s, dismissal pay was used to relieve workers who were displaced by technological change, but few agreements provided for dismissal pay.[88] In 1940, CIO President Phillip Murray argued before the Temporary National Economic Committee that dismissal pay for technologically displaced workers should be secured through collective bargaining, if compulsory federal legislation could not be adopted.[89] In 1944, fewer than 5% of labor agreements provided for severance pay.[90]

Unions achieved company-provided severance pay and supplemental unemployment benefit (SUB) plans through collective bargaining after World War II with the introduction of automation in basic industry. However, the original impetus for such plans occurred during the War, in anticipation of mass unemployment that would result from post-War reconversion to a peace-time economy, and from a perceived inadequacy of state unemployment insurance.[91] In 1943, several CIO unions in the steel, auto, aluminum, electrical, and meat packing industries demanded from the War Labor Board guaranteed employment and wages to cushion the shock of post-war reconversion and continued their demands after the war. In 1947, the Advisory Board of the Office of War Mobilization and Reconversion held that guaranteed wage plans should not be put in legislation and promoted collective bargaining solutions instead.[92]

Severance pay and SUB plans were increasingly negotiated through collective bargaining in the 1950s. The percentage of agreements covering 1000 or more workers with company-provided severance pay increased from about 15% to 30% between 1955 and 1963 and levelled off to 34% by 1980.[93] SUB plans were company-provided payments to displaced workers which were designed to supplement state unemployment insurance benefits. The first SUB plan was negotiated between the United Automobile Workers and Ford Motor Company in 1955. By 1965, almost all states had amended their unemployment insurance laws to allow for SUBs and the number of SUB plans had increased from 12 to 81 between 1956 and 1963.[94] However, SUB plans were less prevalent than provisions for severance pay. Fourteen percent of agreements covering 1,000 or more workers had SUB provisions in 1963 and 1980.[95]

In conclusion, the union role in preventing and relieving technological unemployment has shifted from that of provider to that of advocate. With the advent of continuous employment in the internal labor market of one em-

---

[88]U.S. Bureau of Labor Statistics, *Union Agreement Provisions*, Bulletin no. 686 (Washington, DC: GPO, 1942), p. 71.

[89]Hawkins, p. 36.

[90]U.S. Bureau of Labor Statistics, *Major Collective Bargaining Agreements—Severance Pay and Layoff Benefit Plans*, Bulletin no. 1425-2 (Washington, DC: GPO, 1965), p. 6.

[91]Hawkins, pp. 40–42.

[92]Joseph Becker, *Supplemental Unemployment Benefits* (Cambridge, MA: Cambridge Center for Social Studies, 1967), chapter 1, pp. 1–27.

[93]U.S. Bureau of Labor Statistics, Bulletin no. 1425-2, p. 6 and Bulletin no. 2095, p. 108.

[94]U.S. Bureau of Labor Statistics, *Supplemental Unemployment Benefit Plans and Wage-Employment Guarantees*, Bulletin no. 1425-3 (Washington, DC: GPO, 1965), p. 1; Becker, chapter 2, pp. 2, 30.

[95]U.S. Bureau of Labor Statistics, Bulletin no. 1425-3, p. 78 and Bulletin no. 2095, p. 108.

ployer, the decline of the union labor supply function, and the jeopardization of union benefit programs during the 1930s, the union has increasingly become an advocate, bargaining with employers for preventive and relief measures and lobbying the government for social insurance programs.

However, the union role of advocate in the prevention and relief of technological unemployment during the post-World War II era has been enacted in diverse ways in different industries. Such diversity derives in part from differences in macroeconomic, political, and organizational conditions and in the legacies of labor relations among industries, as shown by the succeeding chapters in this book.

IV. PLAN OF THE BOOK

The analyses of changing labor relations arrangements in the fourteen industries covered in this book suggest two broad processes by which labor and management have attempted to control the implementation of technological change during the post-World War II era. The first, increasing unilateral managerial control, typically reflects a decline of union input into decision making; a transfer in the possession of production knowledge from labor toward management; increasing use of technology by management to monitor and control labor; and/or increasing flexibility for management in the introduction of technology. The second process, increasing labor–management cooperation, involves the proliferation of institutionalized, joint labor–management decision-making forums. These include decision making, political lobbying and research committees, and programs that are often established in and as parallel structures to collective bargaining. They may address such issues as productivity, training, company- and industry-wide job security and profitability, adverse government regulatory and legislative change, occupational safety and health and the quality of work life, and wield advisory or binding decision making authority. Part II, "Toward Increasing Unilateral Managerial Control?" and Part III, "Toward Labor–Management Cooperation?" include chapters on industries whose labor relations trends have taken on the characteristics of one of these two processes, respectively. The question marks following the subtitles denote a presumed impermanence of any labor relations trend as well as the tendency of any trends to comprise, in varying degrees, characteristics of both processes. The concluding chapter addresses the determinants of cooperation and unilateral managerial control based on a comparison of the industries covered in this book.

ACKNOWLEDGMENTS

I am gratefully indebted to William Form and Randy Hodson for their helpful comments on earlier drafts, to Laurie Alioto, Doris Davis and Mamie Padgett for typing the manuscript, to Mark Leners for research assistance, and to the AFL-CIO Department for Professional Employees for providing me with materials.

II

TOWARD UNILATERAL
MANAGERIAL CONTROL?

The chapters in Part II cover industries in which management has been able to deploy strategies for controlling the labor process at the point of production, in the shop or office, during the post-World War II era. These strategies include job deskilling, in which the adoption of new technology simplifies the content of jobs; technical control, whereby management wrests from workers discretion over the determination of work methods and pace, through the design and implementation of new production technology; and/or bureaucratic control, in which worker loyalty and compliance in an internal labor market are gained through the establishment of seniority rules and the provision of fringe benefits.

These control strategies have been applied to diverse occupational groups in various industries. In agriculture, newspaper printing, and longshoring, control strategies have been applied to laborers and blue-collar occupations (Chapters 2–4); in the U.S. Postal Service and the insurance industry, control strategies have been deployed among diverse clerical occupations (Chapters 5 and 6); and, management control strategies have been applied to professional occupations in the public education and air traffic control industries (Chapters 7 and 8).

Each of these industries is characterized by at least one of three features which have facilitated the increase in managerial control during the post-World War II era. First, all of the industries have experienced favorable market conditions, which have facilitated technological change and, in some cases, the provision of severance pay or "buy-out" packages to technologically displaced workers. Second, unionization is relatively rare in most of these industries, providing workers with little or no bargaining strength for controlling the implementation and outcomes of technological change. Finally, with comparatively high rates of quitting and low on-the-job tenure, most of these industries employ "casual" workforces which lack a vested interest in the survival of their employers, giving management greater flexibility in redesigning the workplace.

2

Microchips and Macroharvests
Labor–Management Relations in Agriculture

Robert J. Thomas

Since the early 1960s, many large Southwestern agricultural employers have been working with plant breeders and electrical engineers to recast fruit and vegetable growing into a rationalized production system. Theirs is a vision of agriculture dominated by prosperous firms continuously producing perishable commodities with the aid of the latest advances in bioengineering and manufacturing technologies. Evidence of incremental success in their venture is abundant in California, Arizona, Florida and, increasingly, larger segments of U.S. agriculture.[1] In the early 1960s, for example, the breeding of new tomato varieties, durable enough to withstand the rough and tumble of mechanical harvesting, made it possible for growers to cut the labor force by two-thirds, increase yields, and achieve greater reliability in the timing of deliveries.[2] Tomatoes, once picked and sorted by hand, are now uprooted and "destalked" mechanically and sorted with the aid of electro-optic sensors.[3] Equally impressive, in the early 1970s scientists and engineers employed

---

[1]For a survey of recent developments in agricultural research, see Wayne Rasmussen, The Mechanization of Work," in *Scientific American* special edition, *The Mechanization of Work* (San Francisco: Freeman Publishing Co., 1982), pp. 15–30; Robert J. Kalter, "The New Biotech Agriculture: Unforeseen Economic Consequences," *Issues in Science and Technology* 2(Fall 1985), pp. 125–34; and Jack Doyle, "Biotechnology and Agricultural Stability," ibid., pp. 111–24.

[2]William H. Friedland and Amy E. Barton, *Destalking the Wily Tomato: A Case Study in the Consequences of California Agricultural Research* (Davis, CA: University of California, Department of Applied Behavioral Sciences, Research Monograph #15, (1975).

[3]Ann Scheuring and Orville Thompson, *From Lug Boxes to Electronics: A Study of California Tomato Growers and Sorting Crews* (Davis, CA: University of California, Agricultural Policy Seminar, 1978).

Robert J. Thomas • Sloan School of Management, Massachusetts Institute of Technology, Cambridge, MA 02139.

microelectronics to devise harvesting machines which can "select" mature lettuce heads for cutting, thus allowing multiple passes through a field as the crop ripens.[4]

Although the marriage of genetic and electrical engineering promises to spawn an increase in productivity, these developments tend to conceal two important facts. First, focused concern about productivity is a relatively recent phenomenon in the fruit and vegetable industries of the Southwest. Indeed, with some crops today machete-like knives and spring-action staplers remain the principal harvest tools. Second, the pattern of deployment of new production technologies has been uneven. The mechanical harvest of tomatoes began with those grown for processing (e.g., tomatoes turned into sauce, paste, and related products) but was only slowly adopted for tomatoes destined for the supermarket. Machine harvesting of wine grapes spread rapidly in the late 1970s though the technology had been available as much as five years earlier. And, as will be discussed later, the mechanical lettuce harvester has been available for over a decade but hand labor continues to be the dominant harvest technique.

The relatively late attraction to new production technologies and their uneven deployment have roots in two major factors: (1) the political struggle waged between employers and union forces for control over agricultural labor markets and, by extension, for control over the content of agricultural work; and (2) the changing economic organization of Southwestern agriculture. Beyond their independent effects, these two factors in combination explain a great deal about the organization of work and labor–management relations in agriculture.

As I will argue in this chapter, employers' support for various labor importation programs and, most recently, their vehement opposition to restrictions on the entry of immigrant workers have won for them the capacity to exert political and economic pressure on the labor force and with it a strategy of "simple" control[5] over the work process. By manipulating the political vulnerability of the largely Hispanic and/or non-citizen labor force, employers have effectively dampened the strength of worker organization around the terms and conditions of employment.[6] The low wages and a steady supply of labor generated by successful intervention in the labor market made fruit and vegetable production profitable but relatively backward technologically up through the 1950s and 1960s.

[4]M. Zahara, S. S. Johnson and R. E. Garret, "Labor Requirements, Harvest Costs, and the Potential for Mechanized Harvesting of Lettuce," *Journal of the American Society for Horticultural Science* 99(Spring 1974), pp. 535–7; and William H. Friedland, Amy E. Barton and Robert J. Thomas, *Manufacturing Green Gold: Labor, Capital and Technology in the Lettuce Industry* (New York: Cambridge University Press, 1981).

[5]Richard Edwards, *Contested Terrain* (New York: Basic Books), p. 16–36.

[6]Robert J. Thomas, "Citizenship, Gender and Work: Some Considerations for Labor Process Theories," in *Marxist Inquiries* ed. Michael Burawoy and Theda Skoopol (Chicago: University of Chicago Press, 1982), pp. 86–112; Michael Burawoy, "Functions and Reproduction of Migrant Labor," *American Sociological Review* 38 (October 1976), pp. 1050–87; and Linda and Theo Majka, *Farmworkers, Agribusiness and the State* (Philadelphia: Temple University Press, 1982).

Yet, as I will suggest, the attractiveness of agriculture as a locale for new profits (or tax losses) inspired investments by industrial enterprises in the 1960s. With the influx of non-agricultural firms also came economic re-organization, especially in the form of concentration of production and ver-tical integration. Their efforts spurred imitation among large agricultural firms seeking to remain competitive. Though not inclined toward immediate implementation of new technology, the new agribusiness enterprises sought to combine the inherent advantages of a low wage, malleable, and abundant labor force with a more integrated industrial approach to production.

Most significantly, economic concentration in agriculture provided the opportunity for a new approach to union organization among farm workers. The economic fragmentation and strong local political influence which had characterized agriculture historically gave way in the 1960s and 1970s to high-ly visible firms with financial ties to industry and banking, and enabled one farm worker organization, the United Farm Workers union (UFW), to do what its organizational predecessors could not: threaten real economic harm if workers were not allowed representation. The ability of the UFW to develop local organization—in addition to the highly successful consumer boycotts of grapes, wine, and lettuce in the late 1960s and early 1970s—enabled the union to wrest unprecedented influence in several industries over access to jobs and, therefore, over the terms of employment.

As I will conclude, however, the union's efforts to broaden farm worker representation touched off the drive to increase labor productivity and, in some instances, to replace labor with new technology. For those firms which can afford it, new technology provides the opportunity to institute "tech-nical" control[7]—machine-pacing and a reorganized labor process—as a suc-cessor to traditional simple controls over workers. However, the uneven de-ployment of new production technology rests not simply on which firms can afford it; rather, new technology deployment has been substantially affected by the ability of employers to mute the union's influence by gaining access to new supplies of vulnerable labor—in particular, undocumented workers ("il-legal aliens"). Through two brief case studies, I will analyze the dilemmas facing farm worker unions as they confront the two-edged sword of un-protected labor and technological change in agriculture.

In order to put the trends in labor–management relations in agriculture into perspective, the analysis will be broken into four parts: (a) the structural factors influencing worker organization historically; (b) changes in the eco-nomic organization of Southwestern agriculture and their implications for unionization; (c) the history and present dilemmas of the United Farm Work-ers union; and (d) discussion of two instructive cases in new technology and labor–management relations—the tomato and lettuce industries in Califor-nia. In the conclusion I will return to the broader context of political economy as a basis for understanding the relationship between technology and labor management relations in agriculture.

[7]Edwards, pp. 52–7.

I. POLITICAL ECONOMY OF AGRICULTURE AND UNIONIZATION

Although the United Farm Workers union headed by Cesar Chavez is often referred to as the first successful agricultural workers' union in the nation, it is more correctly termed the longest-running union. That is, as students of agricultural labor history have shown, the UFW was preceded by a sizeable number of unions and less formal worker organizations.[8] The Industrial Workers of the World, a handful of socialist and communist unions, the Teamsters, and a number of AFL and AFL-CIO creations have at one time or another tried their hand in the fields. While they may not have enjoyed the longevity of the UFW, these organizations nonetheless constituted important efforts to develop at least some measure of organization and protection for field workers. In addition to the groups that survived long enough to acquire a place in historical literature were the short-lived but significant collections of workers who banded together to mount a challenge to employers.

The sporadic success of earlier farm worker unions, tallied in occasional wage concessions or momentary protection from bullying, cannot be understood without consideration of the obstacles posed to worker organization by the political and economic structure of agriculture. One immediate and obvious obstacle was the powerful political organization of agricultural employers. At the national level, the American Farm Bureau Federation, particularly in the period of the 1920s–60s, stymied the efforts of industrial labor unions to extend the umbrella of federal labor legislation to include farm work. The Department of Agriculture, even during the New Deal era, was a virtual captive of the Farm Bureau it created.[9] Even when the Farm Bureau failed to develop a coherent strategy for overcoming regional and commodity cleavages in its national membership, it managed to organize a united front of agricultural employers implacable in their hostility to the unionization of farm labor.[10] Wielding the scepter of the Jeffersonian ideology of yeoman agriculture and its alleged centrality to republican democracy, the Farm Bureau pierced all attempts to include farm laborers within the National Labor Relations Act of 1935.[11]

At the local level the Jeffersonian guise was also invoked, but far less frequently. In its place, growers (as they refer to themselves) brandished the

---

[8]Majka and Majka, pp. 113–35; Ernesto Galarza, *Merchants of Labor* (Santa Barbara: McNally and Loftin, 1964), and *Spiders in the House and Workers in the Field* (South Bend, IN: Notre Dame University Press); Merle Weiner, "Cheap Food, Cheap Labor: California Agriculture in the 1930s," *Insurgent Sociologist* 8 (Fall, 1982), pp. 181–90; William H. Friedland and Robert J. Thomas, "Paradoxes of Agricultural Unionism in California," *Society* (May–June 1974), pp. 54–62; Robert J. Thomas and William H. Friedland, "The United Farm Workers Union: From Mobilization to Mechanization?" (Ann Arbor: Center for Research on Social Organization, Working Paper #269), pp. 12–28; and Robert J. Thomas, *Citizenship, Gender and Work: The Social Organization of Industrial Agriculture* (Berkeley: University of California Press, 1985), chapters 5 and 6.
[9]Grant McConnell, *The Decline of Agrarian Democracy* (New York: Atheneum, 1969).
[10]Majka and Majka, pp. 3–20, 51–73.
[11]McConnell, pp. 44–55.

direct force of local police and vigilantes to quash refusals to accept meager wages or 19th-century sweatshop working conditions. Throughout the period 1880–1940, strikebreakers were imported from other areas to replace the discontented; often those who broke the strikes did so out of a need to fight for their own survival. When the opportunity arose, growers pitted ethnic groups against one another, exacerbating the antagonisms, for example, which already existed among equally powerless Mexican and Filipino members in a split labor market.[12] The outcome of such competition, most commonly, was one group's acceptance of lower wages and worse working conditions.

Whereas the Farm Bureau derived its leverage in the period 1920–1940 from its purported representation of agriculture nationally, local anti-union interests derived theirs from the immediate dependency of local merchants, politicians, schools, and churches on the economic fortunes of growers. For example, the rural towns of Salinas, El Centro, Delano, and Bakersfield drew sustenance from the agricultural economy just as much as Southern communities were dominated by cotton plantations.[13]

At both the national and local levels, the concept of "agricultural exceptionalism" served (and continues to serve) as a shorthand rationale for the exclusion of farm labor from industrial legislation and for the direction of national agricultural policy.[14] Exceptionalism, briefly, claimed that agriculture by its very nature could not be equated with industry: farming was small business and the cornerstone of a free polity; and farmers were subject to the vagaries of God, weather, and natural calamity. In other words, agriculture could not withstand the combined stress of upholding democracy, weathering unpredictable acts of God and nature, *and* unionism.

Though the temptation to dismiss these claims might be strong, particularly in light of the historically larger scale and intensity of agriculture in the Southwest, there is an element of truth embedded in the ideology of exceptionalism. In the period 1880–1940, the organization of agricultural production was characterized by relatively small firms growing crops for local markets: they either sold their crops to brokerage agents or they grew commodities under contract with processing firms which transformed the crop (e.g., wine grapes, tomatoes or canning vegetables) into finished products.[15] Most distinctive of agricultural production was its seasonal and localized character. That is, the agricultural economy was typified by independent firms tied to

[12]Edna Bonacich, "Advanced Capitalism and Black-White Relations in the United States," *American Journal of Sociology* 41 (1976): pp. 34–51.

[13]For a glimpse at the remarkable similarity in social structure of southern and southwestern rural towns, see Walter Goldschmidt, *As You Sow: Three Studies in the Social Consequences of Agribusiness* (Montclair, NJ: Allanheld Osmun, 1978); Oliver Cox, *Caste, Class and Race* (Garden City, NY: Doubleday, 1948); and John Steinbeck, *Grapes of Wrath* (New York: Bantam Press, 1966).

[14]Friedland and Thomas, pp. 54–6.

[15]For a more detailed discussion of the varying production and contracting arrangements organized in Southwestern agriculture during this period, see Robert J. Thomas, "Social Organization of Industrial Agriculture," *Insurgent Sociologist* 10 (Winter 1981), pp. 5–20.

particular geographic areas by land ownership, and constrained in their production cycles by the seasonal nature of agriculture. Few if any firms produced in more than one area, even though most produced more than one
crop when weather permitted. Thus, until the 1940s, there were no "mobile
firms"[16] producing lettuce or broccoli on a daily basis throughout the year by
leasing acreage in scattered production areas.

This geographical and organizational discontinuity in production affected the degrees of freedom open to farm owners in organizing production.
For most it meant that the demand for labor was uneven at best. While highly
skilled family labor could be called upon to maintain the farm in the interim
period between planting and harvesting and during the winter season, planting and harvesting chores often far outstripped the capacity of family labor.
Few farm owners found it economically rational to invest in training hired,
seasonal labor to perform more than a few relatively simple chores. The
sensitivity of most farms to market conditions, especially with the high cost of
land and restricted access to capital, further diminished the feasibility of a
more continuous use of labor and heightened the demand for unskilled,
seasonal workers.[17] These two factors—a demand for unskilled labor and the
uneven demand for labor generally—combined to generate a specifically agricultural labor market.

The actual construction of the labor market, however, was an overtly
political process. In order to satisfy a generalized need for labor which would
be continuously available, unskilled, willing to travel in search of employment, and willing to accept meager wages, employers banded together on
regional and state levels.[18] Using their substantial leverage as food producers,
major contributors to the agricultural (and, therefore, state and national)
economy, defenders of democracy, and guardians of traditional morals and
values, employers and their representatives sought to construct continuous
sources of labor which would be available when needed for short periods but
which could be jettisoned when unneeded. During the late 1800s through the
1940s, attractive labor was found largely in a succession of alien workers.
Thus, as London and Anderson so eloquently described: "Indian, Chinese,
Filipino, Japanese, and Mexican workers followed one another's footsteps
into California's fields, there to find working conditions virtually unchanged
since the initiation of commercial agriculture in the mid-1800s."[19] The recruitment of alien labor created a politically-mediated labor market: one which
gave to employers considerable power in determining wage levels and work-

[16]Thomas, *Citizenship*, p. 48.

[17]Paul S. Taylor and Tom Vasey, "Historical Background of California Farm Labor," *Rural Sociology* 1 (September, 1936), pp. 281–95, and "Contemporary Background of California Farm
Labor," *Rural Sociology* 1 (December 1936), pp. 401–19.

[18]See Lloyd Fisher's discussion of employer organizations and their efforts to influence local,
state and national governments, in *Harvest Labor Markets in California* (Cambridge: Harvard
University Press, 1953).

[19]Joan London and Henry Anderson, *So Shall Ye Reap* (New York: Thomas Y. Crowell, 1970), p.
39.

ing conditions and which, through the denial of the political protections of citizenship, severely restricted the capacity of workers to negotiate the labor contract.

These factors combined to produce myriad obstacles to the organization of farm workers. Differences in language, culture, and aspirations among ethnic groups, along with the capacity of employers to set these groups in competition with one another, dampened the efforts of domestic labor organizers to create a common ground for organization.[20] The elastic supply of labor curtailed the potential for any one organization to carry out a successful work stoppage, since dissidents were capable of being replaced by less militant workers. The dispersed character of employment, with unmarked fields separated from rural communities by miles of meandering roads, inhibited traditional "factory gate" leafletting and speech-making. Finally, the migrancy of the workers themselves posed major problems in organization. The short duration of employment often precluded development of real organizational commitments before workers had to pack their belongings and scatter in search of the next job.

Though a later development, the Bracero Program epitomized the politically-mediated labor market. Begun in 1942 as a formalization of past labor recruitment practices, the Bracero Program (officially known as Public Law 78) established an open pipeline of Mexican workers to southwestern fields.[21] The labor contract which brought Mexican workers north was negotiated between growers (through their labor supply associations initially, and later through the U.S. Department of Labor) and the Mexican government, and stipulated wage levels and the duration of employment prior to the beginning of a season. Braceros, lacking any organized means by which to participate in wage negotiations, worked in the fields for the length of their certification and then were returned to Mexico to reenter the pipeline.

Because braceros were readily available at a price favorable to employers, domestic workers were forced to either compete with the contract workers or leave the fields altogether. Despite numerous attempts to publicly demonstrate the adverse affect of non-citizen workers on wages and working conditions, labor organizers (in particular, organizers supported by the AFL-CIO chartered National Farm Laborers Union) could not overcome the sheer political strength of agricultural employers nor could they begin to make even the most elementary advances in organizing the braceros themselves. The intransigence of employers was only bolstered by the increased importance of food supplies to the nation during the Second World War and the Korean conflict.

However, with the election of John Kennedy in 1960, Congressional debate over the termination of the Bracero Program pitched in favor of union

[20]See, in particular, Galarza, *Merchants*, chapters 3 and 4, and Majka and Majka, pp. 136–66.
[21]The most detailed discussions of the operations and local impacts of the Bracero Program are to be found in Galarza, *Merchants*. However, for an analysis of the national political debates surrounding P.L. 78, see Richard Craig, *The Bracero Program* (Austin: University of Texas Press, 1971), and Otey Scruggs, "Evolution of the Mexican Farm Labor Agreement of 1942," *Agricultural History* 34 (1960), pp. 140–49.

and liberal forces. Two anti-Bracero arguments, in particular, found a sympathetic ear: first, with rising unemployment in the nation's cities (a partial consequence of the massive northward migration of displaced black farmworkers and sharecroppers), the potential availability of thousands of unemployed urban residents as domestic replacements for Mexican migrants became a rationale for termination of the program; and, second, with union backers of the new Democratic administration who sought to extend their influence in the rapidly developing food industry (i.e., the growing corporate-dominated food processing and packaging sector) by establishing a solid foundation in the fields.[22] The anti-Bracero campaign gained momentum in the first years of the Kennedy administration, though actual dismantling of the program was not completed until 1964–65.

Ostensibly, the termination of the Bracero Program should have changed the structure and the composition of the agricultural labor market. It did, but not in a direction favorable to modernization of labor–management relations. First, the termination of the Bracero Program was not accompanied by a major change in the legal status of farm labor. Agricultural workers continued to work outside the protections of the National Labor Relations Act. Equally important, individual states remained fully in control of the eligibility requirements for receipt of unemployment and workmen's compensation, food subsidies, and transfer payments. Workers had few alternatives to "moving on" when the season ended in one area since they could not file for unemployment compensation, and welfare eligibility requirements made it difficult to acquire non-work support. Thus, farm workers continued to be bedeviled by agricultural exceptionalism, on the one hand, and by the ability of local politicians to enforce their mobility between agricultural employers, on the other hand.

Second, the replacement of Mexican workers by the domestic unemployed failed to occur. Agricultural employers, angered by the loss of their elastic supply of labor, did little to attract citizen workers into the fields. Wage increases for most jobs were minimal and remained below those available in manufacturing; furthermore, no significant efforts were made to upgrade either the working conditions or the status of farm work. Many of the urban unemployed either refused to accept agricultural working conditions (preferring to stay in the cities) or left the fields after a short trial period. Also, the official demise of the Bracero Program was incomplete. Left behind as a loophole in the McCarran-Walter Immigration Act of 1952 was a clause allowing for the emergency certification of foreign immigration in case of a shortage of specific categories of labor. With the onset of the summer season of 1965 and the apparent shortage of domestic replacements, California growers petitioned the Secretary of Labor for emergency supplies of Mexican nationals to undertake the harvest.[23] The importation of "green-cards" developed into an alternative labor supply in short order.

---

[22]Craig, Chapter 3.
[23]"Editorial," *Western Grower and Shipper*, (May 1965), p. 2.

While the green-cards had greater formal protections than their bracero predecessors (largely in the formal right to choose their employers), they were not the only "new" entrants in the fields. A much larger loophole appeared as employers bemoaned the loss of the braceros: the accessibility of undocumented workers. Although the bracero pipeline was closed, the undocumented worker floodgate opened. With little attention paid to border regulation in the years prior to 1965, the Immigration and Naturalization Service (INS) and its enforcement arm, the Border Patrol, were insufficiently prepared for the massive influx of Mexican nationals who came across the border seeking to recapture the jobs they had occupied (or sought to acquire) as braceros. Even with the infusion of tax dollars into the INS budget (partially stimulated by union lobbying), the Border Patrol proved woefully inadequate in dealing with the problem. Indeed, in light of the Border Patrol's largely unsuccessful efforts since 1965 to effectively control the flow of immigrants north, it would seem that, as Burawoy and others[24] have argued, greater attention (and more vigorous deportation procedures) to the problem has only accentuated the political vulnerability of undocumented labor, not arrested its flow.

II. STRUCTURAL CHANGE AND ITS CONSEQUENCES

Post-World War II changes in the political economy of agricultural production in the southwestern United States changed significantly the environment in which unions attempted to organize farm workers. Two changes are relevant to the analysis: concentration in production, particularly in what had been labor-intensive crops, and changes in the structure of the enterprises engaged in agricultural production. In some cases these changes resulted in an alteration of the labor process in production, particularly toward mechanized harvesting; in other cases, organizational changes more directly affected the susceptibility or vulnerability of enterprises to challenges by farm workers for union representation.

As Fellmeth[25], Villarejo[26] and others have documented, California agriculture has historically led the nation in terms of the size of production units, percentage of fresh and processed fruits and vegetables, and corporate ownership of land and product. During the period 1940–1975, the production of major fruit and vegetable crops steadily increased in volume but decreased in total production units; as more was being grown, fewer firms were growing it. Although few precise figures are available to document the process of

[24]Burawoy, pp. 1066–72; Thomas, "Social Organization," p. 21; and Robert Bach, "Mexican Immigration and the American State," *International Migration Review* 42 (Winter, 1978), pp. 536–58.

[25]Robert Fellmeth, *Politics of Land* (New York: Grossman, 1973), especially the chapters devoted to landownership.

[26]Don Villarejo, *Getting Bigger: Large-Scale Farming in California* (Davis, CA: California Institute for Rural Studies, 1980).

concentration, a few examples provide evidence. Prior to 1960, nearly 4,000 farms produced tomatoes for processing; by 1974, however, fewer than 600 farms grew tomatoes (even though total production had increased significantly).[27] In 1940, the three largest lettuce growers accounted for less than 20% of all the lettuce produced in California and Arizona; by 1978, the top three produced nearly 50% (with individual contributions reaching nearly 40% at some points during the year).[28] In the 1940s, citrus production in California was carried out on several thousand small farms; by the mid 1970s, less than 8% of all citrus producers accounted for 47% of the crop.[29] Similar processes occurred in the wine and table grape industries.[30]

Some of the bigger firms had roots in the more successful competitors who survived the 1930s depression. Many others, however, came in from the "outside" in the much publicized corporate penetration of agriculture during the decades of the 1950s and 1960s. Companies like Tenneco (wine grapes, cotton, assorted vegetables), Santa Fe Land Company (grapes, cotton), United Brands (lettuce, mixed vegetables), Purex (lettuce), Coca-Cola (citrus, wine), Schenley, Heublein, and National Distillers (wine and brandy) joined large local firms such as Gallo and Almaden to significantly change the organizational shape of California agriculture. With the growth of extensive and durable marketing networks, linkages to chemical and fertilizer producers, vast agglomerations of land and production capital, and advances in production technique, the costs of entering the business skyrocketed and the market position of smaller firms eroded further.

At the same time that corporate agriculture expanded its share of production, many large firms sought to establish and expand their market position through aggressive advertizing. Major processing firms like Contadina, Hunt-Wesson, Heinz, Libby's, Gallo, Almaden, Christian Brothers, Campbells and others attempted to fix their names in the public mind and increase the expense of entering into the highly lucrative processing and distilling industry. Other firms, such as Bud-Antle, attempted to create brand-name identification with consumers by putting their company logo on the plastic wrapper found on lettuce in the supermarket;[31] Sunkist expanded the use of ink dies on the skins of their oranges and lemons to cement a consumer association between the brand-name and product quality.

The changing political economy of agricultural production—increased concentration, corporate penetration, and brand-name advertising—altered the stage upon which agricultural labor and capital struggled. Most impor-

---

[27]Friedland and Barton, p. 3.

[28]Friedland, Barton, and Thomas, p. 49; Thomas, *Citizenship*, p. 81.

[29]Vincent Valvano, "Concentration and Centralization in U.S. Citrus Production," paper presented to the Conference on the Political Economy of Food and Agriculture in the Advanced Industrial Societies, Guelph, Canada (August, 1981).

[30]William H. Friedland, unpublished monograph on the social consequences of mechanization in the California grape industry.

[31]Anne Fredricks, "Agribusiness in the Lettuce Fields," *Food Monitor* 10 (May–June 1979), pp. 12–15.

tant, economic concentration brought about a concentration of workers in production. As a consequence, the personal relations between employer and employee tended to be minimized in the face of a much larger labor force and a much more bureaucratic administrative and personnel system. Furthermore, companies found it more rational (if only in budgetary terms) to directly handle their own employment and labor recruitment, thus removing the middleman labor contractor altogether.[32]

Corporate penetration into agriculture also brought with it many firms which based their profitability on other products.[33] For example, firms like Coca-Cola (Coke, Minute Maid), United Brands (Chiquita Bananas), Heublein (Smirnoff Vodka), Seagrams (Seagram's 7, VO), Purex (Bleach), and National Distillers (Gilbey's Gin, Old Grand-Dad) all banked on other consumer items as their principal profit centers. Although they were in a better position to weather the vagaries of agricultural production in general—whether that meant oscillations in weather, market prices, or labor unions—profitability in other product lines did not bring with it a complete guarantee of invulnerability. In particular, the high visibility of these main-line products and their centrality to corporate profits also made them potentially susceptable to "negative" brand-name identification, largely in the form of organized consumer boycotts.

III. A DIFFERENT APPROACH TO UNIONIZATION

Structural change in the political economy of Southwestern agriculture provided an important point of leverage for farm worker unionization, particularly for the fledgling United Farm Workers union headed by Cesar Chavez. Concentration and centralization of production, increased reliance on brand-name identification, and stabilization of employment relations all contributed to the visibility of organizing efforts and, more importantly, to the potential economic impact of a company's resistance to unionization. Although academic accounts of the rise of the UFW have laid great emphasis on the determining role of liberal activism in the 1960s,[34] the ability of the UFW to conduct its now-famous boycotts of wine, grapes, and (to a lesser extent) head lettuce relied heavily on corporate visibility and vulnerability in the public eye.[35]

An equally important, but often overlooked, aspect of the UFW's organizational success resided in its ability to combine a non-traditional organizing style along with its efforts to tap the national media and sympathetic audiences for support.[36] By focusing on community organizing, initially through an

[32]Thomas, *Citizenship,* Chapter 5.
[33]Fellmeth, pp. 26–114; and Daniel Zwerdling, "The Food Monsters," in J. Skolnick and E. Currie (eds.) *Crisis in American Institutions* (Boston: Little, Brown, 1982, 5th ed.), pp. 38–53.
[34]Craig Jenkins and Charles Perrow, "Insurgency of the Powerless: Farm Worker Movements, 1946–72," *American Sociological Review* 42 (October 1977), pp. 249–67.
[35]Arguments in this section draw heavily from Thomas and Friedland, "The United Farm Workers Union."
[36]Ibid, pp. 38–70; and Friedland and Thomas, pp. 54–62.

association of farm workers (the National Farm Workers Association of NFWA), Cesar Chavez and the UFW leadership sought to identify workers' common social and economic needs before launching into direct confrontation with employers. Thus, for example, credit unions, burial insurance, and low-cost gas and car repairs became the organization's first objectives as it sought to create bonds of solidarity within an otherwise fragmented labor force. The organization pursued this strategy in its early years (1962–65) *despite* sentiments among farm workers (members and non-members alike) that unionization was the only real key to better working and living conditions.

An unorthodox but successful approach to organizing helped the UFW transform the *opportunities* for unionization into reality. But, in order to understand how those opportunities were exploited (and turned into negotiated contracts with employers) it is necessary to briefly consider the strategy the union devised to take advantage of structural changes in agriculture. Two aspects of the union's strategy are important: (1) concentrating on pockets in the industry where workers were geographically and/or organizationally stable; and (2) employing product boycotts to exert economic leverage with large enterprises.

A. Stability

The first systematic organizing efforts were directed toward farm workers in Kern County, California (in the southern end of the San Joaquin Valley). During the peak of season Kern County accounts for the bulk of the national output of grapes (as the weather changes and production shifts north from the other major production area, the Coachella Valley). The availability of work, first in the harvest, then in the meticulous process of pruning back exhausted vines, and finally in other phases of production (e.g., weeding), made it possible for some workers to settle in local communities such as Delano and find stable employment throughout much of the year.[37] Organizational and employment stability had resulted from the changing economic organization of the industry. As firms increased in size—through the purchase and combination of smaller farms by larger ones—the number of employers decreased and workers who had formerly moved between several companies came to be employed for longer periods by fewer firms. For many of these workers, migration in search of work was extremely limited and often consisted more in long-distance commuting between home and various work sites.

In contrast to the braceros whose legal status was conditioned by the terms of their temporary labor contract, the workers whom Chavez and the UFW had organized tended to be either citizens or permanent-resident immigrants. Although the alignment of local governments and police agencies

---

[37]This is not to argue that all grape workers were drawn from local labor pools; by contrast, up to the termination of the Bracero Program, the majority of workers were drawn from Mexico under the contract provisions of the program.

with employers often jeopardized the legal rights of even citizen farm workers, claims to the political and legal entitlements of citizenship of an *organized* group proved to be an important resource for the fledgling organization. This was borne out by the victories of the civil rights movement (affirmed in the passage of the Civil Rights Act of 1964) and later demonstrated in political support from the Democratic Party in California and elsewhere for the farm workers movement. More immediately, however, the low wages and poor working conditions which citizen farm workers had suffered (as a result of the flooding of the labor market by braceros) had created a long-standing, shared grievance amongst citizen and documented immigrants. The predominance of braceros in the labor force and the confounding effect of shared culture and national heritage among farm workers (both citizen and non-citizen) had muted the potential for solidarity along the lines of citizenship status; however, the termination of the Bracero Program provided the potential for citizen and documented workers to claim jobs formerly held by braceros and to assert their legal rights to organize unions. This was especially the case among citizen and permanent immigrant workers in the grape industry who had already "invested" in the industry by way of their geographical and employment stabilization.

B. Product Boycotts

In September, 1965, the UFW was drawn into a strike against grape growers when the membership refused to cross the picket lines of the Agricultural Workers Organizing Committee (AWOC), an older union (comprised mainly of Filipino workers) struggling to win concessions from grape growers. The combined efforts of the UFW and AWOC were successful in bringing workers out to stand on the picket lines; the strike was, however, a failure economically. It ultimately failed, as many of its predecessors had over the past century, largely due to the capacity of employers to effectively import strikebreakers from Mexico.

Confronted by the dilemma of being able to successfully organize workers and pull them onto the picket lines but being unable to halt production because of the importation of strikebreakers, Chavez turned to a new technique: the boycott. Boycotts had been a traditional weapon of labor but have not always had outstanding success. However, the UFW changed this situation, resuscitating the boycott as a biting economic weapon. Through very effective public relations, an emphasis on non-violence, dramatic pilgrimages, and highly-publicized fasts, Chavez and the UFW made the plight of the farm worker much more visible. The UFW membership was dispersed to dozens of cities in order to translate the farm workers' message into specific local actions, enabling urban populations to support the farm workers without any great personal cost.

Although it redirected significant amounts of the organization's energy and resources away from the point of production, the boycott strategy did provide a significant lever in obtaining representation and, later, contracts.

During the period 1966–73 the UFW undertook boycotts in three commodities: wine grapes, table grapes, and lettuce. The initial boycott began in
1966 with wine grapes, a commodity grown by a mix of growers ranging from
the giant Schenley corporation to many local enterprises. For Schenley, a
typically vertically integrated corporation that had recently become involved
in agriculture, wine growing was but a small part of the larger corporation.
But Schenley labels such as I. W. Harper were distinct in the public's mind—
the product of decades of advertising to develop brand-name identification.
Thus, Schenley was among the first of the grape growers to agree to a UFW
contract when confronted by a boycott.

Other wine grape growers were less directly vulnerable. Some were producers of table wines that they bottled and distributed under their own labels.
Unlike Schenley, their economic success was almost entirely dependent on
wines; and, while striving for brand-name identification, their advertising
budgets were relatively minuscule and their labels had less prominence. In
these cases, then, the union boycott attempted to develop negative product
identification. The remainder, largely smaller firms growing grapes under
contract to large wineries, were sheltered so long as the wineries did not
suffer adversely from the boycott. Although the process was lengthy, the
boycott organization ultimately achieved its purpose: five contracts with the
major wine growers of the Southern San Joaquin Valley in 1968–69. Between
then and 1973, the UFW extended its base with this type of grower.

The table grape boycott, initiated in 1967, encountered different obstacles. Unlike wine grapes, table grapes were grown mainly by medium-sized
firms, few of which were vertically integrated. Moreover, product identification of table grapes was negligible, since the public did not buy table grapes
by their label. After a protracted educational campaign, the boycott began to
pay off. Consumers began to treat grapes as if they were expensive (e.g.,
foregoing them for other available fruits), which was facilitated by the roughly simultaneous arrival of grapes, apples, peaches, and pears to the supermarket. Although the struggle was a hard and bitter one for the UFW, the
boycott once again proved its utility.

The UFW's boycott of iceberg lettuce had mixed results when the union
took on the lettuce industry in 1969. The demand for lettuce, unlike grapes, is
highly inelastic—few substitutes exist, and consumption rates remain relatively stable within a broad price range. However, among lettuce producers
who were vertically integrated with large corporate entities having strong
product identification in other markets, the threat of a boycott produced three
contracts. Thus, Freshpict (the corporation associated with Purex, Inc., and
its bleaches and detergents) felt threatened by a national boycott of its well-
advertised products, not simply its lettuce. The same held for InterHarvest
(later known as Sun Harvest and owned by United Brands) and Pic-N-Pac
(owned by Del Monte). But by contrast most of the Salinas Valley lettuce
growers, highly specialized growers of lettuce and several related crops, resisted the threat of the boycott and refused to sign with the UFW. Only one
locally-based lettuce grower of any significance signed with the union. The

UFW retaliated with a boycott against non-UFW lettuce, but this largely proved unsuccessful.[38]

Thus, by early 1973, the UFW had been able to successfully organize workers and bring them out on strikes, which could only become economically effective through a boycott—at least in some cases. The tenuousness of its contracts and the constant harassment from growers and their political allies forced the UFW to expend considerable energy mobilizing external support. The boycott campaigns, in particular, began to erode the union's capacity to do extensive community organizing prior to launching campaigns in other industries. With the onset of employer efforts to engage in "union substitution"—through the negotiation of accords (often sweetheart contracts) with the Teamsters union—expansion was curtailed as the UFW sought desperately to protect the ground it had won.

Between 1973 and 1984, the UFW experienced a roller coaster in the number of its contracts and the size of its membership. It had slowly but steadily increased its contract base to 180 firms in 1977,[39] and approximately 50,000 members,[40] only to see that figure plummet to fewer than 80 contracts in 1979. The majority of contracts were lost in the union substitution pursued by employers with a vengeance in the middle and later 1970s. The Teamsters union and off-shoots from various local organizations nibbled away at the edges despite the passage of California's Agricultural Labor Relations Act in 1976.[41] Even when the union won representation elections in the peak years of 1976–77, the UFW encountered employer resistance to establishing contract language. By 1982, the union had lost nearly 40 contracts and 15,000 members.[42]

Despite its struggles with the staunchly conservative Teamsters union for the right to represent farm workers, the UFW emerged in the late 1970s as the most influential agricultural union in the nation. Among its accomplishments (particularly in California, its organizational base) were the following: substantial increases in basic wage packages; the extension of broader unemployment and worker's compensation coverage for employees; development of medical, dental and legal benefits for union members; the creation of a separate Agricultural Labor Relations Board to oversee elections and enforcement of labor laws; construction of an extensive representative system starting at the level of the work unit (e.g., crew) and cross-cutting firms as well as crops; and the cementing of a union-run system of hiring halls and seniority which effectively undercut the frequently exploitative labor contracting system.

[38]Its lack of success was only in part due to the on-again, off-again, series of tactical errors by the union, harassment by employers, alleged heavy purchasing of lettuce by the Defense Department (under the Nixon administration), and other factors. The fact remained inexorable: lettuce was seen by most consumers as "necessary" and non-substitutable.

[39]Thomas and Friedland, p. 68.

[40]Ibid.

[41]William H. Friedland, "From Social Movement to Trade Union: the United Farm Workers in 1984," paper presented to the Society for the Study of Social Problems, San Antonio, Texas, August 14, 1984.

[42]Ibid.

Yet, for all the union's successes, agricultural work inside and outside of California remains far less attractive and secure than that of other economic sectors. Average annual earnings for farm workers hover at a point less than 85% of the average for manufacturing employees.[43] The 1980 and 1982 elections weakened the political influence of labor in state and national legislatures overseeing agricultural labor relations. In California, where the highest proportion of agricultural workers is unionized, less than 40% of farm workers belong to a union; in other states, such as Arizona, Florida, Georgia, South Carolina, Ohio, Texas and New York, the percentages are substantially smaller. And, even where the UFW has had greatest success—e.g., in the wine, table grape, and lettuce industries—numbers of workers are declining through the increased use of new production technologies, especially harvest mechanization.

IV. THE TECHNOLOGICAL CHALLENGE TO LABOR–MANAGEMENT RELATIONS

Unlike entrenched unions in other industries which have negotiated slowdowns in new technology introduction or bargained successfully for early retirement or retraining packages, the UFW has not had great success in curbing the negative impacts of new technology. The 1978–79 lettuce industry strike, intended initially to advance just such an agreement, eventually abandoned a "no mechanization" stipulation in favor of higher wages. Mechanization of the wine grape harvest continues unabated, with the major producers rapidly shifting to machines which reduce the labor force substantially.

As in other sectors of the economy, decisions about the introduction of labor-displacing technology in agriculture have been heavily influenced by their cost and contribution to managerial control over production. These are, of course, the points upon which the UFW and other farm labor unions find themselves hung: the more successful they are as economic and political agents, the more likely it is that companies will attempt to eliminate them as obstacles to organizational performance. However, as was suggested in the earlier historical analysis, an added element shapes the relationship between labor and capital in agriculture: the political vulnerability of most agricultural labor. Where low-status workers—blacks, non-citizens and, most importantly, undocumented workers—are employed, managers retain a greater measure of control even when those workers belong to a union. Thus, the introduction of labor-displacing equipment has not been simply a response to higher wages or the presence of a union; the decision to introduce has also been affected by the availability of politically vulnerable labor.

Two brief cases help illustrate the relationship between new technology and labor relations.

[43]Philip Martin, Richard Mines and Angela Diaz, "A Profile of California Farm Workers," *California Agriculture* (May–June 1985), pp. 16–18.

A. Tomatoes: The Mechanical Solution

The production of "processing" tomatoes (destined for canning, sauces, and other products) emerged as a major contributor to the agricultural economy of the Southwest following World War II. A labor-intensive crop requiring large numbers of workers for hand-picking, the industry involved nearly 4,000 growers and 50,000 workers in 1962. Until 1964, the supply of labor was effectively unlimited; braceros were supplied as needed.[44] However, as the Bracero Program weakened, research underwritten by private industry and the state of California began in an effort to devise an alternative harvesting system. The new system, combining a mechanical harvester and a tomato engineered to withstand it, was introduced by the University of California in 1961.[45]

Yet, until the termination of the Bracero Program in 1964–65, mechanized harvesting remained unpopular with growers. The machines were expensive and awkward and simply not as versatile as a gang of contract workers. With the official cut-off of the regulated labor supply in 1965, however, a rapid transition was accomplished in the space of only 5 seasons—stimulated by the loss of cheap labor and a fear among California growers that processors would shift their tomato purchases to lower-cost Mexican producers. Mechanization reduced employment from 50,000 to 18,000 workers.

While the first stage of mechanization was precipitated by a fear of economic collapse for the industry, the second stage came about under different circumstances. The initial plunge into mechanization involved what would now be termed "low" technology: the machines were largely new combinations of hydraulic and pneumatic equipment; hand labor was still necessary to sort good tomatoes from the unripe fruit and dirt clods also harvested by the machine. The second stage, however, began in the early 1970s with serious efforts on the part of the UFW to begin organizing tomato workers. The UFW's strategy was clear: higher capital investments in equipment made growers more vulnerable to production stoppages.

Faced with advances from a militant union and mindful of the economic clout still held by processors (an element of agricultural economics I described earlier), tomato growers moved quickly to a new technological alternative: electro-optic sorting of tomatoes.[46] The new equipment allowed employers to eliminate all but five or six of the 25 workers employed on the earlier harvesting machine.

B. Lettuce: Squeezing the Labor Market

As in the case of the tomato industry, public and private sources combined to underwrite research on a mechanical harvester for the head lettuce industry in the early 1960s. Experimentation by the U.S. Department of Agriculture and

[44]Friedland and Barton, pp. 22–27.
[45]Ibid., pp. 20–30.
[46]Scheuring and Thompson.

the University of California led to the development, in the late 1960s, of two systems. Each employed a low-level radiation emitter/receiver to measure the density (maturity) of a lettuce head; the devices were necessary to allow "selective" harvesting of the unevenly maturing plants. Equipped with either X-ray or gamma ray devices, the machines proved remarkably efficient and easily competitive with the harvest crews then employed by the industry.[47]

Even with field trials in the early 1970s demonstrating the attractiveness of this mechanical alternative, the industry did not rush to the new technology. And, despite the massive organizational efforts of the UFW (including a highly visible boycott of iceberg lettuce) and the impressive number of contracts won by that union or ceded to the Teamsters, the mechanical harvester did not constitute an attractive alternative to the hand harvest.[48] One factor decisively affected the situation: the availability of a substantial supply of politically vulnerable labor, undocumented workers.

Unlike their counterparts in the tomato industry, lettuce firms produce directly for the market. Lettuce is, for the most part, unprocessed and sold directly from the field to supermarkets and institutional buyers. In the 1930s and 1940s, lettuce growers began integrating forward to the market to cut down on middleman expenses and to establish durable links with retailers. This shift was strengthened with corporate penetration in the 1960s. The infusion of industrial and finance capital also enabled many lettuce firms (or, as I noted earlier, subsidiaries of non-agricultural conglomerates) to break the bonds of seasonality by leasing or purchasing acreage in several areas, and to begin to grow lettuce year-round. The combination of direct market links, more abundant financial resources, and greater resistance to price fluctuation (since income was generated over a multi-season period) gave lettuce producers substantially more degrees of freedom in coping with labor supply and labor cost.

Initially responding to the demise of the Bracero Program by raising wages and attempting to attract indigenous labor for the harvest, lettuce producers found that a modicum of patience would be paid off by the opening of the undocumented worker floodgate. Active recruitment of workers in Mexico and the lax enforcement of border-crossing eventually provided a reliable source of labor for the back-breaking harvest. Precisely because citizen workers did not rush in to fill the bracero vacuum, there was no need to change the labor process. By keeping wages higher than those in other agricultural industries and offering longer-term employment, the lettuce industry quickly became the most attractive place for undocumented workers to work. Thus, as I found in my 1979–80 study of lettuce harvesting, upwards of 60–70% of the harvest labor force was undocumented.[49]

The paradox of labor relations in the lettuce industry—and the crux of the present situation vis-a-vis new technology—is that the lettuce industry is among the most heavily unionized in agriculture *and* substantially populated

[47]Zahara, Johnson and Garrett, pp. 535–6.
[48]Friedland, Barton and Thomas, pp. 31–40.
[49]Thomas, *Citizenship*, Chapter 3.

by undocumented workers.[50] While the UFW used the social cohesiveness of citizen (Chicano) and green-card crews to build an organizational base in the early 1970s and the lettuce boycott to leverage contracts from large, corporate producers, it also constructed a constituency of members with considerable political vulnerability. That is, the signing of contracts with lettuce producers effectively "organized" all the undocumented workers employed by a firm into the UFW. In fact, as I note in the lettuce industry study, the UFW was forced to seek the assistance of the Border Patrol (a traditional nemesis of farm workers) in an effort to strengthen its efforts to stop production in the 1978–79 strike.[51] That effort to restrict access to employment was only partially successful. More important, it exacerbated cleavages in the union's membership and further eroded its leverage in negotiating with employers.

V. CONCLUSION

Thus, in the lettuce industry and other crops, the availability of politically vulnerable labor has made the technological alternative less attractive to employers. When the supply of that labor is threatened—as it was for tomato producers in the early 1960s—or a union uses its leverage to influence how the work is done, mechanization arises as an attractive alternative. For the UFW and other unions in a similar position, the prospects are not at all encouraging. Regularizing employment and improving working conditions cannot be accomplished without politically protecting the labor force, but political protections will likely precipitate mechanization. Employers, not surprisingly, have been quite adept at whipsawing the UFW with the issue of undocumented workers and the threat of mechanization. Wrapping themselves in the colors of agricultural exceptionalism and the resurrected laissez faire ideology of the Reagan administration, many have attempted to lay the responsibility for dealing with undocumented immigration at someone else's feet. The executive director of the Western Growers Association argued in an interview that: "I don't think that the responsibility for handling the issue of illegal aliens should be put on the grower's back. It's not our fault that there's high unemployment in Mexico. It's not our fault that the state and federal government can't keep them from getting across the border. It's not our fault that they can get fraudulent documentation. Why should we be the only ones responsible for them? . . . Hell, we get most of our workers through union hiring halls. Why doesn't Chavez clean up his act?."[52]

Just as they portrayed themselves as hapless victims of a jurisdictional dispute between the UFW and the Teamsters a decade earlier, employers now disclaim responsibility for the operations of the labor market—while lobbying to ensure that legislation which seeks to penalize employers for hiring undocumented workers is defeated or made difficult to enforce.

[50]Ibid.
[51]Ibid, p. 165.
[52]Thomas and Friedland, p. 73.

3

The Eclipse of Craft

The Changing Face of Labor in the Newspaper Industry

Arne L. Kalleberg, Michael Wallace, Karyn A. Loscocco, Kevin T. Leicht, and Hans-Helmut Ehm

I. INTRODUCTION

The newspaper industry provides an ideal context for studying the impact of industrial and technological change on the labor process. Sociologists have long noted the exemplary craftsmanship and occupational pride of the printing trades.[1] These authors viewed printing as "an anachronism in the age of large scale industrial organization,"[2] where the venerable traditions of craftsmanship, pride in one's work, and control over the immediate work process remained virtually undaunted by technological change. Yet recent advances in automating nearly all phases of newspaper production have rendered obsolete Blauner's original portrait of the printing craftsman. Indeed, it is difficult to think of an industry where the transformations wrought by technological change have been so profound. Smith has recently remarked that the newspaper industry is "the dove sent from the ark of mechanical society

---

[1]Seymour Martin Lipset, Martin Trow, and James Coleman, *Union Democracy* (New York: Free Press, 1956); Robert Blauner, *Alienation and Freedom* (Chicago: University of Chicago Press, 1964).
[2]Blauner, p. 56.

Arne L. Kalleberg • Department of Sociology, University of North Carolina at Chapel Hill, Chapel Hill, NC 27514. **Michael Wallace** • Department of Sociology, Ohio State University, Columbus, OH 43210-1353. **Karyn A. Loscocco** • Department of Sociology, State University of New York—Albany, 1400 Washington Avenue, Albany, NY 12222. **Kevin T. Leicht** • Department of Sociology, Indiana University, Ballantine Hall, Bloomington, IN 47405. **Hans-Helmut Ehm** • University of Trier, Postfach 2710, 5500 Trier, West Germany.

to test the waters of computerization."[3] Surely, there are few other industries that, in the span of a single generation, so embody the remembrances of our preindustrial past and prefigure the future of an automated society.

The newspaper industry is generally classified in the "periphery" sector of the dualistic American industrial structure, based as it is on small-scale, labor-intensive production techniques, small establishment size, and geographically dispersed and localized markets.[4] Many newspapers have long-standing traditions of being family-owned enterprises with paternalistic employment practices. Because of the competitive structure of the industry, profit margins have generally been narrow by comparison with "core" industries. Yet, because of the constantly increasing volume of readership, newspaper production is typically insulated from the oscillations of the business cycle, thus providing a measure of economic security that is absent in other periphery industries. This economic security has generally been reflected in patterns of economic growth and stability of profits for employers and a rising standard of living for most newspaper workers.

Newspaper printing involves a craft occupational structure, using a low ratio of capital to labor expenditures and a simple division of labor in which each occupation embodies a constellation of non-routine tasks.[5] Newspaper printing is a classic example of small-batch production technology and unique in that a new product is produced every twenty-four hours (or more frequently in the case of papers with multiple editions). The local character of newspaper markets and the perishable nature of the product have traditionally limited the supply of competent labor to those in the immediate area with the requisite skills. In most of the printing trades, four- to six-year apprenticeships have been necessary to achieve journeyman status, and genuine expertise in all the necessary tasks generally comes only after a period of several additional years. The combination of a highly skilled, functionally essential labor force and a highly perishable commodity (since publishers cannot stockpile news, work stoppages inflict an immediate loss on profits) has given newspaper workers broad control over the labor process and unparalleled power in labor–management negotiations. The strength of printing craftsmen is reflected both in the extensive array of institutionalized "job property rights" which have historically characterized their jobs[6] and the legacy of craft unionism which dates back to 1852 when the National Typographical Union became the first recognized labor union in the United States. This combination of factors, along with the inherent obstacles to

---

[3]Anthony Smith, *Goodbye Gutenberg: The Newspaper Revolution of the 1980s* (New York: Oxford University Press, 1980), pp. 236–237.

[4]See, e.g., Randy Hodson, "Labor in the Monopoly, Competitive, and State Sectors of Production," *Politics and Society* 8 (1978), pp. 429–480.

[5]Robert Max Jackson, *The Formation of Craft Labor Markets* (New York: Academic Press, 1984); See also Blauner, p. 36.

[6]Arthur R. Porter, Jr., *Job Property Rights: A Study of the Job Controls of the International Typographical Union* (New York: King's Crown, 1954).

streamlining many traditional printing operations, has, until recently, limited the capacity of employers to rationalize the production process through technological innovation.

Soon after World War II, and then accelerating in the 1960s, the newspaper industry experienced a transformation of its industrial structure that was to have dramatic consequences for the nature of work and craftsmanship in the industry, and, in turn, for relations between labor and capital. While it is difficult to identify a single precipitating factor in this transformation, many analysts point to the serious "profit squeeze" which occurred soon after World War II.[7] For example, the ratio of after-tax profits to sales in printing and publishing (SIC industry classification 27) fell steadily from 9.3% in 1946 to 2.7% in 1957.[8] Demands by labor for higher wages, which occurred in printing as well as other industries after the war, only exacerbated the financial crisis of many newspapers.

The downward spiral of profits was part of a larger web of post-World War II changes, including the transition from family-owned to corporate-owned newspapers, the shift in readership from afternoon to morning dailies, increased competition from non-print sources of news, and increased reliance on advertising as a source of revenue. Aside from these factors, however, the profit squeeze initiated two essential changes in the industry: first, a "shakeout" of non-competitive newspaper firms and the creation, through merger and consolidation, of a dualistic industrial structure *within* the newspaper industry; and, second, a new business climate in which newspaper publishers had added economic incentive to rationalize the labor process through the introduction of labor-saving and skill-degrading technologies.

In this chapter, we examine the origins of technological changes in the newspaper industry and the consequences for the nature of work and labor relations. First, we discuss the transformations in the corporate structures of newspapers, which form the backdrop for technological change in the industry. Then, we analyze the impact of technological change on the industry's labor process. In particular, we focus on the implications of technological change for the decline of craftsmanship and skills in the manual phases of newspaper production. Finally, we discuss the effect of these changes on labor-management relations in the industry. The percentage of unionized workers in the industry has declined and the surviving union structure has moved away from the craft model towards a "quasi-craft" model.

---

[7]A. H. Raskin, "A Reporter at Large: Part I, 'Changes in the Balance of Power'; Part II, 'Intrigue at the Summit.'" *The New Yorker*, (22 January and 29 January 1979); Michael Wallace and Arne L. Kalleberg, "Industrial Transformation and the Decline of Craft: The Decomposition of Skill in the Printing Industry, 1931–1978." *American Sociological Review* 47 (June 1982), pp. 307–324; Arne L. Kalleberg, Michael Wallace, and Larry E. Raffelovich, "Accounting for Labor's Share: Class and Income Distribution in the Printing Industry," *Industrial and Labor Relations Review* 37 (April 1984), pp. 386–402.

[8]Wallace and Kalleberg, note 8, p. 313.

Table 1. Competition in the Daily Newspaper Industry, 1923–1984[a]

Year	(a) Number of Firms	(b) Total Daily Circulation (millions)	(c) Number of Firms in Multi-Paper Cities	(d) % of Firms in Multi-Paper Cities	(e) % of Daily Papers Sold by Firms in Multi-Paper Cities
1923	1,977	30.5	1,182	59.8	88.8
1933	1,745	36.6	562	32.2	73.9
1943	1,597	44.1	318	19.9	64.2
1948	1,536	51.3	253	16.5	62.0
1953	1,582	54.3	218	13.7	54.2
1958	1,545	57.2	168	10.9	51.7
1963	1,552	59.7	127	8.2	43.3
1968	1,547	60.8	97	6.3	36.1
1973	1,566	61.3	84	5.4	32.2
1978	1,580	59.4	78	4.9	28.3
1980	1,584	60.2	80	5.1	27.7
1984	1,539	63.3	81	5.3	26.0

[a]Source: *Editor and Publisher International Yearbook,* various editions.

II. THE CONTEXT OF TECHNOLOGICAL CHANGE: INDUSTRIAL DUALISM IN THE NEWSPAPER INDUSTRY

The pressure of declining profits after World War II limited the entry of new newspaper firms even though newspaper readership was expanding. While circulation increased by about 44% since 1943, the number of newspaper firms remained stable (see Table 1, columns a and b). The net result is that the added demand for news is absorbed not by new firms, but by existing firms. Moreover, there is a significant trend toward product market monopoly in many cities, reflected in the sharp decline in the percentage of firms (note that these "firms" *may* include more than one newspaper) and daily circulation in multi-paper cities (see Table 1, columns c, d, and e). This is due in large part to the inability of many firms to keep costs competitive with rival papers and their resultant merger or dissolution. By 1980, only about 5% of all firms and 28% of all circulation was accounted for by papers in multi-paper settings.

Declining metropolitan competition was accompanied by growing concentration of newspaper firms at the national level. By 1980, the largest 10% of newspaper firms accounted for 61.0% of all circulation; the largest 5% accounted for 47.1% of all circulation.[9] This pattern of national consolidation is best reflected in the rapid rise in the influence of newspaper chains (or "groups") which combine multiple newspapers under single ownership. For example, Table 2 shows that in 1910 there were only 13 chains, controlling 62

[9]James N. Dertouzos and Kenneth E. Thorpe, *Newspaper Groups: Economies of Scale, Tax Laws, and Merger Incentives* (Santa Monica, CA: Rand Corporation, 1982), p. 94.

Table 2. Chain Ownership, U.S. Daily Newspapers, 1910–1984[a]

	(a)	(b)	(c)	(d) % U.S. Dailies that are Chain-owned	(e) % Total Circulation Sold by Chains	(f)
Year	Chains	Chain[b] Newspapers	Independent Newspapers			Independent[c] Voices
1910	13	62	2140	3	—	2153
1920	55	311	1631	16	43	1686
1930	60	319	1559	17	—	1619
1940	95	485	1300	27	45	1395
1950	109	560	1203	32	46	1312
1960	157	879	869	50	63	1026
1970	167	1047	715	59	71	882
1980	155	1136	609	65	72	764
1984	149	1115	573	66	73	722

[a]Source: *Editor and Publisher International Yearbook,* various editions.
[b]The totals reflect dailies, not separate establishments. Thus a single establishment publishing a morning and evening edition is counted as two newspapers.
This total approximates the number of different owners, that is, the number of chains added to the number of independent newspapers.

newspapers, but that by 1984, 149 chains controlled 1,115 newspapers. During that time, the percentage of newspapers that are chain-owned increased from 3% to 66% with a similar rise in the percentage of circulation under chain publication. After the first chain (Scripps-McRae) was organized in 1896, it took nearly 60 years before chains controlled one-third of U.S. newspapers; but only 20 years later, they already controlled another third.[10] This trend represents not only the consolidation of capital resources among fewer owners, but also a 66% decline in the number of "independent voices" (as measured by the number of chains plus independent newspapers—see column f of Table 2).

Table 3 presents information on the 12 largest U.S. chains as of 1984. The median number of newspapers controlled by this elite group of chains is 21.5. While this tiny group represents less than 2% of the "independent voices" in the country, it controls 21% of all U.S. dailies and over 43% of all newspaper circulation. Also, these twelve chains control more circulation than the remaining 137 chains combined (see lower panel of Table 3). The most recent trend is for chains to buy out other chains, signaling a second wave in the consolidation pattern. For instance, there were 18 fewer chains in 1984 than in 1970, but 68 more newspapers controlled by chains.

Aside from the trend in chain ownership, many newspapers have been absorbed by larger conglomerates in other industries. Some have merged with interests in other media industries, such as cable television and telecommunications. Others have integrated vertically. For instance, the *Times-Mirror*

[10]Smith.

Table 3. Major Newspaper Chains, 1984[a]

Chain	Number of Dailies[b]	Percentage of U.S. Total	Daily Circulation (thousands)	Percentage of U.S. Total
Gannett	86	5.1	4772	7.5
Knight-Ridder	32	1.9	3933	6.2
Newhouse	27	1.6	3236	5.1
Tribune	8	.5	2780	4.4
Dow-Jones	21	1.2	2499	3.9
Times-Mirror	7	.4	2355	3.7
New York *Times*	25	1.5	1609	2.5
Scripps-Howard	13	.8	1413	2.2
Thomson	89	5.3	1408	2.2
Cox	22	1.3	1295	2.0
Hearst	15	.9	1141	1.8
Capital Cities	9	.5	966	1.5
Total 12 chains	354	21.0	27.4 million	43.3
137 other chains	761	45.1	18.8 million	29.7
All chains	1115	66.1	46.2 million	73.0

[a]Source: *Editor and Publisher International Yearbook*, 1985.
[b]For these data, a single establishment publishing both a morning and evening edition is counted as two "dailies."

chain owns substantial interests in lumbering firms which are key sources of newsprint.[11] Finally, many chains are owned by larger conglomerates with interests in oil, finance, and even professional sports teams. Clearly, the small, independently owned, family-centered newspaper is a rapidly vanishing breed in the U.S. newspaper industry.

Antitrust laws are virtually ineffective in slowing newspaper mergers, due to ambiguities in the definition of relevant product markets.[12] Further, with the passage of the Newspaper Preservation Act of 1970, a new type of quasi-merger known as a "joint operating agreement" (JOA) has become prevalent. JOAs are arrangements between competing newspapers in the same city to share production facilities and sometimes production personnel. Although the intent of the Act was to salvage the spirit of journalistic competition in the face of rising production costs, its effect has been to combine newspapers whose economic vitality was never in doubt.[13] This suggests that the Newspaper Preservation Act, in contrast to its original purpose of pre-

[11]See Ben H. Bagdikian, "Newspaper Mergers: The Final Phase," *Columbia Journalism Review* 15 (March/April 1977), pp. 17–22; and Robert L. Bishop, "The Rush to Chain Ownership," *Columbia Journalism Review* 11 (November/December 1972), pp. 10–19.

[12]Toby J. McIntosh, "Why the Government Can't Stop Press Mergers," *Columbia Journalism Review* 16 (May/June 1977), pp. 48–50; Smith, p. 54.

[13]Stephan R. Barnett, "Monopoly Games—Where Failures Win Big," *Columbia Journalism Review* 19 (May/June 1980), pp. 40–47; and Gail L. Barwis, "The Newspaper Preservation Act: A Retrospective Analysis," *Newspaper Research Journal* 2 (February 1980), pp. 27–39.

serving struggling independent dailies, actually served to consolidate further the larger newspaper interests.

Essentially, then, a dualistic corporate structure *within* the newspaper industry has evolved over the past forty years. In the "core" sector of the industry are the large metropolitan dailies which are affiliated with national chains or huge conglomerates. Typically, these firms have a monopoly in the daily print media in their metropolitan market, enabling them to set local standards for wage rates and other factors of production. Newspapers which are part of large chains or conglomerates can achieve economies of scale in production facilities, advertising rates, labor costs, and other necessities of production. Ultimately, these economies of scale help to curtail falling profit margins and/or gain virtual monopolies in local markets. These core firms are the technological pace-setters and the industry leaders in restructuring the industry's relationship with its labor force.

In the "periphery" sector of the industry are the independently owned dailies which may have local monopolies but are more likely to be secondary papers in multipaper markets. Also in the periphery sector of the market are weekly suburban newspapers and independently printed and distributed advertising flyers. Periphery newspapers face an uphill struggle against the financial backing of the chains. The recent experiences of the Cleveland *Press,* the Chicago *Daily News,* and the Washington *Star* provide visible reminders of newspapers which succumbed to the competition from larger, chain-backed competitors.

Increased consolidation of newspaper firms has spurred rapid technological changes, thus erasing the technological backwardness that historically plagued employers. Consolidation has provided the capital necessary for research to develop automated technologies. Moreover, the local nature of product markets, along with the trend toward single-newspaper cities, means that innovations can be quickly disseminated to the newspapers which can afford them. Further, the networking capacity provided by newspaper chains allows member firms to gain access to advanced technologies.

Much of the research for new technologies in the industry has been carried out by the Research Institute of the American Newspaper Publishers' Association (ANPA), which was founded in 1947. This is a major center for newspaper research, development, testing, and training, with an annual budget of about $1 million. Innovations produced by the Institute are made available to all ANPA member newspapers, which comprise most of the core sector of the industry and about 90% of all U.S. daily newspapers. The Institute thus facilitates the cost-efficient development of new technologies and bears costs that would otherwise have to be borne by individual newspapers. Retired ANPA Director Erwin Jaffe estimates that the Institute has been involved in 80–85% of the new technologies developed since the 1940s.[14]

---

[14]Interview with Erwin Jaffe, American Newspaper Publishers' Association, Eaton, Pennsylvania, 20 December 1982.

The ANPA also articulates the ideological interests of newspaper publishers in their struggle with the craft labor unions. The ANPA preaches the industry gospel of higher profits through lower labor costs in its monthly publication *Presstime* and through other materials widely disseminated to newspaper publishers. Far from an end in itself, the technological rationalization of printing processes is the most successful instrument yet devised for implementing managerial control of the labor process.

III. TECHNOLOGICAL CHANGE AND THE DECLINE OF CRAFTSMANSHIP

Newspaper production has been a labor-intensive process dependent on the services of skilled printing craftsmen. For this reason, employers have had an incentive to rationalize the production process through mechanization or other means in order to minimize their reliance on skilled labor. Yet the historical fragmentation of capital in newspaper printing has limited the ability of employers to impose sweeping technological change on the powerful printing craft unions, even when technological solutions to production problems seemed imminent.[15] With the increasing capital consolidation in the industry, however, employers have gained the economic wherewithal to restructure the labor process to their advantage through technological modernization.

In this section, we describe the nature of the new technologies and their impact on the decline of craftsmanship among newspaper production workers. We focus on the transformation of traditional craft occupations in newspaper *printing*, which encompasses about 48% of the employment at a typical U.S. metropolitan newspaper. While technological changes have affected other areas of the newspaper firm—editorial functions, advertising, business and administration, and circulation—these production or so-called "mechanical" functions have been the focal point for the major technological changes.

The actual production of newspapers involves four successive stages: *composition*, whereby copy is set in type and arranged in page form; *platemaking*, in which metal, rubber, or plastic plates or reproductions of the typeset page are produced; *presswork*, where printing impressions are transferred into final copy with the aid of a printing press; and the *mailroom*, where the papers are folded, bundled, and readied for distribution. We now discuss each of these functions.

A. Composing Room

While all phases of newspaper production are labor-intensive, the major bottleneck has always been page composition, the most labor-intensive and highly skilled phase of the printing process. As a result, it is not surprising

---

[15]Blauner.

that employer efforts to restructure the labor process have historically centered on composing room operations. It has been common wisdom among publishers that if the composing room could be streamlined, the modernization of subsequent printing operations would follow suit. This assumption appears justified by recent experience in the industry.

From the time of Gutenberg to the early twentieth century, compositors assembled type by hand, one character at a time, into a composing stick, and then transferred each completed line of type into a galley where stories were laid out in page form.[16] By the late 1800s, a great deal of effort was devoted to developing a mechanical process that could expedite the work of hand compositors and relieve employers of their dependence on this group of workers. Dozens of prototypes for mechanical typesetting machines were developed in the late 1800s, but most of them proved impractical or too expensive. One such device received financial backing and promotional support from Mark Twain, who claimed the machine could do everything six men could do "except drink, swear, and go out on strike."[17]

The most successful machine to emerge from this flurry of inventive activity was the Mergenthaler Linotype machine, so named because it cast a "line of type" at a time into a long narrow strip of molten metal. When the metal cooled, the type was delivered to a galley at the front of the machine where it was proofed and printed just as with handset type. Within a decade of its production for commercial use in 1890s, this new "hot metal" process displaced over 10,000 skilled craftsmen.[18] However, in subsequent years as demand for printed goods expanded, employment eventually exceeded the levels it had achieved before the linotype. The linotype, though it displaced workers and slowly phased out hand composition, did not eliminate the need for traditional printing skills such as typesetting or page layout. The printing craftsman still retained a large degree of autonomy and discretion in day-to-day performance of his tasks.[19] Because it failed to achieve the employers' ultimate aim of eliminating dependence on basic printing skills, the linotype is best described as an example of "simple mechanization,"[20] an effort that fell short of ultimate control of the labor process by employers.

Although it experienced several modifications in subsequent years, the linotype remained the dominant technology in the setting of type for the first half of the twentieth century. But the advent of teletypesetting (TTS) machines in 1950s signaled the coming of "cold type" technology and the eventual obsolescence of the linotype. The first TTS machines produced a perforated tape which the linotype operator threaded through the machine to

[16]Ibid.

[17]Smith, p. 211; see also Harry Kelber and Carl Schlesinger, *Union Printers and Controlled Automation* (New York: Free Press, 1967), p. 3.

[18]Kelber and Schlesinger, pp. 24–25.

[19]Andrew Zimbalist, "Technology and the Labor Process in the Printing Industry," in *Case Studies in the Labor Process*, ed. Andrew Zimbalist (New York: Monthly Review Press, 1979), pp. 103–126.

[20]Richard C. Edwards, *Contested Terrain* (New York: Basic, 1979), p. 112.

create the metal slugs automatically.[21] TTS made it technologically possible (though perhaps inadvisable from a labor relations standpoint) to have typesetting of classified advertising and syndicated news stories done outside the plant, virtually bypassing in-house composing room workers. This technology was adopted very rapidly: the number of typesetting installations increased from 98 in 1964 to 663 in 1968.[22]

Technological innovations accelerated in the 1960s with the introduction of phototypesetting, the second wave of the cold type revolution.[23] This involved the application of computer-based technology to TTS-like systems. Accessing the computer via video display terminals (VDTs), the operator types the unjustified manuscript to produce an "unfinished" tape which is then fed into the photocomposition machine with appropriate justification codes. This eliminates the need for the intermediary step of producing perforated tapes and allows for direct inputting of typeset material by journalists, editors, and other personnel outside the composing room. The computer then justifies and hyphenates the copy and, with a high-speed printing device, reproduces the copy on photosensitized paper, instead of casting metal slugs. Many composing room workers are now relegated to "paste-up" jobs in which they paste column-width strips of copy on page-size mats which are photographically reproduced in the plateroom and transformed into plates for the press runs.[24] A complete transition from hot metal linotype technology to cold type phototypesetting technology with VDTs was accomplished in the 1970s, as shown in Table 4.

Futuristic composing room technologies are currently being developed by the ANPA Research Institute. Optical character recognition (OCR) devices use electro-optical techniques to "read" typewritten or handwritten copy, translate them into characters programmed into the memory of the scanners, and then produce the page-ready copy of news articles. While OCR may eventually permit the conveying of copy directly to the computer-operated typesetting devices and circumventing composing room workers, its present applications are more limited. Pagination, which will use computer-based systems to compose the entire page, including pictures, on a VDT, will have far-reaching implications. Once pagination becomes operational and economically feasible, it will totally obviate the need for the composing room, making page layout a function of the editorial office and/or newsroom. Several prototype pagination systems are currently in use and industry leaders foresee the day in the near future when pagination will be as pervasive in the industry as VDTs are now.[25] A less complex version of pagination known as area spacing accomplishes essentially the same task but without the ability to

[21]Kelber and Schlesinger, pp. 47–49.

[22]Smith.

[23]United States Bureau of Labor Statistics, *The Impact of Technology on Labor in Five Industries.* Bulletin 2137 (Washington, DC: U.S. Government Printing Office, 1982).

[24]Theresa F. Rogers and Natalie S. Friedman, *Printers Face Automation* (Lexington, MA.: D. C. Heath & Co., 1980).

[25]Alan Janesch, "Pagination: The Dream Machine is Real," *Presstime* 3 (1981), pp. 5–9.

Table 4. Conversion from "Hot Metal" to "Cold Type" Technology in the Composing Room, 1970–1980[a]

	1970	1972	1974	1976	1978	1980
"Hot metal": linotype machines	10,290	8,784	3,892	1,877	1,158	465
"Cold type": video display terminals	23	360	1,666	7,038	15,841	27,078

[a]Source: Dertouzas and Thorpe, 1982.

recreate photographs on the VDT screen. The long-term implications of these frontier technologies for the composing room and the role they will play in wresting ultimate control of the labor process have not been overlooked by employers. As one trade journal stated several years ago:

> The next five years will see the development of terminals for interactive composition and makeup of type, live art, and photographs into complete images on a display screen. As a visual page image is being put together on the screen, a digital page image will simultaneously be assembled on the computer. . . . As soon as complete page images can be produced in this way, there will be a strong impetus to bring the whole process of page creation into the publisher's office where it has always logically been. . . . Partial automation of the page production process has not radically altered traditional relationships between publishers, printers, and their distribution channels. Complete automation will change these relationships completely and forever.[26]

The most visible impact of existing technologies is a drastic reduction in the number of composing room workers. According to a recent Rand Corporation study of 493 daily newspapers (about 30% of the total), the number of newspaper composing room workers declined from about 14,500 to about 6,900 between 1970 and 1983, a 52% reduction in this single occupation! Of the 7,600 jobs which were lost, 52.7% were lost through attrition, 29.1% through buyouts (to be discussed in the next section), 10.9% through layoffs, and 7.3% through retraining for jobs in other parts of the plant.[27] Projections by the Bureau of Labor Statistics (BLS) suggest that composing room workers will decrease by another 24% between 1978 and 1990.[28] The BLS expects that the new technology will create some computer programmer and systems analyst jobs but these jobs will account for less than 1% of all employment in the industry by 1990.[29]

New technologies have also affected the skill requirements of composing room workers. One BLS publication suggests that typesetting with a VDT can

[26]Cited in Zimbalist, p. 112.
[27]Study results cited in James Warren, "Technological Changes Smooth at Newspapers, Study Finds," Chicago *Tribune* (16 April 1985), pp. 1, 8.
[28]United States Bureau of Labor Statistics, 1982.
[29]Ibid., pp. 11–12.

be performed by "a secretary with average typing skills" who can produce typeset copy more efficiently and cost-effectively than skilled linotype operators.[30] In a time series study of composing room operators in the printing industry, Wallace and Kalleberg found that relative skill levels compared to other representative workers had declined since 1931, which they attributed to the changing technological environment in the industry.[31]

These dramatic declines in skill have diminished worker autonomy and this, in turn, has reduced overall levels of job satisfaction among printers. Using 1941 data, Blauner found that only 36% of composing room workers would choose an occupation other than printing if they "were 15 years old and starting all over again."[32] But Rogers and Freedman, in a study that was otherwise optimistic regarding the effects of technology on printing skills, found that by 1976, 66% would choose another occupation.[33] Reasons given for choosing another occupation included "there's no future in printing," "printing is a dying craft," and "printing isn't printing anymore."

B. Platemaking

In platemaking, the major change imposed by the transition to cold type has been the virtual elimination of the stereotyping and photoengraving processes whereby heavy metal galleys of type were transformed into 43-pound plates, curved to the contours of the press cylinders. Today, most newspapers photographically reproduce the "paste up" version of the newspaper page made in the composing room and, through a chemical treatment, produce a pliable, lightweight (about 14 ounces) aluminum or plastic plate which can be adapted to either letterpress or offset press techniques (see below). Another innovation is electronic color scanning equipment, which converts light from color copy into electronic signals that can be used to expose the separation films. This will make color photographs more accessible for many newspapers, ushering in an era when "the printed paper will be so commonly colorful that a page of only black-and-white print will seem as strange to you as a colorless 1930s movie once did to your parents."[34] Previously, color separation was time consuming and the quality of the finished product varied with the skill levels of the workers. However, the number of newspapers utilizing color photographs has greatly increased in the last five years, the most obvious example being *USA Today*.

Other innovations which have affected the plateroom include improved data transmission capacity with microwave or satellite technologies. These technologies allow for the transmission of typeset page images to remote printing facilities. The information is received in digital form and converted

---

[30]United States Bureau of Labor Statistics, *Outlook for Technology and Manpower in Printing and Publishing*. Bulletin 1774. (Washington, DC: U.S. Government Printing Office, 1973).
[31]Wallace and Kalleberg, pp. 316–322; See also Zimbalist.
[32]Blauner, Table 37, p. 202.
[33]Rogers and Freedman, p. 149.
[34]Jerry W. Friedham, "Year 2000 Newspaper: Electronic Age in Print," *Presstime* 3 (1981), p. 19.

into conventional photographic negatives or printing plates. In many cases, the plates are created automatically at the receiving site, eliminating the need for plateroom workers. Microwave and satellite technology have greatly facilitated the same-day distribution of many newspapers with national markets, such as the *Wall Street Journal, New York Times, Chicago Tribune,* and *USA Today,* and recently, of smaller newspapers.

Technological changes in the plateroom simplify platemaking skills and reduce the number of required workers. Today, many newspapers employ only a few plateroom workers who are often retrained composing room workers. As a craft, platemaking (especially the hot metal variety) is on the decline and will probably be extinct within a decade.

C. Pressroom

With the development of labor-saving technologies in composition and platemaking, publishers have turned their attention to the pressroom. The major change in pressroom technology was the conversion from letterpress techniques (in which the printed plates consist of a "wrong read" image of the printed page with characters raised above the surface of the plate) to offset lithographic techniques (whereby the plate is a "right-read" image of the printed page and characters are flush against the plate itself). In offset, the printing impression is made by chemically treating the plate and is based on the principle that the oil base of the chemical compound and water do not mix. The era of offset printing was made possible by previous conversions to cold-type processes in the composing room but, because of the expense involved in buying new press equipment, some newspapers retained and adapted their old letterpress techniques even after the transition to cold type. In contrast to letterpress techniques, offset printing allows the reproduction of high quality color pictures and is thus compatible with the electronic color scanning innovations developed in the platemaking process. Other advantages of offset include better print quality, more durability of plates, and faster press runs.

The pressroom "is the only stage of the modern printing operation where some traditional craft skills have been preserved."[35] Pressroom workers continue to be responsible for ensuring proper plate balance on the press, the correct amount of ink, no jams in press operation, and the proper mixture of chemical and water. Numerically controlled and computer assisted presses are becoming more common, though, decreasing press workers' control over the machines. But despite the adjustments required of pressmen to new technologies, their responsibilities and skills have not diminished quite as drastically as those of composing room workers. This means that in relative terms the status and power of pressmen have increased compared to composing room workers.

Eventually, technological innovations may eliminate many pressroom

---

[35]Zimbalist.

functions altogether. The ANPA's Research Institute, for example, is experimenting with the use of lasers which would transfer electronic images stored in a central processing unit onto a belt or drum. Sprayed-ink systems would then form the image directly on paper.[36] This would largely eliminate the need for many of the traditional pressroom functions, and "pressroom" workers would perform the simpler tasks of monitoring the spraying equipment.

D. Mailroom

Streamlining the front-end operations of newspaper production has created incentives to modernize the mailroom facilities. According to ANPA, mailroom modernization remains the "last obstacle to automated newspapering."[37] Until ten years ago, not much had changed in mailroom operations since the introduction of the conveyor belt in the 1940s. But recently, automated counter stackers (which stack papers into bundles of predetermined size), bundle-top, bottom-wrap, and tying machines have become affordable for many newspapers, speeding up mailroom operations.

The increasing role of advertising revenue in the newspaper industry has had a major impact on mailroom technology. Since a large volume of advertising inserts and flyers is contained in newspapers, a high priority has been placed on developing automated inserting machines which can keep pace with the high-speed offset presses currently in use. The average hand inserter can insert about 1000 copies per hour, while state-of-the-art machine inserters can insert up to 40,000 copies per hour. Still, a bottleneck can occur because most modern offset presses can operate at nearly 60,000 copies per hour and, in fact, to operate them at slower speeds frequently detracts from the quality of the print. The ultimate goal is to approximate a "continuous flow" technology in the mailroom where mechanized inserters can keep pace with the presses. The rapid increase in advertising inserts (from 8 million to 27 million in the 1970s) has added to the urgency of the problem for many publishers. As the mailroom is slowly converted from a cost center to a profit center, more attention will be devoted to mailroom technology.

Historically, mailroom workers have been the least skilled and the most poorly compensated of all newspaper production workers. Because of the fluctuating volume of advertisements, mailroom employment is irregular for many workers. Few would consider mailroom work a craft, and unlike the other occupations discussed thus far, no established apprenticeship period exists for these jobs. Nevertheless, the mailroom seems to be one place in the newspaper plant where new technology may lead to a modest upgrading of workers' skills as they are trained to operate the new technology. Still, in the

---

[36]Ibid.

[37]Tom Walker, "Automation Knocks on the Mailroom Door," *Presstime* 4 (June 1982), pp. 4–9. The term "mailroom" is somewhat of a misnomer carried over from the early 19th century when about 90% of newspapers were delivered through the mail.

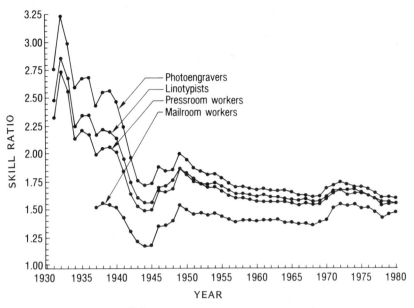

Figure 1. Skill ratios, various newspaper occupations.

fully automated mailroom the workers will be semi-skilled operatives responsible primarily for monitoring equipment. The new technology will also reduce manual work and thus the fluctuations in crew size, and will lead to an overall reduction in the mailroom work force. To date, however, diffusion of mailroom technology has been slow and, as a result, the amount of human labor required to sort and bundle the newspaper has not been dramatically altered.[38]

In sum, changes in composing room, plateroom, and pressroom technologies have lowered the skills required by these functions. Mailroom technologies have not had a major impact on skill levels of workers in those areas. Deskilling is reflected in the 1931–1980 skill ratio trends of four representative newspaper printing occupations, shown in Figure 1. Following Wallace and Kalleberg, a skill ratio is the average occupational union wage divided by the average manufacturing wage.[39] Figure 1 indicates a secular decline in the skill ratios of the three highly skilled occupational groups (linotypists, photoengravers, and pressroom workers). Mailroom workers show virtually no long-term change though they are considerably higher than the "typical" manufacturing worker. The most conspicuous pattern conveyed by these data is the leveling of skill-ratio differences among the major newspaper occupations—a convergence in skill ratios toward that of the least-skilled occupation, the mailroom worker.

[38]Walker.
[39]Wallace and Kalleberg, pp. 314–315.

Technological change in newspaper printing, then, has led to reductions in the production work force and to a decline in skill requirements. As a result, extensive apprenticeships are now unnecessary for performing most newspaper production tasks. The overall impact of these changes has been to restructure the labor process in a manner that shifts power from workers to employers. This has been demonstrated on several occasions in recent years when newspapers have been produced by skeleton crews of management and other white collar employees during strikes by craft unions.

IV. CHANGES IN LABOR–MANAGEMENT RELATIONS

Technological changes in the newspaper industry, along with the trends toward capital concentration and decreased local market competition discussed above, have radically and irrevocably altered labor–management relations in the newspaper industry. While the rapidity of the changes makes it impossible to forecast their eventual outcomes, two major trends are likely to have a lasting impact on the future of labor–management relations in the newspaper industry. First, there has been a gradual erosion of the ability of craft unions to maintain job security in the face of continued automation, a trend that is most evident in the pervasive use of "buyout" packages to eliminate redundant workers. Second, there has been a general decline in the size and influence of the major craft labor unions in the industry, resulting in a frenzied pattern of mergers and overtures to merger among several of them. Both of these trends reflect the increasingly defensive posture of labor in the industry. We discuss each trend in turn.

A. The Decline of Craft Consciousness and Control

The essential ingredient of craft consciousness is the ability of labor as a collectivity to control the destiny of the craft, what Jackson calls the "conceived interests" of a work group.[40] Craft consciousness is an ideology grounded in the concrete experience of the occupation and the ability of its incumbents to maintain their indispensability to the labor process against the encroachments of market forces, technological change, and other circumstances. For generations, the printing trades exemplified a high degree of craft consciousness. But as a result of the technological changes described above, there has been a decline not only in craftsmanship, but also in the craft consciousness of newspaper workers. This tendency is most evident in the growing inability of craft unions to control the impact of new technology on their employment and the nature of their work.

The history of the International Typographical Union (ITU) mirrors these changes in labor–management relations. Founded in 1852 as the National Typographical Union (NTU), the ITU is the oldest national union in the

---

[40]Jackson, pp. 33–39.

United States. The NTU (and subsequently the ITU) originally represented all the printing crafts in the industry. Apprenticeships provided novices with exposure to all aspects of printing, including composition, platework, and presswork. It was only after increased specialization produced by technological changes in the 1890s that clear lines of craft demarcation emerged.[41] This specialization was followed by a withdrawal from the International of other printing crafts and journalists, so that ITU membership became almost exclusively comprised of composing room workers.

Beginning with the introduction of the linotype machine in the 1890s, the ITU sought to control the introduction of new technologies on the shop floor and to minimize the hardship they imposed upon ITU members.[42] New York Typographical Union local No. 6 ("Big Six") established the more or less permanent control over automation that the ITU would have for the next eighty years with its general technology policy of 1890:

> Resolved, That Typographical Union No. 6 . . . welcomes the advent of successful typesetting machines, but maintains the right to establish regulations for the employment of its members upon them that will secure decreased hours of labor at a fair rate of wages.[43]

In later years, the ITU formed committees for learning about new printing technologies before their introduction into the work place. By doing this, the union was able to ensure retraining of its members, thereby limiting the hiring of lower skilled, non-union workers when new equipment was introduced. In 1955, the ITU created a retraining center in Colorado Springs, Colorado to teach union printers the newest techniques, which they could impart to their fellow chapel members. The Colorado Springs center was very active in the 1970s, but it has since been discontinued as the functions of both the technological committees and the training school were transferred to the local chapels.

The ITU remained strong through both world wars. As late as the 1950s, Lipset and his associates observed that the ITU maintained closed shops and had been successful at winning "the most complete control over job conditions of any union in the world."[44] So complete was ITU control that shop foremen were required to hold membership in the local union chapel, and workers instinctively stopped work when management representatives stepped onto the shop floor. Union control of working conditions brought favorable wage and benefit gains and helped printers achieve the status of the "blue collar aristocracy."[45]

However, the technological changes discussed above eventually eroded the strength of the ITU. The growing powerlessness of the union is illustrated by the experience of "Big Six" in the 1960s and the 1970s.[46] In 1962, contract

[41]Zimbalist; Wallace and Kalleberg, p. 309.
[42]Kelber and Schlesinger.
[43]Cited in Kelber and Schlesinger, p. 13.
[44]Lipset, Trow, and Coleman, p. 24.
[45]Ibid.
[46]Much of this account is taken from Raskin, 1979.

negotiations concerning TTS technology commenced between Big Six and the New York newspapers. Big Six sought restrictions on non-union production of TTS tape and demanded a large pay increase. When negotiations on both issues failed, the union called a strike which lasted 114 days and cost the affected New York papers $108 million, local business $70 million, and the union $8 million in strike benefits. In the end, the ITU allowed non-union production of TTS tape for national news stories on the condition that the union would share in any savings that resulted from the new method. This was the first in a series of concessions over shop control that weakened the union's bargaining position. It also set a precedent for the rest of the country as both the union and newspaper publishers began to anticipate the technological obsolescence of the composing room.

In the 1966 contract negotiations, Big Six sought to reassert its control over the introduction of cold type technology. Big Six President Bertram Powers negotiated a contract with the seven New York newspapers which gave the union absolute authority over the types of technology which could be brought into the composing room. Union jobs seemed secure at the time, but by 1974 the six smallest New York papers had folded, largely because they were unable to afford the high wage structure associated with the old hot metal printing processes. According to former New York *Times* labor columnist A. H. Raskin, the large New York papers (the *Times, Post,* and *Daily News*) had gambled that the 1966 agreement would bankrupt their smaller competitors.[47] Moreover, the large papers hoped that the ITU, because of its opposition to new technology, would be perceived by the public as the cause of these failures and the hundreds of lost ITU jobs. This in fact is what happened, so that by 1974 Big Six was under pressure from both within and outside the union to assume a more conciliatory position.

The decreasing strength of the ITU was reflected further in the willingness of the union to negotiate the introduction of automated processes in 1974. The unprecedented 11-year contract created a model for dealing with technological advances throughout the industry. It provided lifetime employment for currently employed typesetters (including substitutes) and an attractive early retirement program. The contract also mandated future workforce reductions through attrition. For the union, the contract limited technological displacement of composing room workers. For publishers, the contract allowed them to embark on a long-range strategy to rationalize newspaper production, gain control of the labor process, and recalibrate the wage structure. This provision and others like it throughout the country signaled the reduction of composing room personnel and the imminent decline of the ITU. According to Raskin:

> The New York publishers' willingness to be so generous in negotiating the 1974 contract stemmed from an awareness of both sides that the packet represented the last hurrah for the typographical union. The union had strength enough to exact a high price for removing its veto power over automated processes, but the advent of

---

[47]Interview with A. H. Raskin, New York, New York, 16 February 1983; see also Smith, p. 46.

automation effectively stripped it of future power. All that the union can now look forward to is a precipitous decline, as old-timers retire or die off and the traditional composing room disappears.[48]

As ITU locals across the country capitulated to the demands of employers to automate the composing room, Raskin's prediction rang true. Since the early 1970s, approximately 120 buyout arrangements or "termination incentive programs" have been made and are currently in effect, most of them in large metropolitan dailies with hundreds of composing room workers.[49] The scale of buyout strategies has been tremendous in many large newspapers. For example, between 1974 and 1981, the Indianapolis *Star and News* reduced its composing room work force from 480 to 259;[50] and between 1974 and 1982, the New York *Times* reduced its composing room from 823 to 441.[51] A recent Rand Corporation study found that in 432 newspapers, 7,600 composing room jobs were lost between 1970 and 1982, 2,200 of which were eliminated through buyouts.[52]

Buyout strategies take a variety of forms, including lump-sum payments, monthly installments paid over a period of years, interest-free loans, and college tuition.[53] Most of these are coupled with lifetime employment guarantees for workers who remain on the job. The size of the buyout payments— which range up to $80,000—generally varies inversely with workers' age, thereby encouraging young workers to retire early. Buyout plans have been costly for newspaper publishers: in the New York *Times* alone, the program was estimated to have cost the paper about $11.5 million by 1982. However, the ultimate savings to employers will be considerable, especially when it is considered that the average *Times* compositor earns over $44,000 in wages and fringe benefits per year.[54]

In newspapers where unions are weak or non-existent (i.e., in the periphery sector of the industry), buyout plans have been less conspicuous and generally one-sided. Redundant workers are laid off or given the alternative of transferring to another position in the plant.

The frequency of buyouts has declined sharply in the 1980s.[55] While the buyouts served their purpose in reducing the work force, they did not provide a permanent solution to the problems of technological adjustment. Indeed, many newspapers have found that some traditional printer skills in page layout and other composition techniques are still required even with photocomposition. Also, many ITU locals have been reluctant to enter into further buyout agreements because of the sharp decline of dues-paying members.

[48]Raskin, 1979.
[49]Clark Newsom, "'Buyouts' of Printers May Have Peaked," *Presstime* 2 (1981), pp. 4–9.
[50]Ibid.
[51]Clark Newsom, "For Printers, Life Varies After Accepting Buyouts," *Presstime* 4 (December 1982), pp. 32–35.
[52]Warren, p. 1.
[53]Newsom, 1981.
[54]Newsom, 1982, p. 32 (inset titled "127 Accept NY Times 'Buyouts'")
[55]Newsom, 1981.

B. Craft Unionism in Transition: Toward Industrial Unionism?

With technological change and work-force reductions, the percentage of unionized workers in printing and publishing has declined from 39% in 1959 to less than 20% today.[56] The current configuration of American printing unions can best be described as "quasi-craft unionism," perhaps in transition to a form of industrial unionism which is similar to that of the West German printing industry.[57] Rather than representing workers from a single craft, some newspaper unions increasingly combine members from diverse crafts and occupations in the industry. In addition, some unions with no history of involvement in the industry (notably, the International Brotherhood of Teamsters) have made inroads among some occupations. Quasi-craft unionism is reflected, then, in the decline in the number and influence of craft unions in the industry. Since World War II, the number of major craft unions has declined from about 10 to 3, mainly because of union mergers. It should be emphasized that most union mergers have been defensive ones, designed to minimize the erosion of craft power which followed technological rationalization.

Table 5 shows membership figures for the major unions in the printing industry (newspaper and commercial sectors) from 1955 to 1983 and conveys the pattern of union mergers in the past 30 years.[58] The following is a summary of the recent union mergers:

1964—The International Photo Engravers Union of North America affiliated with the Lithographers and Photoengravers International Union

1972—The Lithographers and Photoengravers International Union merged with the International Brotherhood of Bookbinders to create the Graphic Arts International Union

1975—The International Printing Pressmens and Assistants Union of North America and the International Stereotypers, Electrotypers, and Platemakers Union merged to create the International Printing and Graphic Communication Union

1979—The International Mailers Union affiliated with the International Typographical Union

1983—The International Printing and Graphic Communications Union merged with the Graphic Arts International Union to create the Graphic Communications International Union

[56]A series on percentage of the industry work force was assembled from two sources: United States Bureau of Labor Statistics, *Directory of National Unions and Employee Associations*, (Washington, DC: U.S. Government Printing Office, various issues); and Leo Troy and Neil Sheflin, *Union Sourcebook*, (West Orange, NJ: Industrial Relations Data and Information Service).

[57]Michael Wallace, "Responding to Technological Change in the Newspaper Industry: A Comparison of the United States, Great Britain, and the Federal Republic of Germany," *Proceedings of the Thirty-Seventh Annual Meetings of the Industrial Relations Research Association*, (1985), pp. 325–332.

[58]This updates data presented by Gail L. Barwis, "The Changing Face of Labor in the Newspaper Industry," *Newspaper Research Journal* 2 (January 1981), pp. 49–57.

Table 5. Printing and Publishing Industry Union Membership, 1955–1983
(Working Membership in Thousands)[a]

Organization	1955	1957	1959	1961	1963	1965	1967	1969	1971	1973	1975	1977	1979	1981	1983
Photo Engravers Union of North America, Int.	16	16	16	16	15	b									
Lithographers & Photoengravers Int. Union	22	25	28	20	42	41	43	45	46	c					
Bookbinders, Int. Brotherhood of	51	54	56	56	53	51	57	60	59	c					
Graphic Arts Int. Union										99	93	83	77	74	d
Graphic Communications Int. Union															154
Printing & Graphics Communications Union, Int.											105	99	94	93	d
Printing Pressmen's & Assistants' Union of North America, Int.	87	92	96	99	100	100	102	106	107	104					
Stereotypers' Electrotypers', & Platemakers' Union, Int.	12	12	12	12	12	11	10	9	8	7	e				
Mailers	3	4	4	4	4	4	4	5	4	3	3	3	f		
Typographical Union, Int.	78	78	79	81	86	87	90	89	87	81	73	61	52	47	43
Newspaper Guild, The	21	22	24	24	23	23	24	25	26	26	26	26	25	25	23

[a]Source: Directory of U.S. Labor Organizations, 1982–83 Edition.
[b]Merged with Lithographers and Photoengravers International Union, September 7, 1964.
[c]Merged to form Graphic Arts International Union, September 4, 1972.
[d]Merged to form Graphic Communication International Union, June 30, 1983.
[e]Merged to form Printing and Graphic Communications Union, Int., October 17, 1973.
[f]Merged with International Typographical Union, 1979.

Today there are three major unions in the printing industry: the Newspaper Guild (Guild), composed of journalists, editors, and a few white collar workers; the International Typographical Union (ITU), composed mainly of composing room workers and mailroom workers; and the recently created Graphic Communications International Union (GCIU), composed of pressroom and ancillary workers.

Surveying the issues of the ITU's *Typographical Journal* from the last ten years reveals the reasons for the spate of mergers and for the current disarray among American printing unions. New technology has radically altered newspaper production roles, eroding craft jurisdiction over many jobs and creating the need for a more united front against employers.

Rhetorically, ITU leaders have called for the formation of "one big union" in the printing industry, but old cleavages have proved difficult to overcome.[59] After the successful merger with the Mailers in 1979, the ITU was twice unsuccessful in consummating mergers with the Guild.[60] In 1983, the second failed attempt set the tone for a turbulent year in which the union's national leadership and its rank-and-file both became deeply divided over the union's future. The incumbent president began merger discussions with the Teamsters, a non-craft union with a multi-industry membership. Fearing that ITU identity would be lost in the Teamsters, other ITU leaders sought a merger with the newly formed GCIU. In 1983, the pro-GCIU challenger for ITU president defeated the pro-Teamster incumbent and his plan for merger. But, seeking to close the impending deal with the Teamsters, the incumbent succeeded in having the union's canvassing board overturn the results of the election on a technicality.

The National Labor Relations Board sponsored a new election to correct irregularities in the 1983 election. In a separate action, six disgruntled ITU members were granted an injunction to block the vote on merger with the Teamsters pending the outcome of the new election. In the new election, held in July 1984, the pro-GCIU faction gained a 3–2 control of the executive board, including the presidency. The new president immediately recanted all past negotiations with the Teamsters and vowed to pursue negotiations with the GCIU. After several months of negotiations, though, the scheduled membership vote on the GCIU merger package was cancelled because of lingering differences between the ITU and GCIU negotiating teams. The failure of the new president to consummate his merger plan with the GCIU led to renewed demands for a merger vote with the Teamsters. Spurred by the two minority members of the executive board and internal dissension by some ITU locals, a referendum on merger with the Teamsters was held in 1985 and voted down by a 2–1 margin.

Even with the result of the referendum, the merger issue remains unre-

[59]The following account is taken from Ralph Kessler, "The Death Agony of the Typographical Union," *Union Democracy Review* 46 (1985), p. 6; and various issues of the *Typographical Journal*, a publication of the International Typographical Union.

[60]John Consoli, "Internal Dissension Delays ITU/Guild Merger," *Editor and Publisher* 116 (8 January 1983), pp. 12–13.

solved. Too weak to resist further employer assaults alone, the ITU is compelled to seek a partnership which would restore its bargaining power. But the divisions between pro-GCIU and pro-Teamster (mainly mailroom workers) factions are deep-rooted and difficult to reconcile. By some accounts, a decision in either direction would lead to mass defections by the losing side. Indeed, there have been recent claims that the Teamsters are "raiding" ITU locals (especially mailroom affiliates for whom they have the most appeal). In a 1984 decertification election held at the Cleveland *Plain Dealer*, the Teamsters gained representational rights from the ITU in the composing room and mailroom.[61] Other Teamster "raids" challenged established ITU locals in Cleveland, Columbus, New Haven, Toronto, Montreal, and Little Rock.[62] ITU leadership warned that this was part of a national campaign by the Teamsters to gain a toehold in the printing industry at the expense of the ITU.[63]

The union merger movement and the painful transition toward industrial unionism in newspaper printing is frought with inter-union conflict which stems from the dying legacy of craft unionism. Longstanding rivalries among composing room workers and pressroom workers have (for now) aborted merger negotiations between the ITU and GCIU. Differences between journalists and composing room workers over jurisdiction of cold-type technology remain a point of friction between the Guild and the ITU. Furthermore, while the ITU and GCIU include increasingly diverse memberships due to previous mergers, each must deal with internal friction along the jurisdictional lines of the previous craft unions (e.g., between mailroom workers and composing room workers in the ITU).

Along with newspaper consolidation and technological change, the belated and defensive nature of the printing union merger movement has facilitated increased managerial control of the labor process in printing. The printing unions, particularly the ITU, were slow to react to the changes wrought by technological change and only turned to merger as a last resort *after* questions of control of the new technology had been decided by the publishers on a plant-by-plant basis. This is in marked contrast to the more far-sighted approach of British printing unions during the 1970s.[64] With a more centralized national structure, the British printing unions anticipated the technological trends and merged *before* newspaper interests could consolidate their power. Hence, although the British union configuration—with three major national unions—bears a superficial resemblance to that of the U.S.,

[61]Donald Sabeth, "PD Printers, Mailers Vote Switch to Teamsters," Cleveland *Plain Dealer* (5 December 1984), pp. 1E–2E.

[62]Kessler, p. 6.

[63]Billy J. Austin, "With Friends Like This . . ." *Typographical Journal* (November 1984), p. 6.

[64]See Tony Griffin, "Technological Change and Craft Control in the Newspaper Industry: An International Comparison," *Cambridge Journal of Economics* 8 (March 1984), pp. 41–61; and John Gennard and Steve Dunn, "The Impact of New Technology on the Structure and Organisation of Craft Unions in the Printing Industry," *British Journal of Industrial Relations* 21 (1983), pp. 17–32.

the British unions are much further along the road to true industrial unionism, thus approximating a "quasi-industrial" structure.[65] Due to the conflict-ridden form of quasi-craft unionism, the U.S. printing unions currently lack a coordinated bargaining strategy at either the local or national levels and therefore remain vulnerable to concerted, unilateral efforts by publishers to rationalize newspaper printing.

V. CONCLUSION

Technological change in newspaper printing has shifted control of the labor process away from craft unions and toward newspaper publishers. The increasingly dualistic structure of the newspaper industry—the uneven consolidation of larger newspaper firms alongside small family-owned enterprises—made technological modernization possible and ultimately facilitated this shift in managerial control.

Newspaper consolidation, technological change, and growing managerial control have had two consequences for labor–management relations. First, the decreasing number of craft jobs has led to a decline in the percentage unionized and, therefore, a decline in the voice of organized labor. Second, declining union strength, skill decomposition and skill homogenization have eroded traditional craft jurisdictions, leading to defensive craft union mergers. The transition to industrial unionism has stalled in a "quasi-craft" stage and should not be regarded as a foregone conclusion. The failure to accomplish this transition in a timely fashion, we have suggested, accounts for the nearly total success of newspaper publishers in rationalizing newspaper printing, while the remaining unions struggle simultaneously to preserve their erstwhile craft identities and memberships.

As an industry which displayed a high degree of worker autonomy and control over the labor process until recently, newspaper printing illustrates Braverman's thesis on skill degradation in its purest form.[66] This process had been accomplished in many mass production industries by the 1930s, but its occurrence in many craft occupations is largely a post-war phenomenon.

But Braverman's thesis neglects the connection between deskilling, the erosion of craft boundaries, and changing structures of union power. The stormy birth of industrial unionism in the 1930s was made possible, in part, by preceding patterns of capital consolidation and technological rationalization which levelled skill differences and homogenized the work force in mass-production industries.[67] But what happens when industries with relatively weak employer systems and well-entrenched craft union structures undergo rapid capital consolidation and technological change, accompanied by deskill-

[65]Wallace, pp. 329–331.

[66]Harry Braverman, *Labor and Monopoly Capital* (New York: Monthly Review Press, 1974).

[67]David M. Gordon, Richard Edwards, and Michael Reich, *Segmented Work, Divided Workers* (Cambridge: Cambridge University Press, 1982).

ing of workers? Our account of the developments in newspaper printing in the last forty years provides one answer to this question, though by no means a complete or exhaustive one. Our answer is not complete because the process of union adjustment to technological change in the U.S. newspaper industry is still unfolding. It remains to be seen whether the ITU's cry for industrial unionism will surmount longstanding craft boundaries or wither in the face of continued automation.

4

Technology and Control of the Labor Process

Fifty Years of Longshoring on the U.S. West Coast

Gordon Betcherman and Douglas Rebne

I. INTRODUCTION

Longshoring on the U.S. West Coast has undergone a technological transformation over the past quarter century. Perhaps the most critical effect of mechanization is the more than nine-fold increase in labor productivity since 1960. Furthermore, the effects of technological change and attendant productivity gains on industrial relations have been considerable. Most obviously, the replacement of men by machines has had a drastic impact on employment levels. In addition, we will argue that a less apparent, but by no means insignificant, implication of the transformation has been a major shift in control of the labor process from the workers to management.

Prior to mechanization, longshoremen possessed the unique, if not complex, skills, knowledge, and resources necessary to load and unload cargo. Labor was the essential ingredient in the process. However, the evolution to cranes, containers, and computers has rendered the traditional skills and knowledge of the longshoremen largely irrelevant. The critical production input now is advanced technology—both the equipment and its application. Only the companies have this resource and with it comes control of the longshoring process. This shift in control, itself, has had a number of effects, including a strengthening of employer bargaining power in relation to the union.

Gordon Betcherman • Institute of Industrial Relations, University of California, Los Angeles and Economic Council of Canada, P.O. Box 527, Ottawa, Ontario KIP 5V6, Canada. **Douglas Rebne** • Graduate School of Management, University of California at Los Angeles, CA 90024.

After discussing the theme of control of work, we examine how technological innovations have transformed traditional longshoring methods over the past three decades. Following this, we analyze the impact of the new technologies on employment and the collective bargaining history of the industry, emphasizing the negotiations on the subject of technological change. Of special interest here are the historic Mechanization and Modernization (M&M) Agreements of 1961 and 1966 which guided automation on the West Coast docks.[1] Finally, we return to the control theme and its application to longshoring.

II. CONTROL AND TECHNOLOGY

The concept of control assumes somewhat competing interests between workers and their employers. Control, in its application to labor relations, has three dimensions: direction over investment and resource allocation, supervision of labor power, and command of the production process.[2] Our interest here concerns the third dimension. Command or control over the production process requires knowledge, resources, and skills: that is, knowledge of the process, its boundaries, and its constituent tasks and the skills and physical resources (or access to them) to carry out these tasks. For both management and labor this control is desirable. From management's point of view, command over the production process allows it to organize work in order to maximize productivity, and thus profits.[3] For workers, on the other hand, control reduces alienation on the job by enabling their labor to be empowering, meaningful, socially integrative, and creative.[4]

According to Braverman, mechanization has contributed to increased managerial control in U.S. business enterprises throughout the twentieth century, especially in the skilled crafts.[5] In the early stages of industrialization, craft workers controlled production with essentially the same skills and knowledge used in pre-industrial settings. Since labor possessed the information and expertise, management assumed the responsibility for financing, sales, and co-ordination, while remaining somewhat distanced from production. Through the nineteenth century, this separation from the labor process became increasingly unsatisfactory for employers. In the first place, control

---

[1]The Mechanization and Modernization Agreements have received considerable attention in the past. For example, see Paul Hartman, *Collective Bargaining and Productivity: The Longshore Mechanization Agreement* (Berkeley: University of California Press, 1969); and Lincoln Fairley, *Facing Mechanization: The West Coast Longshore Plan* (Los Angeles: UCLA Institute of Industrial Relations, 1979).

[2]Stephen Hill, *Competition and Control at Work* (London: Heinemann, 1981).

[3]Control is sometimes viewed as an end in itself. See for example Harry Braverman, *Labor and Monopoly Capital: The Degradation of Work in the Twentieth Century* (New York: Monthly Review Press, 1974).

[4]Robert Blauner, *Alienation and Freedom* (Chicago: University of Chicago Press, 1964).

[5]Braverman views scientific management as the epitome of this process. See Chapter 4 for his explication of this.

over production costs and scheduling became more important as enterprises grew larger and more complex. More fundamentally, management's imperative of cost minimization with productivity maximization was not an imperative for workers. Accordingly, to ensure that their interests were organizational priorities, managers moved to assume greater control over production, typically by increasing the division of labor, pre-planning production tasks, and by mechanizing operations. Yet mechanization occurs for other compelling reasons, such as improving quality and volume, reducing unavoidable errors, and making possible the production of new goods. Nevertheless, the links between technology and control is important. Managerial control is easier when the instruments of production are inanimate. Also, technical innovations can eliminate the skills from which craft workers derived their autonomy and control.

This having been said, it should be noted that it is not clear that more advanced technologies inevitably reduce worker control. For example, Blauner suggests that worker control is greater in automated, continuous process production than in mass production assembly lines. Furthermore, the particular form that technology takes in any situation partly derives from the choices made by managers and workers.[6] While workers and their employers may try to ensure that technological choices serve their interests, social and economic forces in the work place dictate the relative influence of each. As Winner points out, "different people are differently situated and possess unequal degrees of power as well as unequal levels of awareness."[7] Therefore, the form of technological change depends in part on the relative bargaining power of labor and management.

While there are innumerable models of bargaining power,[8] most include some notion of the source of control over the production process. The capacity of workers to control production depends on both the indispensability of labor in the production process and, therefore, on the capacity of workers to disrupt operations by withdrawing their labor. Technology can influence the bargaining power of workers by enhancing or eroding their indispensability in production. Thus, while the legacy of labor relations in an industry may affect the course of technological change, so, in turn, may technological change alter the balance of power between labor and management.

III. TECHNOLOGICAL CHANGES IN LONGSHORING

The function of the port is to transfer goods between land and sea transportation. In the case of sea-to-land transfers, this involves a number of stages between the arrival of the ship to the quay and the eventual departure of the

[6]Stephen Wood, ed., *The Degradation of Work? Skill, Deskilling and the Labour Process* (London: Hutchinson, 1983), pp. 16–17.

[7]Langdon Winner, "Do Artifacts Have Politics?," *Daedalus* 109 (Winter 1980), p. 127.

[8]Thomas Kochan, *Collective Bargaining and Industrial Relations* (Homewood: Richard D. Irwin, 1980), p. 39.

land vehicle from the port area. According to Jansson and Shneerson, these include five linked operations: discharge of cargo from the ship's hold to the pier, moving the cargo from there to a storage area, storing the cargo in transit, moving cargo from storage to a loading platform and, finally, loading the cargo on to a land vehicle.[9]

Using Woodward's classification of technology, we characterize the transformation of longshoring from unit and small batch production toward large batch and mass production and, now with global computer technology, toward a continuous process.[10] Technological changes in longshoring may be further understood by considering two principles which are fundamental to the economics of the port: "time is money"[11] and "the chain is as strong as its weakest link".[12] The first underscores turnaround time as the central objective of longshoring operations. Shipping companies make their money by moving cargo and since the time their ships spend in ports is not revenue-producing, minimizing the duration of loading and unloading is part of their profit function. The second axiom pertains to the operational stages involved in port activity which were identified above. As is the case with any production process, bottlenecks are created because some phases are more efficient than others. Given these principles, then, the evolution of the longshoring process can be seen for now as a series of largely technical solutions to eliminate production bottlenecks and, thus, decrease ship turnaround time.

For centuries the longshoring process underwent little change.[13] Experience guided the stowage design and the actual loading and unloading of ships was carried out by large gangs of dockers with the assistance of ropes and hooks. According to Jansson and Shneerson, the impetus for innovation emerged with the development of bigger boats early in the 1900s.[14] The increased scale of these vessels made the minimization of turnaround time more economically compelling. The principle behind more rapid loading and unloading rested then, as now, with the unitization of cargo, thereby reducing the number of items to be handled. Unitization, of course, implies larger, heavier packages which necessitate more sophisticated transfer processes. This requirement led to preslinging, palletization, and the increasing use of fork lifts, conveyors, and jitneys in the first half of this century.

While these innovations improved the stowage-unstowage operation, they brought with them new problems which stimulated additional tech-

[9]Jan Owen Jansson and Dan Shneerson, *Port Economics* (Cambridge: MIT Press, 1982), p. 10.

[10]Joan Woodward, *Industrial Organization: Theory and Practice* (London: Oxford University Press, 1965).

[11]Lane C. Kendall, *The Business of Shipping*, 4th ed. (Centreville: Cornell Maritime Press, 1983), p. 137.

[12]Jansson and Shneerson, p. 9.

[13]For descriptions of traditional longshoring, see David F. Wilson, *Dockers: The Impact of Industrial Change* (Bungay: Fontana, 1972); Stephen Hill, *The Dockers: Class and Tradition in London* (London: Heinemann, 1976); and Herb Mills, "The San Francisco Waterfront: The Social Consequences of Industrial Modernization", in *Case Studies in the Labor Process*, ed. Andrew Zimbalist (New York: Monthly Review Press, 1979), pp. 127–55.

[14]Jansson and Shneerson, p. 14.

nological changes. For example, the new equipment required more land space than was available in the traditional finger-pier configuration, which led to the design of wide, lineal wharves. Moreover, the efficient use of fork lifts and other equipment required the larger cargo units to be on the dock prior to loading, thereby raising damage risks and stimulating the subsequent use of containers.

Initial efforts were made to employ containers in the 1930s. The technical obstacles impeding the regular use of larger units rested with the design of the containers and cargo ships.[15] Cranes with massive hoisting capacity were available, but their cost effectiveness depended on the availability of containers that were sufficiently large to permit the realization of economies of scale. Also, a container design was needed to simultaneously allow for efficient stowage on ships and adaptability to land transportation vehicles. Cargo ships, too, required redesign so that massive containers could be stored safely and efficiently.

Standardized flat-bottomed containers and cellular container ships were developed in the mid-1950s to solve these technical problems.[16] The productivity gains stemming from the economies of scale associated with this system have been enormous. The correlation between package size and handling capacity is substantial: while a longshore gang can load two-ton palletized units at a rate of 60 tons per gang-hour, 10-ton (20-foot) containers can be loaded at over 300 tons per gang-hour, and 20-ton (40-foot) containers can be put on board at the rate of 650 tons per gang-hour.[17] Productivity has also spiralled upward because of the direct adaptability of the containers to ground carriers, which has integrated land and sea transportation.[18]

The technological innovations are reflected in the changes in the types of cargo handled in West Coast ports (Table 1). The dry bulk (grain, ores, etc.), lumber and logs, and automobile categories have maintained a relatively stable share of between 45 and 60 per cent of the market since 1960. While the container and general cargo groups generally involve the handling of similar commodities, they represent high and low technologies, respectively. In 1960, the general cargo category, based on traditional labor-intensive, break-bulk methods, predominated. Container traffic, capital-intensive and highly mechanized, was virtually non-existent. Ten years later, containers had become much more common but, in terms of volume, general cargo remained primary. During the 1970s and into the 1980s, containers rapidly took over and, by 1984, they accounted for almost six times more tonnage than general cargo.

[15]While large containers needed advanced material handling equipment, this in itself was not a problem. Ibid., p. 17.
[16]The technical problems and the eventual development and implementation of containers and container ships are discussed in detail in Kendall.
[17]Jansson and Shneerson, p. 17.
[18]The integrated container system by no means represents the only technological development in longshoring in recent decades. Other technological changes include the computerization of cargo tracking, stowage design, and crane operation.

Table 1. Percentage Distribution of Tonnage by Category, West Coast Longshore Industry, 1960–1984[a]

			Tonnage category[b] (% of total)			
Year	Dry bulk	Lumber and logs	Autos	Containers	General	All cargo[c]
1960	37.8	5.8	4.1	2.5	49.8	100.0
1965	41.9	8.0	5.8	10.3	34.1	100.0
1970	42.7	9.6	7.5	14.6	25.5	100.0
1975	44.2	8.8	8.3	26.6	12.0	100.0
1980	44.5	5.1	11.3	30.8	8.3	100.0
1984	36.2	4.2	11.1	41.2	7.3	100.0

[a]Source is Pacific Maritime Association, *1984 Annual Report*, p. 35.
[b]Tonnage is defined as "manifested cargo upon which ocean revenue is computed." Note that tonnage assessment methods have changed several times over the years, and thus these latest figures may differ from those cited in earlier publications.
[c]Totals may not add up to 100.0 due to rounding errors.

IV. LONGSHORE EMPLOYMENT

Longshoremen and clerks are the two occupational groups with which we are most concerned. Longshoremen are responsible for the physical transfer of cargo between ship and dock. A number of specific skills, including winch drivers, crane operators, and fork lift truck operators, to name just a few, fall under the general longshoreman category. Clerks have traditionally been charged with stowage design and the registration and inspection of goods as they are loaded and unloaded. As we will see, technological change has transformed the way in which both longshoremen and clerks carry out these functions. Modernization of methods has even altered the responsibilities themselves, particularly in the case of the clerks.

Since the 1930s, available longshoring and clerical work has generally been distributed to workers registered by joint action of the union, the International Longshormen's and Warehousemen's Union (ILWU), and the employers' association, now the Pacific Maritime Association (PMA).[19] Typically, longshore work has been assigned on a "single-job" basis through local hiring halls, although steady employment relationships between workers and companies are now becoming more prevalent.

Technological change has contributed to declining employment among both longshoremen and clerks (Table 2). From 1952 until 1984, cargo tonnage passing through U.S. West Coast ports increased seven-fold from about 18

[19]The few unregistered casual workers have been employed to absorb short-run fluctuations in the variable cargo load. Longer-run increases in labor demand have been met by additional registration rather than prolonged use of casual labor.

Table 2. Number of Registered
Longshoremen and Clerks, United States
West Coast, 1952–1984[a]

Year	Registered Longshoremen[b]	Registered Clerks[c]
1952	13,953	n/a
1956	13,735	n/a
1961	13,941	1,791
1966	13,224	1,701
1971	12,277	1,922
1976	8,795	1,431
1981	8,059	1,307
1984	7,457	1,469

[a]Sources are Pacific Maritime Association, *Annual Report,*
various years; Lincoln Fairley, *Facing Mechanization: The
West Coast Longshore Plan,* Appendix Table 1; PMA/NRD
No. 2 January, 1973.
[b]Includes all Class "A" and "B" registrants.
[c]Includes all Class "A" and "B" registrants.

million tons to 133 million tons. Nevertheless, the number of registered long-shoremen has been nearly halved in this period, falling from just under 14,000 in 1952 to 7,457 in 1984. While the employment decreases among clerks have not been as striking, registration in this occupation has also been on a downward trend.

All registered longshore workers on the West Coast are ILWU members. Longshoremen and clerks are generally organized into separate locals at major ports.[20] The two occupations negotiate separate collective agreements with the PMA which, for both groups, cover the entire U.S. West Coast.[21] Currently, the ILWU has an overall membership of approximately 55,000.[22] In addition to the longshore workers on the U.S. continental West Coast, this total includes warehousemen on the West Coast, longshoremen and other workers, particularly in food processing, in British Columbia, Alaska, and Hawaii, and inland water transportation workers. The occupational and geographical diversity of ILWU membership has dampened the effect of declining West Coast longshore employment on union membership. Nevertheless, membership in the West Coast bargaining unit has diminished with the shrinking registered work force.

---

[20]It should be noted that this general pattern of occupationally distinct locals does not apply in a
few ports where combination locals including all ILWU members exist.

[21]There are also ILWU port locals representing foremen, or "walking bosses," who supervise
loading and discharging operations. The foremen negotiate their own coast-wide collective
agreement with the PMA.

[22]Information on current membership was supplied by ILWU officials.

V. COLLECTIVE BARGAINING AND TECHNOLOGY

The technological transformation of longshoring described in section III must not be seen as deterministic but rather, the result of choices and decisions emerging out of the labor–management relationship. The employers have bargained collectively through the PMA and its predecessors for the past half century. The most important managerial actors are the shipping companies. These firms own and operate the cargo-carrying ships and, as such, they decide which routes and ports will be used. Thus, the volume and distribution of activity along the West Coast is affected in no small part by these companies. The ship-operators' decision-making power extends to the longshoring process as well, primarily because they are responsible for most of the capital investment in the ports. Although there are a few very large companies, overall the number of ship operators involved in West Coast shipping is considerable and, accordingly, the industry is competitive. It should be noted that the shipping companies have not traditionally been the direct employers of the workers. Rather, they made arrangements with stevedoring contractors who engaged the workers required for loading and unloading. The other group of firms in the industry, the terminal companies, offer cargo-handling services. With modernization, these typically small stevedoring and terminal operations have been increasingly controlled by the shipping companies.

The history of collective bargaining in longshoring can be organized into three periods. The first, beginning with the coast-wide strike in 1934, witnessed the emergence of the union, the employers' association, and the institutionalization of bargaining arrangements between the two. The second period, from 1961 to 1971, was a decade of industrial relations reorganization, made possible by the Mechanization and Modernization Agreements of 1961 and 1966. Technological change, and its impact on employment, have accelerated in the third period, which encompasses the years since 1971.

A. The Early Years (1934–1960)

At the turn of the century, longshoring employment was transacted in a "casual" labor market in which employers hired workers on an hourly or, at best, daily basis to load and unload cargo ships. While this "shape up," as it was called, was advantageous for the shipping companies, it was not so for the longshoremen.[23] With the supply of labor far exceeding demand, employers enjoyed the fruits of absolute power in hiring and utilizing workers. Corruption, speed-ups, back-breaking work, and poverty characterized life on the docks on the West Coast and elsewhere.

By the 1930s, these working conditions were exacerbated by the depres-

---

[23]Some description of the "shape-up" can be found in Irving Bernstein, *Turbulent Years* (Boston: Houghton Mifflin, 1970), pp. 254–56. For more detail of the same process in the British context, see Wilson, pp. 17–28.

sion economy. In 1933, well over half of the Pacific Coast longshoremen were on relief, and for the few who could get work, wages barely exceeded $10 per week.[24] It was in this setting that the International Longshoremen's and Warehousemen's Union was born. At the time there was no employee representation, save for the company-dominated "Blue-Book" union. By 1934, worker support spread on the docks for a nascent, and quite radical, union movement led by a young Australian, Harry Bridges. With the employers unwilling to recognize Bridges and his organization, longshoremen up and down the coast stopped working. The 1934 strike, ultimately settled by arbitration, was a violent chapter in American labor history.

The work stoppage, and its resolution through arbitration, marked an important turning point in longshoring labor relations.[25] The conflict spawned the new union which, at first, was part of the International Longshoremen's Association (AFL), but then broke away in 1937 to join the CIO, renaming itself the ILWU. The 1934 settlement had two features that were to take on long-standing significance. First, the foundation was set for coast-wide uniformity in collective bargaining and, second, hiring halls supplanted the casual labor market.

The first step towards uniformity came with the establishment in 1934 of port-specific and coast-wide joint (union–employer) labor relations committees. Negotiations regarding contract interpretation and enforcement were to come under the purview of these committees, with disputes subject to arbitration. Uniformity was furthered in 1937 with the founding of an employers' organization, now the Pacific Maritime Association, which continues to represent West Coast shipping companies, stevedore contractors, and terminal operators in all industrial relations matters. The final step in establishing a uniform industrial relations arrangement from Seattle to San Diego was NLRB recognition in 1938 of the West Coast as an appropriate bargaining unit. It should be recognized that coast-wide uniformity was particularly significant from a strategic point of view for the union. For shipping companies, ports tend to be acceptable substitutes for one another. Attempts to improve the labor situation in any single locale, then, could merely lead to changes in the flow of trade to low-wage ports. Coast-wide standards, on the other hand, ruled out such employer responses.

The other significant feature of the 1934 arbitration award was the institution of hiring halls in every port. While hiring halls were not novel to the industry, earlier efforts had been employer-dominated. The halls, as they were mandated by the arbitrator, however, quickly became controlled by the ILWU. The 1934 award allowed the union to supply the dispatchers, and subsequent arbitral decisions strengthened the ILWU position in the hall. By 1940, the employer role in labor allocation ended with its request for a certain

---

[24]Bernstein, p. 257.

[25]It should be noted that today the 1934 strike plays an almost mythical role in the occupational culture of the longshoremen, particularly that of the old-timers. For them, the 1934 strike ended the degrading days of employer domination and ushered in a new era characterized by strength through collectivism.

number of men. All labor supply decisions were made in the union hiring hall on the basis of union-determined principles.

The union could now exert some control over the supply of workers and, hence, the chronic labor surpluses. Traditional hiring practices, and the attendant discrimination, favoritism, and corruption were also minimized through the hall. Not only did an early arbitral award ban the "preferred gang" arrangement whereby employers hired favored teams of longshoremen but, in addition, the union adopted a rotating dispatch policy. That is, union members with the lowest number of hours worked were given the first opportunity to fill company requests for labor.

One final legacy of the early days deserves mention as well. In arbitration and job actions following the strike, the union won a number of work rules pertaining to maximum load limits, handling of cargo, gang sizes, and other manning provisions. These increasingly took on a disruptive and restrictive character from the employer point of view and, during the late 1940s and throughout the 1950s, the PMA attempted, for the most part unsuccessfully, to increase operational flexibility. Not only did the work rules inflate labor costs and dampen productivity, but they also placed severe constraints on the ability of the employers to take advantage of new unitization technologies that were appearing on the horizon.[26]

B. The Mechanization and Modernization Agreements (1961–1970)

Beginning in 1961, the ILWU and the PMA operated for a decade under successive Mechanization and Modernization (M&M) Agreements. The contract preamble to the first M&M Agreement, which covered the period from 1961 to 1966, affirmed "the Employers' right to operate efficiently and to change methods of work and to utilize labor saving devices."[27] Specific changes in the work rules regarding manning, handling, and sling-load units were implemented to this end. In reciprocation, the employers contributed $27.5 million to union members in the form of a pay guarantee plan and an early retirement incentive fund. The former was available as short-run protection for any work earnings lost due to labor-saving innovations. The latter, by far the more substantial in magnitude, was intended as an adjustment mechanism for any disemployment resulting from the changes.

For the most part, both parties prospered under this new approach. Employers reaped significant gains in productivity which led to a 12% decrease in real labor cost per ton between 1960 and 1965, despite the fact that real labor compensation rose over 20% during the period (Table 3). These increasing labor compensation rates, on the other hand, along with the enriched retirement and other benefits, were attractions for the workers. Moreover, the union's apprehensions regarding disemployment did not mate-

---

[26]Considerable detail of this is provided by Hartman, pp. 46–70.
[27]As quoted in Fairley, p. 151.

Table 3. Tonnage, Longshore Hours, Productivity, Labor Costs, and Compensation, West Coast Longshore Industry, Selected Years, 1960–1984[a]

Year	Tonnage handled[b]	Longshore hours worked	Productivity index[c] (1960=100)	Hourly longshore labor cost[d] (nominal)	Real compensation index[e]	Real ($ 1960) labor cost per ton[f]
1960	28,495,619	23,757,382	100	$ 4.13	100	$3.44
1965	40,151,909	24,387,133	138	5.31	121	3.02
1970	60,025,612	19,693,920	254	6.94	128	1.73
1975	66,968,534	12,130,379	460	12.28	164	1.22
1980	113,682,374	13,376,301	708	19.77	172	.84
1984	133,282,925	12,276,802	905	30.10	208	.79

[a]Source is Pacific Maritime Association, *Annual Report*, various years and calculations made by the authors.
[b]For a definition of tonnage and recognition of changes in assessment methods over time, see note b, Table 1.
[c]Calculated on the basis of tonnage-per-longshore hour.
[d]Included in the labor cost are wages (for hours worked plus travel time) and employer contributions for benefits (pension, welfare, vacation, holiday, pay guarantee plan, and voluntary travel).
[e]Calculated on the basis of nominal hourly labor costs deflated by the Consumer Price Index.
[f]Calculated on the basis of total real labor costs (hourly costs in $ 1960 times hours worked) divided by tonnage handled.

rialize. Indeed, as Table 3 indicates, longshore hours actually increased over the first M&M tenure.

The M&M Agreement was extended in 1966 when a second five-year contract was signed. The essential principles introduced by its predecessor were continued. The PMA successfully pushed for more freedom to operate efficiently, largely through increasing discretion and flexibility in manning. In return, the pension scheme and the entire fringe benefit plan were sweetened. The major departure from the first agreement concerned the replacement of the pay guarantee plan by higher wages. The plan had not been used during the first five years and, accordingly, the union felt it could be traded off during the 1966 negotiations.

The significance of the M&M Agreements was twofold. In the first place, they marked the beginning of a "modern" labor market characterized by employment guarantees and attractive compensation packages which contrasted sharply with the conditions in the pre-M&M period. Second, by agreeing to relax the work rules in return for a share of the wealth generated by the productivity gains, the union opened the way for the technological transformation of the docks.

C. Post-Mechanization and Modernization (1971–1984)

The issue of job security dominated the 1971 contract negotiations. As a result of impressive productivity gains, longshore hours worked in 1970 were only 80 per cent of those five years earlier. Discussions of the union position in *The Dispatcher*, the ILWU paper, emphasized that the fundamental issue was "the growing mechanization of waterfront work and the resultant decline of work opportunity and job security."[28] A resolution adopted by the 1971 ILWU convention recognized an employment "crisis" and proposed a more militant platform to challenge the threat to employment. This proposal, which featured a reincarnation of the pay guarantee plan and measures to preserve longshore employment, formed the basis of the ILWU negotiating stance in 1971.

In order to maintain jobs the union made two major demands. First, and above all, the ILWU demanded that there be no further manning reductions. Second, to create more work opportunity, it pursued exclusive longshore jurisdiction over the stuffing and unstuffing of containers within 50 miles of West Coast ports.[29]

For the companies, on the other hand, the right to introduce new methods and practices without manning constraints continued to be paramount. In addition, the PMA sought "steady man" rights to guarantee the availability of trained workers to operate the increasingly sophisticated equipment. During the second M&M tenure, availability of skilled labor had emerged as a problem for the employers who, ideally, wanted to be able to employ their own skilled workers on a regular basis.

Negotiations failed to produce an agreement, and in July 1971 the ILWU began what became a nine-month strike.[30] After a Taft-Hartley injunction and a resumption of the strike, the parties arrived at a settlement in February 1972. One month later, however, the wages and benefits component of the contract was rolled back by the Pay Board. The agreement established a new pay guarantee plan (PGP), which became an important mechanism for adjusting to technological change for ILWU members. The 1972 plan guaranteed 36 hours of pay weekly for class A workers (fully registered) and 18 hours for class B men (registered casual). In addition, the union's demands regarding jurisdiction over container stuffing were accepted by the PMA. This provision (the Container Freight Station Supplement), however, has never really been implemented.[31]

A final note on the 1972 pact concerns the crucial manning issue. Questions such as "steady men" were set aside for resolution through the griev-

---

[28]*The Dispatcher*, 8 January 1971.

[29]Various issues of *The Dispatcher* in 1971 provide the source for the discussion of the union's position in the negotiations.

[30]It should be noted that this strike was carried out during a period in which there was great debate in the Nixon Administration regarding labor conflict within transportation. Attempts were being made at the time to limit or discontinue the right to strike in that sector. For more details regarding the initiatives considered, see Robert C. Lieb, *Labor in the Transportation Industries* (New York: Praeger, 1974).

[31]The stuffing provision was challenged by the Teamsters, and since 1972 it has been the subject of numerous NLRB and court cases and appeals. At any rate, it should be recognized that the provision would apply only to "less-than-full-loads" and, as such, would have only a minor effect on employment.

ance-arbitration procedure. These issues continue to be redefined, renegotiated, and arbitrated, particularly as new methods are introduced.

Despite continuous technical innovations, technology was not an important bargaining issue during most of the 1970s. Presumably, the companies were pleased with their freedom to innovate. Productivity continued to rise, increasing nearly three-fold over the decade. By 1980, West Coast ports were handling nearly double the tonnage they had ten years earlier with only two-thirds as many longshore hours worked (Table 3). For the union, this reduction in work opportunities undoubtedly represented a concern. Nevertheless, the impacts of the ongoing technological changes were scarcely mentioned as an issue at ILWU conventions or in *The Dispatcher*. It seems likely that the pay guarantee plan offered considerable security for the membership. Moreover, with accelerating inflation, attention shifted to pursuing real wage gains. As we can see from Table 3, real compensation continued on an upward trend.

While compensation has persisted as an important question, the issue of technological displacement of workers has resurfaced in the contract negotiations during the 1980s. The union has successfully sought transfer and travel programs in order to place members in those ports where work is available. Also, the "steady man" has reemerged as an important issue. Designed to insure the availability of skilled labor for employers, this provision has always been resisted by the union due to the threat it poses to the hiring hall and the cherished ILWU principle of sharing available work. Aware of the low likelihood of eliminating the "steady man" provision, the union has attempted since 1978 to influence the operation of the plan. In particular, it has tried to retain as much work in the hall as possible by negotiating ceilings on the number of hours companies can use steady men. Moreover, seniority rather than company choice has become the primary criterion for selection.

Sensitivity regarding the distribution of work has been part of a larger concern for the future of labor on the docks. The trend towards capital intensification has carried on into the 1980s. The upward spiral of productivity, as shown in Table 3, offers testimony to the continuing implementation of increasingly sophisticated technology which requires less and less labor. Certainly, one cannot ignore the worker displacement issue. Discussions with ILWU members and officials conveyed their concern that if present trends continue, longshoring, as an occupation, will largely disappear. Decades before the accelerating mechanization, Harry Bridges, trumpeting the ILWU cause, said that even if there was only one longshoreman left on the West Coast, he would be a union member. Nobody at the time could have had any idea that Bridges' contention, in spirit at least, might one day be tested.

VI. THE SHIFT IN CONTROL

For the employers, capital intensification of longshoring has brought considerable benefits in the form of growth and productivity gains. The workers have benefited through much-improved compensation and income security and the virtual elimination of arduous and dangerous work. On the other hand, as we have seen, the modernization has drastically reduced longshoring employment. While the displacement has been limited by a "no layoffs" policy, new job opportunities have been scarce.

The technological changes have also altered the work process itself. In this section, our focus will be on how this has resulted in a shift in control from labor to management. This shift in control, in turn, has increased the relative bargaining power of employers.

Before containerization, labor was the primary vehicle for the loading and unloading of ships. Small cargo units predominated, and these tended to be "man-handled" by longshoremen. While the "science" of this process, in the sense of technical complexity, was quite primitive, the dockers and clerks possessed and utilized considerable knowledge and skills. Manual handling of the cargo required experience, dexterity, and resourcefulness. Coordinated teamwork was essential. In addition, the design of safe, efficient stows was a complex problem because of the irregular shapes of both ships and cargo units.

While the longshormen possessed the knowledge and skills to control the labor process, the shipping companies were distanced from the longshoring phase of their overall operations. This separation was evident from the arrangements which characterized the employment relationship. The labor (and minimal equipment) required for unloading and loading a ship while in port was subcontracted for through a stevedore who, more often than not, had come from the longshoring ranks in the community. Furthermore, since they were paid on a cost-plus basis, the stevedoring contractors had little incentive to intervene in the production process to represent the interests of the shipping companies. The situation seems somewhat analogous to the "inside contracting" found in the machining industry in the late nineteenth century. Under this arrangement, as described by Shaiken, "ultimately, management had little precise knowledge, let alone control, over what was happening in production".[32]

Indeed, the art of a good stow was somewhat akin to the product of a craftsman. While longshoring lacked the technical complexity associated with many crafts, such as machining, it embodied particularistic knowledge and skills not readily available to management. Consequently, longshoremen (or, more correctly, longshore gangs) were able to maintain considerable independence and discretion and, thus, control over their work.

From 1934 until the M&M Agreement in 1961, the control of the workers over the longshoring process actually seems to have increased. While mechanization was beginning to appear on the docks in the form of fork lifts and jitneys, for example, it did not erode the longshoremen's possession of their work. Indeed, the fundamental nature of the task was not altered by the new

[32]Harley Shaiken, *Work Transformed: Automation and Labor in the Computer Age* (New York: Holt, Rinehart and Winston, 1984), p. 21.

machines which remained completely under the guidance of the docker and, if anything, served to expand his capabilities.

However, the impact of containerization and computerization on long-shoring differs from that of the earlier mechanization. In the first place, the recent technologies have increasingly come under managerial control. The epitome here is the computer-controlled crane transferring containers to specific cells on board which have been assigned on the basis of a computer-generated stowage design. The movement in this direction clearly renders the traditional knowledge and skills of both the dockers and the clerks largely irrelevant. Standardized units and ships eliminated the need for the longshoring techniques required to handle asymmetric and heterogeneous cargo and vessels. Containers and computers have had an analogous effect on the work of the clerks by attenuating their cargo inspection and stowage design responsibilities.

The high-technology production systems have also created new skills and knowledge. Stowage design now requires sophisticated engineering and information processing skills for positioning the standardized containers in the cellular container ships on the basis of their destination and weight and in accordance with principles of structural dynamics. Cargo handling requires the skills to operate large-scale, technologically sophisticated machinery and to intervene when technical problems emerge. Furthermore, the new skills, knowledge, and resources are in the possession of management. The vocational requirements of the high-technology production systems are now met by the transfer of technical knowledge from management to labor through employer-sponsored training programs. The capital equipment, itself, is controlled by the shipping companies, either directly through ownership or indirectly as major users of terminal operations. Finally, the ongoing incorporation of stevedoring services by the shipping companies has furthered shipping company control over the production process.

The shift in control has eroded the cohesive social relations among the longshoremen. Prior to mechanization, this cohesion partly stemmed from the high degree of interdependence experienced by the workers on the job. The technology of traditional longshoring necessitated collective efforts. Loading and unloading ships with little if any mechanization consisted of task-sharing, physical and social proximity, and group decision-making. The empowerment and meaningfulness which derived from self-control in work promoted a strong fraternal spirit within the gangs. This cohesion, which has been captured well by Mills, extended beyond the docks into what has been characterized as a highly integrated community.[33]

In contrast, modern longshoring has reduced the need for co-operative work efforts, has created ranks within the workforce and, ultimately, has eroded the longshoring community.[34] Social contact has been minimized by

[33]Mills' description fits well with those of other authors, like Hill and Wilson, which suggests it would probably be an error to impute it with more than slight over-romanticization.

[34]These observations were made to a considerable extent from interviews with longshoremen and ILWU officials during January–March, 1983 in Los Angeles and San Francisco.

the magnitude of the operations and the scale of the heavily automated machinery. Individual workers now carry out their duties in considerable isolation of one another. With task specialization accompanying the technological changes, collective activity has decreased. Decision-making has been progressively removed from the docks as operations have become more machine-paced. The fraternal ethos—at one time exemplified not only by collective efforts on the job, but also by the sharing of available work through the hiring hall—has been threatened by the increasing use of "steady men." Moreover, the orientations of steady men and those who are hired through the halls differ substantially. The former tend to be younger, "instrumental" workers aiming to maximize individual employment and earnings. This clashes with the "solidaristic" orientation of the latter group which tends to maintain an historical appreciation for the importance of a collectivism based on the equal sharing of available work.[35]

The shift in control has also been accompanied by a change in the relative bargaining power of management and labor. Indeed, control of the work process emerges as a critical variable in understanding the industry's bargaining relationship. Before mechanization, labor was the necessary input in the loading and unloading of ships. Once the union had acquired control of the work force through the hiring hall mechanism, the indispensability of labor quickly translated into bargaining power. This power was evident in the ability of the ILWU in the 1930s and 1940s to further worker control over the longshoring process through the establishment of extensive work rules pertaining to manning, cargo handling, and the pace of work. These practices were won largely through short walkouts which tended to be successful because they completely halted operations.

After World War II, increased union job control had become a major problem for the employers. Many of the work rules inflated labor costs and inhibited changes, which was particularly important in light of the emerging technological possibilities. Worker control of the longshoring process continued to make the companies vulnerable to job actions.

In the post-M&M era, worker indispensability has been markedly reduced. With each technological development, the companies increased their capacity to load and unload ships with less labor input. The effectiveness of strikes and other job actions has been reduced accordingly. There are already examples of advanced technology enabling managers to continue port operations during labor disputes.[36]

Control of the longshoring process has shifted bargaining power toward the employers. This has been evident in recent negotiations. At first glance this might not seem to be the case, given the compensation gains received by the workers. However, labor now represents only a minor portion of total operating costs for the PMA members and, accordingly, compensation raises

[35]The "instrumental-solidaristic orientation" dichotomy is from John Goldthorpe et al., The Affluent Worker (Cambridge: University Press, 1968).

[36]For example, non-bargaining unit personnel kept the port of Anchorage operating for a few days during a labor dispute earlier in this decade. The port was not organized by the ILWU but nevertheless the incident had a significant effect on union officials.

do not necessarily mean major cost increases. More critical are issues affecting how longshoring work is carried out. The employer interest is in operational flexibility so that increasingly productive equipment and methods can be introduced. This objective clashes with the union's current priority of maintaining an adequate level of employment. The ILWU has been unable to negotiate any provisions which might increase the input of labor in production, thereby significantly increasing work opportunities. Provisions which offer the workers protection from disemployment—most notably, the pay guarantee plan—may be seen from the employers' point of view as (albeit expensive) side-payments which do not interfere with their operational control.

VII. CONCLUSIONS

The technological transformation of longshoring on the West Coast has shifted control of the production process toward the employers. Traditional dockwork relied on the knowledge, skills, and resources of the longshore gangs. This process has undergone major changes since the Mechanization and Modernization Agreements of the 1960s. The managerial flexibility guaranteed by the pacts has enabled the shipping companies to successively incorporate new technological developments into reorganized longshore operations. The current technology of loading and unloading containers, increasingly the dominant longshoring activity, and the standardization of unitized cargo have rendered anachronistic the man-handling skills of the traditional docker. The requisite knowledge for efficient and safe stowage resides no longer with the longshoremen, but with management, who possesses or imparts to the workers such skills as sophisticated information processing, spatial engineering, linear programming, and operating advanced material handling equipment.

Bargaining power in the industry has been altered by the shift in control of production. Once the workers had been effectively organized in the 1930s, the union negotiated major gains over the next twenty-five years. Not only was the ILWU able to obtain compensation increases, but it developed considerable influence over production methods and employment levels. Much of the union's power came from the indispensability of its members in the production process. With the shipping companies dependent on labor for the loading and unloading of their cargo, the ILWU successfully implemented job actions to fulfill their goals.

In the past twenty-five years, the essential role of labor in production has been diminished by the successive technical and procedural innovations made possible by the Mechanization and Modernization Agreements. As machines have replaced men on the docks, relative bargaining power has shifted toward management. While the union has received substantial gains in wages and benefits, the ILWU has been unable to negotiate more than minimal influence in production and thus has been unsuccessful in halting the erosion of employment which is now its primary concern.

5

Technological Change and Labor Relations in the United States Postal Service

Vern Baxter

I. INTRODUCTION

Fundamental changes in labor relations and the widespread implementation of mechanized and automated mail processing technology were both associated with the structural reorganization of the United States (U.S.) post office in 1971. The Postal Reorganization Act created a public corporation to replace the Post Office Department (POD). Postal reorganization grew out of the failure of the old structure to reconcile the competing demands of business mailers for faster mail service, postal management demands for increased mechanization and greater control over postal operations, and postal labor demands for higher wages and collective bargaining rights.

The purpose of this paper is to explain the importance of technology as a cause of changes in postal labor relations since 1971. The thesis of the paper is that technological change is a central component of a scientific management strategy which was designed and implemented to reduce labor costs and facilitate the transition from politically administered to collectively bargained labor relations. Subsequent labor–management conflict has produced favorable economic results for postal labor, while the strategic implementation of new technology has increased management authority to direct workers in the labor process. After presenting a theoretical framework for the analysis of technology and labor relations, I outline recent, major technological changes in the post office, review postal labor relations before reorganization, and,

Vern Baxter • Department of Sociology, University of New Orleans, New Orleans, LA 70148.

finally, examine the effects of technical change on postal labor relations since 1971.

II. THEORETICAL ISSUES IN THE ANALYSIS OF TECHNOLOGY AND LABOR RELATIONS

A. Labor–Management Relations in Public Sector Organizations

The postal service is a central part of the state sector of the contemporary political economy. Compared to private sector employees, public employees are less likely to fear job losses which stem from adverse market conditions such as declining employer market shares and bankruptcies.[1] Despite the greater job security in the public sector, state organizations that participate directly in the economic production process tend to adopt labor–management relations similar to those of private enterprises, and principles of profit are more prominent than the principles of allocation evident in much of the state bureaucracy.[2] Postal reorganization replaced the political process of allocative budgeting and labor relations based in Congress with a more businesslike system of direct negotiation between postal labor and management, separate from ratemaking and other allocative deliberations of the state.[3]

Postal collective bargaining involves the conflicting interests of labor and management in a state sector organization. The privatization of the post office has altered the employment status of postal employees from civil servants to quasi-private employees of a corporation which may attempt to reduce labor costs in order to maximize profits.[4] The parties bargain collectively over control of the labor process and resources of the organization. Resources are the raw materials of organizational activity, including labor, tools, and liquid assets. The labor process is the process by which raw materials or other inputs are transformed into products which have some use-value.[5]

[1]Recent research into the status of public employees includes: Joseph Reid and Michael Kurth, "The Organization of State and Local Government Employees: Comment," *Journal of Labor Research* 5, no. 2 (Spring 1984), pp. 191–200; and Amy Dalton, "A Theory of the Organization of State and Local Government Employees," *Journal of Labor Research* 3 (Spring 1982), pp. 163–177.

[2]James O'Connor, *The Fiscal Crisis of the State* (New York: St. Martin's Press, 1973); and Guglielmo Carchedi, *On the Economic Identification of Social Classes*, (London: Routledge and Kegan Paul, 1977), pp. 14–16. Carchedi argues that the proximity of state activities to the production of profit in the private economy influences the nature of employment relations in state sector organizations. Employment relations in public corporations like the Postal Service can therefore be expected to mirror those in private corporations.

[3]John Tierney, *Postal Reorganization: Managing the Public's Business* (Boston: Auburn House, 1981).

[4]Ibid., p. 99.

[5]Howard Aldrich, *Organizations and Environments* (New York: Prentice-Hall, 1979); and Stewart Clegg and David Dunkerley, *Organization, Class, and Control* (London: Routledge and Kegan Paul, 1980).

B. Technology and Labor Relations

Defined as the techniques used to transform inputs into outputs on a predictable basis, technology is an important organizational resource which partly determines variation in labor relations in organizations.[6] Open systems and population ecology theories conceive of technology as an external source of uncertainty in the environment that requires adaptive behavior by the organization. Aldrich and Pfeffer argue that technology structures social relations inside organizations and serves as a primary mechanism for environmental selection of successful organizational forms.[7]

Technical change can promote conflict between labor and management. Workers in jobs which become routinized by technological change may collectively pressure management for more money in order to minimize the loss of craft skills. The organization may adapt to pressure from labor by expanding the task environment to include labor unions and collective bargaining as a way to reintegrate the organization.[8]

However, technological determinist arguments inadequately treat the effects of the organizational political process and conflict over organizational control on the relationship between technology and labor relations. Recent work from the social-action and class perspectives holds that market competition and conflict over control of the labor process shape organizational structure and the choice and implementation of technology.[9] From this perspective, managers seek to monopolize research and development, field testing, and the implementation of technology, in addressing conflict with labor.

Three issues pertaining to control of the organizational labor process are important for the analysis of technology and labor relations: (1) economic issues; (2) political issues; and (3) health and safety issues. Economic issues concern the basic conflict between labor and management over the price of labor, which has consequences for both the viability of the organization and

[6]John W. Slocum and Henry P. Sims, "A Typology for Integrating Technology, Organization, and Job Design," *Human Relations* 33, no. 3, (1980), pp. 193–212.

[7]Howard Aldrich and Jeffrey Pfeffer, "Environments of Organizations," in *Annual Review of Sociology*, ed. Alex Inkeles, (Palo Alto: Annual Reviews, Inc., 1976) vol. 2, pp. 79–106.

[8]The task environment of the organization includes: suppliers; customers; and competitors; in short, any unit with which the organization has input and output transactions. See James D. Thompson, *Organizations in Action* (New York: McGraw-Hill, 1967), p. 27. In the same book, Thompson argues that the organization environment consists primarily of technology and a task environment. Aldrich maintains that the environment selects successful organizations for survival, largely based on successful adaptation of the organization to technological and communication-based constraints. Howard Aldrich, *Organizations and Environments* (New York: Prentice-Hall, 1979).

[9]Among the most important contributions in this tradition are: Michael Burawoy, *Manufacturing Consent* (Chicago: University of Chicago Press, 1979); Stewart Clegg and David Dunkerley, *Organization, Class, and Control* (London: Routledge and Kegan Paul, 1980); Richard Edwards, *Contested Terrain* (New York: Basic, 1979); Stephen Hill, *Competition and Control at Work: The New Industrial Sociology* (Cambridge, MA: MIT Press, 1981); and David Noble, *Forces of Production* (New York: Alfred Knopf, 1984).

worker livelihoods. Political issues concern the capacity to direct labor in the organization. Political control strategies include: (1) direct control by supervisors; (2) technical control—whereby the skills, pace, and procedures for performing work are embedded in the production technology; and (3) bureaucratic control—in which formal rules and internal job structures are used to elicit worker loyalty and compliance.[10] Health and safety issues concern the maintenance of safe and healthy work conditions.

The contention of this paper is that changes in labor relations result from labor–management struggles over these three control issues that accompany technological change. In the case of the Postal Service, technological change was part of a scientific management strategy that was developed to reduce labor costs, improve efficiency, and increase political control and control of health and safety work conditions. Technology thus shapes the conflict in labor relations to the extent that management incorporates technological change in its strategy for controlling the labor process.

III. TECHNOLOGICAL CHANGE IN MAIL PROCESSING

Postal reorganization unleashed a rapid evolution in mail processing technology. The technology of mail processing has progressed from unit output by manual laboring clerks, who completed 25 letters per minute, to large batch and mass production with letter sorting machines, and toward an automated continuous process system with optical character-reader technology.[11]

The specific operations of mail processing include: (1) *culling*—separating various classes and sizes of mail, including machineable from non-machineable mail; (2) *facing*—placing letters so the address can be read; (3) *cancelling* the stamp; (4) *sorting*; and (5) *transportation*. Prior to 1953, conveyors linking a variety of manual operations constituted the extent of mechanization in mail processing. Sorting tasks were widely dispersed and the manual distribution of letter mail required by large post offices involved three distinct sorts into cases containing seventy-seven separations.[12] The skills of postal clerks, who memorized a limited number of sorting schemes, consisted of knowing the schemes and the ability to rapidly coordinate hand and brain.

The facer-canceller machine (1953), designed to cancel 12,000 manually faced letters per hour, was the first major technological advance in mail processing. The newer Mark II (cancels 18,000 letters per hour), M-36 Advanced Facer-Canceler (30,000 letters per hour), and Micro-Mark (1982), automatically face and cancel the mail. The Burroughs Air Culler culls the mail and automatically feeds the facer-canceler machines.

---

[10]Richard Edwards, *Contested Terrain;* and Michael Burawoy, *Manufacturing Consent.*

[11]*The typology of technology is taken from Joan Woodward, Industrial Organization: Theory and Practice* (London: Oxford University Press, 1965).

[12]Paul Browne, *The Roles of Top Management in Shaping Organizational Design: Evidence From the USPS,* unpublished dissertation, Harvard University, Cambridge, MA, 1981.

A. Mechanized and Automated Mail Processing

The cornerstone of postal mechanization is the letter sorting machine (LSM), prototyped in 1957 by the Bell Corporation for one operator to sort 2,250 letters per hour into one hundred separations. The multiple position letter sorting machine (MPLSM) was developed from 1959 to 1961 by the Burroughs Corporation and sorts 28,000 letters per hour into 277 separations or bins.[13] Each machine-paced MPLSM requires eight to twelve keyboard operators, two loaders, three sweepers, and a supervisor. The first MPLSM's were deployed in the early 1960's and by 1968, 145 MPLSM's were in operation nationwide. There are over 900 MPLSM's in operation today.[14]

The MPLSM was designed and implemented to expedite the sorting of mail, reduce handling costs, and generally improve mail processing procedures.[15] Prior to reorganization, postal workers resisted the widespread implementation of MPLSM technology because they feared the elimination of clerk craft jobs. Labor resistance to the MPLSM took several forms: (1) Congressional lobbying to curtail appropriations for postal research, development, and procurement of the MPLSM; (2) lack of labor cooperation during field testing of the MPLSM; (3) a large number of keying errors and missent letters; and (4) demands for system modifications and reduced operating speeds.[16]

Modifications to the MPLSM were designed to reduce labor costs, further speed up mail processing, and overcome operator resistance to the machine. In 1969, the Zip Mail Translator (ZMT) was added to the MPLSM. The ZMT is a computerized box that allows mail distribution on LSM's by zip code, thus eliminating the need for distribution scheme knowledge by the operators. The Engineering Data Isolation Technique (EDIT) was developed in 1973 to isolate operator from machine errors on the LSM, allowing closer supervisory control of the keying speed and accuracy of individual operators.

Despite improvements in the MPLSM, the human operator is considered by management and design engineers to be the "weak link" in the system. There are limits to how rapidly a person can read addresses and key in accurate codes. The elimination of operators and the automation of mail processing is being accomplished with the Optical Character Reader (OCR) technology. The OCR is connected to an integrated mail preparation system with manual loading of the OCR.

Currently, 250 advanced OCR's (OCR II's) electronically "read" the zip

[13]United Federation of Post Office Clerks, *Mechanization Committee Minutes* (Washington, DC: UFPC, 1968–69), pp. 15–16.

[14]Ibid., p. 16; and Personal Interview with Alvin Patterson, President, New Orleans APWU, New Orleans, LA, May 27, 1985.

[15]U.S. Postal Service, *Maintenance Handbook for MPLSM* (Washington, D.C.: USPS, 1978), p. I–1.

[16]Wesley Baker et al., *Exploratory Study of Selected Factors Which May Influence Fatigue and Monotony Associated With the Letter Sorting Task* (Dallas, TX: SMU Department of Management, 1967); and Sylvania Electronics Corporation Research Staff, *Human Factors in Letter Sorting Machine Operation* (Washington, DC: USPS, 1969), pp. 16–17; U.S. Post Office Department and AFL-CIO Postal Unions, "Mechanization Committee Minutes," (Washington, DC: USPOD, 1968).

code on a letter and spray a magnetic bar code on the envelope. A Bar Code Sorter (BCS) then matches the bar code to a computer program that automatically sorts the letter to one of sixty separations without the involvement of an operator. Mail equipped with the new nine-digit zip code can be automatically sorted directly to streets on a letter carrier's route, greatly reducing the carrier's office time.[17] A two person crew, one for loading and clearing jams and one to sweep the BCS, is required for the automated OCR-BCS system.

The long-range plan for processing flats (magazines and newspapers), small parcels, and rolls includes a fully integrated system featuring mechanized processing (single and multiple position flat sorters) with computer control and automated storage and retrieval of destination codes.[18] The Multiple Position Flat Sorting Machine (MPFSM), deployed in 1979, is configured exactly like the single operator LSM. 236 MPFSM's are currently in operation. Automated flat preparation systems to edge, feed, face, and cancel flats and divide machineable from nonmachineable pieces are also being developed.

B. The Nationwide Bulk Mail System

After passage of the Reorganization Act, the national mailstream was divided into two networks: preferential mail (letters and magazines) and bulk mail (advertising matter and parcels). In 1972, a modular system of twenty-one Bulk Mail Centers (BMC's) was approved by Postmaster General (PMG) Klassen and the postal Board of Governors. The centralized, high volume, highly mechanized system was constructed during 1972–75 in line with the following design concepts: (1) use process control computers to maintain a constant processing rate; (2) incorporate high speed parcel/sack sorting machines; and (3) minimize hands-on sorting labor by incorporating operator scheme knowledge into the processing equipment.[19] Operators introduce parcels and sacks into the computer-controlled, conveyor-run system by keying a three to five digit code into the parcel or sack sorting machine. The machine then feeds the mail into run-outs for loading and transportation to the destination.[20]

C. Computerization of Mail Forwarding and Window Service

In 1973, computer technology was first applied to the process of forwarding or "mark up" of letters that are undeliverable as addressed. Computer

[17]See, Comptroller General of the U.S., *Implications of Electronic Mail for the Postal Service Workforce* (Washington, DC: Comptroller General, 1981). USPS, *Outlook For Mechanization in the U.S. Postal Service* (Washington, DC: USPS, 1975), p. 13; APWU, "Mechanization and Technology Files," (Washington, DC: APWU, 1981).

[18]United States Postal Service, *Outlook For Mechanization in the Postal Service* (Washington, DC: USPS, 1975), pp. 11, 13.

[19]Giffels and Associates, "Work Group Report For Washington, D.C. Bulk Mail Facility" TISR no. 1801 (Washington, DC: USPS, 1971); Personal Interview with William Foster, Design Engineer, USPS, Washington, DC, March 29, 1982; and Bernie Knill, "Surprise. There Were Design Concepts For the Bulk Mail System," *Materials Handling Engineering,* (Sept. 1976), pp. 61–66.

[20]Personal Interview with William Foster, March 29, 1982; Bernie Knill, pp. 61–6.

labels are generated by microcomputers for letters that require forwarding from a carrier's route.[21] An integrated and computerized calculator and scale have been developed (1981) to automatically weigh and calculate postage for packages and letters presented for mailing to postal window clerks. The new machine will save time for clerks who must currently weigh mail and consult rate and zone charts before punching the postage meter.[22]

IV. LABOR RELATIONS IN THE POST OFFICE PRIOR TO REORGANIZATION

The first uniquely postal labor organization was the National Association of Letter Carriers (NALC), formed in 1889. The National Association of Post Office Clerks (NAPOC) was formed in 1890 to seek civil service classification for all clerks, the eight-hour day, and pay increases.[23] In response to legislative and press campaigns staged by the unions over wages, safety and health, and union affiliation, President Theodore Roosevelt issued his "gag rule" in 1902. The "gag rule" prohibited federal employees from taking their grievances to Congress or to public forums.[24]

The administration wanted no formal relations with postal labor organizations, claiming that postal workers were public servants. According to President Taft, speaking in 1911:

> Government employees are a privileged class, upon whose entry into government service it is entirely reasonable to impose conditions that should not and ought not be imposed upon those who serve private employers.[25]

The fight against the "gag rule" culminated in the passage of the Lloyd-LaFollette Act of 1912, which protected worker rights to join unions and petition Congress.

Postmaster General Burleson opposed the Lloyd-LaFollette Act and responded with calls for repeal of the Act and the dissolution of all postal unions in 1913. Burleson fired the national officers of all the postal unions except the NAPOC from their postal jobs.[26] These policies moved the postal

---

[21]USPS, *Outlook For Mechanization in the U.S. Postal Service*, p. 10.

[22]USPS, "New Automated Systems Approved by Board of Governors," *Postal Bulletin* (Washington, DC: USPS, February 8, 1985), p. 1.

[23]Sterling Spero, *The Labor Movement in A Government Industry* (New York: Remsen, 1924). NAPOC and the NFPOC merged in 1961 to form the United Federation of Post Office Clerks (UFPC). On July 1, 1971, the American Postal Workers Union (APWU) was formed from the merger of the UFPC, Special Delivery Messengers, AFL-CIO Mailhandlers, and the Maintenance and Motor Vehicle Employees. The independent National Postal Union later merged with the APWU. See Murray Nesbitt, p. 316.

[24]The post office experienced rapid growth in mail volume around the turn of the century as the nation's industrial economy took-off. Wage earning postal clerks and letter carriers were hired and gained job security, and also began to demand union recognition and the end of direct political control in the postal workplace.

[25]Gerald Cullinan, *The U.S. Postal Service* (New York: Praeger, 1973), p. 123.

[26]Gerald Cullinan, *The U.S. Postal Service*; Murray Nesbitt, *Labor Relations in the Federal Government Service* (Washington, D.C.: Bureau of National Affairs, 1976); and Sterling Spero, p. 137.

unions to hire their officers as full-time Congressional lobbyists and to concentrate their efforts in Congress.

From 1912 to 1969, the postal unions battled the POD over every postal appropriations bill and established a reputation as one of the most effective lobbying groups in Washington. Persistent union lobbying coupled with imprudent attacks on a Democratic Congress by Republican PMG Summerfield in 1955 combined to keep postal research and development budgets low until well into the 1960s.[27]

A. Executive Orders 10987 and 10988 and Formal Union Recognition in the Post Office

A contradiction existed in postal labor relations during the 1960s in that postal workers were directed by the POD, but redressed their grievances to Congress. The POD resisted union calls for collective bargaining of wages and working conditions as an infringement on state sovereignty. President Kennedy finally responded to union inspired demands for collective bargaining rights when he issued Executive Orders 10987 and 10988 in 1962. The orders provided for a grievance procedure, formal union recognition, and limited collective bargaining between federal agencies and exclusively recognized unions.[28] The Orders prohibited negotiations or grievances on the mission, budget, and organization structure of the post office, technology, and assignment of personnel.

Neither management nor the unions was satisfied with the system of labor relations governing the post office in the late 1960s. Management was too constrained by Congress in the areas of policy and finances and by the federal bureaucracy in the area of personnel relations. The unions had no real clout in the workplace and demanded full collective bargaining rights.

By 1968, serious breakdowns occurred in contract negotiations over issues of employee discipline, mechanization, and reassignment. Negotiations were complicated by the emergence of a postal management and private business coalition whose purpose was to reorganize the post office as a public corporation. The movement for reorganization was motivated by demands from large mailers for faster service and POD demands for a self-contained and businesslike structure for postal operations.[29] Among the paramount elements of business operation required by postal management was authority and money to overcome the "mechanization gap" in the post office, which resulted from "a chronic shortage of funds for capital investment."[30]

The reorganization plan was designed to remove Congress from its policy-making role over the post office and to implement mechanized mail processing technology, principles of scientific management and collective bar-

[27]Gerald Cullinan, 1973; John Tierney, 1981.
[28]Murray Nesbitt, p. 316.
[29]The President's Commission on Postal Organization, *Report of the President's Commission on Postal Organization* (Washington, DC: President's Commission on Postal Organization, 1968).
[30]Ibid., p. 33.

gaining in the postal labor process. Satisfied with their power in Congress, and fearful of the displacement of workers by new technology, the unions opposed reorganization. In January, 1970, the Nixon administration moved to tie postal reform bills to postal pay raise bills in Congress.[31] The resulting legislative impasse fueled strike talk among postal workers.

Two hundred thousand postal workers closed six hundred post offices with an illegal wildcat strike in March, 1970. The strike settlement officially linked postal pay raises and postal reform, thus removing the political impasse that blocked reorganization. After the size of the postal pay raise and the framework of the postal corporation were hammered out, the final stumbling block preventing passage of the Reorganization Act was POD and administration demands that issues pertaining to technological change should not be negotiable with labor.[32] A joint House-Senate Conference Committee finally ruled that technological change was a bargainable issue and President Nixon signed the Postal Reorganization Act on August 12, 1970.

V. CHANGES IN THE POSTAL ORGANIZATION STRUCTURE AFTER PASSAGE OF THE REORGANIZATION ACT

Passage of the Postal Reorganization Act created an eleven member Board of Governors (nine appointed by the President and two from postal management) to replace Congress as the ultimate authority over the post office. A five member Postal Rate Commission was empowered to hold hearings and make recommendations regarding rates to the Board of Governors. Postal Service managers were now authorized to: (1) enter into and perform contracts and determine the character and necessity of expenditures; (2) construct, operate and maintain buildings and equipment; (3) issue debt obligations; and (4) enter into collective bargaining contracts with employees and their representative unions for the purpose of establishing compensation and working conditions.[33]

VI. POSTAL LABOR RELATIONS, 1971–1985

A. Conflicts over Wages and Job Security

The impact of technological change on postal operations since 1971 has been considerable, but management control of the economic conditions of the

---

[31]Congressional Quarterly, "Postal Unions Settle For Two-Stage Pay Increase," *Congressional Quarterly*, (Washington, D.C.: Bureau of National Affairs, Inc., April 3, 1970), p. 787; Harold Dolenga, *An Analytical Case-Study of the Policy Formation Process: Postal Reform and Reorganization*, unpublished dissertation available from University Microfilms International, Ann Arbor, MI (1973), p. 533.

[32]United Federation of Postal Clerks, "Memo on Technological Change," (Washington, DC: UFPC, 1970), p. 3.

[33]U.S. Congress, "The Postal Reorganization Act," public law 91-373, 39 U.S.C., (Washington, DC: U.S. Government Printing Office, 1971).

postal labor process has been mediated by the efforts of workers to protect jobs and secure substantial wage increases. Mail volume has increased by 50%, while the number of pieces of mail handled per employee per work year has increased by 43% since 1971 and the percentage of first-class mail handled by machine has risen from 25% to 75%. The resulting 20,000-person decrease in the work force since 1971 has not had a commensurate impact on the proportion of postal expenditures attributed to personnel costs, which have risen from 82% in 1970 to 83% in 1983.[34]

Postal collective bargaining has led to broad managerial political control in the labor process, including increasing power to introduce new mail processing technology and organize work. Postal labor has secured substantial economic advantage through wage increases, cost of living allowances, and job security. The following functions were included in Article IV of the 1971 contract as management's rights: (1) to direct postal employees; (2) to determine the methods, means, and personnel for carrying out operations; and (3) to take whatever action is necessary to carry out its mission in an emergency situation.[35]

Postal wages were increased by $1,710 from 1971 to 1973, and a limited Cost of Living Allowance (COLA) was initiated. These pay increases were clear victories for postal labor, as well as part of a management strategy which was designed to use material incentives to raise morale and integrate workers into the mechanized postal corporation.[36] Postal wages have increased nearly twice as fast as wages for other federal civil servants since the full COLA was enacted in 1973. Recent studies show that postal wages are at least comparable to those in organized private-sector industries and much higher than wages in unorganized, secondary industries and labor markets.[37] Wages for non-white and women bargaining unit postal workers are higher than wages for non-white and women workers in any other industry.[38]

Job security led to the major impasse in negotiations for the 1971 contract. Article III, Section 2-C under management's rights in the 1968 contract had granted management the power "to relieve employees from duty because of

[34]USPS, *Comprehensive Statement of Postal Operations* (Washington, DC: USPS, 1983), p. 46; Postmaster General of the United States, *Annual Report of the Postmaster General* (Washington, DC: USPS, 1970); Postmaster General of the United States, *Annual Report of the Postmaster General* (Washington, DC: USPS, 1983).

[35]APWU and USPS, *Collective Bargaining Agreement* (Washington, DC: APWU, 1984), pp. 4–5. President Richard Nixon set the modern precedent by ordering the Army and National Guard into the New York City Post Office to handle the mail during the 1970 postal strike. See James B. Jacobs, "The Role of Military Forces in Public Sector Labor Relations," *Industrial and Labor Relations Review* 35, no. 21 (January, 1982), p. 163.

[36]Clark Kerr, "National Arbitration Award for 1984 Postal Labor Agreement" (Washington, DC: National Labor Relations Board, 1984), p. 20.

[37]Jeffrey Perloff and Michael Wachter, "Wage Comparability in the USPS," *Industrial and Labor Relations Review*, 38, no. 1 (Oct. 1984), pp. 26–37.

[38]Martin Asher and Joel Popkin, "The Effects of Gender and Race Differentials on Public-Private Wage Comparisons: A Study of Postal Workers, *Industrial and Labor Relations Review* 38, no. 1 (Oct. 1984), pp. 16–24.

Table 1. Results of the First Vote on the 1978 Postal Labor Agreement[a]

Union	For Contract	Against Contract
National Association of Letter Carriers	56,342	78,832
American Postal Workers Union	78,487	94,491
Laborer's International Union of North America	7,749	8,441
Total for the three unions	142,578	181,764

[a]Source: "Postal Workers Reject Contract," *New York Unity News,* February 9, 1979, p. 1.

lack of work or for other ligitimate reasons."[39] The certain push by management to eliminate jobs by introducing new technology made a no-layoff clause essential for the unions. Labor prevailed as Article VI, "No Layoffs or Reductions in Force," was added to the 1971 contract.

Management went after the un-capped COLA and the no layoff clause in negotiations for the 1978 contract. Workers who were dissatisfied with attacks on the no-layoff clause, the wage package, and other provisions in the tentative 1978 agreement staged a wildcat strike in the New York and San Francisco BMC's. The Los Angeles BMC was hit by a smaller strike, while workers at the Washington, DC BMC only picketed one shift and returned to work. Two-hundred postal workers were fired for involvement in the illegal wildcat strikes.[40]

The memberships of all three major postal unions voted to reject the tentative agreement (See Table 1). Union leaders decided to allow a federal arbitrator to settle the contract dispute. The resulting settlement provided for improvements in the wage package, but an attenuation of the no-layoff clause for employees hired after September 15, 1978. There was no postal strike following the second contract settlement. There were no further contractual developments regarding wages until 1984.

Postal management entered negotiations for the 1984 contract with a clear strategy: (1) cut wages and benefits; (2) end the COLA; and (3) divide workers with a two-tier pay system designed to pay new employees one-third less than continuing employees.[41] Contract negotiations were ineffectual. Management goaded workers to strike so they could fire workers and hire new workers at the reduced pay scale. The unions, meanwhile, held fast in their demands for increased wages, continuation of the COLA, and improved benefits.

[39]USPOD and Seven AFL-CIO Postal Unions, *Agreement Between USPOD and Seven AFL-CIO Postal Unions* (Washington, DC: USPOD, 1968, Article 3), p. 5.

[40]Pat Moore, "Postal Unions: Balance of Forces." Unpublished Paper, Postal Contract Coalition, Berkeley, CA., (1978), p. 6. Rank and File Postal Worker Caucus, *The Rank and File Postal Worker,* (July 28, 1978); APWU, "Contract Proposals," *The American Postal Worker,* (May, 1973), p. 25.

[41]Bill Keller, "Deadline Near, Postal Negotiators Are Far Apart," *New York Times,* July 15, 1984, p. A-22.

The unions broke off contract talks without any job action on July 21, 1984, sending the contract to a federal fact-finding panel and, ultimately, to binding arbitration. The Postal Service took advantage of the expired contract to hire new workers at 20% less pay than employees hired under the 1981 agreement.

The arbitration of the 1984 postal labor agreement affected more workers than any arbitration in U.S. history. The award, handed down on December 24, 1984, added three steps at the bottom of the pay system, but also approved a 2.7 percent pay increase and continuation of the COLA for postal workers.[42]

B. Further Conflict over Economic Control: Hiring, Promotion, Overtime, and Training

Mail processing was centralized from 1971 to 1978 to ensure the cost-effectiveness of MPLSM's, and 60,000 postal jobs were eliminated.[43] Staffing levels on the MPLSM were decreased from 18 to 17 in 1980, further reducing the demand for labor in mechanized mail processing operations.[44] The no-layoff clause led management to use early retirement programs and hiring freezes in 1972–73 and 1982–83 as the installation of new mail processing systems reduced the demand for labor. The adoption of the automated OCR-BCS technology is expected to lead to further work force reductions. PMG Bolger estimated that automation and the nine-digit zip code could eliminate 60,000 man-years of work from the post office by the year 2,000.[45]

The disruptive effects of hiring freezes and the mechanization and automation of mail processing on an industry characterized by fluctuating workloads have periodically generated problems with the use of overtime in the post office. Mandatory overtime greatly increased labor costs during the early mechanization period (1972–73), the shakedown period for the new bulk mail system (1975–78), and in the first phase of automation (1983–85). Most recently, excessive overtime was required when mail volume increased unexpectedly and slow public acceptance of the nine-digit zip code produced inadequate volumes of mail that were properly prepared for the newly installed automated technology. Thousands of grievances were filed and struggles occurred around the nation over the assignment of overtime. Overtime costs soared to $1.4 billion, or 5.7% of total postal costs in 1983, an increase of

[42]Bill Keller, "Postal Officials Plan to Impose 2-Tier Pay Scale," *New York Times*, July 26, 1984, P. A-1.

[43]Postmaster General of the United States, *Annual Report of the Postmaster General* (Washington, DC: USPS, 1976).

[44]American Postal Workers Union, "Memo on LSM Staffing," (Washington, DC: APWU, 1981), p. 3.

[45]Federal Times Staff, "Impact of Electronic Mail on the Postal Workforce," *Federal Times*, (Washington, DC: Army Times Publishers, February 16, 1981), p. 1; and, Memos from, USPS, Department of Employee and Labor Relations to APWU, "Operational and Workforce Impacts of OCR-BCS Deployment," (Washington, DC: USPS, February 23, 1983 to January 18, 1984).

25% over 1982. Overtime costs rose to 8% of total postal costs in 1984.[46] The strict contractual procedures for the assignment of overtime frustrate supervisors who are responsible for moving mail and workers who either depend on overtime to maintain their standard of living or detest working extra hours.

The allocation of employees to highly skilled maintenance and other technical jobs created by mechanization and automation constitutes another economic issue in postal labor relations. In the 1971 contract, labor secured language which guaranteed that training and appointments to new jobs were to be provided to continuing employees who would receive rate protection during training. Management, in turn, won the right to use the criterion of "best qualified" for promoting employees in the Postal Service.[47]

Management attempts to minimize training costs have influenced the pace of technological change in the Postal Service. Before 1978, postal clerks learned processing schemes on their own time. In a 1978 case before the Department of Labor under the Fair Labor Standards Act, the American Postal Workers Union (APWU) successfully argued that clerks must be paid for scheme training.[48] The resultant increases in training costs spurred the deskilling of clerical labor and hastened the implementation of mechanized and automated mail processing technology.

C. Deskilling and Degradation of Postal Jobs

The logic underlying the implementation of new mail processing technology produced systems in which the skills of mail processing employees were embedded inside the technology. Jobs were downgraded, thereby reducing labor costs. Job deskilling also promoted technical control for managers who set the pace of mail-processing systems that determine the physical motions of workers on the job. The implementation of ZMT, computerized forwarding and OCR-BCS technologies illustrate conflict over economic and political issues in the control of job deskilling consequences of technological change.

Upon implementation of the ZMT, MPLSM clerks were no longer required to memorize processing schemes for outgoing mail. In 1971, postal

---

[46]USPS, *Comprehensive Statement on Postal Operations* (Washington, DC, 1983), p. 10.

[47]Postal clerks, mailhandlers, and maintenance crafts are the major occupational groups involved in mail processing, while letter carriers dominate the carrier craft. Bargaining unit postal employees occupy pay levels one to ten. There are twelve steps within each pay level. Management rates jobs at a specific pay level in terms of skills and responsibilities attached to the job. Workers move through the steps within the level at which their job is rated on the basis of seniority. Most clerk jobs are rated at levels four to six, most mailhandler jobs are rated at levels three to five, most carriers are rated a level five, and most maintenance jobs are rated at levels six through nine. See, USPS, *Administrative Support Manual* (Washington, DC: USPS, 1978), pp. I–3. USPS and Four AFL-CIO Affiliated Postal Unions, *Agreement Between the USPS and Four AFL-CIO Affiliated Postal Unions* (Washington, DC: USPS, 1971), Articles 12, 33.

[48]The 1978 Fair Labor Standards Act Victory for the APWU is summarized in Paul Browne, p. 170.

management created a new position for ZMT clerks called Distribution Clerk-Machine Operator. While the new position was rated at either pay level five or six, many ZMT operators were reduced from level six to level five. In the field, many local postmasters classified all ZMT jobs as level five, forcing the union to grieve every case where scheme knowledge still applied. Conflict over job classification for clerks in mechanized mail-processing led the APWU to demand in 1973 and 1975 that all LSM operators receive level six pay status. The unions won in 1975, forcing management to restrict level five pay to ZMT operators working the LSM without scheme knowledge.[49]

The 1978 contract contained new language on the criteria and procedures to be followed when assigning new positions to the appropriate craft and pay level. The issue has created jurisdictional conflicts between the unions as reorganization and mechanization have changed and created jobs. Clerks now forward or "mark-up" letters, a job formerly performed by carriers. Computerization of mark-up work has reduced the skill level of the job, justifying a reduction in pay grade for the position of Mark-Up Clerk-Automated from level five to level four.[50]

OCR-BCS automation is designed to eliminate the more highly paid but "slower and error prone" LSM operators with faster and more efficient electronic mail processing systems. Operators are now machine-tenders with reduced pay levels for the newly created jobs. In June, 1982, postal management announced the creation of a new standard position in the clerk craft, "Mail Processor, PS-Level 3," for OCR-BCS operators. The APWU immediately filed a grievance and later an unfair labor practice with the National Labor Relations Board (NLRB), charging the Postal Service with unilateral and unfair changes in technology that would downgrade 44,000 jobs.[51] The Laborer's International Union of North America (LIUNA) filed an unsuccessful grievance charging that the new position should be assigned to the mailhandler craft.

Testimony during the arbitration hearing by J. Robert Shoop, General Manager of the Postal Service Job Evaluation Division, revealed that the existing key position considered most comparable to the new Mail Processor was Elevator Operator, PS-3.[52] As further justification for the level three status of the position, Ned Braatz, Senior Distribution Procedures Specialist in Mail Processing, testified that the OCR-BCS operator requires no scheme knowledge because the machine decides whether or not mail is machine-readable. Braatz also argued for new supervisory responsibilities:

> All keyboard interface with the computer systems, whether bringing the logic system up, changing from one sort program to another, or the request for management

[49]APWU, "Letter on Rate Protection," (Washington, D.C.: APWU, 1973); USPS and Four AFL-CIO Affiliated Postal Unions, *Agreement Between the USPS and Four AFL-CIO Affiliated Postal Unions* (Washington, DC: APWU, 1975, Articles 9, 12, and 14).

[50]National Labor Relations Board (NLRB) Arbitrator, "Arbitration Award in Dispute Between the USPS and APWU," Case AC-NAT-11-991 (Washington, DC: NLRB, 1979).

[51]Benjamin Aaron, "Arbitration Award in Dispute Between USPS and APWU," Case H1C-NA-C26, (Washington, DC: NLRB, April 26, 1985), p. 12.

[52]Ibid., pp. 9–10.

information, is the responsibility and duty of the supervisor in charge, not that of the clerk craft employees assigned to operate this (OCR-BCS) equipment.[53]

The unions argued that the new OCR-BCS operators should be rated at level five, like operators on the previous OCR-I systems.

OCR-BCS II operators do not have to verify mail as machine-readable (as OCR-BCS I operators did), and the streamlined OCR-BCS II operates much faster than the earlier model, with a crew of two compared to seven or nine on the earlier model.[54] Comparing her experience on both generations of OCR technology, one OCR operator testified as follows:

> The difference I see between the two is that on the new machine, . . . one person is doing almost twice the work as on the old. The new machine reads much, much faster than the old, and there's less people and everything about the new machine is so much . . . faster than the old.[55]

The arbitrator ruled that the Postal Service had the right to unilaterally create the new position but that the position was unfairly rated at level three and should be upgraded to level four.

A new position called Mail Distributor, PS-level 4, was created in 1982 for manual distribution clerks who possess no mail processing scheme knowledge. Management had planned to cull out non zip-coded mail for distribution by clerks with scheme knowledge, classify these clerks as level five, and classify clerks with no scheme knowledge as level four.[56] However, the arbitrator ruled that the latter job should be rated at level five, which pays $1.14 more per hour than a level four job.[57]

The distribution of postal employees occupying level four and five positions from 1973 to 1985 is presented in Table 2. These data indicate that level four incumbents, as a percentage of all postal employees in levels four and five, decreased from 1973 to 1978, and then increased from 1979 to the present. Until 1978, most new jobs created by mechanization were claimed by the clerk craft and were rated level five. In 1978, postal management issued Regional Instruction 399 which clarified the craft jurisdiction of jobs, paving the way for increases in the number of level four mailhandler jobs that required only the separation and not the distribution of mail, an important basis for the distinction between level four and level five jobs. Postal hiring since 1979 has included more level four positions, reflecting the deskilling of jobs through automation.

D. Political Control: The Pace of Change and Work Standards

The negotiability of the pace of technological change and changes in work standards is at the heart of conflict over political control of the organiza-

[53]Ibid., p. 13.
[54]Ibid., pp. 6, 16.
[55]Ibid., p. 16.
[56]Ibid., pp. 23, 39.
[57]Richard Mittenthal, "Arbitration Award in Dispute Between USPS and APWU," Case H1C-NA-C28, (Washington, DC: NLRB, May 18, 1984), pp. 12–13.

Table 2. Distribution of Postal Employees in Pay Levels Four and Five, 1973–1985[a]

Year	Level 4	Level 5	Total in Levels 4 & 5	Level 4 as % total Levels 4 & 5
1973	61,555	447,445	509,000	12.0
1974	53,671	459,648	513,319	10.4
1975	52,516	446,588	499,104	10.5
1976	44,897	417,479	462,376	9.7
1977	42,871	407,323	450,194	9.5
1978	42,326	400,292	442,618	9.5
1979	41,132	392,758	433,890	9.4
1980	41,845	388,680	430,525	9.7
1981	42,279	387,490	429,769	9.8
1982	42,468	387,699	430,167	9.8
1983	43,176	384,921	428,097	10.0
1984	47,106	400,669	442,775	10.5
1985	55,411	427,809	483,220	11.4

[a]Source: Frank Jacquette, Senior Labor Relations Specialist, United States Postal Service, Washington, DC, September, 1985.

tion of work. Since the beginning of the LSM program, labor has sought input into the process of technological development and change. The labor agreement requires management to inform the unions "as far in advance of implementation as practicable of technological or mechanization changes which affect jobs . . ."[58] Postal labor demanded and won the establishment of a national joint labor–management technological change committee during deliberations over the 1965 contract. The Postal Service used the labor–management committee meetings to officially notify the unions before impending jobs changes due to new technology. The meetings were labelled "exercises in futility" in 1975 by APWU Director of Industrial Relations Emmett Andrews, as management continually said they would take union suggestions "under consideration."[59]

The 1971 contract provided for arbitration of unresolvable issues arising from technical change. The APWU demanded improved protection against the disruptive aspects of technological change in their 1973 contract proposals to postal management. The unions had learned that arbitrating the effects of technological change after a system was in place was futile. Therefore, they demanded more responsibility and participation in the design and implementation of new mechanization systems. Similarly, the union wanted disputes settled before new work standards were imposed.

It was clear that arbitrators were hesitant to undo accomplished programs that displaced and sped up workers. The APWU developed contract proposals in 1975 which would have placed a moratorium on technological or

[58]USPS and APWU, *National Collective Bargaining Agreement*, 1971, Article 4, p. 5.
[59]APWU, *The American Postal Worker* (Washington, DC: APWU, May, 1973), p. 25.

mechanization changes which in any way affected wages, hours or working conditions, except by agreement between the employer and the union.[60] The 1975 contract contained no moratorium on the disruptive impact of technological or mechanization changes.

The joint labor–management committees to oversee technical change increasingly faded into obscurity and essentially stopped functioning altogether by 1982, as management sought to incorporate the development and implementation of new technology into their private province of "Management's Rights." The unions are dutifully notified in advance of any changes in technology, but management effectively controls the pace of change. Three separate arbitration decisions have sustained management's right to unilaterally create new positions that are made necessary by technological changes in the middle of a contract.[61]

Postal reorganization involved a transformation in job standards and employee classifications which engendered labor–management conflict. While Civil Service occupational codes had been used to determine salary levels, the Postal Service established its own job evaluation department. The unions have the right to be kept informed during time and work studies and to grieve any work measurement system or work standard that is unfair, unreasonable, or inequitable. Immediately following reorganization, production control personnel from the Westinghouse Corporation performed a massive time and motion analysis of all jobs in the Postal Service in order to develop new position descriptions.[62] The 1972 APWU National Convention specifically authorized a strike if the Westinghouse job evaluation study resulted in new job classifications that downgraded postal jobs. No strike occurred over the subsequent downgrading of jobs, though the unions won the right to perform their own time and motion studies of jobs created in the process of technical change.[63]

E. Reassignment

The displacement of the work force that has accompanied technological change is an important object of political conflict in the postal labor process. The centralization of mail processing has required thousands of workers to relocate their families and give up familiar work surroundings and work culture because the BMC's and most other newly constructed mail processing facilities are located in suburban areas near interstate highways and airports that have replaced rail lines as the major postal transportation arteries.[64]

[60]APWU, "Draft Paper on Technology and Mechanization," (Washington, DC: APWU, 1975).

[61]NLRB Arbitrator, Case AC-NAT-11-991, 1979; Benjamin Aaron, Case H1C-NA-C26, 1985; Ricard Mittenthal, Case H1C-NA-C28, 1984.

[62]U.S. House of Representatives, "USPS Contract With the Westinghouse Corporation for A Job Evaluation Study," (Washington, D.C.: U.S. Government Printing Office, March–April, 1971).

[63]APWU, "Resolutions From 1972 Convention," *The American Postal Worker* (Washington, D.C.: APWU, Sept.–Oct., 1972), p. 11; APWU and USPS, *Collective Bargaining Agreement*, 1984, Article 34, p. 99.

[64]Peter Rachleff, *Moving the Mail*, (Morgantown, W.V.: Work Environment Project, 1982), p. 19.

In 1971, management agreed to the use of seniority in employee reassignment and an elaborate protocol was erected to govern the process. In the 1975 contract, workers won an increase from ninety days' to six months' advance notice before major personnel relocations take effect. Nonetheless, the staffing of mechanized postal facilities continues to generate conflict in the postal labor process. In the fall of 1975, mailhandlers at the Philadelphia General Post Office staged a slowdown over staff reductions. One thousand workers from all crafts in San Francisco and six hundred in Los Angeles rallied to protest job cutbacks accomplished through forced transfer, excessing of employees for reassignment, speed-ups, and cutting the hours of substitutes.[65]

F. Safety and Health

The conflict between safety and productivity arising from the implementation of mechanized and automated mail processing technology has been evident in postal labor relations since 1971. Management is responsible for providing a safe working environment and joint labor–management committees at the national, regional, and local levels established in 1968, 1973 and 1981, respectively, enforce the safety provisions in Article Fourteen of the labor agreement.[66] Postal Service accident rates peaked in 1979–80, but remain higher than the rates in private industry.[67]

Upholding the responsibility to provide a safe working environment can conflict with the drive for productivity and the postal motto that "the mail must go through." Labor demands for an expanded role in ensuring a safe working environment in the Postal Service have been a constant source of conflict with management. Management resisted on-site inspections by local safety committees and the Occupational Safety and Health Administration. Labor has still failed to win the broad right to refuse to work under conditions defined as unsafe by the legitimate representatives of the workers.[68]

The system of BMC's has been the hotbed of dissent over safety and health in the post office ever since the system came on line in 1975. The worst safety hazards in the BMC's are: (1) inadequate protection from overhead conveyors; (2) extender belts on docks; (3) overweight parcels; and (4) noise. BMC safety conditions reached their nadir in 1979 with the death of Michael McDermott, a mailhandler at the New York BMC. McDermott was "sucked into" the parcel induction system after a jam relay that allowed employees to

---

[65]Rank and file protests included thirty-two ZMT clerks leaving work in a "sick-out" to protest mandatory overtime, and a twenty minute walk-out by workers at the Washington, D.C. BMC in July of 1977. See, Rank and File Postal Worker Caucus, *The Rank and File Postal Worker* (Philadelphia, PA, and San Francisco, CA: Rank and File Postal Worker Caucus, April–May, 1976), p. 1; (August, 1976), p. 1; and (November, 1977), p. 1.

[66]USPOD and Seven AFL-CIO Postal Unions, 1968, Article 19, p. 106; USPS and Four AFL-CIO Unions, 1973, Article 14, p. 23; USPS and APWU and NALC, *Agreement Between USPS and APWU and NALC* (Washington, DC: USPS, 1981, Article 14), p. 46.

[67]Peter Rachleff, p. 33.

[68]Ibid., p. 39.

stop the machine was bypassed to maintain system throughput.[69] Twenty-six other postal workers died at work in 1979 and 1980.[70]

Injury compensation claims in the post office increased from $134 million in 1971 to $656 million in 1977, largely due to the debugging of the BMC's.[71] Management charged that postal employees were abusing the workman's compensation program as a tactic to get out of work and that abuse of workman's compensation claims was the primary cause of the postal deficit. Employees were disciplined for having too many accidents in the Philadelphia and San Francisco BMC's. Worker reaction included rallies at the San Francisco BMC over speed-ups and safety and the July 24, 1976 walkout at the Philadelphia BMC over mandatory overtime and safety.[72] Slowdowns were also common in the BMC's over safety, schedule changes, and mandatory overtime.

Stress, noise, eye strain, and wrist injuries are among the occupational hazards associated with the operation of the MPLSM. Management and labor continue to use experts and grievances to fight over the causal relationship between LSM operation and the health problems experienced by operators. The combination of the stressful nature of MPLSM operation and a July, 1981 heat wave prompted a one hour walkout by two hundred MPLSM operators in Chicago who left their jobs chanting, "it's too hot, it's too hot." Seven union stewards were fired for failing to order members back to work during the work stoppage, but all seven eventually won back their jobs through arbitration.[73]

VII. SUMMARY AND CONCLUSION

Postal reorganization represents the privatization of an important state sector organization. The mediating authority of Congress over postal labor relations was replaced by direct negotiations between labor and management. Management control over technological change was increased with the termination of political deliberations over the postal budget that had allowed labor to block funding for new technology.

From the outset of the postal corporation, postal management has sought to "own" and control the technological resources that are so critical to changes in the postal labor process. Postal reorganization has been guided by a logic of scientific management, designed to speed up mail processing and reduce labor costs. Mechanization and automation serve as central components of management plans to wrest control of the methods and pace of work

---

[69]Ibid., p. 40.

[70]Ibid., pp. 37–38.

[71]APWU, The *American Postal Worker*, January, 1978, p. 20.

[72]Rank and File Postal Worker Caucus, *The Rank and File Postal Worker*, (October, 1977), pp. 2–3; (May, 1976), p. 1; and (July, 1976), p. 1.

[73]National Labor Relations Board, "Arbitration of Dispute Between USPS and APWU," Case C8C-4D-D (Washington, DC: NLRB, Dec. 31, 1981), pp. 9, 35, 43.

away from postal workers and embed mail distribution skills within the new technology. The economic costs of the scientific management strategy have been great as labor demands for wage increases, job security, and a COLA were successful, yet failed to produce significant cooperation from workers during the transition to automated mail processing.

The unions have tried to bargain over the pace of technological change, but management has resisted and has used new technology to build political control in the labor process. The demise of the joint labor–management committees on technological change represents an advance in unilateral political control by management in the postal labor process. The deskilling of clerk jobs has enhanced technical control in the labor process, though labor has successfully protected the pay levels of many deskilled jobs. Deskilling implies less reliance on mail processing scheme knowledge possessed by postal clerks, which has blurred the distinction between clerks and mailhandlers, thus dividing workers, to the political advantage of management in conflict over control of the labor process.

Labor's reliance on the grievance-arbitration system has not curtailed significant increases in political control by postal management. Arbitrators have proven hesitant to order fundamental changes in management programs designed to deploy new technology in mail processing. During periods of rapid change, the grievance-arbitration system is too slow and reactive to adequately represent the interests of workers in conflict over political and health and safety issues in the labor process.

The strategic use of technological resources as the private property of management has proven an effective tool for increasing management control in the labor process. Labor resistance to management strategies has been formidable and the uneven economic performance of new technology in reducing labor costs attests to the importance of labor–management conflict for analyzing the relationship between technology and labor relations. The current stagnation and ongoing conflict over economic control in the postal labor process suggests that stability and unilateral management control have not been attained, nor uncertainty curtailed, in postal labor relations.

6

Office Automation, Clerical Workers, and Labor Relations in the Insurance Industry

Daniel B. Cornfield, Polly A. Phipps, Diane P. Bates, Deborah K. Carter, Trudie W. Coker, Kathleen E. Kitzmiller, and Peter B. Wood

I. INTRODUCTION

As "a major white-collar industry which pioneered in the application of office automation"[1] in the early 1950s, the insurance industry altered the conditions of office work and the relations between clerical workers and management. A growing disjunction between office clerical workers and management in the insurance industry has accompanied office automation during the post-World War II era. As management automates the office to raise worker productivity and rationalize the clerical labor process[2]—that is, to formalize, standardize and quantify the control of labor—clerical workers, most of whom are women, increasingly express concern over employment conditions and sex discrimination. Moreover, women clerical workers are beginning to unionize and affiliate with working women's organizations, prompting management

---

[1]U.S. Bureau of Labor Statistics, *Impact of Office Automation in the Insurance Industry*, Bulletin no. 1468 (Washington, DC: GPO, 1966), p.iii.
[2]Evelyn Glenn and Roslyn Feldberg, "Degraded and Deskilled: The Proletarianization of Clerical Work," *Social Problems* 25 (October 1977), pp. 52–64.

Daniel B. Cornfield, Diane P. Bates, Deborah K. Carter, Trudie W. Coker, Kathleen E. Kitzmiller, Peter B. Wood • Department of Sociology, Vanderbilt University, Nashville, TN 37235. **Polly A. Phipps** • Department of Sociology, University of Michigan, Ann Arbor, MI 48109-2054.

111

to introduce a human relations, social psychological managerial philosophy in order to preempt collective action of clerical workers. The disjunction, then, concerns the implementation of office automation, employment conditions and the divergent methods clerical labor and management have developed for management-labor discourse. In a context of occupational sex segregation, the disjunction is occurring simultaneously along class (management and labor) and gender lines.

Our purpose is to explain the nature and emergence of the disjunction between clerical labor and management in the insurance industry. As office automation occurred in the context of occupational sex segregation, we begin with a discussion of this feature of the industry. This is followed by an analysis of technological change in insurance and its effect on occupational structure, employment, employee attitudes and earnings. Finally, we present a model of insurance labor relations, the disjunction between clerical labor and management, and how the disjunction arose from forces within the insurance industry, as well as from greater economic and political forces in the finance sector, the women's movement, and the labor movement.

II. OCCUPATIONAL SEX SEGREGATION IN INSURANCE

During the post-World War II era, women made inroads into professional, managerial and agent jobs in insurance, but the majority continued to be employed in clerical jobs, as shown in Table 1. Columns one and two show that the percentage of women in professional, managerial, and agent occupations increased between 1950 and 1980, while that in clerical occupations remained stable. Carson estimates that women accounted for about 2% of insurance directors and 1% of executives in the late 1970s.[3]

Occupational sex segregation in insurance is shown in columns three through six. While the percentage of women employed in clerical occupations declined, over 70% of women were employed as clerical workers between 1950 and 1980. More than two thirds of men were employed as agents or managers in the same period.

Many of the women who have attained insurance management jobs began their organizational careers in clerical jobs such as typists and file clerks or as insurance raters and were assisted by the National Association of Insurance Women (NAIW). Founded in 1940 to improve the careers of professional insurance women, NAIW has served as a support system for insurance women and, recently, men by providing employees with career counseling and insurance-related educational programs. The organization claims a mem-

---

[3]Ellis Carson, "Women Directors and Officers of Insurance Companies," *Best's Review*, Property/Casuality ed., 78 (December 1977), p.10.

Table 1. Percentage Women and Percentage Distribution of Women and Men Employees by Occupation in the Insurance Industry, 1950–1980[a]

Occupation	(1) % Women 1950	(2) % Women 1980	(3) % of Employed Women 1950	(4) % of Employed Women 1980	(5) % of Employed Men 1950	(6) % of Employed Men 1980
Professionals	21.4 (28)[b]	46.5 (158)	1.8	6.8	5.3	10.3
Managers	15.5 (73)	29.2 (197)	3.4	5.3	14.6	16.9
Insurance agents[c]	8.7 (290)	25.7 (558)	7.6	13.3	63.1	50.4
Clerical workers	84.7 (333)	84.2 (932)	85.1	72.5	12.2	17.9
Secretaries, typists and stenographers	97.1 (140)	99.1 (292)	40.9	26.8	1.0	0.3
Other clerical	75.7 (194)	77.3 (639)	44.2	45.7	11.2	17.6
Other	25.8 (27)	37.5 (59)	2.1	2.0	4.8	4.5
Total	44.2 (751)	56.7 (1905)	100.0	99.9[d]	100.0	100.0
N[e]	—	—	332	1081	419	824

[a]Source: U.S. Bureau of the Census: 1950 Census, Vol. IV, Special Reports, Part I, Chapter C, Occupation by Industry; 1980 Census, Vol. 2, Subjects Reports, PC80-2-7C, Occupation by Industry.
[b]Ns in thousands in parentheses.
[c]Includes agents, brokers and underwriters.
[d]Does not sum to 100.0% due to rounding.
[e]In thousands.

bership of over 18,000 with almost 400 chapters in the United States and Canada.[4]

Despite the efforts of the NAIW, aspiring, qualified women professionals and managers often encounter barriers to their mobility from sexist attitudes in a management considered by some insurance industry analysts as conservative, protective, and cautious.[5] These attitudes include labeling women as too aggressive and condemning women for being advocates of change or "ambitious to become something more than 'a hewer of wood and a drawer of water'."[6]

[4]Ibid.; Linda Kocolowski, "Join Ins. Mainstream, Women Told," The National Underwriter, Property/Casualty ed., 4 June 1982, p.56.
[5]Carson; William Krupman and Patrick Vaccaro, "Labor Relations for Today's Insurers," The National Underwriter, Property/Casualty ed., 8 August 1981, p.11; Charles Reckley, "How Women Can Be More Successful in Business," The National Underwriter, Life/Health ed., 15 August 1981, p.15; Terrence Deal and Allan Kennedy, Corporate Cultures (Reading, MA: Addison-Wesley, 1982), pp. 119–120.
[6]Carson, p.80.

III. THE IMPACT OF TECHNOLOGICAL AND ORGANIZATIONAL CHANGE ON THE INSURANCE INDUSTRY WORK FORCE

Prophesying about the process of office rationalization, C. Wright Mills wrote in 1956:

> As machines spread, they began to prompt newer divisons of labor to add to those they had originally implemented. The new machines . . .require central control of offices previously scattered throughout the enterprise. This centralization . . .is again facilitated by each new depression, through the urge to cut costs, and each new war, through increased volume of office work. The present extent of office centralization has not been precisely measured, although the tendency has been clear enough since the early 'twenties . . .it is clearly the model of the future.[7]

Insurance offices have fulfilled Mills' prophecy. The "integrated office system," impersonally managed with multi-purpose computers operated by clerical workers, has long supplanted the turn-of-the-century manual office.[8]

The insurance industry must contend with massive amounts of data and paperwork. This is reflected in the composition of its work force (see Table 2). Clerical workers account for nearly one half of those employed. Insurance carriers have led in the adoption of office automation—those technological advances which promise a more efficient, less costly way to handle paperwork.

A. Technological Change and Diffusion in the Insurance Industry

Technological change in the insurance industry has occurred in four stages, constituting a shift from batch toward continuous-flow production.[9] In each stage, computers have been installed to replace manual office functions. Throughout these stages, multi-purpose computers have been increasingly adopted, thereby linking formerly separate computerized clerical functions into an integrated office system.

1. Stage I: Pre-1950

As early as the 1890s, the Prudential Life Insurance Company used mechanized tabulating machines. The insurance industry at this point was already making widespread use of the typewriter and electric card-punching and adding machines for coding of routine billing services.[10]

---

[7]C. Wright Mills, *White Collar* (New York: Oxford University Press, 1956), p.195.

[8]Glenn and Feldberg; Maarten de Kadt, "Insurance: A Clerical Work Factory," in *Case Studies on the Labor Process*, ed. Andrew Zimbalist (New York: Monthly Review Press, 1979), pp. 242–256; David Lockwood, *Black-Coated Workers* (London: Allen & Unwin, 1958); Harry Braverman, *Labor and Monopoly Capital* (New York: Monthly Review Press, 1974).

[9]Joan Woodward, *Industrial Organization: Theory and Practice* (London: Oxford University Press, 1965).

[10]William Corliss, *Computers* (Washington, DC: U.S. Atomic Energy Commission, GPO, 1973).

Table 2. Percentage Distribution of Employment by Occupation in the Insurance Industry and American Work Forces, 1950–1978[a]

Occupation	1950		1960		1970		1978	
	Insurance	U.S.	Insurance	U.S.	Insurance	U.S.	Insurance	U.S.
White-collar	97.1	36.8	96.6	41.2	97.6	48.2	98.0	50.0
Professional	3.7	8.7	3.9	11.2	5.7	14.8	6.0	15.1
Managers	9.7	8.8	11.1	8.4	9.2	8.3	12.1	10.7
Sales	39.3	7.0	33.9	7.2	33.5	7.1	34.5	6.3
Clerical	44.4	12.3	47.7	14.4	49.2	18.0	45.4	17.9
Blue-collar	1.7	39.7	1.3	36.7	1.4	36.0	1.2	33.4
Craft	1.2	13.8	1.0	13.5	1.0	13.9	0.8	13.1
Operative	0.4	19.9	0.2	18.4	0.3	17.6	0.3	15.3
Laborer	0.1	6.0	0.1	4.8	0.1	4.5	0.1	5.0
Service	1.0	10.2	1.3	11.1	1.1	12.8	0.8	13.6
Farm	0.0	12.0	0.0	6.1	0.0	3.1	0.0	3.0
Not reported	0.2	1.3	0.9	4.9	—	—	—	—
Total[b]	100.0	100.0	100.1	100.0	100.1	100.1	100.0	100.0
N[c]	751	55804	1072	64647	1331	76554	1608	94373

[a]Source: See Table 1 and U.S. Bureau of Labor Statistics, *The National Industry-Occupation Employment Matrix, 1970, 1978, and Projected 1990*, Bulletin No. 2086, Vols. I and II, Government Printing Office, 1981.
[b]May not sum to 100.0% due to rounding.
[c]In thousands.

The IBM 077 Collator was introduced in 1936 to sort and tabulate data gathered in initiating the new Social Security Program and was immediately found to be useful in insurance. This same year the automatic typewriter became available, as well as the use of magnetic tape as a means of information storage and retrieval. Metropolitian Life Insurance Company utilized the "auto-typist" to process full letters and paragraphs stored on paper tape. Ten years later the same company combined its automated typing equipment with a centralized transcription department, creating in essence the first word processing center.[11]

2. Stage II: 1950–1964

In 1951, Remington-Rand, later to become Sperry-Rand, delivered the first production-line computer to the Bureau of the Census, and by 1953 at least 13 companies were manufacturing computers for commercial application.[12]

The insurance industry first adopted computers in the early 1950s. The U.S. Bureau of Labor statistics' (BLS) study of computer diffusion in the insurance industry collected data from over 400 insurance companies representing about 90% of the industry's employment. Two companies acquired computers in 1954. Over the next two years fifteen more followed suit, and by 1960 well over 100 companies had installed computers. By 1963, a majority of the companies surveyed by the BLS were using computers, with an average of three computers per company.[13]

Computers were used to perform a variety of insurance-specific tasks, especially premium billing and accounting, commission accounting, experience rating, valuation of reserves, and actuarial analysis, as well as such administrative tasks as payroll, general accounting, and personnel record-keeping. Moreover, according to the BLS, the number of functions performed by computers increased from three, for computers installed in 1955, to more than seven for those installed between 1961 and 1963.[14]

A trend in departmental consolidation within insurance companies accompanied the growth of multipurpose equipment. Prior to computer adoption, separate departments were usually responsible for billing, loan accounting, dividend accounting, claims, and agents' commissions. One company in the BLS study, for example, had 14 separate files per policy, which were maintained by seven departments. Computers began to store and process simultaneously the files of three departments, typically premium billing,

---

[11]Charles Eames and Ray Eames, *A Computer Perspective* (Cambridge: Harvard University Press, 1973; T. J. Anderson and W. R. Trotter, *Word Processing* (New York: AMACOM Press, 1974).
[12]U.S. Bureau of Labor Statistics, Bulletin no. 1468.
[13]Ibid., p.11.
[14]Ibid., p.18; U.S. Bureau of Labor Statistics, *Adjustments to the Introduction of Office Automation*, Bulletin no. 1276 (Washington, DC: GPO, 1960).

loans, and dividends, thereby eliminating "bulky card files," tabulating equipment, and many first-line supervisory and clerical jobs.[15]

Greater links between home and branch offices began to be forged with increased utilization of data transmission equipment which could transmit computerized information over telephone or telegraph circuits. As of 1963, 18 companies in the BLS study had installed this equipment and 29 had actually ordered or "definitely planned to order" these systems.[16]

The most frequently mentioned reason for introducing computers in this period, according to the BLS, was clerical labor-saving. One insurance company reported a post-computerization reduction of 80% in the time needed to prepare a report on agency experience, enabling it to prepare monthly instead of quarterly reports. Another reported a 64% reduction in unit time requirements for premium billing processing.[17] Among 17 life insurance companies that had installed computers between 1954 and 1956, according to the BLS, the number of policies in force increased by 3.5% between 1956 and 1959 and by 3.7% between 1959 and 1962. The percentage changes in the number of office employees in these two periods were 6.8% and 1.6% respectively, and those of policies per office employee were -3.1% and 2.1% respectively.[18]

By the end of this period, most large-and medium-size insurance companies had installed computers. The BLS estimated that between 1954 and 1963, 300 insurance companies had acquired over 800 computers.[19]

3. Stage III: 1964–1972

This stage is characterized by a rapid diffusion of the computer throughout the insurance industry to smaller insurance companies (especially with the availability of minicomputers). Burnett's interindustry analysis of the computer penetration ratio (CPR), the ratio between the numbers of computers in use and establishments in an industry, shows that the computer had become widely diffused in insurance (especially in "home offices") in relation to other industries by the late 1960s. In 1968, the insurance CPR was 1:80 compared to 1:200 for all industries.[20]

4. Stage IV: 1972–Present

Technological developments in the 1970s and 1980s have furthered earlier trends in insurance industry computer applications and home office cen-

[15]U.S. Bureau of Labor Statistics, Bulletin no. 1468, p.23.

[16]Ibid., p. 22.

[17]U.S. Bureau of Labor Statistics, Bulletin no. 1276, pp.11–12.

[18]U.S. Bureau of Labor Statistics, Bulletin no. 1468, pp. 36–37.

[19]Ibid., p. 7; U.S. Bureau of Labor Statistics, *Technological Trends in Major American Industries*, Bulletin no. 1474 (Washington, DC: GPO, 1966), p.249.

[20]Ed Burnett, "Computers in Use—Part 1," *Computers and People* 24 (May 1975), p. 28; "Computers in Use—Part 2," *Computers and People* 24 (June 1975), pp. 27–30; "Computers in Use—Part 3," *Computers and People* 24 (July 1975), p.29.

tralization. Premium billing and collection, for example, is often performed through the "turnaround" billing system. After a machine-readable notice and payment are returned by the policyholder, the computer stores the payment data for the accounting department, calculates the agent's commission on each premium, and credits the policyholder's account. These computerized billing systems handle about 5000 remittances an hour and the capacity of new equipment is over 40,000 remittances an hour. Computers are used in all other insurance functions including actuarial research, underwriting, and claims.[21]

Greater use of consolidated computer systems has continued the trend of departmental consolidation and centralization of home office control over field offices. Insurance computers now store approximately 12 separate records per policy which are distributed across departments and duplicated in field offices.[22]

The use of sophisticated data input devices such as optical character recognition and the "Mark Sense" system, which were first used in insurance in the early 1960s, reduces data entry time by 30% and raises clerical worker productivity.[23]

Home office centralization is expected to increase, because insurance companies are beginning to integrate horizontally through mergers and to conglomerate with other financial institutions. Centralization is also facilitated by developments in telecommunications linkages between home and field offices and between insurance companies. The insurance industry recently contracted with IBM to install a communications network linking insurance companies and agencies nationwide. The Insurance Institute for Research expects some 200 companies and over 60,000 agencies to make use of this system.[24]

The insurance industry appears to be entering a fifth stage of technological change. This stage is characterized by the increasing use of business satellites. In 1980, Satellite Business Systems launched its first business satellite and now rents space on the satellite to companies which desire to improve their communications networks. Companies with major offices in distant locations can now have instant satellite communications, person-to-person and computer-to-computer.[25]

With these changes, insurance industry ouput per employee increased by 27% (in constant dollars) from about $26,000 in 1958 to $33,000 in 1976. The average annual percentage change in output per hour almost tripled after

---

[21]U.S. Bureau of Labor Statistics, *Technology and Labor in Five Industries*, Bulletin no. 2033 (Washington, DC: GPO, 1979), pp. 42–44.

[22]Ibid.

[23]Ibid., p.45; U.S. Bureau of Labor Statistics, Bulletin no. 1468.

[24]U.S. Bureau of Industrial Economics, *1983 U.S. Industrial Outlook* (Washington, DC: GPO, 1983), p. 51–5; "IBM Picked to Install Communications Link by Insurance Institute," *Wall Street Journal*, October 7, 1982, p.6.

[25]Richard Smith, "Telecommunications in the 1980's," *Best's Review*, Life/Health ed. 82 (September 1981), p.54.

1964 as the computer became widely diffused in the insurance industry.[26]

In sum, computer application in insurance has progressed from the automation of task-specific functions to the development of the modern integrated office system. Further, intra-office systems will become integrated in inter-office systems through telecommunications networks. Speculating on the life insurance industry's near-future, one government analyst recently wrote:

> Computers will be used much more extensively for field operations. By linking home offices with branch offices, sophisticated terminals and minicomputers will make it possible to . . .perform many other functions in the field . . .At the beginning of the 1990's there will be fewer life insurance companies, they will become more consolidated and diversified, and there will be more joint ventures in attempts to broaden markets.[27]

B. Technology-Related Shifts in the Insurance Occupational Structure

The rising volume and complexity of business transactions and their records led to a continuous demand for clerical workers through the late 1940s.[28] However, office automation, unlike its predecessors, has slowed the overall growth rate of the insurance clerical work force. Clerical occupations represent the largest subset of white-collar workers within both the U.S. and insurance-industry work forces. But while the share of clerical workers within the U.S. work force had stabilized by the late 1970s, it had begun to decline in insurance (see Table 2).

In general, clerical occupations which involve a variety of tasks, individual decision-making, and face-to-face communication have been least affected by office automation. Those which require routine and repetitious work have proven most vulnerable. With the diffusion of voice recorders, improved copying machines, word processing, and computerized document storage and retrieval systems during the 1960s and 1970s, the proportions of typists, stenographers, secretaries, bookkeepers, and file clerks declined and the number of bookkeeping, billing, calculating, duplicating, and tabulating machine operators absolutely declined since 1970.[29]

Employment in insurance computer occupations—computer operators, programmers, and systems analysts—has increased since the 1950s and grew rapidly in the 1970s. Demand for these occupations is projected to decline by 1990 with the development of small, easy-to-run computers and standardized

---

[26]U.S. Bureau of Labor Statistics, Bulletin no. 2033, p.69.

[27]U.S. Bureau of Industrial Economics, *Industrial Outlook*, p. 51–5.

[28]U.S. Bureau of Labor Statistics, *Occupational Outlook Handbook*, Bulletin no. 940 (Washington, DC: GPO, 1949).

[29]U.S. Bureau of Labor Statistics, *Occupational Outlook Handbook*, Bulletin no. 1215 (Washington, DC: GPO, 1957); *Occupational Outlook Handbook*, Bulletin no. 1375 (Washington, DC:GPO, 1963); *Occupational Outlook Handbook*, Bulletin no. 1785 (Washington, DC: GPO, 1974); *Occupational Outlook Handbook*, Bulletin no. 1955 (Washington, DC: GPO, 1978); *The National Industry-Occupation Employment Matrix, 1970, 1978, and Projected 1990*, Bulletin no. 2086, 2 vols. (Washington, DC: GPO, 1981).

computer software packages. The proportion of keypunch operators, which initially increased, has declined since 1970 with the diffusion of computerized data entry systems.[30]

Despite the application of computers to most insurance functions, growing business volume increased employment in such higher-skill, insurance-specific occupations as actuaries and underwriters and claim approvers during the 1970s. However, employment in lower-skill, insurance-specific occupations, such as policy evaluation clerks and premium-ledger-card clerks, declined with office automation.[31]

In sum, the insurance occupational structure is changing in three ways. First, clerical occupations are declining and becoming more homogeneous. Second, computer occupations are emerging and differentiating into a skill hierarchy. Third, insurance-specific, higher-skill occupations are growing while their lower-skill counterparts are being eliminated by office automation.

C. Displacement, Reassignment and Retraining

High employee turnover, a characteristic of many clerical occupations, and a growing volume of business have been key factors in averting layoffs in insurance. According to the BLS, early computer adopters—large insurance companies—left job vacancies unfilled as computers were installed. Attempts were made to place remaining workers in comparable clerical positions within other company departments. Retraining was brief, usually lasting no more than two weeks. Largely recruited from tabulating machine operators, the new computer and peripheral equipment operators were chosen on the basis of their work records, supervisor recommendations, and aptitude tests. Similar means were used to select programmers and systems analysts, most of whom were former accountants and related professionals. Training, at company expense, was provided by the computer manufacturers. However, since the early 1960s, companies have begun to hire a growing share of university-trained computer professionals.[32]

This is demonstrated by our study of a small insurance company, TWI (pseudonym), based on interviews with managerial and non-supervisory personnel. TWI currently employs about one dozen clerical workers. Starting in the late 1970s, TWI progressed through several stages of office automation, including batch and on-line time-sharing, and the addition of a separate, in-

[30]U.S. Bureau of Labor Statistics, *Occupational Outlook Handbook*, Bulletin no. 1255 (Washington, DC: GPO, 1959); Bulletin nos. 1375, 1468, 1785, 2033, 2086; *Occupational Outlook Handbook*, Bulletin no.2200 (Washington, DC: GPO, 1982).

[31]U.S. Bureau of Labor Statistics, *Industry Wage Survey, Life Insurance, December 1971*, Bulletin no. 1791 (Washington, DC: GPO, 1973); *Industry Wage Survey, Life Insurance, February 1980*, Bulletin no. 2119, microfiche (Washington, DC: GPO, 1981).

[32]U.S. Bureau of Labor Statistics, Bulletin nos. 1276 and 1468; Ida Hoos, *Automation in the Office* (Washington, DC: Public Affairs, 1961); Diane Werneke, *Microelectronics and Office Jobs* (Geneva: International Labour Office, 1983); Joan Greenbaum, *In the Name of Efficiency* (Philadelphia: Temple University Press, 1979).

house minicomputer system. Recently, TWI installed a new computer which will replace and integrate the separate group-billing and claims systems. At one time TWI employed a university-trained programmer. However, with the array of computer software now available, the company does not plan to hire another.

There have been no layoffs due to office automation at TWI. Employee attrition has been due to personal, not personnel decisions. Several senior office workers attended training sessions offered by the computer manufacturers and, in turn, instructed other employees. During all stages of office automation, technological decline in labor demand has usually been more than offset by the growing volume of business. Between 1976 and 1983 the clerical staff has expanded from two to twelve workers.

D. Job Satisfaction and Interpersonal Work Relationships

With each stage of office automation, worker dissatisfaction has shifted from a concern with job security toward a concern with the intrinsic aspects of jobs. Four stages in this attitudinal process, corresponding to the stages in the technological process, will be discussed.

1. Stage I: 1950–1964

As automation was first introduced in the insurance industry, workers and management alike began to feel that their careers were in jeopardy. In her study of several insurance companies in the San Francisco Bay Area, Hoos found that many employees feared job loss, decreased promotion chances, skill downgrading, stricter supervision, reduced interpersonal interaction, and the possibility of geographical relocation. She also found that supervisors were threatened by job downgrading, loss of status, and job insecurity due to rescheduling and decreasing numbers of employees. Vice-presidents feared the transfer of their functions to a new hierarchy of data-processing personnel who were more knowledgeable about automation decision. Mann's findings are similar to those of the Hoos study. However, employees who had been given job security assurances tended to be dissatisfied with the intrinsic aspects of their jobs after automation.[33]

2. Stage II: 1964–1972

Between 1964 and 1972, as employers retrained office machine operators for new computer operator jobs and reduced the workforce by attrition, layoffs were avoided and employees began to examine and express dissatisfaction with the intrinsic aspects of their jobs. However, employees of companies which were just beginning to automate during this period were con-

---

[33]Hoos; Floyd Mann, "Psychological and Organizational Impacts," in *Automation and Technological Change*, ed. John Dunlop (Englewood Cliffs, NJ: Prentice-Hall, 1962), pp. 43–65.

cerned with job security, like the employees of the early computer adopters.[34]

In his study of five Boston insurance companies and one bank, Shepard concluded that feelings of powerlessness among clerical workers in automated offices derived from a decrease in job skills and responsibilities and the "factory-like" conditions under which most clericals work. Whisler's study of computerization in 23 life-insurance companies further highlights these factory-like conditions which accompanied computerization. Decision-making became increasingly centralized, rationalized, and quantified, controls and discipline over lower-level employees were tightened, and clerical jobs became more routinized while supervisory jobs were enlarged. Further, interpersonal communication decreased for clericals but increased for management, and about one-third of clerical workers experienced downgrading of skills.[35]

3. Stage III: 1972–Present

The period from 1972 to the present corresponds to what Zisman calls the "maturational" stage, a period of stabilization in organizational adaptation to office automation. In the insurance industry, job satisfaction declines, especially among clerical workers, employees continue to be dissatisfied with the intrinsic aspects of the job, and they begin to express concern about the loss of control over their jobs.[36]

Glenn and Feldberg argue that clerical work in general is becoming "proletarianized," in part because management has automated the office to control labor. They maintain that clerical work now requires skills that are more mechanical, simplified, and narrow; that work is subdivided and standardized to allow for supervisory control and inspection; and that physical separation and job title differentiation inhibits interpersonal interaction. Cummings' study of an insurance company found that computer technology not only increases productivity, but leads to a more complete control of the workplace through deskilling and elimination of jobs.[37] One health claims processor at Equitable Life Assurance Society bemoaned the simplification of her job after computerization, stating, "It's kind of an insult to anyone's intelligence."[38]

However, our study of TWI suggests that clerical worker proletarianiza-

---

[34]Simon Marcson, ed., *Automation, Alienation and Anomie* (New York: Harper & Row, 1970).

[35]Jon Shepard, *Automation and Alienation* (Cambridge: MIT Press, 1971); Thomas Whisler, *The Impact of Computers on Organizations* (New York: Praeger, 1970).

[36]Michael Zisman, "Office Automation: Revolution or Evolution?" *Sloan Management Review* 19 (Spring 1978), p.6; Elliot Richardson, *Work in America* (Cambridge: MIT press, 1973); Graham Staines and Robert Quinn, "American Workers Evaluate the Quality of their Jobs," *Monthly Labor Review* 102 (January 1979), pp.3–12; Paul Andrisani, *Work Attitudes and Labor Market Experience* (New York: Praeger, 1978).

[37]Glenn and Feldberg. Also, see Braverman; James Driscoll, "Office Automation: The Dynamics of a Technological Boondoggle," paper presented at the International Office Automation Symposium held at Stanford University, 1980; Laird Cummings, "Workers, Management and Computers," paper presented at the 27th annual meetings of the Society for the Study of Social Problems, Chicago, 1977.

[38]John Andrew, "Terminal Tedium," *Wall Street Journal*, May 6, 1983, p.1.

tion and job fragmentation are processes that mainly occur in large companies with bureaucratic structures. At TWI, office automation has led to few changes in the way clerical workers perform their jobs. Although claims workers now enter data directly into the computer, each remains completely responsible for several accounts. Faced with growing workloads and un-changing deadlines, TWI's clerical staff has welcomed technological change. This suggests, then, that any proletarianizing effects of office automation are likely to be most pronounced in large offices which maintained a complex division of labor before office automation. As a core industry, insurance em-ploys a disproportionately large number of people in large establishments. In 1981, 63.4% of the insurance workforce was employed in establishments with 100 or more employees, compared to 45.6% for the United States workforce.[39]

Employees in computer occupations have experienced the same fate as clerical workers. Kraft and Greenbaum argue that computer programming has become fragmented, routinized, and deskilled, like clerical work, and for the same reason: to allow management easier supervision and closer control over these employees. Kraft goes on to say that developments such as "canned" programming have downgraded computer workers' skills, while the creation of different job titles for employees who do similar work creates social subdivisions between computer workers. Although some believe that systems analysts still do the bulk of the skilled computer work, Brill found that they often feel alienation due to their separation and independence from other workers. Another study found that computer workers often feel over-educated for their job, causing them to feel underutilized.[40]

4. Stage IV: Present

Recent attention has been given to the effect of physical work conditions on the health of clerical workers. With greater use of video display terminals (VDT's) in the insurance industry, reports of health problems among em-ployees and allegations that VDT's emit dangerous levels of radiation have increased. Studies show that 25% of secretarial/clerical workers suffer severe muscular distress in the arms, neck, and shoulder, especially among clerical workers who work with VDT's. Other studies show that women clerical workers experience higher levels of stress on the job than men or women in most other occupations, and that VDT operators experience higher levels of stress and dissatisfaction than general clerical workers. A 1980 study by NIOSH found that VDT radiation levels were below the standard set by the

[39]Charles Tolbert, Patrick Horan and E. M. Beck, "The Structure of Economic Segmentation," *American Journal of Sociology* 85 (March 1980), pp. 1095–1116; U.S. Bureau of the Census, *County Business Patterns 1981*, United States, CBP-81-1(Washington, DC: GPO, 1983).

[40]Greenbaum; Phillip Kraft, *Programmers and Managers* (New York: Springer-Verlag, 1977); Alan Brill, "The Alienation of the Systems Analyst," in *Highlights of the Literature: Worker Alienation*, ed. Loren Meltzer (Scarsdale, NY: Work in America Institute, 1978), pp. 7–8; Donileen Loseke and John Sonquist, "The Computer Worker in the Labor Force," *Sociology of Work and Occupations* 6 (May 1979), pp. 156–179.

Occupational Safety and Health Administration, but that visual, postural, and stress-related complaints were high in the insurance industry, especially for VDT operators. According to District 925 of the Service Employees International Union, vision-related problems are among the most common complaints of VDT users.[41]

E. Declining Real Earnings in Insurance

Despite the increase in labor productivity associated with office automation, the real earnings of many life insurance office jobs, while they increased during the 1960s, declined in the 1970s. For all of the 37 life-insurance office occupations covered in the BLS industry wage surveys of 1971 and 1980, the real weekly earnings declined, averaging -17.5% and ranging from -7.5% for premium-ledger-card clerks to -30.2% for entry-level underwriters.[42]

In order to explain the variation in the 1971–80 growth (decline) rate in real earnings across these 37 occupations, we calculated zero-order correlation coefficients among 1971–80 percentage change in real earnings, 1971 real earnings, and seven other variables which describe the type of occupation and occupational trends in gender composition and employment with BLS wage survey data. For type of occupation, we used the BLS distinction between insurance, clerical and computer occupations, assigning a dummy variable to each. The trend in gender composition is measured by the 1971 percentage women in the occupation and the 1971–80 difference in the percentage women. Employment trend is measured by 1971 employment and 1971–80 percentage change in employment. The correlation coefficients are presented in Table 3.

The correlation coefficients show that the occupations with the highest rates of decline in real weekly earnings tended to be those with relatively: high 1971 earnings, especially such insurance occupations as actuaries and underwriters; few women employees in 1971; large increases in the percentage women by 1980; few employees in 1980; and high rates of employment growth between 1971 and 1980. Moreover, these variables are intercorrelated. The high-growth occupations tend to be the high-earnings occupations which employed few women in 1971, had large increases in the percentage women by 1980, and experienced large rates of decline in real earnings.

We regressed the 1971–80 percentage change in real weekly earnings on

---

[41]Adele Hoffmeyer, "VDT Safety: Is There a Problem?" *Best's Review*; Life/Health ed. 82 (March 1982), pp.66–72; Roger Hotte, "User Comfort, Safety Now Major Issues in U.S.," *Computer World*, October 26, 1981, p.5; Working Women, *Race Against Time: Automation of the Office* (Cleveland: Working Women, 1980); "Working with Video Display Terminals: A Preliminary Health-Risk Evaluation," *Morbidity and Mortality Weekly Report*, June 27, 1980, p. 307; "VDT Study Challenged on Conclusions," *AFL-CIO News*, August 20, 1983, p.3.

[42]U.S. Bureau of Labor Statistics, *Industry Wage Survey, Life Insurance, May–July 1961*, Bulletin no. 1324 (Washington, DC: GPO, 1962); *Industry Wage Survey, Life Insurance, October–November 1966*, Bulletin no. 1569 (Washington, DC: GPO, 1967); *Industry Wage Surveys: Banking and Life Insurance December 1976*, Bulletin no. 1988 (Washington, DC: GPO, 1978); Bulletin nos. 1791 and 2119.

Table 3. Zero-order Correlation Coefficients, Means and Standard Deviations for 37 Life Insurance Office Occupations

	(2)	(3)	(4)	(5)	(6)	(7)	(8)	(9)	X	S.D.
1. 1971–80 % change in real weekly earnings[a]	-.58*	-.49*	-.30*	-.05	.34*	-.40*	.43*	.46*	-17.5	5.3
2. 1971–80 difference in % women	—	.75*	.22	.29*	-.48*	.53*	-.43*	-.64*	4.9	9.5
3. 1971–80 % change in employment		—	.41*	.21	-.59*	.78*	-.56*	-.77*	18.5	56.2
4. Insurance occupation			—	-.45*	-.51*	.27	-.44*	-.18	0.297	0.463
5. Computer occupation				—	-.54*	.26	-.14	-.52*	0.324	0.475
6. Clerical occupation					—	-.51*	.56*	.67*	0.378	0.492
7. 1971 real weekly earnings[a,b]						—	-.59*	-.84*	4.8	0.4
8. 1971 employment[b]							—	.57*	6.8	0.7
9. 1971 % women								—	67.6	37.0

[a]In 1967 dollars.
[b]Natural logarithmic value.
*$p < .05$.

Table 4. Regression of 1971–1980 Percentage Change in Real (1967 Dollars) Weekly Earnings on Selected Independent Variables for 37 Life Insurance Office Occupations

Independent Variables	Metric Regression Coefficients
1971–80 difference in % women	−.29*
1971–80 % change in employment	.02
Insurance occupation	−.63
Computer occupation	2.44
1971 real weekly earnings[a]	1.01
1971 employment[a]	1.20
1971 % women	.05
Constant	−33.22
Adjusted R^2	.28

[a]Natural logarithmic value.
*$p < .05$.

all of the variables in order to discern the net effects of type of occupation and trends in gender composition and employment on the occupational variation in the real earnings growth (decline) rate. The regression equation is shown in Table 4. The only statistically significant regression coefficient is 1971–80 difference in percentage women. Occupations with the largest increases in the percentage women tended to be those with the highest rates of decline in real earnings, all else being equal.[43]

The findings suggest three patterns in the life insurance occupational earnings structure that accompanied office automation in the 1970s. First, the real earnings of all office occupations declined. Second, while the real earnings of the majority-women, clerical occupations declined, those of the higher-pay, fast-growing, non-clerical occupations declined at the highest rate, especially as women came to account for a larger share of employment in these latter occupations. Third, changing occupational gender composition is the strongest determinant of the occupational earnings growth rate. Occupations which experienced the greatest increases in the percentage women—or, occupational "feminization"—were those with the greatest declines in real earnings. In sum, with office automation and increased employment of women in high-pay, non-clerical occupations, all occupational earnings declined, with higher rates of earnings decline among the high-pay, non-clerical occupations and, therefore, a compression of the occupational earnings structure.

[43]In order to test for multicolinearity in the Table 4 findings, we calculated a regression equation—not reported here—without the 1971 measures of earnings, employment and percentage women. The results were almost identical to those in Table 4.

IV. CLERICAL LABOR RELATIONS IN INSURANCE

Managerial philosophies on collective bargaining are classified by Sloan and Witney on a scale ranging from conflict to collusion, the intermediary points being an armed truce, power bargaining, accommodaton (where many industries are today), and cooperation.[44] The insurance industry is located at the conflict point on the scale, being an industry where collective bargaining is quite new and as yet unacceptable to management. We now turn to clerical workers, management, and the growing disjunction between them.

A. Clerical Workers: Organization and Issues

Unionization is not new to the insurance industry. As early as 1895, Metropolitan Life and Prudential insurance agents joined the American Agents Association, affiliated with the American Federation of Labor (AFL). Unions affiliated with the AFL, such as the Insurance Agents International Union, with the Congress of Industrial Organizations (CIO), including the United Office and Professional Workers of America and the Insurance Workers of America, and with the AFL-CIO, such as the Insurance Workers International Union (IWIU), as well as independent unions have attempted to organize the insurance industry and, beginning in the 1930's, succeeded mainly in the large insurance companies. However, less than 10 percent of the insurance workforce is unionized and unionization is concentrated among the sales agents of large insurance companies.[45]

Unionization is low but increasing among insurance office workers. According to the BLS, the percentage unionized among life insurance office workers increased from 2 percent to almost 5 percent between 1961 and 1980.[46]

Until recently, collective bargaining and collective action by insurance clerical workers have been rare, while quitting and absenteeism have been the main methods used to express dissatisfaction. The normal tenure in some insurance occupations is about two years. Foner suggests that the annual turnover rate may be between 25 and 45 percent.[47]

Clerical worker unionization in insurance has partly been impeded by the identification of office workers with management. According to Kassalow, the physical work conditions, job security, benefits, and other conditions of

[44]Arthur Sloane and Fred Witney, *Labor Relations*, 3rd ed. (Englewood Cliffs, NJ: Prentice-Hall, 1977).

[45]Harvey Clermont, *Organizing the Insurance Worker* (Washington, DC: The Catholic University of America Press, 1966); Edward Kokkelenberg and Donna Sockell, "Union Membership in the United States, 1973–1981," *Industrial and Labor Relations Review* 38 (July 1985), pp. 497–543.

[46]U.S. Bureau of Labor Statistics, Bulletin nos. 1324, 1569, 1791, 1988 and 2119.

[47]Matthew Goodfellow, "Is Insurance Unionization Inevitable? (Part 2)," *The National Underwriter*, Property/Casualty ed., March 7, 1981, p. 11; David Armstrong and Christian Nuttal, "Managing the Efficient Automated Workplace," *Best's Review*, Life/Health ed. 82 (May 1981), p. 48; Philip Foner, *Women and the American Labor Movement: From WWI to the Present* (New York: Free Press, 1980), pp. 556–557.

white-collar work tend to be superior to those of blue-collar work, leading white-collar workers to oppose unionization. Writing in 1966, when office automation became widespread in insurance, Kassalow suggested that office automation may erode the superiority of white-collar work conditions as they become more routine, regimented, and factory-like. The increase in insurance unionization suggests, like the changing work conditions in banking, that white-collar work conditions in insurance may no longer prevent clerical worker unionization, especially if office automation is accompanied by occupational downgrading, declining real earnings, and curtailed promotion opportunities.[48]

Although women clerical workers have traditionally not been unionized, research suggests that women are unionizing as their labor force participation increases and more women have full-time jobs and careers. According to LeGrande, the number of women union members in the United States increased at a rate almost three times greater than that of all union members between 1956 and 1976. Goldberg (1983) found pro-union attitudes among women office workers in her study of Baltimore Working Women.[49]

Another eroding impediment to office worker unionization is organized labor's disinterest in organizing insurance clerical workers and women. Since the beginning of the twentieth century, insurance labor unions have been dominated by a craft-consciousness which led them to organize sales agents while virtually ignoring clerical workers. The AFL-affiliated unions such as the Industrial and Ordinary Insurance Agents Council and the Insurance Agents International Union (IAIU) restricted their organizing efforts to sales agents. Even such CIO-affiliated unions as the Insurance Workers of America and the United Office and Professional Workers of America succeeded in organizing sales agents, despite the CIO's philosophy of industrial unionism. Evidence of a decline in craft-consciousness is that in 1966 the Insurance Workers International Union (IWIU) hired an organizer to study the process of white-collar unionization.[50] Furthermore, on October 1, 1983, the IWIU merged into the United Food and Commercial Workers (AFL-CIO) to help launch "a full-scale organizing effort in the insurance and financial industry."[51] According to Joseph Pollack, one of the main reasons for this merger was to improve the effectiveness of organizing clerical workers in insurance.[52]

With declining membership in blue-collar unions and the founding of the Coalition of Labor Union Women (CLUW) in 1974, the man-oriented gender-

---

[48]Clermont, pp. 211–218; Everett Kassalow, "White-Collar Unionism in the United States," in *White-Collar Trade Unions*, ed. Adolf Sturmthal (Urbana, IL: University of Illinois Press, 1966), pp. 355–359; Charles Coleman and Jane Rose, "Bank Unionization: Status and Prospects," *Monthly Labor Review* 98 (October 1975), pp. 38–41.

[49]Kassalow, p.356; Jean Tepperman, *Not Servants, Not Machines* (Boston: Beacon Press, 1976); Linda LeGrande, "Women in Labor Organizations: Their Ranks are Increasing," *Monthly Labor Review* 101 (August 1978), pp. 8–14; Roberta Goldberg, *Organizing Women Office Workers* (New York: Praeger, 1983).

[50]Clermont.

[51]"Insurance Union, UFCW Merger Set for October 1," *AFL-CIO News*, September 10, 1983, p. 1.

[52]Personal telephone communication with Mr. Pollack.

consciousness of many AFL-CIO and other unions has declined and unions are beginning to organize sectors of the economy which are occupied predominantly by women. One of CLUW's chief goals for advancing the rights and status of women is increased union efforts to organize women.[53] Unions which seek to organize insurance clerical workers are beginning to hire women as organizers. For example, the Brotherhood of Railway and Airline Clerks hired a woman in 1980 to organize insurance clerical workers, and the Service Employees International Union (SEIU) has recently increased the number of its women organizers by 15%. Several unions have successfully organized insurance clerical workers. In 1977, the IWIU signed a contract with Metropolitan Life covering clerical workers in seven states. The Office and Professional Employees International Union recently organized clerical workers at Blue Cross/Blue Shield in an interstate agreement. In 1979, the Teamsters negotiated a contract covering clerical workers with John Hancock.[54] SEIU won an election among the health benefit claims clerks at Equitable Life Assurance Society in Syracuse, NY in 1982, and after refusing to bargain for about one year the company has recently signed a contract with the union. Among the provisions in the contract are extra break time from VDT's, the right of pregnant workers to request transfers to non-VDT work, and requirements for safety equipment such as glare-reduction devices and adjustable chairs.[55]

The methods and issues connected with organizing clerical workers in insurance reflect the emergence of a dual consciousness. Clerical worker consciousness includes not only a craft-consciousness, in that organizing is often directed to clerical workers as an occupational group which cuts across industry lines, but also, given occupational sex segregation, a woman-oriented gender-consciousness. Goldberg refers to these forms of consciousness as "job consciousness" and "feminist consciousness."[56]

The dual consciousness of insurance clerical workers has led them not only to unionize, but to join working women's organizations. Strongly influenced by the women's movement and the neglect of women workers by

[53]Foner, p. 514; Sloane and Witney, p.97.

[54]Doris Fenske, "Another Union Readies a Run at the Insurance Industry," *Best's Review*, Life/Health ed. 81 (October 1980), p. 12; "Unions Move into the Office," *Businessweek*, January 25, 1982, pp. 90–92; Goodfellow, "Insurance Unionization (Part 2)" and his articles: "What's New in Union Organizing Companies?" *Best's Review*, Life/Health ed. 76 (October 1975), p. 10; "Avoiding Unions in the Insurance Clerical Field," *Best's Review*, Life/Health ed. 81 (October 1980), p. 13; "Is Insurance Unionization Inevitable? (Part 1)," *The National Underwriter*, Property/Casualty ed., March 7, 1981, p.11; Andrew (n. 38, above); John Kilgour, "Unionization: Is the Insurance Industry Vulnerable?" *Best's Review*, Property/Casualty ed. 83 (August 1982), pp. 34–93.

[55]"Labor Letter," *Wall Street Journal*, February 16, 1982, p.1; "Equitable Boycott," *Wall Street Journal*, March 15, 1983, p.1; "Labor Letter," *Wall Street Journal*, October 4, 1983, p.1; Cathy Trost, "Equitable Life Accord with Service Union Marks Breakthrough," *Wall Street Journal*, November 13, 1984, p. 10.

[56]Goldberg, pp. 89–108; Tepperman; Louise Howe, *Pink Collar Workers* (New York: G. P. Putnam's Sons, 1977).

organized labor, working women's organizations, which have burgeoned since the founding of Nine to Five in 1973, direct much of their attention to women clerical workers in finance industries. Using educational outreach tactics, conciliation, and litigation, working women's organizations address such women's employment issues as sex discrimination in wages and promotions, sexual harassment on the job, and occupational safety and health problems.[57]

Among the chief concerns of working women's organizations and labor unions, which often organize in tandem, is the effect of office automation on the wages, employment levels, promotion chances, job autonomy, and health of women clerical workers. In 1980, Working Women, a working women's organization with affiliates in 12 major cities and members in 45 states, published a report, *Race Against Time*, which deplored low wages, occupational downgrading, declining employment, strict managerial controls, and health hazards, and attributed them to "management choices" in implementing office automation. The report makes frequent references to the insurance and banking industries.[58]

In sum, office automation and accompanying trends, such as declining earnings, clerical employment and job satisfaction, occupational downgrading, increased awareness of occupational health problems, and employer sex discrimination, have begun to fashion a dual consciousness—an occupational and a gender consciousness—among insurance clerical workers. Major catalysts of clerical organizing are the women's movement, especially as expressed through growing working women's organizations, and the labor movement, which is broadening its constituency to include women clerical workers. Finally, the emphasis on organizing women clerical workers stems from the persistent pattern of occupational sex segregation in the insurance industry and the combined occupational and gender-based effects of office automation on this group of employees.

B. Management's Stance toward Clerical Labor

The actions of insurance management toward the clerical work force have been motivated by a desire to reduce clerical labor costs and to raise clerical worker productivity. This desire is manifest in the pioneering and continuous efforts taken by management to automate insurance offices throughout the post-world War II era.

Management adopted two approaches in succession for managing the clerical workforce as offices were automated. The succession of managerial philosophies parallels the shift from Scientific Management to Human Rela-

---

[57]Foner; Goldberg; Fenske; Steve Cocheo, "Head of Women's Group Discusses Fledgling Union," *ABA Banking Journal* 73 (November 1981), pp. 148–159; Karen Koziara and Patricia Insley, "Organizations of Working Women Can Pave the Way for Unions," *Monthly Labor Review* 105 (June 1982), pp. 53–54.

[58]Working Women, p.12; "Health Fears on VDT's Spur Union Action," *Wall Street Journal*, October 27, 1981, p.31; Andrew.

tions.[59] This succession has yielded an admixture of the two in many insurance companies today and is another reason for the relatively low level of unionization in the insurance office.

The first approach is unilateral in that management imposes impersonal and personal controls on clerical workers to measure and maintain clerical worker productivity. A variety of computerized, impersonal techniques are used to control insurance clerical workers. Computer terminals, for example, record the volume of work performed by claims processors and data entry operators (work volume is measured in keystrokes per minute or lines processed per day), count mistakes, and reject inaccurate forms. Many workers are paid by piece rates in accordance with productivity standards called rate expectancies.[60]

Non-computerized, impersonal control techniques are also common. For example, Advanced Office Controls is "a library of engineered standard time values covering virtually every aspect of work performed in an office, with all data summarized on a single card."[61]

Personal surveillance of workers by supervisors and managers is another unilateral control device. It is unilateral in that supervisors often fail to listen to clerical workers. In a survey of insurance supervisors, Goodfellow found that 70% either never listen to subordinates or listen imperfectly (i.e. responding to comments by saying "tsk, tsk"). Costello found that disrespectful, sexist indifference or hostility toward insurance clerical workers is manifested, for example, in managerial dismissals of employee complaints on the grounds that the employee is experiencing menopause or pregnancy. Personal surveillance may include such techniques as monitoring employee phone calls, written reprimands for talking, and following employees into the bathroom. Further, personal control in insurance is frequently administered capriciously as in arbitrary disciplining and violation of seniority rules for layoffs, job assignments, and distribution of overtime.[62]

The second approach for managing insurance clerical workers is an integrative human relations managerial philosophy. Control practices which derive from this philosophy are used to integrate the employee into the company by creating a sense of community among clerical workers in relation to management.

A sense of community is instilled by opening channels of communication between clerical workers and supervisors and by increasing employee par-

[59]Ivar Berg, Marcia Freedman and Michael Freeman, *Managers and Work Reform* (New York: Free Press, 1978).

[60]Glenn and Feldberg; Working Women, p. 7; Cynthia Costello, "Office Workers, Collective Action, and Social Consciousness," paper presented at the Society for the Study of Social Problems, Detroit, 1983, p.12.

[61]Robert Nolan, "Work Management Programs Really Work," *The National Underwriter*, Property/Casualty ed., February 15, 1980, p. 25. Also, see Harry Wiemann, "Administrative Improvement Program," *Best's Review*, Property/Casualty ed. 80 (August 1979), pp. 94–97.

[62]Goodfellow, "Insurance Unionization(Part 2)," p. 31; Costello, "Office Workers, Collective Action," pp. 5–7. Also, see Goodfellow, "Avoiding Unions" and "Insurance Unionization(Part 1)."

ticipation in decision making. These techniques are often used to raise worker productivity and reduce staff, overcome employee resistance to the introduction of office automation, and to lower what is regarded as high employee turnover and absenteeism among clerical workers. Community-instilling devices used in insurance include training supervisors to listen carefully to employee complaints, creating quality control circles, informing employees of technological change and seeking their advice, writing and explaining disciplinary rules, disseminating sophisticated company news in the house organ, hiring expert interviewers recognized as representing top management to interview employees regularly, establishing job enrichment programs, and holding regular meetings with staff.[63]

Insurance management opposes unionization, as reflected in recent actions taken by insurance companies. Anticipating increased union organizing activity in insurance, major insurance companies such as John Hancock and Boston Mutual opposed the recent merger of the IWIU into the United Food and Commercial Workers. American National Insurance Co. hired a consultant to send an eight-page letter, written in English and Spanish, to sales agents encouraging them to oppose the merger.[64] During the union election campaign at Equitable Life discussed above, the company hired 2M, a management consulting firm which specializes in union prevention, to dissuade workers from joining SEIU local 925.[65]

In summary, insurance management's stance toward clerical labor is to reduce its cost and raise its productivity. To this end, insurance companies continue to automate and rationalize the office with unilateral impersonal controls on clerical workers. Beset by recent narrow profit margins and the beginnings of clerical worker unionization, management is also substituting integrative control for unilateral personal control of the clerical work force to preempt clerical worker unionization.

C. The Disjunction between Clerical Labor and Management

Accompanying insurance office automation is a growing disjunction between clerical labor and management along class and gender lines. The dis-

---

[63]Frank Santangeli, "Improving Productivity through Job Enrichment," *Best's Review*, Life/Health ed. 77 (August 1976), pp. 74–77; Jill Casner-Lotto, "Management Choices Will Be the Key to Success," *World of Work Report* 8 (April 1983), p. 25; Ellen Klimon, "Future is Now for Agency Automation," *The National Underwriter*, Property/Casualty ed., May 16, 1980, p. 55; Goodfellow, "Avoiding Unions," and "Insurance Unionization(Parts 1 and 2)"; Krupman and Vaccaro; Kenneth Miller, "Sagging Productivity Besets Insurance Business," *The National Underwriter*, Property/Casualty ed., February 23, 1980, p.2; Armstrong and Nuttal; "Lincoln National Life Stresses Work Restructure, Employee Involvement for Greater Quality, Productivity," *World of Work Report* 4 (June 1979), p. 41; "Those New Employees- and Unions," *The National Underwriter*, Life/Health ed., February 2, 1980, p. 12; "Lists Causes of Unionization," *The National Underwriter*, Life/Health ed., February 9, 1980, p. 10; Alfred Haggarty, " 'Quality Circles' Approach to Greater Productivity Viewed," *The National Underwriter*, Life/Health ed., October 3, 1981, p.30.
[64]"Insurance Union, UFCW Merger," *AFL-CIO News*.
[65]Personal telephone communication with an SEIU organizer.

junction is evident in their issues toward one another and in their methods for resolving their differences.

With respect to their issues, clerical labor and management either oppose one another or ignore the issues of the other. On the issue of wages, the two parties oppose one another. Management gives little attention to such women's issues as sex discrimination in wages and job assignments or disrespectful treatment by supervisors and managers. Clerical labor shows little concern for management's interest in high worker productivity.

In their methods for resolving their differences, clerical labor and management are each building arenas for management–labor discourse that are based on divergent theoretical principles. This divergence is between what Berg *et al.* refer to as institutional and human relations approaches. By unionizing, clerical workers are beginning to evolve an institutional framework in which they can collectively bargain with management to gain enforceable, contractually-based improvements in their working conditions. Desiring unilateral control of the clerical work force, management resists the development of this institutional framework. Furthermore, as management resists this institutional framework, it uses a human relations approach to build an integrative, social psychological framework in which the parties are not contractually-bound adversaries but members of the same community. In this community, labor can express mainly its emotional concerns to management who, in turn, may offer "educational or therapeutic solutions."[66]

The growing disjunction derives in part from two trends in insurance which have occurred in the context of persistent occupational sex segregation: office rationalization and the emerging dual consciousness among clerical workers. As the insurance office was rationalized through office automation and the imposition of impersonal labor controls, many clerical jobs were eliminated or downgraded and the material and emotional livelihoods of many women clerical workers deteriorated. Consequently, a dual consciousness among women clerical workers, an occupation- and gender-based awareness of deteriorating work conditions, has emerged. This dual consciousness has played a role in mobilizing women clerical workers to seek a collective solution to problems which they experienced as an occupation-gender group of insurance employees. The mobilization of women clerical workers, in turn, serves to mobilize a male-dominated management to maintain its control of the clerical workforce and to raise clerical worker productivity.

Office rationalization and the emerging dual consciousness among women clerical workers are not specific to the insurance industry and are caused by greater economic and political forces. Insurance office rationalization has accompanied and facilitated the growth and diversification of insurance companies. Increased interindustry competition within the financial sector, especially between banks and insurance companies, also leads insurance companies to cut labor costs and automate the office further.[67]

---

[66]Berg et al., pp. 23–34, 173.
[67]U.S. Bureau of Industrial Economics, *Industrial Outlook;* "Insurance Squeeze," *Wall Street Journal,* September 20, 1983, p.1.

The emerging dual consciousness among insurance clerical workers is being catalyzed by the women's and labor movements. The women's movement, through working women's organizations, is organizing women clerical workers. With the changing occupational structure of the American workforce, the decline of manufacturing, and the subsequent erosion of the traditional male, blue-collar source of labor union membership, the labor movement is mustering its resources to organize women clerical workers in insurance and, generally, white-collar workers in the growing service sector.

The disjunction in insurance labor relations, then, grows out of a confluence of technological and occupational changes and declining real earnings in the insurance industry, increased interindustry competition in the financial sector, and heightened organizing activity by the women's and labor movements In the context of occupational sex segregation, these trends cause clerical labor and management to diverge as women and men and as economic adversaries. As office automation spreads throughout other white-collar service industries, and in the offices of large corporations in all industries, the pattern of labor relations in the insurance industry may become replicated among other unorganized women clerical workers and managers who are unaccustomed to dealing with organized workers.

ACKNOWLEDGMENTS

We gratefully acknowledge the assistance of Kitty Conlan, an SEIU organizer for Local 925, TWI (pseudonym), Ernest Campbell, Joan Burton, Roslyn Feldberg, Linda Karwedsky, Linda Williamson, Mary Anne Guschke, Roy Young, Joseph Pollack, and Jo Anne Bradford.

7

Computerized Instruction, Information Systems, and School Teachers
Labor Relations in Education

Kent D. Peterson

I. INTRODUCTION

The increasing application of computerized instructional and information management systems in elementary and secondary schools is beginning to transform relationships between teachers and principals. Still in its infancy, this technological change is already affecting the norms of the occupation, the process of supervision, and the professional control of classroom processes.

Computers are reducing the professional autonomy of teachers as well as producing resistance and conflict over the use of this new technology. With the application of computers to educational functions, teacher–principal relations are becoming strained; teachers are increasingly fearful of the newly acquired monitoring power of administrators. The deployment of the new technology reduces teacher control over the selection of curricula, instructional materials, pacing, and student assessment. Consequently, national teachers' associations are reviewing and rewriting their policies toward teacher evaluation and dismissal. Moreover, growing national concern over the quality of American schools has contributed to a greater desire to prescribe, monitor, and assess teachers on the basis of quantitative measures of student performance.

Kent D. Peterson • George Peabody College, Vanderbilt University, P.O. Box 514, Nashville, TN 37203.

The purpose of this chapter is to analyze the effects of emerging educational technologies on teacher–principal relations in U. S. elementary and high schools. After discussing the nature and causes of educational technological change, I assess the impact of this change on teacher autonomy, accountability, evaluation, and supervision, as well as changes in labor relations in national and local settings.

II. CONCEPTUAL APPROACH

Sociotechnical organizational theory is helpful for understanding the effects of technological changes on teacher–principal relations. Important in this perspective are (a) the beliefs held concerning the core technology, (b) the nature of organizational goals, (c) the characteristics of the occupation, and (d) the modes of organizational assessment used to supervise and evaluate managers and workers. Resistance and conflict may arise when technology alters the relationships among these organizational features.

According to Parsons, organizations have three basic levels, each of which performs a discrete set of tasks in the organization, but which is connected to the other levels by exchange of resources and authority linkages. First, the *technical level* produces the goods or services of the organization. Termed the "technical core" by Thompson, this part of the organization is the place where the central work of the enterprise is accomplished. It must be buffered from outside forces, perturbations in the flow of inputs, and bottlenecks to the flow of outputs.[1] Teachers work in the technical core of schools and use computers at this level.

Second, the *managerial level* organizes, coordinates and directs the work of the technical core. Administrators select technologies, smooth flows of resources, and monitor and assess the work of the technical level.[2] In professional and semi-professional organizations the managerial level works with the technical level to select technologies and processes.[3] Principals work in the managerial level of schools and use computers to control and structure this level and the technical level.

Third, the *institutional level* sets the broader mission of the organization, interacts with major forces in the environment, and selects overall strategies and structures. The school board, superintendent, and staff comprise the institutional level.

I turn now to the effects of computerization on the relationships between the technical (classroom), managerial (principal), and institutional (superintendent and school board) levels. The linkages between all of the levels are

[1]Talcott Parsons, *Structure and Process in Modern Societies* (New York: Free Press, 1960); James Thompson, *Organizations in Action* (New York: McGraw-Hill, 1967).

[2]Ibid.

[3]Amitai Etzioni, "A Basis for Comparative Analysis of Complex Organizations." in *A Sociological Reader on Complex Organizations*, ed. Amitai Etzioni (New York: Free Press, 1969), pp. 59–79.

substantially affected by the nature of the core technology, organizational goals, and the specific means used to assess performance.

III. THE NATURE OF EDUCATIONAL ORGANIZATIONS AND PROFESSIONAL AUTONOMY

Public schools in the United States are governed by the separate states. The states provide financial support, commonly based on average daily attendance figures, and determine standards for licensure of personnel. Local boards of education are the immediate governing agencies of schools. Local boards govern school districts, whose coverage may range from one to hundreds of schools. They set policy on local curriculum, hire and fire teachers and administrators, negotiate contracts, and decide on the means for assessing organizational performance.

Individual districts consist of separately bounded schools, each of which includes a principal and 10–20 teachers.[4] This cellular, "egg crate" school structure was developed in the last century and prevails in most schools today.[5]

In most schools, teachers have considerable autonomy over instruction and classroom management.[6] Task specification, supervision, and evaluation of teachers are often ceremonial and ambiguous rather than goal oriented and specific.[7] Teachers remain relatively free of close surveillance and have considerable discretion in selecting the means to achieve ends (for example, the pacing of lessons, whether to use recitation or seatwork, the composition of reading groups, topics for the day's work) while being held accountable for broadly defined results.[8] Moreover, these results are seldom precisely measured or quantitatively assessed for evaluation purposes.[9]

The limits of teacher autonomy are shaped by the properties of educational technology, the goals of schools, and institutional norms regarding discretion. Unlike many of the industries discussed in this book, education does not enjoy a precise technology or clear goals. The technology of education—the set of activities used by teachers to produce cognitive learning and socialization (the two central goals of schools)—remains largely uncodified,

[4]Dan Lortie, Gary Crow, and Sandra Prolman. *Elementary Principals in Suburbia: An Occupational And Organizational Study* (Washington, DC: National Institute of Education, 1983).

[5]Dan Lortie, *Schoolteacher* (Chicago: University of Chicago, 1975).

[6]John Goodlad, *A Place Called School: Prospects for the Future* (New York: McGraw-Hill, 1984).

[7]Lortie, *Schoolteacher*: Anne Trask, "Principals, Teachers and supervision: Dilemmas and Solutions," *Administrator's Notebook* 13 (1964), pp. 1–4; Donald Willower, "Schools as Organizations: Some Illustrated Strategies for Educational Research and Practice," *Journal of Educational Administration* 7 (1969), pp. 110–126.

[8]Charles Bidwell, "The School As a Formal Organization," in *Handbook of Organizations*, ed. James March (Chicago: Rand McNally, 1965), pp. 927–1023.

[9]Kent Peterson, "Mechanisms of Administrative Control Over Managers in Educational Organizations," *Administrative Science Quarterly* 29 (1964), pp. 573–597.

with few proven ways for teachers to achieve specified ends.[10] In Thompson's terms, educators do not *believe* that there are clear, known cause–effect relationships in classroom teaching and that specific sets of activities, materials, and processes will produce the desired learning in students.[11]

Teacher beliefs about the technology of teaching and the structure of curriculum reinforce and support extensive professional autonomy. Teachers often view teaching styles and behaviors as an outcome of their own psychological traits, personal idiosyncracies and social skills, rather than as a result of pedagogic knowledge and technical skill.[12] The teaching–learning process is perceived as an indivisible whole which others cannot understand or evaluate by empirically studying and assessing its component parts.[13] This belief supports a high degree of professional autonomy for teachers.

Given the unclear technology and professional norm of autonomy, educational goals are generally diffuse and multiple.[14] When educators and the public discuss the purpose of schooling they use terms which are often fraught with ambiguous, global concepts that have few behavioral indicators. Schools are expected to produce everything from literate individuals to good citizens, from professional athletes to heart surgeons.

Attainment of educational goals is difficult to measure. While it is relatively simple to measure whether a student has learned an historical fact or an arithmetic operation, measuring the development of complex problem-solving skills, the quality of a written composition or the development of "character" is more difficult.

Social and technical contacts between classrooms and administrators are attenuated, with "loose coupling" of units common in most schools.[15] Teachers are responsible for most of the decisions about the daily content, pace, purpose, and assessment of their work; administrators on the other hand control non-instructional domains such as budgeting, attendance, and building maintenance.[16] Classroom and administrative work are often independent.

Like teachers, the work of principals is characterized by considerable autonomy, an uncodified technology, diffuse goals, and a complex relationship with the environment.[17] Early studies of principals' work note that these administrators, like other managers,[18] must cope with brevity, variety,

---

[10]Robert Dreeben, *The Nature of Teaching* (Glenview, IL: Scott Foresman, 1970); Lortie, *Schoolteacher.*

[11]Thompson.

[12]Lortie, *Schoolteacher.*

[13]Ibid.

[14]Bidwell; Dreeben; Lortie, *Schoolteacher;* James March. "American Public School Administration: A Short Analysis," *School Review* 86 (1976), pp. 217–250.

[15]Bidwell; Karl Weick, "Educational Organizations As Loosely Coupled Systems," *Administrative Science Quarterly* 21 (1976), pp. 1–19.

[16]Dan Lortie, "The Balance of Control and Autonomy in Elementary School Teaching," in *The Semi-Professions and Their Organization.* ed. Amitai Etzioni (New York: The Free Press). pp. 1–53; Peterson, "Mechanisms of Administrative Control."

[17]March.

[18]Henry Mintzberg, *The Nature of Managerial Work* (New York: Harper & Row, 1973).

and fragmentation in their daily interactions.[19] For elementary school principals, the average duration of each task is less than four minutes. Principals must deal with simple and complex tasks, an enormous range of social and technical problems, and constant interruptions. The rhythm of work, the pacing of activities, and the flow of crises brought on by the community are not carefully documented nor easily understood by these administrators.[20] The complexities and demands of principals' work increase the autonomy of teachers, as it is difficult for principals to direct, supervise, and evaluate large numbers of teachers under these circumstances.

In summary, teacher autonomy is influenced by the semi-professionalized nature of the occupation, the structure of the school, the properties of the technology, and the nature of organizational goals. Teachers work in what Scott calls "heteronomous" organizations, in which they have some autonomy for selecting instructional tools, deciding on pacing of lessons, and timing student assessments. School boards, superintendents, and principals have allowed teachers much leeway in making these decisions.[21] Also, teachers have maintained their professional autonomy by establishing teacher associations.

IV. TEACHERS AND THEIR ASSOCIATIONS

Teachers belong to two major associations. The National Education Association (NEA) is the nation's largest labor organization with 1.7 million members. The American Federation of Teachers (AFT), in contrast, has 700,000 members. In 1982, 64.3% of public school teachers were members of a labor organization.[22] During the late 19th and early 20th centuries, school populations grew dramatically, increasing the numbers of people involved in the teaching occupation. High school enrollment increased from 200,000 to 2,000,000 between 1890 and 1920, with a concomitant increase in the number of teachers. Teacher associations also grew, but it was not until the early 20th century, that teachers actively sought to improve salaries and to have some input in policy matters.

From the mid-1950s on, both teacher unions focused more of their attention on civil rights, women's issues, legislative action, and collective bargaining. Both the AFT and the NEA sought to increase their memberships and to

---

[19]Harry Wolcott, *The Man in the Principal's Office* (New York: Holt, Rinehart & Winston, 1973); Kent Peterson, "The Principals' Tasks," *The Administrator's Notebook* 26 (1978), pp. 1–4; John Kmetz and Donald Willower, "Elementary School Principals' Work Behavior," *Educational Administration Quarterly* 18 (1982), pp. 1–29; W. F. Martin and Donald Willower, "The Managerial Behavior of High School Principals," *Educational Administration Quarterly* 17 (1981), pp. 69–89.

[20]David Dwyer, *Contextual Antecedents of Instructional Leadership*, Paper presented at the Annual Meeting of the American Educational Research Association (San Francisco, CA, 1985).

[21]W. Richard Scott, "Field Methods in the Study of Organizations," in *A Sociological Reader on Complex Organizations*, ed. Amitai Etzioni (New York: Free Press, 1969), pp. 558–576.

[22]U.S. Bureau of the Census, *1982 Census of Governments, Labor-Management Relations in State and Local Governments*, GC82(3)-3 (Washington, DC: GPO, 1985), p. vi.

gain higher wages for teachers. Strike activity increased during the early 1960s. Between 1960 and 1964, 40,000 teachers took part in strikes, twice as many as the number which had participated in strikes between 1940 and 1960. The NEA won 26 collective bargaining elections involving 26,000 teachers between 1961 and 1965, while the AFT, which concentrated its energies on organizing teachers in cities, won 14 elections involving over 74,000 teachers.

Beginning in the late 1960s, many states enacted public school teacher collective bargaining legislation. The number of states requiring collective bargaining increased from 3 to 12 between 1965 and 1966; by 1979, 31 states had collective bargaining laws covering some 60% of all public school teachers. Union memberships had grown from 700,000 in 1957 to 1.7 million in 1979.

During the late 1960s and throughout the 1970s, declining enrollments, teacher layoffs, and decreasing real wages led to increased strike activity. Also, the NEA and AFT lobbied extensively in state legislatures and Congress for protective legislation. Furthermore, growing dissatisfaction with the quality of schools has dampened teacher career commitment and decreased the level of support afforded to teachers and schools. Computerization, therefore, comes at a time of teacher unrest and public demands for change.

V. TECHNOLOGICAL CHANGE IN EDUCATION

During the last 50 years, technical innovations in education have been made in the basic tools of teaching (overhead projectors, dustless chalk, and green blackboards, for example), in the method of organizing instruction ("discovery learning," "mastery learning," programmed instruction, and individualized instruction), in the structure and content of curriculum (the "new math," PSSC physics, "Man: A Course of Study") and in the organizational arrangements of classes and schools (team teaching, open space schools). Few of these technological innovations have been long-lived . The overhead projector is one of the few innovations which continues to be widely used.

Two potent forces are pressing schools and school systems to purchase and use computers for instructional and administrative tasks. First, federal and state politicians are demanding improved student performance, often through the use of standardized curricula and greater student testing. Second, local educators and lay boards are demanding improved student performance and tighter control over schools.

A growing national concern about the quality of American education is another impetus for the adoption of computerized, educational technologies. Beginning in 1983 with the National Commission on Excellence in Education report, "A Nation at Risk," which criticized the mediocrity in public schools, politicians and educators have been demanding reform. Governors of southern states, where student achievement has traditionally been the lowest in the nation, have made educational reform a top political priority. Tennessee,

Florida, North Carolina, and Arkansas have already passed major legislation supplying millions of dollars for improving the quality of education in their states. All include computer use as a central element of the reform.

Also, educators are raising demands for change. Quality control and productivity problems in the automobile and steel industries during the early 1980s raised citizen awareness which was transferred to education in the form of concerns over declining SAT scores. Consequently, superintendents are taking action to improve the quality of teaching in their districts.

Several policy changes developed from these concerns which have increased bureaucratization, centralization, and standardization of classroom processes in efforts to increase teacher accountability and control over teachers.[23] First, many state and local education agencies have developed standardized curricula for states and districts with clearly specified curriculum objectives for each grade. Second, some districts have established a standard model of teaching across the district.[24] Third, states and districts have centralized control by gathering measures of student performance and using them to assess schools, principals, and teachers.

Wise refers to these developments as the "hyperrationalization" of schooling, a process of standardizing the technology of teaching and the assessment of organizational productivity through rational decisions based on concrete goals and objectives. Computer usage is one outgrowth of hyperrationalization.[25]

A. Computers in Education

Computer-assisted instruction (CAI), computer-managed instruction (CMI), and computer-based management information systems (MIS) are the main computer applications in education. CAI includes a wide variety of activities such as direct instruction in a subject area, drill and practice of a skill, educational games, and the training of students in typing and computer programming. In these cases, computers replace or supplement the work of teachers or teaching assistants. CMI is used to monitor the amount of work completed by students, to record the skills they have mastered, and to specify grouping patterns. MIS is used by school districts for storing data on students such as skill mastery levels, performance on quarterly or annual tests, and progress in standardized curricula. Some principals use these data to supervise teachers and to group students for instruction[26]—what Williams and Bank have recently referred to as "information driven instruction" (IDI).[27]

[23]Arthur Wise, *Legislated Learning: The Bureaucratization of the American Classroom* (Berkeley: University of California Press, 1979).

[24]Kent Peterson, Joseph Murphy, and Phil Hallinger, *Perceptions of Superintendents Regarding the Control and Coordination of the Technical Core in Effective Districts*, Paper presented at the Annual Meeting of the American Educational Research Association (San Francisco, CA: 1986).

[25]Wise, *Legislated Learning*.

[26]Brian Rowan, R. Edelstein, and A. Leal, *Pathways to Excellence: What School Districts Are Doing to Improve Instruction* (San Francisco: National Institute of Education, 1985).

[27]Richard Williams and Adrianne Bank, "School Districts in the Information Society: The Emergence of Instructional Information Systems," *Administrator's Notebook* 31 (1983), pp. 1–4.

B. Development and Diffusion of Computers

Beginning in the 1950s, larger and more wealthy school districts often purchased their own machines or bought time-sharing from a larger computer company. These computers were used to store the massive amounts of data on students, record and track purchasing and inventories, and perform such complex calculations as scheduling of classes in large high schools.[28]

In 1960 Stanford University and others began developing and testing programs for teaching mathematics and reading to school children. By the late 1960s, experiments at Stanford, the University of Illinois, Florida State University, Texas, and several foreign universities showed that some forms of computer-based instruction had positive effects on student achievement.[29]

The cost of the terminals and computer time remained high for smaller school districts until the late 1970s, when developments in micro-electronics reduced the cost of mainframe computers and led to small, powerful "personal computers" (PCs). Most recent adoptions of classroom computer applications utilize PCs. The University of Illinois PLATO instruction system, which employs a large mainframe attached to individual terminals, is in place in several locations.[30]

The timing of computer adoptions varies by several school district characteristics. According to one study, the median year of adoption was 1972. Both district size, as measured by student enrollment, and wealth, as measured by per pupil expenditure, are related to date of introduction, with larger and wealthier districts being the earliest computer adopters. While the complex administrative problems motivated larger districts to adopt computers, the availability of financial resources facilitated adoption by the wealthier districts. Computers were adopted rapidly during the early 1980s. According to a survey conducted by Johns Hopkins University, the percentage of elementary schools with at least one computer increased from less than 7% to 42% between December 1982 and February 1983; among secondary schools, the percentage increased from under 25% to 85%.[31] A majority of schools now own microcomputers and the proportion is growing.

A nationwide survey found that computers were used for a wide range of administrative tasks. In a sample of 1,484 districts, 91.5% reported either administrative or instructional use of computers.[32] Of those districts reporting some use, 89.1% used them for payrolls and 83.5% used them for receipts and expenditures accounting. Only 65.8% reported complete test scoring and analysis by computer. In summary, school districts confine most of their

[28]Fred Hofstetter, *Computer Based Instruction: Roots, Origins, Applications, Benefits, Features, Systems, Trends and Issues*, (ERIC ED 231 343).

[29]Ibid.

[30]C. Victor Bunderson, "Courseware," in *Computer-Based Instruction*, ed. Harold F. O'Neil, Jr. (New York: Academic Press, 1981), pp. 114–115.

[31]Henry Jay Becker, "How Schools Use Micro-Computers," *Classroom Computer Learning* 2 (September 1983), pp. 41–44.

[32]Nancy Protheroe, Deirdre Carroll and Tracey Zoetis, *School District Uses of Computer Technology* (Arlington, VA: Educational Research Service, 1982).

Table 1. Percentage of Teachers Reporting "Regular" or "Intensive" Uses of Microcomputers at Their School[a]

Elementary	Percentage	Secondary
	85%	. . . . . Introduction to computers
	76%	. . . . . Programming instruction
Introduction to computers	64%	
Drill and practice	59%	
Programming instruction	47%	
Tutoring for special students	41%	
	31%	. . . . Drill and practice
	29%	. . . . Business ed/vocational
	29%	. . . . Programming to solve problems
Programming to solve problems	27%	
Recreational games	24%	
	22%	. . . . Demonstrations, labs, simulations
Demonstrations, labs, simulations	20%	. . . . Tutoring for special students
	19%	. . . . Recreational games
	15%	. . . . Teacher record keeping
	14%	. . . . Administrative use
Administrative use	10%	. . . . Teacher tests, worksheets
Teacher record keeping	7%	. . . . Student papers, word processing
Teacher tests, worksheets	5%	
Student papers, word processing	3%	

[a]From Henry Jay Becker, "School Uses of Microcomputers," *The Journal of Computers in Mathematics and Science Teaching* 3 (1983), p. 31. Reprinted by permission.

administrative computer use to the most rudimentary functions which require either storage of large data bases or analysis of complex mathematical problems (scheduling, for example).

Although many districts have computers, the number of students and teachers using these computers is relatively small. Nonetheless, computers are working their way into school districts and into the instructional lives of teachers, first as supplementary course offerings in computer literacy and then as part of the instructional process.

The actual use of microcomputers in schools is quite varied. In some instances, teachers use computers to teach students subject area knowledge and skills through drill and practice. Computers are also being sued for learning *about* the nature and applications of computers.

The application of microcomputers in schools varies by the type of school as shown in Table 1. In elementary schools, the most common uses are introducing students to computers, drill-and-practice, and teaching computer programming. In secondary schools, the most common uses are introducing computers to students, the teaching of programming, and drill-and-practice. Computers are less commonly used for instructional management activities such as producing worksheets and developing tests.

Computer usage patterns suggest that computerization is likely to have a greater impact on professional autonomy in elementary schools than in secondary schools. Elementary school teachers are more likely than secondary school teachers to use computer software with predetermined lessons in the teaching of subject areas. However, the proportion of classroom time devoted to computer use is relatively small. Microcomputers are used, on average, two to three hours per day (11 hours per week in elementary schools and 13 hours per week in secondary schools).[33]

In both elementary and secondary schools, the largest proportion of time seems to be spent in *computer*-specific, rather than *subject*-specific, activities. However, computer applications are rapidly increasing and are likely to occupy more and more instructional time.

VI. THE EFFECT OF TECHNOLOGICAL CHANGE ON TEACHERS AND PRINCIPALS

The effects of computerization, educational change, and pressures for increased control over classrooms and accountability for student performance are played out at both the national and the local levels. At the national level, computerization is beginning to raise labor relations issues for teachers. AFT and NEA statements and actions indicate "rumblings" over the potential loss of professional autonomy for teachers. As Scott has noted with other professionals, teachers may resist several changes in work, including the imposition of bureaucratic rules, standards, and increased supervision. As indicated by recently collected school district data, the issue of professional autonomy is also being addressed at the local level.[34]

A. Computers, Educational Reform and Teacher Autonomy: National Developments

Recently, the national educational reform movement has fostered considerable movement in the philosophical and strategic positions of the NEA and AFT. The NEA has increasingly taken a traditional collective bargaining approach, while the AFT has been calling for a "professionalization" of teaching. For example, while the NEA lobbied against educational reform programs in Tennessee and other states, the AFT, after initial neutrality, has supported many features of the reforms which are designed to enhance the professional status of teachers. Pronouncements by presidents of the NEA suggest that they oppose programs which include any form of differential salaries (a type of merit pay system for teachers), statewide or national testing of teachers, or career levels similar to those of university professors.

According to AFT President Shanker, increased professionalization of

---

[33]Becker, "How Schools Use Micro-Computers," p. 42.
[34]Scott.

teachers would foster greater involvement of teachers in the control of computer use and in the monitoring of colleagues. In April 1985, Shanker made several proposals to enact this reform which would move teachers closer to professional control of the occupation, and further from the traditional unionism espoused by the AFT.[35] These proposals include: (a) a national examination before entrance into the teaching profession; (b) a system to allow students to choose public schools they want to attend; (c) impartial panels of veteran teachers to evaluate the work of teachers accused of incompetence; (d) career ladders for teachers which would include teacher peer review; and (e) a restructuring of education which would encourage bright, young individuals to become teachers. Shanker argues that teachers must transform their traditional collective bargaining stances into professional structures in which teachers have a major role in setting educational policy and monitoring the profession.

Although there are no studies of the effect of computerization on NEA members or AFT actions, the different stances of the unions suggest that they may address the effects of computerization on teachers in different ways. The NEA, with its more protective, unionist stance, may desire small pay differentials and attempt to restrict the use of computers to the gathering, storing, and assessing of student performance data. Teacher classroom autonomy may be defended through collective bargaining and strike threats. In contrast, if Shanker is able to convince the rank and file of the AFT to professionalize the occupation, computerization may be used to rid the teacher of nonprofessional clerical work and to provide objective data on teachers with substandard performance for peer review.

Shanker has argued that teachers should identify and maintain control over those tasks which are uniquely complex and challenging. He argues that as a professional work force, teachers ". . . would be engaged not mainly in lecturing students but in actively coaching students, teaching thinking skills, stimulating creativity, working with students on rewriting papers, helping students learn to reason, argue, and persuade. No machine can replace teachers in these tasks . . ."[36] This implies further that computers would perform such mundane tasks as drill and practice and teaching simple concepts. Under these conditions, the challenge of the work, the status of teachers, as well as professional autonomy would be enhanced, rather than degraded.

As Shanker has written: "We will never convince the public that we are professionals—unless we are prepared honestly to decide what constitutes competence in our profession and what constitutes incompetence and apply those definitions to ourselves and our colleagues."[37] Computer-based data on student performance provide an objective measure of teacher effectiveness

[35]Gene Maeroff, "Teachers Told to Strive for Professional Status," *The Tennessean,* 28 April 1985; Albert Shanker, *The Making of a Profession* (Washington, D.C. American Federation of Teachers, 1985).

[36]Shanker, p. 22.

[37]Ibid, p. 18.

and could be used to evaluate teachers. If evaluation is controlled by the union, computer-based performance data provide objective and accurate means for peer review, a key step in the professionalization of the occupation. This suggests that the AFT may support diffusion of this technology more readily than the NEA, which views its role as protecting teachers from close evaluation.

B. Technological Change and Schools: The Local Level

While computerization may affect the ways the national associations exercise influence, it also affects the professional autonomy of teachers and their relations with superiors in local settings. Of particular interest are resistance and conflict that accompany technological change and the ways superiors have reduced conflict and stress. This analysis is based on data collected by Rowan and his colleagues[38] as well as data I gathered in 1985 from interviews with administrators, their assistants, and teachers in districts with extensive computerization. The districts were not randomly selected, but they constitute a purposive sample of unionized and non-union districts in several regions of the country.

When computers are used to teach new information, to practice skills, and to manage instruction, teachers face a new set of norms about their work and the autonomy they have traditionally enjoyed. Embedded in computer programs are the traditional decisions teachers make about the form, sequencing, and pacing of material as well as the ways students will be assessed and rewarded.

School principals in the districts studied reported that when school administrators incorporated CAI and MIS in their schools, initial teacher reactions were negative, distrustful, and fearful. Teachers distrusted the capacity of the computer to decide what to teach the student, how to react to wrong answers, and so forth. Also, they feared the loss of student–teacher attachments. Superintendents reported that teachers were less distrustful when teachers were included in the design or selection of the computer applications; granted the discretion to decide when and how to use the computer in their classrooms; and shown the importance of maintaining student–teacher attachments. For example, respondents in a Western district reported that resistance was lessened in schools where a new program led to improvements in student achievement. In another district, in which teachers developed teaching materials and monitoring processes for court-ordered academic improvement of minority students, early complaints turned to support when the materials and monitoring fostered higher student performance. It appears that technological changes which lessen professional autonomy are initially rejected by teachers. However, teachers may eventually support these changes if their involvement demonstrably improves student learning.

Nonetheless, conflict developed even when some teachers were involved

[38]Rowan *et al.*

in designing CAI and MIS programs. For example, in one district where teachers participated in the development of a computerized, elementary basic skills program, teacher opposition has been sustained by the continuing criticism of the local NEA chapter.

The administrators in the districts I sampled reported that initial teacher reaction to computerization was more positive when a teacher committee was directly involved in the decisions about choosing curriculum and teaching methods. In many districts, superiors allowed individual teachers to select the time when the computer program was to be used with their class. Negative teacher reactions to computerization, then, are reduced when teachers design the programs and have some discretion over their use in the classroom. In short, the issue of professional autonomy is lessened when teachers maintain control of teaching.

Using computers to collect, store, and assess data on student performance has affected teacher–principal relations. Teachers' traditional freedom from close, objective monitoring and evaluation is lost when student test results are used for teacher supervision. In districts with MISs, teachers spend much time teaching skills which are being measured, and exhibit stress from increased demands for performance. In several of the districts studied by Rowan and his colleagues, teachers and administrators mentioned increased stress, conflict and resistance when discretion in the selection of curricular content was lessened and monitoring of student performance was increased. Information from the districts I examined also supports these patterns. In virtually all the districts, such problems as fear, resistance, and conflict emerged when administrators implemented extensive new student testing programs and a centralized, standardized curriculum. Teachers feared job loss and declining professional autonomy.[39]

Local administrators have used several approaches to lessen fear, resistance, and conflict when instituting the use of computer-generated student performance data in the supervision of teachers. Four different approaches have been used, according to Rowan and his colleagues and my own observations.[40] First, in several districts, teachers saw that the use of this information was related to improved student performance, a goal they shared with their superiors. Second, the use of student performance data was restricted to informal supervision and was not included in final evaluations of teachers. Third, some districts involved teachers in decisions on the use of student performance data. Finally, several districts provided extensive assistance to teachers whose students were not performing well.

C. Computers and Professional Autonomy

Prior to having student performance data available on computers, teachers and principals had considerable control over the standards and data used

[39]Ibid.
[40]Ibid.

in teacher evaluation. With the advent of computers, this control is devolving to central administrators, district committees, or state departments of education.

Most teachers have considerable autonomy in selecting curricular goals or objectives. They decide on the knowledge that students should learn in the various subject areas and they select the skills to impart to students. In schools without computers, teachers and, at times, principals decide how frequently and in what ways to assess student performance. Following the advent of CAI and information-driven instruction, these decisions are often part of the computer program or established centrally by superiors alone or with teachers. "Mastery" levels are set and immutable and frequency of student evaluation is predetermined. Teachers have objected to the loss of this discretion by arguing that, as professionals they should make these decisions. In cases where the state has mandated these reforms, state teachers' associations have fought their imposition. Where local districts have instituted such standardization, local unions have attempted to limit their impact. In only a handful of the districts that I studied did teachers actively and wholeheartedly support these changes.

Also, before computerization, teachers decided how often superiors and others received these assessments. With the installation of management information systems, the decision-making about the accessibility of assessment data is transferred to administrators. Many of the superintendents I interviewed said that in order to avoid conflict they have not publicized this capability except in unusual cases of teacher incompetence or poor school-wide performance. Nonetheless, teachers were fearful that the data would be used to fire teachers whose students were not performing well.

All of these changes in the conditions of instruction, goal setting, and the monitoring of student performance affect teacher–principal relations, mainly because they are key components of teachers' work and beliefs about work. Increased standardization of goals and objectives for classroom teachers may adversely affect principal–teacher relations as teacher autonomy in selecting classroom goals decreases. Conflict arises over which teaching goals should be assessed in the tests. Little conflict occurred in the districts I studied where teachers helped to develop the goals. Standardization decreases teacher discretion in selecting classroom goals. However several of the districts I studied have allowed teachers to decide how to use computer programs and activities; in other cases, teachers sat on committees which made these decisions, granting teacher representatives at least partial control over teaching objectives and minimizing conflict. Declining teacher discretion has increased conflict. Conflict often develops when states or local boards try to standardize curriculum objectives across grade levels for all classes. Involvement of teachers in these decisions lessens that conflict.

While employees are usually reticent to receive negative feedback, some teachers accepted computer generated feedback more readily than previous subjective evaluations from principals who were not seen as instructional experts. Teachers were more accepting of feedback when they perceived that the information came from objective, reliable sources such as standardized tests. In addition, several of the districts combined performance evaluation with extensive assistance and support for teachers who wanted to improve their teaching skills.

All of these changes strain the relations between principals and teachers as professional autonomy is lessened. Though we have no specific data on the degree of professionalism of the teachers in the districts studied, it seems reasonable to assume that when teachers saw themselves as professionals, feedback about performance from valued superiors was more acceptable.[41] Under the conditions mentioned above, conflict has been lessened or even avoided when teachers retained some control over the use of the technology and could improve the quality of their work.

The increased use of management information systems to monitor and assess student performance increases the conflict between teachers and principals because it decreases professional control. Increased surveillance of this type increases teachers' fear about performance and job security, straining relations with their superiors. Indeed, most of the districts I studied abjure evaluation and have used these data only for supervision and feedback. In addition, this type of computer use increases centralization of control, which increases the tension between first-line supervisors and their employees. Again, when teachers are involved in determining these processes and the ways to assess outputs, initial fears and resistance sometimes turn to passive acceptance or support.

Resistance and conflict over computerization have been minimized when student test scores were used for diagnosing teaching and curricular problems and providing professional feedback about performance, rather than for accountability purposes. As Rowan and his colleagues note: "Because of the politically charged context of formal evaluation, many districts concentrate on revising supervision practices rather than formal evaluation practices."[42] In addition, informal norms of autonomy limited the degree to which superiors could change formal evaluation without incurring additional conflict over reforms in curriculum and instruction. The use of student performance data in this way may be viewed as a legitimate form of feedback by professionally oriented teachers. This is similar to what Scott discovered in his study of social workers.[43] Professionally oriented social workers accepted feedback from superiors if they viewed superiors as knowledgeable and objective. Teachers with professional orientations tend to view this information in a similar manner.

In summary, resistance and conflict over computerization has been minimized when superiors help teachers to see how these data can improve student performance; use student performance data only during informal supervisory conferences; involve teachers in the decisions regarding the use of

[41]Scott.
[42]Rowan *et al.*, p. 43.
[43]Scott.

these data; and provide assistance to teachers whose students are achieving at less than acceptable standards. Under these conditions computerization may, after initial resistance, be accepted by subordinate and superior alike. Without concomitant increases in the opportunity to engage in decisions and policy making and without the understanding that student performance data will help them to improve student learning, teachers will increasingly find working in schools less satisfying and more stressful, and their involvement with principals may become strained as their autonomy over basic work processes declines with increased supervision and evaluation.

VII. CONCLUSIONS

The fate of professional autonomy in organizations staffed by semi-professionals is yet to be decided. Traditionally, teachers, social workers, and nurses have been accorded considerable autonomy in their work. Few technological changes have occurred in organizations employing these workers. The recent increased use of computers in education has, for the first time, put the professional autonomy of teachers in jeopardy. Their use threatens to increase the control superiors have over teachers and decrease discretion over what is taught. Two central questions emerge when one examines the implementation of this technology. First, to what extent does the threat to professional autonomy stimulate actions by teacher unions and local associations to protect autonomy? Second, does implementation of this technology always lead to loss of autonomy?

The two national teacher associations have responded differently to the same problem—the loss of professional autonomy. The NEA has continued its collective bargaining approach in order to maintain teacher autonomy. In contrast, the AFT, while not discarding union action, is in the early stages of professionalizing the teaching occupation and wresting power from state and local authorities. At the local level, teachers have either resisted the use of computers or demanded a voice in determining how computers are used.

However, computerization has not necessarily jeopardized professional autonomy. Teacher responses to technological change are strongly affected by the manner of computer implementation. Conflict and resistance are lessened when teachers actively participate in decision making about the use of computers in classrooms and the way student performance data are assessed and communicated. In addition, when computer information on student performance is coupled with administrative support of teaching, teachers are often willing to accept computer-generated performance assessments.

The future course of labor relations in education will be affected not only by computerization, but, more importantly, by the amount of control enjoyed by teachers and administrators over the implementation of computers. Whether computerization engenders conflict or cooperation will depend on the efforts of the teachers' unions to preserve professional autonomy, as well as administrative efforts to involve teachers in computer implementation.

ACKNOWLEDGMENTS

While many have aided me in preparing this paper, I would like to thank Kathleen Burke for work in tracking down numerous sources, and Dan Cornfield, whose comments were helpful in an earlier draft of this chapter.

8

Technology, Air Traffic Control, and Labor–Management Relations

Arthur B. Shostak

Few episodes in modern labor–management relations so clearly illustrate the precarious nature of industrial peace and the ineradicable opposition of labor and management as does the 1981 strike of 11,500 air traffic controllers against the federal government.[1] Technological changes since the advent of this occupational role in the 1920s generated a labor relations situation that pitted the union's advocacy of professional (craft) self-determination against management's advocacy of bureaucratic/unilateral control . . .and the showdown in 1981 allowed for only one clearcut winner. Seldom before and never since in federal labor–management relations have the parties allowed their contract-bargaining strife to get so far out of control, and to require the unthinkable in mature collective-bargaining scenarios—or the pursuit of total victory. Seldom before and never since has the American labor movement been judged so harshly by the media, the lawmakers, the public, and even many dues-paying unionists.

I. INTRODUCTION

As the essay itself will help make clear, the evolution of controller technology explains much of the ensuing turmoil and eventual all-out confronta-

---

[1] I draw extensively hereafter on a book I have co-authored with a former controller and PATCO staffer, Dave Skocik, entitled *The Air Controllers' Controversy: Lessons from the PATCO Strike* (New York: Human Sciences Press, 1986).

Arthur B. Shostak • Department of Psychology and Sociology, Drexel University, Philadelphia, PA 19104.

tion between the labor relations equivalent of deadly enemies. Management, or in this case, the Federal Aviation Authority (FAA), operates under strong insistance by Congress and the public that risks in air travel be greatly reduced and the air control system have an extraordinarily high level of reliable performance over a considerable time period. The FAA has responded by upgrading hardware reliability, downgrading the discretion of controllers, and pursuing nearly error-free management and highly reliable organizational performance.

Labor, or in this case, the Professional Air Traffic Controllers Organization (PATCO), has naturally placed the highest possible value on user safety and risk reduction. But PATCO charged from its 1968 formation through to its 1982 decertification that the FAA was actually undermining the integrity of the air traffic control system, a charge that infuriated FAA careerists and sparked comparably bitter counter-charges in turn. PATCO insisted that everbetter hardware was increasingly available, but the politically-sensitive FAA shied from pressing Congress for multi-million dollar appropriations entailed in modernizing controller technology. PATCO also insisted that the discretion controllers had on the job was *the* key to split-second decisions that might save hundreds of lives, and the union therefore railed against the FAA's preference for a very tightly-run operation, a "top-down" authoritarian work culture that sought to keep controllers fully in line.

Not surprisingly, therefore, the White House decision in August of 1981 to push for the very destruction of the union drew on 13 years of acrimonious strife over how best to secure increasingly error-free performance in air traffic control. In pursuit of perfection in organizational performance the FAA had come to rely on information-rich computer-aided electronics, and the agency used this hardware to deskill and hamstring human controllers. PATCO, however, insisted this choice of managerial style robbed the workforce of exactly the craft, elan, and leeway earnestly demanded by the job. And the union urged concerned parties to realize that the social psychology of attentive behavior recommended reliance on high-spirited, well-rewarded, power-sharing professionals, rather than on the sort of docile, powerless, and utterly compliant employees the FAA seemed to prefer. PATCO charged that the interest of accurate navigation and the elimination of mid-air collisions were best assured by upgrading *human* resources, and not trusting instead to fancy high tech equipment, a fascination of FAA careerists who spoke longingly of a futuristic system free of all human controllers.

Given these deepset differences in perspective, the normality of conflict in air control labor-management relations becomes clear, as does also the problematic nature of cooperation in such relations. PATCO and the FAA were enmeshed in technological and economic relations which, by their very nature, contained powerful oppositional relations. The parties were unable to reach agreement or compromise on the answers to three overarching questions: How much leeway should human agents retain in an increasingly machine-reliant work process? How much input should the union have in management decisions about technological change? And how should labor and management treat negative stressors rooted in air control technologies? FAA answers represented one of the clearest declarations of "machine-over-man" ideology present on the contemporary scene, while PATCO took the opposite tack. When combined in 1981 with the advent of a new Republican presidency eager to send labor a "message," the elements were present for a historic clash of lasting significance to modern labor–management relations.

II. DEVELOPMENTS IN AIR CONTROL TECHNOLOGY

Every day of the year the nation's air traffic controllers practice a profession that "routinely makes them individually responsible for more lives than the practioners of any other occupation in the United States."[2] These "traffic cops" and "choreographers" handle nearly 200,000 takeoffs and landings daily, with over 415,000,000 passengers annually trusting totally to their craft . . .and to the remarkable technological infrastructure of the modern air control system.[3]

Back in the 1920s, however, the technology consisted largely of hand-held lanterns waved by anxious rural dwellers employed by the nation's first airmail carriers to help guide intrepid biplane aviators. The proto-controllers shooed cows off of primitive landing strips, lit bonfires when fog obscured the field, and telephoned occasional weather reports back and forth along the mail plane routes.[4] By the end of the 1920s, however, electric tower-mounted beacons had been placed along the routes, and rural dwellers had been upgraded to maintain 1,000-watt searchlights and radio timely weather reports the length of the route.

Technology made its first major impact on air traffic control (ATC) in the early 1930s with the development of a satisfactory aeronautical voice radio. This led the airlines to establish a single radio license for all member companies, and each line hired its own personnel for air–ground voice transmission. Selected, trained, and supervised differently by each airline, the nation's first air traffic controllers provided landing instructions, information on other traffic in the area, and wind direction and velocity data. By 1934 a rising volume of passenger traffic led the government to issue its first rudimentary regulations of air-ground voice transmission (as it pertained to directional altitude separation), and this initiative began the modern ATC regulatory system.

[2]Don Biggs, *Pressure Cooker: The Story of the Men and Women Who Control Air Traffic* (New York: W. W. Norton & Co., 1979), p. 11.

[3]See in this connection, House Committee on Public Works and Transportation, "Rebuilding of the Nation's Air Traffic Control System: Has Safety Taken a Back Seat to Expediency?", *Report of the House Subcommittee on Investigations and Oversight* (Washington, DC: Government Printing Office, 1985).

[4]For a thorough review of this history, see David Lowry Paden, "Air Traffic Control," Unpublished Ph.D. dissertation (Bloomington, Ind.: Indiana University, Graduate School of Business, 1962).

Two years later, in 1936, the government purchased America's first air route traffic control centers from the airline companies that had opened three in 1935. With the addition of five more by 1939, the system soon became nationwide, and the eight original controllers on board in '35 were eventually joined by several thousand others (13,000 by 1959, and nearly 17,000 at the time of the '81 strike).

Traffic densities in the 1930s were already beyond what visual flight rules (VFR) could sustain, and Instrument Flight Rules (IFR) were implemented to supplement the earlier "see-and-avoid" concept. Under IFR a pilot was to navigate by referring to cockpit instruments and by strictly following instructions from air traffic controllers on the ground: This new system guaranteed separation from other IFR aircraft and, to the extent practical, helped alert an IFR pilot to threatening VFR aircraft.

The "first generation" of separation service relied solely on radio and telephone communication, and it was not until the 1950s that this was significantly improved upon. Airport surveillance radars (ASRs) developed during WWII were introduced at all major airports, and by 1965 the Civil Aeronautics Authority (predecessor to FAA) had completed radar coverage of the continental United States. Radar contact is now kept with almost every IFR flight, though equipment failure occasionally forces fallback on the old pilot-controller radio system.

Throughout the 1950s controllers (and others) complained that reliance on raw radar returns entailed two major deficiencies, as both the altitude and identity of aircraft could not be learned. Remedied in 1958 by the addition of a transponder to aircraft themselves (capable of sending a code reply to ground ATC stations), this innovation was followed in short order by the development of digitized information systems and computer-driven traffic displays. A third technological breakthrough—known as automated flight plan processing and dissemination—joined the others in being known collectively as "the third (post-radar) generation of air traffic control."

All of these improvements, according to the Office of Technology Assessment, have led to a reduction of controller workload and have simplified and speeded up the acquisition of information. But they "have not substantially altered the decision-making process itself, which still depends upon the controller's skill and judgment in directing aircraft to avoid conflicts."[5]

More recently the FAA has increased its "R & D" investment in the "fourth generation" of separation service, one which could radically transform, if not substantially displace the vaunted contribution of human controllers; e.g., an improved form of radar would display much of the routine ATC information in the plane's cockpit, and thereby provide more complete and rapid exchange of information than the present voice radio method.

As well, collision-avoidance systems placed on board aircraft would effectively transfer to an IFR pilot some of the see-and-avoid responsibility that

[5]Office of Technology Assessment, *Airport and Air Traffic Control System* (Washington, DC: Government Printing Office, 1982), p. 35.

now governs VFR flight. Computer-dominated methods would also replace the traffic spacing and sequencing techniques now used by controllers to prevent traffic buildups or an undesirable mix of aircraft. The essence of the "fourth generation" is to transfer certain "routine" functions—such as separating or metering aircraft, and formulating and delivering clearances—away from controllers and over to computers.

Proponents believe a scenario of computer replacement could achieve several major benefits; e.g., significant gains in controller productivity; sizeable reductions in controller ranks (and related reductions in FAA personnel costs); reduction in user costs, thanks to wider use of fuel-efficient flight profiles; accommodation of more operations; and reduction in system errors (near-misses, mid-airs, etc.). Relieved of yesteryear's routine tasks, the "fouth generation" controller would serve primarily to handle exceptions and emergencies, and also oversee the automated ATC system . . .a far cry from the far more decisive and animated role still being played by controllers in the mid-1980's.

III. GROWING CONCERN WITH HARDWARE ADEQUACY

From its formation in 1968 through to its demise in 1982 PATCO was deeply concerned with the challenge posed by ATC technology and technological change.

Indeed, anxieties about the adequacy of ATC hardware predated the union's (related) formation. Twenty years earlier, in 1948, a major government report ("SC-31") caused quite a stir when it "blew the whistle" on an unsafe air travel system, even while exonerating the hard-pressed controllers: "The ATC tools available . . .are marginal, even by prewar standards . . .the only position information available to controllers . . .may be in error by many miles . . .the position estimates are manually posted, and estimates are made from these postings to effect separation of aircraft . . .the current system is cumbersome, but the controllers have conscientiously tried to keep it safe."[6] Congress rushed to increase upgrading appropriations in 1949 and '50, though at a level far below what the government investigators had recommended.

Not surprisingly, therefore, a second major government report seven years later (1955) found ATC technology less adequate than ever before: " . . .the risks of mid-air collisions have already reached critical proportions, and . . .the collision hazard is becoming greater as the increases in civil and military air traffic outpace the capabilities of outmoded traffic control facilities. The technical knowledge which is available has not been fully utilized, and the programs needed to meet our traffic control requirements have not been formulated."[7] The ATC equipment (ex-military radar systems stripped

---

[6]Quoted in U.S. Aviation Facilities Study Group, *Aviation Facilities* (Washington, DC: AVS Group, 31 December, 1955),p. 21.
[7]Ibid., pp. 1–4.

from naval aircraft carriers and terminated air force radar facilities) drove controllers wild with its unreliability and inadequacy. Moreover, although the jet age was clearly dawning in commercial aviation, over 99% of America's entire civil aviation system nevertheless remained on a *non*-radar basis . . .to the great unease of working controllers.

In June of 1956 two avoidable air tragedies in a 12-day period took 202 lives, and led an investigation team to conclude the system was "outmoded and overloaded" far beyond safety limits.[8] Public outrage forced Congress to authorize substantial funds to update ATC hardware (and add many more controllers to the rolls), a task turned over in 1958 to a new branch of government, the Federal Aviation Administration (FAA).

Within two years the FAA was warning Congress it still could not meet the needs of the ATC system: "On a typical day in 1960, there were nationwide more than 100,000 aircraft flights: FAA's capacity for providing instrument flight rule separation on a peak day was about 22,500."[9]

At about the same time the airline industry began to complain to the FAA about its fears of hardware-linked incidents; e.g., " . . .as traffic builds up there is a tendency to reduce the physical area for which each man is responsible. You introduce a need for coordination. And before long you have to coordinate the coordinators. This has been one of the most serious problems that we have been faced with—human frailties, over-burdening people with coordination."[10] As the volume of traffic expanded dramatically, and the mix of commercial versus pleasure craft grew more volatile, the call for technological improvements grew louder and more urgent . . .though Congress remained exceedingly reluctant to allocate new funds to meet the challenge.

It took still another avoidable air tragedy, a major mid-air collision in 1963, to awaken an interest in FAA policies among lawmakers, and what was uncovered shocked many concerned parties. An investigation team concluded that air travel remained unsafe because the FAA, the very body established to beef up the system, was operating instead to block overdue reforms and cover up a record of penny-pinching neglect. The team condemned the failure of the FAA to hire any new controllers for the past two years, and sharply criticized the agency's continued reliance on archaic and unsafe hardware (used and obsolete military castoffs).

Congress endorsed the report, and once again urged the FAA to use a new financial authorization to modernize ATC technology and provide controllers with the quality of hardware and software warranted by their responsibilities. By this time, however, the nation's air traffic controllers had grown

---

[8]Paden, "Air Traffic Control," p. 116.

[9]FAA, *Second Annual Report to the President and the Congress, 1960* (Washington, DC: Government Printing Office, 1961),p. 14.

[10]Francis M. McDermott, Executive Director, Air Traffic Control Association. Testimony in *Hearings* ("Air Safety", 1961), of the U.S. Senate (Washington, DC: Government Printing Office, 1961),pp. 848–9.

increasingly disillusioned with the FAA, and the ranks seethed with grievances; e.g., understaffed everywhere, controllers doubled up on sectors of airspace, although that left no one else to turn to when assistance was suddenly required. As the unofficial "law" of each facility was "never stop departures or arrivals," controllers took every aircraft they could . . .and many more than they should.

Controllers were still reliant on old-fashioned sweep radar screens, a throwback that pictorially represented aircraft moving at hundreds of miles per hour as indistinct blobs of light. At the busiest facilities they often struggled to hold in mind the position and details of a dozen or so aircraft, a task made no easier or safer for the public by ATC reliance on outmoded hardware. As well, FAA chiefs were allegedly under (unofficial) pressure not to report safety incidents or problems. Instead, they were to convey the impression of a smoothly running operation, the better to permit a relieved FAA to report as much to an appreciative Congress.

While knowledgeable parties recognized that accidents were the result of system errors, and that the air control system depended on a mix of weather, pilot reaction, aircraft performance, the controller, and luck, among its other components, the FAA invariably tried to place the primary responsibility or blame for mishaps on the controller involved. While longstanding bonds of friendship between controllers and their immediate supervisors helped mitigate some of this, the FAA's continued refusal to address complaints about counter-productive equipment and working conditions demoralized employees (and dedicated supervisors) at the local level.

Controllers who tried in vain to improve the situation found their professional associations reliant on very meek, mild, and thoroughly "wimp-like" methods—such as polite pleas for reforms delivered at congressional hearings, timid exploration of legal remedies, and the very cautious like. The FAA, in turn, singled out persistent "troublemakers" and whistle-blowers among the controllers for special treatment that led many to resign in disgust or defeat.

Slowly, however, a very small number of especially feisty and safety-conscious controllers, increasingly nervous about the adequacy of their equipment, began to organize in defense of their notion that public safety required better ATC staffing, superior system equipment, and FAA respect for controllers' needs. They noted that air operation traffic had increased about 100% in the 1960s, while the number of qualified controllers had increased only 10% (since the FAA had frozen ATC hiring from 1963 to 1967).[11] Similarly, although the system had lurched from disaster to disaster, the FAA and Congress were far too slow bringing it up to technological standards controllers judged indispensable.

---

[11]U.S. Congress, 91st Congress, 2nd Session, "Air Traffic Controllers." (*The Corson Report*), (Washington, DC: Government Printing Office, 1970).

IV. CHANGES IN AIR CONTROL LABOR RELATIONS

By 1967 the frequency and seriousness of equipment failure at the FAA's New York facility was more than could be tolerated by the leaders of a controllers' local (National Association of Government Employees). When radio frequencies failed or the radar went down, Jack Maher, the NAGE local president, took to blowing a loud and sustained blast on a horn to register his outrage with FAA facility management. Unable, however, to win hardware reforms in this way, Maher called his first-ever press conference, and "blew the whistle" about safety risks being needlessly run by the flying public in the New York City area.

While the local media appreciated Maher's facts, the FAA was furious, and he and others were threatened with dismissal for being disloyal troublemakers. They responded by forming the first regional organization of NAGE locals (albeit confined to the Greater New York area) and initiated unprecedented talks with other controller groups in Atlanta, Chicago, Newark, and Philadelphia. In January of 1968 Maher and a handful of colleagues drew over 600 controllers from across America to a kick-off function for their new creation, the Professional Air Traffic Controllers Organization (PATCO), a replacement for NAGE affiliation renounced now as far too placid and diffuse for controller loyalties.

PATCO signed up over 4,000 controllers within 30 days, and, at its 1968 constitutional convention, took two decisive steps linked to previous frustration with the FAA: A delegation of FAA supervisors lobbied to be allowed to remain as PATCO members, but were turned away in a narrow vote that hinged on anger over FAA failure to upgrade ATC equipment. And, in a related way, PATCO convention delegates approved a plan for an unprecedented nationwide "rulebook" slowdown, dubbed "Operation Air Safety," to help force the FAA to improve the ATC system. PATCO warned the public that current FAA standards on aircraft separation were inadequate, given the failure rate of existing ATC hardware, and from July 4th through late August the fledgeling organization conducted America's first controller job action.

Much to the delight of the anxious controllers "Operation Air Safety" was a success on every count, and the FAA felt obliged to meet several PATCO demands, chief among which was the reopening of the ATC Academy, closed for the previous seven years, and the recruitment of trainees to help relieve the dire under-staffing of the system. Congress was asked for $14 million for this by the FAA, and 1,000 new controllers were also hired.

On the heels of this welcome success PATCO moved in June of 1969 to conduct a nationwide sickout on behalf of further hiring and FAA reforms. This time, however, a poorly coordinated job action utterly failed, and 477 PATCO activists were suspended, fined, and humiliated by an outraged FAA. In addition, the union lost its highly valued dues checkoff privilege, the FAA contending that this recent job action proved PATCO was no longer a "professional association," but had transformed itself instead into a militant labor organization. As PATCO had not yet earned recognition by the Department of Labor as a bona fide labor union, the FAA felt itself under no obligation to go along with the prevailing dues checkoff system.

Morale received a welcome boost in January, 1970, with the release of the Corson Committee Report. Established in April of 1969 by the Secretary of Transportation to investigate the PATCO-FAA tension, the blue-ribbon group endorsed many of PATCO's major contentions; e.g., controllers were judged a unique professional group whose jobs required more of them than was true of most federal employees. Their work schedules were thought unnecessarily cruel in their impact on an individual's personal and family life. And the Corson Report concluded that controller morale was undermined by a fear of "burnout" between ages 40 to 50, and an inability to work thereafter at the one job they really wanted.

Reforms urged on the FAA included a sharp reduction in required work hours and required overtime, along with the substantial upgrading of ATC hardware and facilities. While PATCO was censured for "ill-considered and intemperate attacks on FAA management," the Corson Committee made much more of the failure of the FAA "to understand and accept the role of employee organizations."[12]

Unfortunately, the Corson Report produced little in the way of concrete results, though it may have helped PATCO rally initial rank-and-file support for its third national job action, a March 1970 sickout of five days' duration. Little went well with this ill-conceived campaign, however, and PATCO thereafter lost its status as a bargaining agent for 126 days. The union was left owing one million dollars in court fines and fees, and also came under a permanent injuncture barring it from ever again striking against the federal government.[13]

With the election in April, 1970, of PATCO's second president, John F. Leyden, the union's uncertain fortunes finally began to turn for the better. Leyden started his decade-long leadership tenure by spearheading the affiliation of PATCO with a powerful and well-off AFL-CIO international union, the 95-year old Marine Engineers Beneficial Association (MEBA). He then announced a 10-point program, one that included revitalization of PATCO by seeking victories without reliance on escalating job actions, and a greater voice for controllers in procedures, training, and the selection of new ATC technologies. Leyden proceeded next to secure official recognition for PATCO from the Department of Labor, thanks in part to the union's ties to MEBA, and to settle for $100,000 the $100,000,000 "sickout" damage suit filed by the Airline Transportation Association.[14]

In June of 1971, PATCO asked the Department of Labor to conduct its first-ever mail ballot in the public sector, and when 87% of the FAA's controllers voted in its favor, PATCO was granted exclusive recognition. The FAA

[12]Ibid. See also U.S. Department of Transportation, *The Career of the Air Traffic Controller—A Cause of Action* (Washington, DC: Government Printing Office, 1970).

[13]See the *Government Employee Relations Report*, No. 370, 12 October, 1970.

[14]Helpful in this connection is the 14 September 1970 issue of the *PATCO NEWSLETTER*.

reacted with pique, however, and reminded PATCO that only "professional societies," rather than labor unions, were thought suitable for discussion of such matters as technological reforms, equipment choices, and the like: Labor unions were restricted instead by the FAA to discussion only of work load terms, grievance processing, general working conditions, and so on. (As Congress alone could authorize wage increases, and as the Civil Service Commission governed the wage levels of federal workers, the FAA barred all talk with PATCO of wage increases and compensation reforms.)

PATCO moved next to win passage of a unique piece of "technology-taming" federal legislation, the Second Career Retirement Bill. The union insisted that an avoidable combination of negative job stresses and frequent equipment failures presently led many controllers to premature burnout, and these victims were owed a second chance at employability through two years of post-burnout subsidized vocational retraining. Whereas federal employees could retire at 60 years after serving 20 years, PATCO asked for eligibility for controllers at any age after 25 years, or age 50 at 50% of base salary, along with the Second Career aid. Although the bill passed in 1972, abuse that PATCO blamed on FAA mis-administration soon had Congress halt necessary funding, and the Second Career "cause" became a permanent feature of PATCO's new contract "wish list."

Early in 1973 PATCO initiated its first contract negotiations with a wary FAA, and won more than Leyden had dared hope; e.g., a dues checkoff, an improved grievance procedure, and contract language that allowed for on-site investigations of accidents by specially trained representatives of PATCO. This last concession bolstered the expertise of certain PATCO activists in ATC technologies, and helped invigorate the union's long-standing concern with the adequacy of FAA standards for hardware and software.

Relations between PATCO and the FAA took a strange turn in 1974 when a long-standing perk—the ability of a controller to fly free in the cabin of any domestic aircraft—was suddenly cancelled by the airline industry and the FAA acting together. PATCO characterized the perk as a valuable way for controllers to update their grasp of plane crew realities and changing aircraft technology. Detractors, however, dismissed it as a joyride frivolity, and it took a fourth (illegal) job action, a five-day PATCO "rule book" slowdown in September, to force the reinstatement of the controversial "familiarization" option.

After another brief and successful "rule book" slowdown in June of 1975, and a major PATCO victory on the wage front, the union negotiated its third contract with the FAA. This three-year agreement contained almost no gains of note, save one: PATCO secured a pledge that the domestic "familiarization" option would now be extended to overseas flights, and PATCO members could now extend their knowledge of aircraft technology to include ocean-crossing jumbos.

Unexpectedly, however, shortly after the contract's signing certain major airlines decided not to go along with the FAA on the overseas "FAM" option, and they refused to honor this vaunted new contract provision. Leyden saw this as a serious attack on the integrity of the entire contract, and warned that PATCO would not accept any meddling by the aircraft industry in the agreement it had hammered out with the FAA. Many PATCO members disagreed with Leyden's interpretation, and an ensuing "rule book" slowdown in the summer of 1978 was so poorly supported that the union finally conceded the matter.

Leyden's administration suffered a related setback thereafter when developments compelled it to renounce an FAA initiative, "Project Professionalism," which the union had initially welcomed. Leyden had long desired a chance to demonstrate that PATCO and the FAA could cooperate to their mutual advantage. He was especially interested in reaching joint agreements about upgrading the quality of FAA facilities and ATC technology, as he was convinced working controllers had many sound ideas and insights to contribute to decision-making in these matters. Certain anti-PATCO facility chiefs, however, allegedly used "Project Professionalism" to disregard the labor contract and harrass PATCO supporters. After six months of monitoring implementation, PATCO reluctantly withdrew its support . . .and Leyden's advocacy of collaboration with the FAA was decisively hurt.

Relations soured throughout the rest of 1978, and provocations followed rapidly on one another's heels, or so PATCO militants insisted; e.g., agreement reached two years earlier with the FAA to liberalize the dress code for controllers ran into more and more management resistance, and it became necessary to arbitrate the use of blue denim, khaki slacks, and other departures from the "IBM"-style of dress preferred by the FAA. While PATCO won many of its grievances, relying on the "neat-and-clean" provision of the contract, Leyden insisted this entire flap distracted urgent attention from more vital matters like hardware inadequacies and other threats to the public's safety.

Congress cut off all funding for PATCO's Second Career Program, and the FAA rushed to attribute this to anger on the Hill over the union's FAM slowdown. Leyden vigorously denied any connection, and urged the FAA to join PATCO in saving this program . . .an idea the FAA ignored and Leyden's detractors within PATCO held up to ridicule. Indeed, after months of equivocation the FAA came out clearly against any resumption of the Second Career option with testimony that, according to outraged PATCO writers, "impugned" the reputation of the controller workforce by characterizing them as "thieves or con men . . ."[15]

Still more troublesome were FAA changes that bore directly on PATCO's many grievances with ATC technology; e.g., the FAA's 1980 budget asked for more than a doubling in the number of Terminal Radar Service Areas, and an expansion of control in the enroute portion of flight. At the same time, however, the FAA proposed only a token increase in the number of air traffic controllers. Additionally, a three-year-old program that assured controllers immunity from reprisals for reporting "incidents" and unsafe conditions was

[15]*PATCO Newsletter*, August, 1979,p. 2.

targeted by the FAA for termination. PATCO urged its retention as the only way to get an accurate "reading" on the strengths and weaknesses of existing ATC technology—but the FAA persisted with its cancellation plans.

Little wonder, accordingly. that the 1979 PATCO Convention cheered in angry agreement with keynote speaker Congressman William Clay (D-Mo.) when he insisted there was no great American dream for federal employees, but ". . . just a series of annually unfulfilled priorities which add up to one gigantic nightmare."[16]

Unrest grew steadily in the ranks throughout 1979, as Leyden's inability to stem PATCO's backward slide became more vexing. Talk grew bolder and more frequent about the need to switch to increasing militance rather than rely on a mixture of occassional militant acts diluted by a predominantly conciliatory stance, as preferred by Leyden.

Controllers disillusioned with the FAA response to Leyden's approach found a champion in PATCO's 10-year Executive Vice-President, Robert E. Poli. Matters came to a head in January, 1980, when a very troubled Executive Board voted "no confidence" in the incumbent, and turned the leadership over to Poli, a far more feisty and assertive type of leader.

PATCO now had 90% of the ATC work force in voluntary union membership, a remarkable vote of support from its 14,500 members (whose dues provided the union with over $5,500,000 annually). As well, the union boasted a $3,500,000 cash balance, with almost as much in its strike fund.[17] All was in readiness, in short, for a major test of Poli's contention that the FAA had to be taught a decisive lesson, once and for all, about where power *actually* resided in the modern ATC system . . .and how indispensable were experienced, dedicated controllers.

The FAA, in turn, waited only two months after Leyden's ouster to create an unprecendented Strike Contingency Force, and both sides hunkered down to do battle.

V. THE 1981 NEGOTIATIONS

PATCO put a list of 99 contract demands on the table in 1981, and tried thereby to make the point that its legitimate needs had gone unmet for so long that the negotiations agenda had to be a *very* lengthy one. In truth, as is standard in the theatrics and give-and-take of collective bargaining, the union hoped to win major concessions only where the top three or so demands were concerned. And, in keeping with the frustrations controllers had expressed to PATCO activists, the top three issues all focused on technological matters of consequence.

For openers the union demanded wage parity with pilots of commercial

[16]*PATCO Newsletter,* June, 1959,p. 15.

[17]Herbert R. Northrup, "The Rise and Demise of PATCO," *Industrial and Labor Relations Review* 37, no. 2 (January 1984),p. 173.

airlines, an issue that translated into an opening bid for a $10,000 across-the-board wage increase. PATCO knew the sum looked ridiculously high, and many officers had misgivings about media and public hostility. But a vast majority of rank-and-filers firmly believed the technologies of the cockpit, the tower, and the radar room were more similar than different, and controllers resented a ceiling of $50,000 on their FAA earnings while pilots drew $80,000 or more annually.

A second major demand sought to reduce the number of work hours required every week of the controllers. PATCO cited the example of its counterparts overseas who had far shorter requirements, as in Switzerland (38 hour work week), Australia (35 hours), Canada (34 hours), West Germany (33 hours), France (32 hours), and Eurocontrol (29 hours). Since the technology was the same or similar in all of these countries, PATCO insisted its 40-hour work week be reduced to a four-day 32-hour schedule, a far-reaching demand that irritated the media and public almost as much as did the $10,000 salary demand.

Finally, PATCO asked for the liberalization of provisions for retirement from FAA service. Under the expired contract a controller could retire with half pay at age 50 if he had 20 years service, or at any age if he had 25 years. PATCO insisted FAA technology was now so out of date and inadequate to the situation that controllers were losing their capacity to do the job at an even earlier age. Accordingly, the union asked for retirement eligibility after only 20 years of service at any age, and at 75% of base salary.

Not surprisingly, the FAA loudly and harshly rejected all three main union demands. Instead, the management team countered with an offer of $2,200 (plus $1,800 that was being promised to all government workers), a refusal to reduce work hours at all, and a refusal to change retirement terms. Convinced that any liberalization of these matters would violate President Reagan's insistance that expenses be held down, the FAA stonewalled without apology.

PATCO fared no better with a second tier of demands known as "social contract" issues, all of which connected to deepset technological stressors; i.e., (1) *Voluntary Re-assignment:* The union sought to establish transfer rights for controllers unable to take the pressure of any particular post; PATCO insisted that this option include full protection for present salary and benefits, regardless of the financial specifics of the requested post. (2) *PATCO Office Space:* The union, fearing that local FAA supervisors could evict PATCO locals from the tiny offices allowed them at large facilities, sought an ironclad guarantee of office space from which to conduct on-site union–management discussions. (3) *Equipment Choice:* PATCO asked for a role in the selection of all new technology (hardware and software), the better to incorporate the savvy and experience of on-line controllers in the upgrading of the entire system. Each of these contract demands was summarily rejected by the FAA negotiating team, and the union announced a strike deadline (June 22).

At the very last moment, in early-morning bargaining only hours before the strike was scheduled to begin, the FAA reluctantly agreed to three concessions. In place of the $10,000 increase PATCO sought, the FAA would ask Congress for a 10% pay hike for the controllers (or about $4,200 stretched out over three years), and a 5% boost in the night pay differential (to 15%, from the present 10% level). In place of a 32-hour shorter work week, the FAA would pay time-and-a-half after 35 hours (but still require 40). And, in place of liberalized retirement, the FAA would ask Congress to improve retraining benefits for "burned out" controllers (as part of a program Congress had stopped funding a year earlier). PATCO reluctantly gave tentative approval (after the rank-and-file had narrowly rejected a strike vote hours earlier), and it briefly looked as though a resolution had actually been achieved . . .though a formal contract vote by controllers still lay ahead.

Union members who campaigned in favor of ratification hailed the fact that PATCO had achieved a milestone: the union had gotten the FAA to actually negotiate about compensation, something the agency had always previously refused to do, insisting that only the Civil Service Commission could set and change compensation terms. PATCO had now achieved an unprecedented degree of (apparent) separation from the dictates of an aloof and unsympathetic Commission, even while remaining within the federal sector—a victory of real value (provided, however, that Congress later went along with any ensuing FAA request for funds to make good the new contract terms).

Opponents of ratification pointed out the absence of significant FAA concessions on PATCO's top three contract demands. They insisted the union would lose credibility and vital support if it meekly accepted the grossly inadequate FAA version of a reasonable contract. They warned that PATCO would be ridiculed both within and outside the air control system, and they anticipated harsh treatment of union activists at the local level by gloating FAA personnel if the union meekly "surrendered." Without winning reduced work hours and a more liberal retirement plan, along with a long overdue say in technological decision-making, PATCO could not face its membership—or so the militants argued.

When the entire matter was put to a vote of the membership on July 30, 1981, some 95% endorsed the arguments of the PATCO militants—and turned thumbs down on the proposed contract.

Both sides returned to negotiations, with the FAA declaring from the start that it would make no further concessions. PATCO lowered its bargaining demands from the intial $775 million price tag down to $490 million, and dropped its request for a new top-level salary from an initial $79,000 down to $59,000, but the FAA continued to offer only its earlier $40 million settlement and no meaningful changes elsewhere in the contract.

Particular attention was paid by both sides to the acrimonious issue of debilitating job stress and its pragmatic relief. PATCO insisted that controllers deserved benefits given no other federal employees because their stress toll was unique, toxic, and preventable. The union castigated the FAA for forcing controllers to rely on outmoded radar and computer hardware; to serve on night shifts on a rotating, rather than on a voluntary basis; to fill in for ailing co-workers on an obligatory, rather than on a voluntary basis; and in other capricious ways, to exacerbate the negative stress inherent in the job.

The FAA, in turn, ridiculed the union's entire position in the matter, and insisted that work place reactions to stress were simply a matter of individual coping styles, simply a personal reaction. The agency noted that its five-year, $2.5 million study of controller stress had found no direct link of hypertension to the job (an interpretation the author of the study, Dr. Robert M. Rose, publicly refuted!).[18] The agency asked how the job could be so debilitating and yet still command the strong allegiance of jobholders, even as thousands annually sought to join their ranks. And the agency insisted that medical proof of the job's stress hazards remained "conspicuously elusive."[19]

Stymied in this way, the opposing sides gave no ground. And, on August 3, 1981, PATCO succeeded in drawing 85% of its 14,500 members into the first-ever 50-state strike of the nation's controllers against the FAA.

VI. PATCO DECERTIFICATION

As is now well known, President Reagan almost immediately moved against PATCO on several fronts; e.g., Justice Department lawyers had the courts freeze the $3-million union strike fund, and PATCO was never able to draw on these critical dollars; Justice Department agents arrested 30 PATCO local activists across the country, and thereby struck at morale in the ranks; and a federal court hit the union with a $4,750,000 contempt-of-court fine for violating a 1970 injunction against ever again striking, while another court slapped a fine of $100,000 an hour as long as the strike ran, and also ruled that PATCO was liable for millions of dollars in daily losses suffered by the carriers.

President Reagan himself went on television to warn just four hours into the strike that any controllers who did not report for work within 48 hours would be fired. Off camera the President authorized a request to the Federal Labor Relations Board to initiate decertification proceedings against the union.

PATCO had anticipated, and had prepared to sustain most of these blows, though its lawyers had thought the $3 million strike fund would be immune to seizure, and its leadership had not expected the President (who had received the union's election endorsement eight months earlier) to come down as hard as had happened. PATCO's ranks remained firm, however, and only 1,300 strikers scurried back in before the 48-hour "window" slammed closed. With over 11,400 men and women continuing to stay away from their posts, the union still hoped for a swift and decisive victory.

---

[18]See in this connection, the House Committee report, "Rebuilding of the Nation's Air Traffic Control System," as cited in footnote 3. See also Frank Van Riper, "Doc: Controllers Don't Hate Jobs," *N.Y. Daily News*, 7 August 1981, p. 20.

[19]As cited in *PATCO Newsletter*, August 1979, pp. 5, 7.

What PATCO had *not* anticipated was the newfound ability of the FAA to turn technology decisively against the strikers.

In 1980 the FAA had published a strike contingency plan that set very low targets for strike-time air traffic, and would have meant very severe disruptions in passenger, mail, and freight service. After the June 22 down-to-the-wire drama of the near-strike, the FAA secretely assigned staff specialists to revise the 1980 document, with the advice, this time, of the major airlines. The new plan, completed only hours before the August 3 strike began, was a substantial improvement, in that the FAA now could use its computers to spread out the sharp concentration of arrivals and departures it had previously tolerated in daily operations. Its new "flow control" plan, one that PATCO had unsuccessfully advocated for years, flattened the "peaks" and "valleys" of traffic, and substantially improved the FAA's ability to keep the system going without the aid of the striking controllers.

PATCO had expected the FAA to fail when it became reliant on the well-known 1980 contingency plan. The agency took the union completely unawares with its flow control update, and this computer-driven, 24-hour, controlled-from-headquarters schedule enabled the FAA to handle 83% of the system's former traffic load with less than 50% of its pre-strike work force.

Effectively neutralized by the FAA's flow control surprise, PATCO was left with only three other possible routes to victory: AFL-CIO unions could force the FAA to shut down the system, or overseas unions of controllers could produce the same outcome, or desperate PATCO members could resort to "dirty tricks" to force a resumption of collective bargaining.

Considerable debate ensued among labor's leadership, as most immediately recognized the strategic importance to all of this first-ever showdown with the new Republican president. PATCO, however, was widely disliked for its notorious haughtiness, its blithe indifference to the airport picket lines of other unions, and its recent endorsement of Reagan. In short order the Airline Pilots unions sided with the FAA, while the Machinists Union indicated it would strike to back PATCO *only* if other relevant unions also pulled their people out. This lack of support from two unions which, alone or together, could have won the strike for PATCO in 24 hours, shut off this route . . .and forced PATCO to settle for only $840,000 in strike aid, sympathy picketing, and supportive rhetoric, in place of the decisive sympathy *strikes* the controllers desparately needed.

Overseas unions of controllers in Canada and Europe responded just as years of PATCO spadework had planned, and for two highly-charged days in mid-August it looked as though the FAA might have to concede to this outside pressure. Taking a note from the Reagan example, however, governments abroad quickly cracked down on their own controllers, and harsh threats of firings and fines soon had air travel flows back to normal. Briefly, all too briefly, it looked as though the dream of achieving concerted and effective action by allied jobholders across national borders might be realized . . .but the reality proved quite fragile. And PATCO was forced once again to settle for mere financial contributions, messages of fraternal support, and sympathetic rhetoric, in place of the decisive, flow-disrupting aid the controllers desparately needed.

As for the third and last desperate option, the use of sabotage and other ultra-militant acts, very few PATCO activists took this seriously enough to consider it aloud. By temperament and training the strikers were thoroughly committed to the safety of the "S.O.B.'s" (Souls-on-Board) they routed daily through the skies, and would therefore do *nothing* that might jeopardize air travel. As for damaging the cars, homes, or person of the "scabs" now undermining the strike's slim chances, the risk of public censure and jail sentences discouraged all such mean-spirited gestures . . .although FAA publicists made the most of isolated incidents of misbehavior.

Instead, PATCO turned its energies toward TV and press relations, lobbying on the Hill, using secret intermediaries to seek a deal with the White House, and, most of all, propping up the morale and (dwindling) resources of the strikers.

Little changed over the following months, as the FAA steadily rebuilt a post-PATCO system into a seemingly smooth-running (flow control) operation. Many strikers persisted in believing the system could not operate safely and economically without their talent, experience, and craft, though the harsh denial of unemployment benefits, food stamps, and public assistance took a heavy toll on their morale. In October, 1981, the 13-year-old union was formally decertified, the first time the new Federal Labor Relations Authority had stripped a union of its bargaining rights. In December, 1981, PATCO president Robert E. Poli resigned in hopes that his leave-taking might make reinstatement discussions possible (the FAA refused to budge on the matter). And in July, 1982, the organization Poli had earlier characterized as not so much a union as it was a "religion" to its 14,500 members, stopped being at least an operating union altogether.[20]

VII. LABOR–MANAGEMENT CONFLICT OVER WORK PLACE CONTROL

While the PATCO saga warrants far more detail and discussion, some of which can be found in my co-authored 1986 book, *The Air Controllers' Controversy,* enough has been told above to permit an attempt now at answering the overarching questions posed at the start of this essay.

To begin with, the FAA and PATCO differed profoundly in their notion of how much leeway human agents should retain in an increasingly machine-reliant work process. The FAA sought a very high level of reliable organizational performance over a considerable length of time. The agency believed that this required fully deployed, high risk technologies that operated without significant error, a prescription with which PATCO would agree. But the

---

[20]As quoted in Fuerbringer, Jonathan. "Militant Controller Chief." *N.Y. Times,* 4 August 1981, p. B-8.

FAA also believed this required a "spit-and-polish" regimen of tight control and minimum discretion on the part of employees, a prescription with which PATCO ardently disagreed. The union insisted that only human agents, and not "smart" technology, could adapt to unpredictable deviations from the norm that ceaselessly threatened the fragile and complex operation of the system.

Second, the FAA and PATCO disagreed about the input the union should have in management decisions about technological change. Over the course of its 13-year history PATCO made much of the fact that its members regarded the job as a "calling," loved its zest and challenge, and took considerable pride in knowing every last mechanical detail possible about system hardware and software. Accordingly, the union urged the FAA to recognize that controllers could make a unique and invaluable contribution to decision-making about technology purchases. Indeed, controllers subscribed to industry magazines, traded technical info with overseas counterparts, and in other relevant ways strove to have a high-quality grasp of technological options confronting the FAA, despite the agency's stubborn refusal to recognize or utilize any of the (unauthorized) expertise of its front-line air traffic controllers.

Finally, the FAA and PATCO strongly disagreed about how to treat negative stressors rooted in air control technologies. The FAA denied any link between system hardware and role stress. The agency scoffed at stories of excessive stress in the health profile of controllers, though it denied being indifferent to PATCO's contrary assertions in the matter. The union, in turn, linked debilitating stress to the unreliability of outmoded FAA hardware, the absence of flow control regulations, and the paramilitary supervisory style of the agency. Neither side recognized any merit in the other's position, and little or no progress was possible in the relief of unnecessary stress in the occupation.

With the complete and utter defeat of PATCO, the FAA was left totally in charge of the nation's air traffic control system: Two ensuing developments have shed valuable light on the pivotal role technology has continued to play in the systems' work realities.

While still insisting that stress levels here are unexceptional, the FAA has implemented a thoroughgoing program of personnel relations reforms. Agency facilities across the country now have Human Relations Committees and Facility Advisory Boards, along with outside consultants hired to advise and educate both management and staff on how to improve employer–employee relations. A revised program of management training places fresh emphasis on cordial techniques for handling people, and an employee rights handbook has been developed.

Critics, however, dismiss all of this as gimmickry, window-dressing, and fraud. They point to Congressional testimony in 1984, '85, and '86 from angry working controllers who feel betrayed by the FAA, controllers who rejected PATCO in the belief that the agency would do well by them if only the union disappeared. These individuals now report that their lack of collective countervailing power has left them entirely at the mercy of local supervisors who treat them much like cogs in an (inhuman) machine.[21]

In a related development, while still insisting that everything is just fine and perfectly under control, the FAA has announced its intention to hire 1,000 more controllers (no strikers!) as soon as possible.[22] And, while still insisting that the computer equipment PATCO damned remains perfectly adquate, the FAA has asked Congress to approve new taxes to cover $20,000,000,000 in capital improvements over the next 20 years . . .as in replacing "horse-and-buggy" computers of 1960s vintage at 20 traffic control centers.[23]

Since the PATCO debacle, in short, the FAA has sought to address leading PATCO criticisms without appearing to do so . . .a guileful strategy that has led to scathing congressional criticism for not going far enough toward participatory reforms, and to persistent unrest among working controllers themselves. Coursing through all of this has been word of new "R & D" gains toward the logical end of the FAA's historic approach to air traffic control, or the perfection of artificial intelligence systems capable of linking airborne computers with ground control computers, independent of human intervention.[24] This man-less technological wonder may be another decade or more in development, but the FAA has long before signalled its willingness to wait it out . . .so appealing is the prospect.

VIII. CONCLUSION

From the earliest years of air traffic control to the present, the nature of the system's dominant technology has profoundly altered employer–employee relations. More than any other labor union in modern American history, the controllers' union risked everything to promote its ideas about man–machine relations . . .and lost.[25] PATCO sought a significant role for its members in technological decision-making, the better to help ensure system productivity, safety, and dynamism. Its defeat in an epic struggle has left the FAA entirely to its own devices, a major test of the ability of a large bureaucracy to do without a labor union with which to "co-manage" the workplace. More significant yet is the agency's campaign for a workerless air control system, a futuristic possibility with far-reaching, job-destroying implications in and outside of the air control system.

There is much to watch carefully in this ongoing matter, for the near

---

[21]See testimony in the House Committee report detailed in footnote 3.

[22]Reginald, "FAA to Increase Air Controllers," *N.Y. Times,* 20 September 1985,p. A-16.

[23]Richard Witkin, "Revamping of Air Control System in Next 20 Years Proposed by U.S." *N.Y. Times,* 29 January 1982,p. A-14.

[24]See in this connection, Paul Kinnucan, "Building a Better Cockpit," *High Technology* (January 1986),pp. 48–54; Kevin McKean, "A Traffic Cop in the Sky." *Discover* (August 1984),pp. 26–29.

[25]For another assessment, one which argues that the strikers were actually the only "winner," see Arthur B. Shostak, "Second Thoughts about the PATCO Strike," *Social Policy* (Winter, 1986),pp. 22–28.

future should reveal whether the FAA's reforms are adequate to hold off the re-unionization of its workforce. We will also learn whether the system can safely handle the *doubling* of air traffic expected over the next 20 years. And we will find out whether a rapidly expanding system is best served by the steady dilution of the controllers' leeway—as the FAA prefers—or, by a fresh renaissance in the role of a *human* air traffic controller, one represented by a union successor to PATCO committed to keeping talented people, rather than high tech, essentially in charge.

III

Toward Labor–Management Cooperation?

The chapters in Part III cover industries in which labor and management have established diverse forums for labor participation in company- and industry-wide managerial decision making, especially during the 1970s and 1980s. These forums for labor–management cooperation include joint committees for researching and resolving productivity, job security, finance, marketing, and quality of work life problems; joint efforts at lobbying the government for legislation and policies that would buffer the industry from marketplace adversity; and/or worker representation on company boards of directors.

All of these industries are characterized by three features which together have motivated and facilitated the development of labor–management cooperation. First, each of these industries has recently faced an external threat to industry profits and job security. Among the many external threats are increased foreign competition in national or world product markets which were once dominated by U.S. producers, as in the coal mining, automobile, steel, construction equipment, and aircraft industries (Chapters 9–13); and government disinvolvement in an industry through the "privatization" of services or the deregulation of entry, which have increased domestic, non-union competition for the major, unionized producers in some industries such as public sanitation and telecommunications (Chapters 14 and 15). Second, all of these industries have stabilized employment in internal labor markets with elaborate systems of non-portable seniority rights, vesting the long-term interests of workers in the survival of their employers and motivating workers to participate in managerial decision making during periods their industry is in jeopardy. Finally, these industries have been highly unionized for some 40 to 50 years, providing workers with the bargaining strength to demand representation in managerial decision making.

Under these conditions, technological innovation is one method for restoring industry competitiveness, and thereby serves the interests of both management and labor. However, technological innovation also displaces workers, threatening labor's interest in maintaining job security. Labor–management cooperation, then, has emerged in industries where both parties are motivated to restore industry competitiveness and where labor has sufficient bargaining strength for gaining some control over the implementation and outcomes of technological change.

9

Changing Technologies and Consequences for Labor in Coal Mining

Richard A. Couto

I. INTRODUCTION

The relations of coal miners and coal managers have always been of central importance in American industrial history. The production of coal measured America's industrial growth and economic power[1] and the relations of miners and managers marked the changed relationship of workers and owners as America's industry changed. This history is familiar. Miners began to organize during the Civil War and were among the first workers to do so. Their efforts met with unexceeded force and resistance from owners. Battles and even "wars" in the coal fields mar American industrial history.[2] Later, the union of coal miners led in the formation of the Congress of Industrial Unions and produced leaders of the AFL and CIO in the 1930s and 1940s.[3] At the same time, the United Mine Workers of America (UMWA) acquired a degree of organization among workers in a single industry tantamount to a closed shop. Through this achievement miners acquired unprecedented wage and benefit agreements. The power of the union was so great that in November

[1]David S. Walls, *Central Appalachia in Advanced Capitalism: Its Coal Industry Structure and Coal Operators' Associations*, dissertation (University of Kentucky, Department of Sociology, 1978), pp. 123–153.
[2]Joseph E. Finley, *The Corrupt Kingdom: The Rise and Fall of the United Mine Workers* (New York: Simon & Schuster, 1972), pp. 120–35.
[3]Ibid., pp. 26–7.

Richard A. Couto • Center for Health Services, Vanderbilt University, Station 17, Nashville, TN 37232.

1946, the *New York Times* had this worried headline, "25,000,000 (Workers) May Be Idle If Coal Strike Is Prolonged."[4]

The power of the UMWA during and after World War II worried some and gave hope to others. Miners struck regularly during World War II and their action and power were largely responsible for the National Emergency provisions of the Taft-Hartley Act which was used three times against the UMWA between 1948 and 1950.[5] John L. Lewis, president of the UMWA, was widely recognized as the leader of the coal industry and blamed for its decline. These claims inspired scholarly rebuttals that the union did the economy no harm and that such claims were related to political attempts to undermine unions.[6] Many came to the defense of the UMWA because they saw in unions in general, and the UMWA in particular, hope for a democratic and progressive America in which working class Americans would have the means to improve the conditions of their labor and achieve a higher standard of living.[7] The controversy surrounding the UMWA immediately after World War II has echoes which can be heard today in discussions about the health of the American economy and balances of power between workers and managers.

The relations of coal miners and coal managers since World War II in the bituminous coal industry remain of central importance because they continue to mark the course of American industrial development. The coal industry dealt with and continues to deal with a set of challenges facing workers and managers in other industries. These include market dislocation, competition from imports, product substitution, a serious decline in production, and a corresponding demand for new technologies and increased labor productivity. Managers organized associations to foster technological change and to limit competition among themselves. Miners cooperated with managers in an effort to introduce new production techniques and today American coal mining ranks high in labor productivity among American industries and far above coal mining in other countries. After this cooperation and transition, the major union of mineworkers, the United Mine Workers of America (UMWA), has only a fraction of its former power. Indeed, on the eve of the nation's longest coal strike in 1977–8, the *Wall Street Journal* had this assuring headline—"Coal Miners May Walk Out in December, But Impact Won't Be What It Used To Be." A *New York Times* editorial made the same assessment and measured the difference 30 years had made.

> Whereas once the United Mine Workers of America and its autocratic president John L. Lewis could tie the nation in a knot with the mere threat of a strike, this

[4]Curtis Seltzer, *Fire in the Hole: Miners and Managers in the American Coal Industry*, (Lexington: The University Press of Kentucky, 1985), p. 58.

[5]John A. Ackerman, "The Impact of the Coal Strike of 1977–8," *Industrial and Labor Relations Review* 32, no. 2 (January 1979), pp. 175–7.

[6]Morton S. Baratz, *The Union and the Coal Industry* (New Haven: Yale University Press, 1955), p. 151.

[7]Finley, *The Corrupt Kingdom*, p. 9.

week Arnold Miller . . . called a strike, but the nation is not particularly worried—indeed it is hardly concerned.[8]

The change of the UMWA's power is only one part of a set of important and unintended consequences in the response of miners and managers to their industry's needs. The efforts of miners and managers also illustrate that the costs of industrial transitions in terms of structural unemployment may be exorbitant. In addition, the accord of miners and managers which permitted the extensive technological change in mining also changed the relations of union officials toward their own members. The union experienced a degree of corruption and of democratic reform which are unique.

The organizations of miners and managers and their relationships changed in response to changes within and external to the coal industry. It is important to stress that managers in the coal industry have changed as well as miners and that technology was only one factor in their relations. Other factors which changed relations among and between miners and managers that are discussed here include the following. First, coal was faced with competition in existing markets from alternative fuels. Second, the coal industry had internal competition for new markets. Third, coal managers achieved a new level of cooperation among themselves in 1950 that limited competition and fostered oligopoly in the industry. Finally, since their initial accord in 1950, both the union and the corporate structure of the coal industry have changed and continue to change. Interwoven among all these events are technological changes which coal miners and managers accommodated to or implemented. The implementation of new production technologies as well as unforeseen changes in the industry had unintended consequences which in turn created pressure for new forms of relations between miners and managers.

II. A CHANGING INDUSTRY

After World War II, the bituminous coal industry was beset with a set of changes that required miners and managers either to accommodate to each other and forge cooperative relationships or to risk the demise of the coal industry through renewed patterns of cut-throat competition and a downward spiral of lower prices and lower wages. The precedent for such a demise was already apparent in the history of the anthracite coal industry, which had lost its traditional markets and declined in production from 84 million tons in 1926 to 15 million tons in 1940. In 1980, only 6 million tons of anthracite coal were produced.[9] Bituminous coal replaced anthracite coal in part and had several geological advantages over the higher quality anthracite coal which contributed to lower production costs. By the end of World War II, it was

---

[8]Ackerman, "The Impact of the Coal Strike of 1977–8," p. 178.
[9]Seltzer, *Fire in the Hole,* pp. 40, 213 n. 19.

apparent that an entire, well established, heavily unionized sector of the coal industry was in serious decline. This fact made it urgent to deal with changes facing the bituminous coal industry lest it follow suit for some of the same reasons. Significant changes in the use of coal made it necessary to make adaptations in the production of bituminous coal if it was to compete with alternative fuels.

A. Changes in the Use of Coal

A major dislocation in the market for coal after World War II drastically reduced the demand for bituminous coal. The industry was in general decline until 1964 when a pattern of fairly steady growth in consumption emerged and continued until the present time. The use of bituminous coal for home heating dropped from 18% of coal production in 1950 to only 1% in 1984. Railroads consumed 13% of all coal production in 1950 but after 1961 consumed virtually no coal. Likewise, industrial use of coal declined from 45% of all coal production to 15% from 1950 to 1984. New production processes in steel making and a decline in the demand for steel, after the Korean War, also contributed to this reduced demand. In most cases, the traditional users of coal switched to alternative fuels such as natural gas for home heating and diesel fuel for railroads. Both fuels could also serve industrial users of coal. Technological changes in the production and transportation of alternative fuels increased their competitive position with coal. This was particularly true of Mideast oil and natural gas.

However, this decline in demand from some traditional coal users was offset eventually by the increased demand for bituminous coal from electrical generation plants. Their demand began increasing about the same time other users were shifting away from coal. In 1984, electric utilities consumed 7.5 times the amount of coal they had consumed in 1950. The importance of this new demand for the coal industry is made clear by the coal consumption pattern. Electrical utilities consumed 18 percent of all coal produced in 1950 and 76% in 1984.[10]

But coal faced competition for this new market of electrical generation as well. Electrical utilities, like other energy users, had a choice among competing fuel sources including oil, natural gas, and uranium. Coal's portion of electrical production actually fell in a vastly expanded market from 66% in 1950 to 50% in 1979. The share of oil in this market grew from 8 to 18% between 1950 and 1979. The share of natural gas declined during this time from 26 to 16% but this portion of the market was absorbed by nuclear power. Between 1950 and 1979 nuclear moved from 0% to 14% of electrical power production.[11]

Political changes also affected coal's competitive position. Since the acci-

[10]U. S. Bureau of Labor Statistics, *Technology, Productivity, and Labor in the Bituminous Coal Industry, 1950–79*, Bulletin No. 2072 (Washington, DC: U.S. Government Printing Office, 1980), pp. 33–4.
[11]Ibid., p. 62.

dent at the Three Mile Island nuclear reactor, for example, coal's competitive position with nuclear power has improved. It was not a change in nuclear technology at Three Mile Island but the public demand for more regulation of the technology after the accident which increased the cost of constructing nuclear reactors and thus improved coal's competitive position with nuclear power. Similarly, the regulation and deregulation of natural gas production and prices influence coal's competitive stance with that fuel. Coal's competitive stance with oil greatly increased in the 1970s with the formation of OPEC and the oil embargo and declined in the 1980s with OPEC's instability and the increased production of oil.

Since World War II, the American coal industry has become more closely tied to the steam generation of electricity. As Americans consumed more kilowatt hours they indirectly fed a demand for more and more coal. By 1964, the increased demand for coal and coal's improved competitive position began a period of steady growth and recovery. By 1970, the coal industry had reached the production level of 1947 which had been the peak year previously. But even with this recovery, coal's portion of the energy market dropped from 38% in 1950 to 19% in 1979.[12] The coal industry lost its competitive stature in its old markets but has been increasing its competitive status in a new market for energy and electricity in particular.

B. Technological Changes in the Production of Coal

The competitive position of coal vis-à-vis other energy sources stimulated technological change in coal production processes. The first change was increased mechanization of underground mining. Hand production virtually disappeared between 1945 and 1980. At the same time, conventional mining—drilling, blasting, and loading—declined from 92% of all underground coal in 1950 to 25% in 1978. The continuous miner, a machine that rips coal from its seam, carries it by conveyor belt and loads it on shuttle cars, produced 1% of underground coal in 1950 and 75% in 1978.[13]

Technological change in coal burning boilers spurred additional changes in the production of coal. Electric utilities designed boilers to burn cheaper, surface-mined coal of lesser quality and with more dirt and rock. Electrical utilities began to contract for coal with producers for periods of 15 and 20 years. These long-term contracts provided producers a guaranteed market, reliable prices and thus the incentive to purchase specialized, costly, and extremely large earthmoving equipment. Surface-mined coal, as a proportion of all coal produced, began a steady increase in 1950 from 24% in 1950 to over 60% by 1978, where it has remained since.[14]

The competition from surface-mined coal simply reinforced pressure to

[12]Ibid., p. 4.
[13]Ibid., p. 14.
[14]U.S. Department of Energy, *Coal Data: A Reference* (Washington, DC, Energy Information Administration, 1985), pp. 32–3.

lower production costs of underground mining by mechanization. Since 1950, much more of the underground mining is mechanized. By 1975, two-thirds of underground mining was totally mechanized, compared with less than 1% in 1950. In addition, conventional mining was partially mechanized by new loading procedures.[15]

The new demand from electrical utilities was tied to industrial growth and population increases which occurred in increased proportion in the South and West, giving the new coalfields in the West a comparative advantage over older coalfields in the East. Also, Western coal is cheaper to produce than Eastern coal because it is found in large seams and in terrain which permits large-scale surface mining. In addition, most Western coal seams have lower sulfur content, facilitating electrical utility compliance with federal standards for emissions from their boilers. Western coal has increased its share of national coal produced from about 4 percent in 1965 to about 25% in 1980. Its share of the Midwest utility market has increased from about 3% in 1965 to about 33% in 1981.[16] If these trends continue, it is projected that by 1995 about half of the nation's coal supply will come from the Western coalfields; it will be almost entirely surface-mined coal; and Eastern coal will be almost entirely deep-mined coal.[17]

III. CHANGES AMONG MINERS AND MANAGERS

The technological changes in the production of coal coincided with profound changes in the numbers of coal miners and coal mines. Productivity increased tremendously due to the mechanization of deep mines and the introduction of surface mining. Far fewer miners were necessary to produce the same amount of coal with these new processes. Thus, there are now far fewer miners. At the same time, these new processes required extensive capitalization which only large companies could afford. Consequently, there has been a change in the coal industry with fewer producers controlling a larger portion of the production in 1985 than in 1945. These large producers have demonstrated varying degrees of cooperation with each other since 1950. All of these factors have influenced the numbers of miners in the UMWA and the influence of that union.

A. Changes among Miners

How coal was produced rather than how much coal was produced adversely affected the employment of coal miners since World War II. Between 1950 and 1960, employment among miners dropped by 60%, from 415,600 to 169,400.

---

[15]U.S. Bureau of Labor Statistics, *Technology, Productivity, and Labor in the Bituminous Coal Industry, 1950–79*, p. 13.

[16]Peter Navarro, "Union Bargaining Power in the Coal Industry, 1945–81," *Industrial and Labor Relations Review* 36, no. 2. (January 1983), pp. 229. See also, Thomas C. Campbell and Ming-Jeng Hwang, "Spatial Analysis and the Identification of Coal Markets," *Journal of Energy and Development* 4, no. 1 (Autumn 1978), pp. 104–25.

[17]Seltzer, *Fire in the Hole*, p. 212.

Table 1. Employment, Productivity, Production and Underground Production
Selected Years, 1945–1983[a]

Year	Total Miners Employed	Underground Miners as % of miners employed	Total Production (tons)	Underground Production as % of Total Production	Average Tons Per Miner Per Day
1945	383,100	nd	577,617	80.9%	5.78
1950	415,600	89.8%	516,311	76.1%	6.77
1955	225,100	87.9%	464,633	73.9%	9.84
1960	169,400	83.9%	415,512	68.6%	12.83
1965	133,700	82.0%	512,088	65.0%	17.52
1970	140,100	76.9%	602,932	56.2%	18.84
1975	180,900	70.9%	648,438	45.2%	14.74
1980	251,700	67.4%	823,644	40.9%	16.32
1983	173,543	64.5%	778,003	38.5%	21.19

[a]Source: U.S. Department of Energy, *Coal Data: A Reference* (Washington, D.C., Energy Information Administration, 1985), pp. 32–3; and U.S. Bureau of Labor Statistics, *Technology, Productivity, and Labor in the Bituminous Coal Industry, 1950–79*, Bulletin No. 2072 (Washington, D.C.: U.S. Government Printing Office, 1980).

During this same time, coal production dropped by 13% from 477 million tons to 417 tons. What affected the employment of miners most was the mechanization of deep mines and increased production from surface mines. The proportion of mechanized deep-mined coal and surface-mined coal increased from about 25% of all coal produced in 1950 to about 50% in 1960. By 1983, total coal production exceeded 1950 levels by about 50% and about 90% of all coal produced came from mechanized deep mines or from surface mines. The total number of coal miners employed in 1983 was only 42% of those employed in 1950.[18] The figures of Table 1 also indicate a slower decline in the proportion of underground coal miners than in the proportion of underground coal production. Thus, the largest portion of coal miners remains in the segment of the industry with a much smaller, and declining, portion of production.

Moreover, surface mining has changed the skills of some miners, setting them apart from deep miners and their tradition of union organization. The UMWA has had competition in organizing Western coal miners in part because Western miners see themselves as heavy equipment operators and not miners.[19] Miernyk asserts, "The technology of Western strip mining might have as much to do with the workers choice of the Operating Engineers (as their union) as their attitude toward the UMWA."[20]

[18]U.S. Bureau of Labor Statistics, *Technology, Productivity, and Labor in the Bituminous Coal Industry, 1950–79*, p. 39.

[19]Walls, *Central Appalachia in Advanced Capitalism*, p. 264.

[20]William H. Miernyk, "Coal," in *Collective Bargaining: Contemporary American Experience* (Madison, WI: Industrial Relations Research Association, 1980), p. 47. There is an irony that the UMWA is competing also with the Progressive Mine Workers in the West, because the latter group was an insurgent reform group within the UMWA that Lewis defeated. Finley, *The Corrupt Kingdom*, pp. 72–3, 86, 112.

B. Changes among Managers

As the number of coal miners and the nature of their work were undergoing profound changes, the corporate structure of the industry was also changing. Along with mechanization, increased productivity, and unemployment came increased concentration of fewer, larger producers in the coal industry. The largest 50 coal producers increased their share of the coal produced from 45% in 1950 to more than 60% by 1960.[21] By 1970, this corporate sector of the industry produced 68% of the total coal production and has maintained this share up to the present time.

But this is only one measure of the concentration that was occurring. The largest 15 companies increased their share of production from 26% in 1950 to 40% in 1960 and to 52% in 1970. Thereafter, their share of the coal produced dropped and they produced only 40.5% in 1980. Finally, the four largest companies increased their share of coal produced from 13.6% to 30.5% between 1950 and 1970.[22] We shall refer to the sector of large coal producers as the oligopoly sector to indicate a set of larger producers with higher labor standards and which are economic powers on a national level. This should not be taken to mean that these producers set prices or influence market mechanisms in the conventional sense of oligopoly or that there is no competition in this sector.[23]

The oligopoly sector of the industry grew not only through the expansion of the operations of the large firms, but by their acquisition of middle-size operations. These latter companies faced increased labor costs, declining prices for coal, and a need for capital to mechanize. Many companies could not compete in these circumstances and sold out to larger companies.[24] After 1970, the requirements of the Coal Mining Health and Safety Act placed further pressures on the middle-size producers to end operations.

The makeup of the oligopoly sector began to change in the 1960s. Oil companies began to buy coal companies while coal companies in the West, some of which were owned by oil companies, grew in production size. After 1970, coal companies tied to electrical utilities became more prominent, while companies tied to steel companies became less prominent. Many of the top 15 coal companies were bought by oil companies and new companies formed by

[21]Walls, *Central Appalachia in Advanced Capitalism*, pp. 154–61.

[22]Ibid., pp. 154–65.

[23]Analysts have difficulty in locating the coal industry in a scheme of oligopoly and competitive industries. On the one hand, the producers do not exhibit the concentration of other oligopoly industries. Also, there is no national market of coal as there are national markets for other commodities produced by oligopoly industries. On the other hand, the labor force in coal mining has exhibited a degree of organization and compensation that one expects in an oligopoly industry. What analysts overlook is the link between the coal industry and other industries which are clearly oligopolies. This link is capital and it binds steel, oil and electric utilities with coal. See Charles Tolbert, Patrick M. Horan and E. M. Beck, "The Structure of Economic Segmentation," *American Journal of Sociology*, 5, no. 5 (March 1980), pp. 1095–1116; Randy Hodson, *Workers' Earnings and Corporate Economic Structure* (New York: Academic Press, 1983), esp. chapter 4; and Walls, *Central Appalachia in Advanced Capitalism*, pp. 154–85.

[24]Walls, *Central Appalachia in Advanced Capitalism*, pp. 154–85.

oil corporations appeared among the top 15 coal producers. Also, Western coal companies became more prominent and now constitute a majority of the largest 15 coal producers.

However, a competitive sector of small, relatively unmechanized coal operations developed alongside of the oligopoly sector after 1950. The large producers were either mechanized, underground mines or large surface mines with specialized equipment. The small producers were unmechanized, conventional underground mines or small surface mines utilizing heavy equipment such as bulldozers and trucks that could be used in any land excavating work, such as road building. This growing division of the industry into oligopoly and competitive sectors occurred unevenly across geographic areas. The Eastern coalfields had many more and smaller mines than the Western coalfields. Entry into small-scale, relatively unmechanized production was far easier in the East because of the smaller concentration of land ownership than in the West. The Western coalfields had fewer and larger mines and displayed the greatest trend to oligopoly.

A number of factors facilitated the continuation of the competitive sector of the industry. Many small mine operators ended union contracts in the 1950s in order to reduce costs and to compete with larger, mechanized, more efficient producers. Also small producers often found a market with electrical utilities on the "spot market" where they could sell limited quantities of coal for a short period of time.

IV. THE RELATIONS OF COAL MINERS AND COAL MANAGERS

The changes in the production technologies of coal, the employment of coal miners, and the number and size of coal mines are all related to agreements between the UMWA and the large coal producers. Since World War II, these relations went through three stages. The first, 1945 to 1950, was a post-war adjustment and a transition from frequent government intervention in the relations of miners and managers to a pattern of competition which was destructive of management and labor relations and self-destructive for the producers, especially in the face of competition from other fuels. The coal producers' "strikingly slack" group discipline, as compared to the UMWA's "monolithic structure," sharply diminished the producers' bargaining power at this time.[25]

The second stage of relations of miners and managers, 1950 to 1972, was one of cooperation; an exchange of increased wage scales for increased labor productivity.[26] The UMWA and the large coal producers cooperated in the mechanization of underground mines and the increase of wages and benefits for the miners who remained employed, as well as in benefit programs for former miners. This cooperation was possible only because a new association

[25]Baratz, The Union and the Coal Industry, p. 79.
[26]James O'Connor, The Fiscal Crisis of the State (New York: St. Martin's Press, 1973), pp. 22–3.

of large producers created new organization and discipline within the industry.

After 1972, the relations of miners and managers changed in response to a reform movement in the UMWA, changes in the corporate structure of the large coal producers and the westward shift in coal production. The association of producers which was so instrumental in the accord of 1950 to 1972 has less control over large producers at present because of changes among them. In addition, UMWA miners control far less of the total production of coal and consequently national strikes have less influence on the industry except to erode the competitive position of the producers with UMWA contracts. Presently, the union and the producers with union contracts are engaged in a process of establishing new relationships and new tactics for influence within a changed industry.

A. Miners, Managers and Mediation, 1945–1950

Federal government actions changed the management of the mines and the relations of miners and managers between 1933 to 1945. With the National Recovery Administration of the New Deal, Lewis acquired leverage for new organizing drives and brought 90% of American coal miners into the UMWA, most of them in a single year, 1933–4.[27] In addition, the federal government took control of the mines three times from 1943 to 1945 and ran the mines for about half the time in those years. Government action brought Lewis and the UMWA closer to industry-wide bargaining, a position towards which Lewis had worked since the 1920s. One indication of the changed relations of power in the coal industry was Lewis' move of the UMWA headquarters from Indianapolis to Washington, DC in 1934.[28]

With explicit and indirect support from the federal government during the New Deal and World War II, Lewis achieved virtually a closed shop in coal mining and unprecedented gains for miners, indeed for blue collar workers in general. Between 1940 and 1948, miners' wages doubled, they achieved vacation pay, a half-hour lunch, and pay for travel time within the mine.[29] By 1948, the UMWA produced 90% of the nation's coal and its members were the best paid blue collar workers in America, with unequalled fringe benefits.[30] Lewis used government's management of the mines from May 1946 to June 1947 to acquire a royalty on each ton of coal produced in order to finance a health program for miners and their families and a pension program for retired miners and for the dependents of sick, injured, or killed miners. Lewis made his major new demand for the Welfare and Retirement Fund of the operators in 1946. He gained the Fund through an agreement with the government, however. Lewis and the operators could not come to terms, the miners

---

[27]Seltzer, *Fire in the Hole*, pp. 52–3; and Finley, *The Corrupt Kingdom*, pp. 78–82.
[28]Melvyn Dubofsky and Warren Van Tine, *John L. Lewis: A Biography* (New York: Quadrangle/The New York Times Book Co., Inc., 1977), pp. 371–2.
[29]Finley, *The Corrupt Kingdom*, pp. 116.
[30]Navarro, "Union Bargaining Power in the Coal Industry, 1945–81," pp. 217–9.

struck, and President Truman took control of the mines to prevent interruption in the post-War economic recovery. The Fund is still considered the most important gain miners made in this period[31] and is often described in terms just short of hyperbole: "There could never be any more impressive testimonial to the benefits of unionism where there was a unanimity of purpose."[32]

But the end of World War II brought important changes in the relationship between the UMWA and the federal government. The Truman Administration grew increasingly impatient with Lewis' continued militancy, especially after the 1946 elections that sent Republican majorities to Congress.[33] On December 3, 1946, the UMWA, and Lewis personally, were found in civil and criminal contempt for resisting a back-to-work order from the government, which was operating the mines at the time. The fines were unprecedented, $3.5 million and $10,000, respectively. In addition, between 1948 and 1950 the National Emergency provision of the Taft-Hartley Act was invoked three times against Lewis and the UMWA. Current studies are in agreement that this provision was inappropriately applied.[34] However, the administration's action and the court's findings made it clear that, as Seltzer has observed, "federal power could no longer be swung against coal management in collective bargaining."[35]

Lewis, "the acknowledged leader of the coal industry in America" who "could be restrained only by the government and the United States Supreme Court" had met his match.[36] He enjoyed a superior bargaining position[37] and he undertook action to regulate the industry, such as a two-week shutdown in 1948 to reduce the supply of coal. But Lewis' strategy needed adaptation to changed conditions. His control over the supply of union coal was formidable, but less important when demand for coal was decreasing, renewing the traditional problem of excess capacity. In fact, his strategy of frequent work stoppages made matters worse, because the labor unrest reminded coal users of the threat of interrupted supply implicit in the troubled and strike-prone relations of miners and managers. This added to coal's reduced competitive position with other fuels. Aggravating all of this was the obvious willingness of the government to deal severely with Lewis and the UMWA.

Despite the important gains he had made for the union while the government operated the mines or interceded regularly in the affairs of miners and managers, Lewis was publicly opposed to government operation of the mines but not opposed to returning the management of the mines to private ownership.[38] But Lewis did not welcome the possible repetition of cut-throat competition in a leaderless industry, which had been a frequent pattern in coal. A

[31]Ibid., p. 219.
[32]Finley, *The Corrupt Kingdom*, pp. 116.
[33]Dubofsky and Van Tine, *John L. Lewis*, pp. 464.
[34]Miernyk, "Coal," p. 40; Ackerman, "The Impact of the Coal Strike of 1977–8", p. 176.
[35]Seltzer, *Fire in the Hole*, p. 59.
[36]Finley, *The Corrupt Kingdom*, p. 108.
[37]Baratz, *The Union and the Coal Industry*, p. 83.
[38]Ibid., pp. 83–5.

new relationship of miners and managers seemed to be needed, and became possible with a new initiative among managers in 1950.

B. Miners and Managers in Accord, 1950–1972

The industry-wide agreement with the UMWA in 1950 ushered in 22 years of relative peace with only three national strikes, compared to the ten national strikes from 1935 to 1950 and the turmoil from 1946 to 1950. Both miners and managers would strive for fewer, better-paying jobs in a mechanized, efficient, and competitive coal industry which would provide some of the highest wages and most generous health and retirement benefits in American industry. Mechanization was not specifically mentioned in the contract, yet the 1950 agreement is often referred to as the "Mechanization Agreement."[39] *Fortune* also noted the relationship of the 1950 agreement to new production technologies: "In the coal industry 1950 may be remembered as the year of the great shakeout—and also as Year One of its technological revolution."[40] By Year Six of that revolution, 1955, *Fortune* observed, "Collective bargaining in the soft-coal industry, once a colorful pagaent in which political fireworks, editorial dragon slaying, and judicial jousting were variously mingled, has been altered beyond recognition."[41]

Lewis' primary goals after World War II were to increase coal's competitive position with other fuels and to decrease competition within the coal industry. His primary means was the mechanization of coal production. Larger, mechanized and more efficient mines would not only compete better with other fuels but would eliminate small, less mechanized coal producers. Lewis testified before Congress, in 1947, that mechanization would increase the living standard of miners and the profitability of coal producers.[42]

Testifying before Congress as early as 1927, Lewis placed the blame for cut-throat competition and excess capacity in the coal industry directly on the coal operators' inability to regulate themselves.[43] The problem of the industry, widely conceded, was excess capacity: the ability to produce more than was needed. This excess capacity drove down prices, wages and benefits, the number of miners, and the number of miners under union contract. Excess capacity also drove down profits and guaranteed that boom times in the industry would be short-lived, as producers rushed in to acquire profits, and that slumps in the industry would be exacerbated by producers underselling each other, in a market without a floor to prices, until they went out of business. Without a floor to prices, wages and benefits could plummet as

[39]John Peter David, *Earnings, Health, Safety, and Welfare of Bituminous Coal Miners Since the Encouragement of Mechanization by the United Mine Workers of America,* dissertation (West Virginia University, Department of Economics, 1972), p. 65.

[40]Seltzer, *Fire in the Hole,* p. 65.

[41]Ibid., p. 76.

[42]Lewis cited in David, *Earnings, Health, Safety, and Welfare of Bituminous Coal Miners Since the Encouragement of Mechanization by the United Mine Workers of America,* p. 64.

[43]Ibid., p. 52.

well. The ability of small, non-union producers to compete in good times eroded the position of the large, union mines and kept the coal industry on a cycle of boom and bust.

Lewis wrote in 1925, "It seems that it is now up to Labor Unions to compel capitalists to act like capitalists, and to discharge the social functions of capitalists."[44] Indeed, his actions after 1946 exemplified that earlier opinion. But now, in 1950, Lewis found in management a partner with whom he could work. Several major coal producers organized the Bituminous Coal Operators Association (BCOA) to conduct industry-wide agreements with labor in order to achieve some goals which were compatible with Lewis'. First, the BCOA wanted to establish greater leverage in bargaining with the UMWA and to reduce the UMWA's ability to whipsaw individual producers or groups of producers in bargaining.[45] Second, the BCOA wanted to enforce a floor for wages and working conditions in order to prevent the cut-throat competition that characterized the industry at times, such as 1950, when production capacity exceeded demand.[46] Third, the BCOA wanted to establish wages and benefits with the UMWA which were sufficiently high to motivate the coal companies to mechanize and to acquire the acquiescence of the UMWA in the introduction of technology.[47]

Lewis acceded to this strategy because he had long believed that the surest way to improve living and working standards for miners was to achieve fewer and more efficient mines. Lewis understood this to be impossible in view of the operators' inability to regulate themselves, and welcomed the self-regulation which the BCOA represented. The BCOA was dominated by the few giants of the industry, the steel-related companies and the northern operators of Pennsylvania, West Virginia, Ohio, and Illinois. The standard they set for the industry had been high and could be expected to remain so.[48] However, demand was in severe decline from 1950 to 1962 and some coal seams were too small to be mined with the new machinery, so the mechanization accord actually ushered in a period of "orderly decline"[49] rather than new prosperity.

Lewis assisted the large operators and made few demands of the BCOA during this time to assist them in their competition with other fuels and the accumulation of capital for mechanization. Royalty payments remained the same during this time and while wages increased modestly and regularly, UMWA members fell behind other blue collar workers in wages and benefits.[50] Lewis negotiated secret "sweetheart" deals with some mines to delay

[44]Lewis cited in Walls, *Central Appalachia in Advanced Capitalism*, p. 169.

[45]Interview with Joseph Brennan, President, Bituminous Coal Operators' Association, July 30, 1985.

[46]Baratz, *The Union and the Coal Industry*, p. 72.

[47]C. L. Christenson, *Economic Redevelopment in Bituminous Coal*, (Cambridge: Harvard University Press, 1962), pp. 275–6.

[48]Finley, *The Corrupt Kingdom*, p. 171; and Dubofsky and Van Tine, *John L. Lewis*, pp. 502, 520–1.

[49]Miernyk, "Coal," p. 25.

[50]Navarro, "Union Bargaining Power in the Coal Industry, 1945–81," pp. 220–1.

or suspend royalty payments in order to permit mechanization or to continue operation. He centralized decision making within the union and secretly negotiated contracts in with the BCOA. District and local union officers were selected for their loyalty while critics were purged. Peace at the national level was to extend to the local level and consequently Lewis showed little support or tolerance for wildcat strikes.[51]

Lewis accepted the unemployment of a majority of his union's members as a consequence of his accord with the BCOA. In 1950 there were 416,000 miners but in 1959 only 180,000. Moreover, he took extraordinary actions which put miners out of work. He used money from the Welfare and Retirement Fund to finance the secret purchase of nonunion coal mines in Western Kentucky. These companies were large, mechanized operations that became unionized upon purchase by Lewis and competed with union mines in southeast Tennessee for the coal purchases of the Tennessee Valley Authority (TVA). By refusing to negotiate separate contract terms with these competitors, as he had done secretly with larger operators, he sought to end the operations of small, unmechanized mines. When the small Tennessee operators attempted to produce in violation of the contract terms the union struck them. In one instance, TVA barged in coal very likely from UMWA owned and organized mines in Western Kentucky past UMWA miners in Southern Tennessee coal fields who were on strike and had cutoff a portion of TVA's coal supply.[52] Seltzer describes the choice Lewis gave to the small coal operators as: comply with the BCOA contract and go out of business or refuse to comply and be forced out of business by strikes.[53] On the one hand, Lewis was fighting for higher standards for his miners. On the other, he was working to force many of their employers out of the industry.

Nonunion mines represented another and increasing problem for Lewis. The UMWA-BCOA accord was based on the assumption that the union would be able to impose uniform labor costs on all producers. However, some nonunion mines persisted for two reasons. First, a surplus of unemployed coal miners were willing to work in non-union mines. Second, by the mid-1950s, a growing number of non-union operators were supplying the TVA which was expanding its steam-generated electrical capacity at a time of a declining demand for coal. TVA was the largest coal customer in the growing electric utilities sector of the coal economy and used its influence to drive down the costs of coal. It bought coal on the spot market in large quantities for the first time in the industry, allowing small non-union producers to bid on limited quantities of coal at prices lower than that of large, mechanized producers with

[51]Dubofsky and Van Tine, *John L. Lewis*, p. 502.
[52]Richard A. Couto, "Metaphysical Pathos of Peripheral Economics: TVA and Region and Regional Development in Appalachia," Paper presented at the annual meeting of the British Sociological Association (1983) Cardiff, Wales, pp. 25–6. See also, Nat Caldwell and Gene S. Graham, "The Strange Romance Between John L. Lewis and Cyrus Eaton," *Harper's Magazine*, Vol. 203 (December 1961), pp. 25–32 and Richard Harshberger, *TVA Coal Buying Policies*, dissertation (Indiana University, Department of Economics, 1964), pp. 115–6.
[53]Seltzer, *Fire in the Hole*, p. 80.

long term contracts. From 1950 to 1958, the number of coal mines around TVA's Kingston steam plant in East Tennessee almost doubled while the average annual production of these mines declined from 38,000 to 10,000 tons.[54]

To prevent this and other nonunion coal production, Lewis took two extraordinary steps in 1958. First, he negotiated a contract with the BCOA that prohibited signators from processing or marketing non-union coal. This was a substantial blow to small, nonunion producers since they could not replicate the processing and marketing facilities of the large producers and still stay in business. Second, he increased a campaign of terror and violence in District 19, in East Tennessee and East Kentucky, against nonunion operators.[55]

Eventually, court action stopped Lewis and the UMWA from continuing both steps. By 1971, the UMWA and some BCOA coal companies had been found in restraint of trade in several federal court cases. By 1959, the campaign of terror had been halted but not before the UMWA stood alone, "as the only union in America's history to undertake a concerted, directed, planned, financed and calculated campaign, over a sustained period of time, of violence, terror, dynamite and killing of other men."[56]

The period of orderly decline had consequences which continued into the period of 1963 to 1972, one of growth for the coal industry. Industry concentration continued and the acquisition of small coal companies by large coal companies was followed by the acquisition of large coal companies by other corporations, most notably oil corporations. UMWA cooperation with the large producers continued despite calls for higher pay and benefits and improved safety from the rank and file in light of a healthier industry.

The first major challenge to UMWA leadership rekindled the legacy of terror in the UMWA's history during the period of "orderly decline." Joseph Yablonski, who had opposed UMWA president Boyle in the election of December 1969, was murdered with his wife and daughter weeks after the contested election. Eventually, Boyle was found guilty for ordering the murder of Yablonski. The men who arranged the murder were the same officials from District 19 who had carried out the orders of violence from Lewis and Boyle earlier.

C. Miners and Managers without Accord, 1972 to Present

A new set of relationships between miners and managers reflected the substantial changes in each of them. The most apparent change occurred

[54]Harshberger, TVA Coal Buying Policies, pp. 115–6.
[55]Dubofsky and Van Tine assert that the violence ended with the contract of 1958 but Finley offers more convincing evidence that the contract and the violence were parts of an effort to eliminate small producers. Dubofsky and Van Tine, *John L. Lewis*, p. 512 and Finley, *The Corrupt Kingdom*, pp. 136–58.
[56]Finley, *The Corrupt Kingdom*, p. 154.

within the UMWA. A rank and file insurgency coupled with a movement to address the health risk of black lung led to a radical reform of the UMWA by 1972. Far less visible, but equally profound, were the changes among the large producers of the coal industry. Oil and other corporations purchased large coal corporations and insisted on new terms in their relations with the union. Coincidental with this change was a shift in production from the Eastern coal fields to the Western coal fields where few producers had contracts with the UMWA. Most producers in the West either had no union contracts or contracts with other unions such as the International Union of Operating Engineers. These changes have meant that less coal is produced under UMWA contract; that fewer large producers are part of the BCOA; that industry wide-agreements are more difficult to obtain; and that the UMWA and BCOA individually and together have less influence on industry standards. Both the union and the BCOA are looking for new relations in an industry now dominated by companies without UMWA contracts or membership in the BCOA.

1. UMWA Reform and Change

In 1972, a rank and file insurgency movement, Miners for Democracy, capped about ten years of protest with an election which ousted Tony Boyle as president of the UMWA and instated Arnold Miller. This movement was related to the accord between the UMWA and the BCOA and the mechanized production processes which prompted it. Stirrings among the rank and file began shortly after Lewis' departure as president in 1960. Miners in Western Pennsylvania conducted wildcat strikes in protest over the national contract negotiated in 1964 and the lack of job security within it. Boyle was challenged in the election of 1964 and in 1969. The last election was a more serious challenge to Boyle and was led by Joseph Yablonski, who had been a member of the UMWA's executive board until 1969.

Yablonski's murder shortly after the election served to coalesce several groups which had been protesting UMWA policies. Widows and disabled miners began protests of the restrictive policies of the Fund and picketed union mines in the mid-1960s. Their protest, stimulated in part by the War on Poverty and its call for maximum feasible participation, was designed to acquire union action towards the Fund and its beneficiaries and policies. Joining this stream of protest was another group, the Black Lung Association (BLA). Retired and disabled miners began to work in the mid-1960s for the recognition and compensation of coal miners' pneumoconiosis, a lung and breathing disorder brought on by the inhalation of coal dust, which can be totally disabling and fatal.

The BLA was significant for several reasons. It was symptomatic of the UMWA's neglect of health and safety measures during the period of mechanization. Second, black lung was a problem aggravated by deep-mine mechanization, which had increased dust levels. Third, the BLA succeeded without the UMWA. Wildcat strikes and other actions among the rank and file, retired miners, and their supporters, many of whom were women, were the primary means of BLA's success. The BLA had little organized leadership and no union sanction, but had become popular in the Eastern coalfields where it represented a pent-up reservoir of reform.

In 1972, new leadership in the UMWA disavowed the accord with the BCOA and decentralized union decision making. Items to negotiate with the BCOA were identified in convention and all contracts had to be ratified by a vote of a bargaining council and then by a rank and file vote. Health and safety matters were promoted. The UMWA made new efforts to organize non-union miners in Central Appalachia including Eastover in Harlan County, Kentucky, and Stearns in Whitley County, Kentucky. In general, there was a feeling that the time had arrived to be compensated for the costs of that accord. As one study of the industry between 1945 and 1972 concluded:

> The question that remains is whether miners obtained any benefits from the Mechanization Agreement and its later amendments. The evidence suggests that they did not, due in part to the lack of union interest or ability to obtain the benefits and in part to the union's miscalculation of the immense social costs that would result from the mechanization and the resulting worker displacement.[57]

2. The BCOA and Change

By the 1970s, the BCOA was losing its industry-wide influence. With the advent of Western coal companies and new coal companies which produced for electric utilities, the number of non-BCOA companies among the top 15 producers increased from 3 to 8 between 1970 and 1980. These large, non-BCOA, mechanized producers enjoyed a cost savings over producers with the UMWA contract. Their wages and benefits were often as high or higher than those of UMWA producers and in some cases, especially in the West, coal miners were represented by other unions. But these non-UMWA producers could always depend on a lower price per ton of coal because of the cost of the royalty required by the UMWA contract. These changes in the oligopoly sector decreased the BCOA share of coal production from 80% to 70% between 1950 and 1970 and to 40% by 1983.[58]

In addition, as large coal companies became a part of larger energy or other corporations, decision making about coal companies became enmeshed in a set of considerations separate from the coal industry. The operations of coal companies were synchronized to events and profit making within the parent corporation as well as the coal industry.[59] Some of these companies, the oil companies in particular, have substitute products for coal. In other cases, they have a set of completely different products. In still other cases,

---

[57]David, *Earnings, Health, Safety, and Welfare of Bituminous Coal Miners Since the Encouragement of Mechanization by the United Mine Workers of America*, pp. 64.

[58]Seltzer, *Fire in the Hole*, p. 127.

[59]Charles Craypo, "Introduction to the Special Issue: The Impact on Labor of Changing Corporate Structure and Technology," *Labor Studies Journal* 3, no. 3 (Winter 1979), p. 197.

companies have coal holdings in other American coalfields and overseas.[60] This diversity of profit sources allows corporations to synchronize decisions regarding any particular company in light of profits and needs of other companies within the parent company.[61] This diversity also permits parent corporations "deep pockets" from which to draw revenues to support coal subsidiaries during periods of conflict with labor.[62] At the same time, this diversity often reduces a coal company's finances to a modest portion within the parent corporation and changes the reporting requirements for the coal company because corporations are not required to report on subsidiary companies which produce less than 15 percent of the corporation's revenues on the 10-K form required by the Securities and Exchange Commission. Without such information on coal companies the union has less information on the financial position of the coal company subsidiaries and are at a major disadvantage in dealing with that company.[63]

3. The UMWA and the BCOA, 1972 to Present

The changes in the UMWA, among the large producers of the coal industry, and in the membership of the BCOA have had a profound influence on the relations of miners and managers. Both the UMWA and the BCOA entered the 1970s with new expectations of themselves, of each other, and of an industry that was undergoing far-reaching change. The strikes and contracts since 1972 make it clear that this relationship revolved about factors related to technological change: royalty payments to the Fund, job protection, and competition with non-UMWA producers.

(a) The Contract of 1974. The UMWA made substantial gains in the contract in 1974. The terms to be negotiated were decided in the convention of 1973 and researched well by new staff members who came into the UMWA with Miller. Coal companies were reporting substantial profits from the higher prices for coal which the oil embargo influenced. Wages and benefits were increased 54% over the three years of the contract, the largest increase ever. A cost-of-living adjustment was introduced and brought coal miners a benefit achieved by auto workers in 1948 and steel workers in 1956.[64] The previous benefit and pension Funds were reorganized with increased benefits and revenue. In addition, new pension and benefit plans were established with revenues from a royalty per ton and an assessment on worker hours.[65] The

---

[60]John F. Schnell, "The Impact on Collective Bargaining of Oil Company Ownership of Bituminous Coal Properties," *Labor Studies Journal*, 3, no. 3 (Winter 1979), p. 205.

[61]Craypo, "Introduction to the Special Issue: The Impact on Labor of Changing Corporate Structure and Technology," p. 197.

[62]Schnell, "The Impact on Collective Bargaining of Oil Company Ownership of Bituminous Coal Properties," p. 212.

[63]Ibid., p. 209.

[64]Navarro, "Union Bargaining Power in the Coal Industry, 1945–81," p. 220.

[65]Seltzer, *Fire in the Hole,* pp. 134–5; and *National Bituminous Coal Wage Agreement of 1974,* pp. 83–94.

contract established Mine Health and Safety Committees and protected the individual miner's right to withdraw from a workplace the miner judged unsafe.[66]

The new contract did not come easily. The new, democratic procedures of the UMWA required approval by a bargaining council of district presidents and executive board members. This council voted down the contract twice before approving it for rank-and-file endorsement which came in early December after a nationwide strike of several weeks. In addition, the process renewed divisions between the reformers and the Boyle loyalists and fostered new divisions among those reformers who wanted more and those who thought the contract represented all that was attainable. These divisions coupled with the inexperience of union officials in dealing with a more complex coal industry jeopardized UMWA unity and strength.

(b) The Contract of 1977–1978. The UMWA lost much in the contract negotiations of 1977–8, and sought to prevent large concessions. Despite a 111-day strike, the longest in the UMWA's history, the union ended up with a contract that the rank and file did not want, but was the best they could get. Seltzer argues persuasively that, "The 1977–8 strike was a watershed in coal politics that recast the balance of power between labor and management."[67] It was a watershed for several reasons. First, recent union gains were modified. The cost-of-living adjustment was recalculated and capped at a straight $.30 per hour supplement to wage increases. Second, long-standing union benefits were lost. The thirty-year old health program of the Fund was eliminated for everyone except pre-1976 pensioners, and company-provided health insurance programs were instituted in its place. Third, bonus plans which linked wages to production and which were historically opposed by the UMWA were permitted by the 1978 contract for the first time since 1945.[68]

These UMWA losses and the lengthy strike resulted from new divisions among coal producers, especially pressures on the BCOA companies to level the difference in labor costs between themselves and other major producers without UMWA contracts. One determinant of the cost differential was the royalty paid by BCOA producers to the Fund. Large, non-UMWA producers had demonstrated their willingness to pay wages at or above UMWA contract levels[69] in order to prevent worker dissatisfaction and unionization. Such producers, especially in the West, could still undersell UMWA mines because they had no royalty payments. For the UMWA to concede the health program of the Fund meant not only losing the main apparent advantage that the union had over non-union miners, but also sacrificing part of the union's achievement, an achievement that had in some measure justified the suffering and sacrifice mechanization represented for miners. On the other hand, it was a concession prompted, if not dictated, by the changes in the oligopoly

---

[66]National Bituminous Coal Wage Agreement of 1974, pp. 8–10, 14–5.

[67]Seltzer, *Fire in the Hole,* p. 165.

[68]Navarro, "Union Bargaining Power in the Coal Industry, 1945–81," p. 224.

[69]U.S. Bureau of Labor Statistics, *Earnings and Other Characteristics of Organized Workers,* Bulletin 2015, (Washington, DC: U.S. Government Printing Office, 1980), p. 31.

sector and the continuation of the competitive sector which threatened BCOA profits.

Wildcat strikes in the East were another cost differential between UMWA and non-UMWA mines. Wildcat strikes, which were miners' primary means to deal with management on the local level, had become common in the aftermath of the Black Lung Movement and the mass movements of the 1960s. The average annual number of wildcat strikes between 1975 and 1977 reached 3,000, double that of the preceding three years despite improved contract language in 1974. Miners used wildcat strikes for broad social purposes, such as to protest school textbook policies in Kanawha County, W.VA. and gasoline rationing policies. But the root cause of the wildcat strikes was the cumbersome grievance procedures and the inability to mediate grievances, formally and informally, at the local level. The major study of wildcat strikes during this time shows that local miners viewed the wildcat strikes as effective and, in mines with large numbers of wildcat strikes, as necessary in order to gain management's attention.[70]

Miners and managers disagreed on how to deal with the wildcat strikes despite their consensus that the strikes were detrimental. The union proposed a right-to-strike clause in the contract that would permit miners to determine a local strike by majority vote. The BCOA sought sanctions for miners on wildcat strikes. In the end, each side gained a little of what it wanted. Miners who honored a wildcat strike received increased protection from management sanctions, but managers received increased power to sanction miners who advocated or promoted a wildcat strike.[71]

Miners and managers reached an impasse in resolving their differences because each side was factionalized. The UMWA had to deal with differences between Eastern and Western miners and among Eastern miners. The agreement that the UMWA signed with major coal companies in the West one day after the "national" strike began is indicative of differences between Western and Eastern companies and miners. Western UMWA miners continued work under contract while the majority of UMWA members, Eastern miners, were out on strike for a national contract. UMWA President Miller was a minority president, having survived a three way race in 1977 with about 40% of the vote. Dissension and purges within the UMWA left him without competent staff assistance and little unity. He largely ignored the UMWA convention's position for a right-to-strike clause and proposed it late and half-heartedly. This was an important alteration of the union's solidarity between the convention and the negotiations as exemplified in 1974. Miller weakened the UMWA's solidarity further when he hired an inexperienced Washington consulting staff to assist in the negotiations.

Although the BCOA was united in its desire for labor stability and lower labor costs, individual companies were prepared to break up the BCOA and to

---

[70]Jeanne M. Brett and Stephen B. Goldberg, "Wildcat Strikes in Bituminous Coal Mining," Industrial and Labor Relations Review, 32, no. 4 (July 1979), passim.
[71]Seltzer, Fire in the Hole, p. 163.

end industry-wide bargaining in order to achieve their demands.[72] The coal industry and the BCOA now had three distinct sectors: underground metallurgical coal; underground steam coal; and surface steam coal. To some it seemed more logical to bargain on the basis of region or industry sector rather than on an industry-wide basis.

The divisions on both sides and their impasse led the Carter administration to intervene. White House pressure ultimately forged an agreement between the UMWA and the BCOA, but the contract was rejected 2 to 1 by UMWA rank and file union members. On March 24, 1978 the UMWA members ratified a BCOA-initiated contract with similar terms to the contract they had rejected.

The strike and settlement illuminated the impact of industry changes on declining UMWA strength. A 111-day strike did not adversely affect the U.S. economy. The steel industry, a traditional and important customer of coal, was down in production and so was its demand for coal. Coal supplies were sufficient for steel and for the most important coal customer, electric utilities, from non-UMWA producers in the Eastern coal fields. Although the supply from the competitive sector had been an "offset factor" to UMWA power to stop the supply of coal since the 1950s,[73] it had become critical and extended into the oligopoly sector of the industry among companies without UMWA contracts by 1978. Only 50% of coal production was UMWA produced in 1978, as compared with 67% in 1974. Furthermore, UMWA power was offset by the growth of Western coal and coal imports from Australia, Poland, and South Africa.[74] Electric utilities could not only acquire coal, they could supply electricity to utilities that had coal shortages. Finally, the UMWA strike was less effective because many coal companies were sheltered by their parent corporations from the financial strain of the prolonged strike.

The UMWA and BCOA agreed in this contract to joint action on broad issues within the industry which affected them both. They began a joint UMWA Industry Development Committee. The committee of six appointees, three each from the UMWA and the BCOA, had a budget of up to $100,000 and the task of addressing labor relations and productivity. UMWA and BCOA officers as well as company presidents were excluded from serving on the committee.[75]

(c) The Contract of 1981. Both the UMWA and the BCOA underwent further change between 1978 and the contract talks of 1981. Sam Church replaced Miller as UMWA president. Unity within the union increased, and the union developed new tools to deal with the new industry. A selective strike fund was approved in 1979 which would support union miners at

---

[72]Ibid., p. 153.

[73]Navarro, "Union Bargaining Power in the Coal Industry, 1945–81," p. 222, footnote 19.

[74]Schnell, "The Impact on Collective Bargaining of Oil Company Ownership of Bituminous Coal Properties," p. 222.

[75]*National Bituminous Coal Wage Agreement of 1978*, pp. 7–10.

companies which did not agree to the national contract.[76] The changes within the BCOA were more dramatic. A reorganization entrusted three large producers to negotiate for the BCOA and to coordinate an eleven-member committee made up of chief executive officers from parent companies of the coal subsidiaries. This had the practical consequence of maintaining the BCOA after the threat of splintering brought on by Consolidated Coal's temporary and brief departure from the BCOA in 1979; restoring the predominant pattern of the influence of U.S. Steel and Consolidated Coal within the BCOA that had been disrupted in 1978; and involving nine corporate executives in negotiations even though they were not exclusively or primarily in the business of coal.

The UMWA signed a contract with Pittsburg and Midway for their Western operations without a strike in 1981. This settlement was a pattern for the Western mines and established a goal lower than what was expected for Eastern coal companies. The ease of union ratification in the West was related to the UMWA desire to avoid a strike in the West and in order to promote its Western organizing efforts.[77]

However, the issues between the BCOA and the UMWA were more complex and related to job protection and royalties for the Fund. BCOA's original proposal called for subcontracting certain work in and around the mines and leasing coal properties to non-union firms. This latter measure was a new encouragement to the competitive sector whose operations would be tied to BCOA companies. The operators also sought to reduce the royalty payment on coal from such leased operations.[78]

The pattern of 1978 rank-and-file reaction repeated itself in 1981. UMWA rank-and-file members rejected a contract with the terms requested by the BCOA. A subsequent two and a half month strike had little effect on the general economy. It did affect the smaller BCOA producers, who threatened to negotiate separately, and thereby divided the BCOA, which then reopened negotiations and reached a settlement with the union.

The approved contract once again demonstrated the strength and sacrifice required of the UMWA to minimize its concessions to management. Job protection was written into the contract to protect miners in leasing arrangements. Royalty payments on non-BCOA coal remained the same. The miners gained a dental plan and some pensions were increased.

(d) The Contract of 1984. In September 1984, the UMWA and the BCOA agreed on a contract without a strike for the first time since 1968. The UMWA had a new president, Richard Trumka, and greater unity. He asked for and acquired new negotiating powers from the UMWA convention. Bargaining council ratification was eliminated, and the proposed contract was to go di-

[76]Paul F. Clark, *The Miners' Fight for Democracy: Arnold Miller and the Reform of the United Mine Workers* (Ithaca: New York State School of Industrial and Labor Relations, Cornell University, 1981), p. 150.
[77]"A Western Coal Pact Bodes Well for the East," *Business Week*, no. 2676 (February 23, 1981), p. 37.
[78]Seltzer, *Fire in the Hole*, p. 195.

rectly to the rank and file for ratification. In addition, Trumka authorized selective strikes against holdouts to the national agreement, a strategy which actually assisted the BCOA to maintain discipline among its members. Trumka limited his bargaining goal to "no backward step." The UMWA was united, despite some concessions in the contract. For example, the contract implicitly condoned subcontracting practices by establishing first priority in hiring at subcontractors' operations for UMWA miners.[79] The BCOA in the same year was still threatened with a splinter. Island Creek Coal Company, a subsidiary of Occidental Petroleum, withdrew from the BCOA in 1983 although it quickly signed the 1984 agreement with the UMWA. In general, the UMWA terms were considered favorable to producers.[80]

Changes in the Joint Committee whose name was changed to the UMWA-BCOA Joint Interests Committee, indicate the new attempts at cooperation and harmony within the industry. The budget of the committee was no longer specified, and its membership, now including UMWA and BCOA officers, was increased from six to eight. Most importantly, the contract language of this agreement broadened the tasks of the new committee and articulated the challenge before the industry and a new accord in search of a course of action:

> The parties are concerned that the operations covered by this Agreement, as well as the coal industry generally, increasingly face many challenges in supplying the energy needs of this nation. They recognize that both employment security and return on substantial capital investment in these operations depend on the underlying ability of the operations to be cost-competitive with other energy suppliers. It is also the parties' belief that the development of domestic coal as an energy resource and the development of a coal-based national energy policy are critical components of national security and the ability of the United States to maintain its position of industrial competitiveness at home and abroad.[81]

(e) The Future. The relations of the UMWA and the BCOA face further challenges, as events in 1985 illustrate. There is a shift overseas in coal production. Although this does not affect the U.S. coal market appreciably, it does play a part in the calculations of the corporations which produce coal here and abroad. Occidental Petroleum, for example, announced plans to develop the world's largest surface mine in the People's Republic of China. The Exxon Corporation entered the ranks of the top fifteen producers of coal in 1983 in the form of the Exxon Coal Group, which is not a BCOA member. It operates coal mines in the Western states, where its parent company began and then abandoned a multimillion dollar oil shale project. Exxon closed a UMWA deep mine in West Virginia in 1985 while its production in the Western coal fields continued. More importantly, the first production of coal in Colombia, developed by Exxon, began in 1985. That coal is intended for the Western European steam coal market, a prime export market for coal from the

[79]"Chaos in the Coalfields May Finally Be Over," *Business Week*, no. 2863 (October 8, 1984), p. 162; *National Bituminous Coal Wage Agreement of 1984*, pp. 8–9.
[80]"Chaos in the Coalfields," p. 162.
[81]*National Bituminous Coal Wage Agreement of 1984*, p. 11.

Appalachian coal fields.[82] In addition, Exxon's Colombian coal is imported and used in Southern states around the Gulf of Mexico and, in late 1985, an electric utility in Virginia began a test-burn of the Colombian coal. The introduction of this coal occurs at a time when large numbers of UMWA miners, including those in Virginia, remain unemployed.

Foreign operations compete with American coal in other ways. For example, in 1984, the UMWA began a selective strike against the A.T. Massey coal company in West Virginia. Massey Coal Company is the parent company of A. T. Massey and is run jointly by a partnership group of Fluor Corporation and Royal Dutch Shell. With capital from these parent firms, Massey became the fifth largest producer of coal in the United States in 1984, and second in export sales. At the same time, Fluor developed the second synthetic fuel plant in South Africa and Royal Dutch Shell developed the Reitspruit surface mine in South Africa. A modest amount of South African coal reaches the Gulf States, but more importantly, the capital to develop this foreign coal production is tied to American coal production as well. The lower production costs of new foreign operations pressure domestic companies to lower their own production costs, especially labor costs, in established production sites such as the Eastern coalfields in the United States.[83]

The large producers within the coal industry are companies with global operations. Their decisions about profit revolve about the relative costs of production including technologies, transportation, and labor. The same dynamic that drove the American coal industry to surface mining and to the Western coal fields is at work driving coal operations around the world. That dynamic rent asunder the accord of miners and managers forged after World War II and the association of miners and managers. The international aspect of the dynamic is adversely affecting the American coal industry at present and reduces the short-term prospects for reestablishing the former accord or even establishing a new one within their existing organizations.

The UMWA began recently to forge new links with other labor organizations in addition to defending their own traditions. On October 30, 1985, Trumka became the first UMWA president ever to address the AFL-CIO convention, and the two labor organizations organized and led a boycott of Shell products in protest of the Shell operations in South Africa. Two unions that did not endorse the boycott, significantly, were the International Union of Operating Engineers and the Oil, Atomic, and Chemical Workers Union. South African miners traveled to the United States in 1985 and one of them, James Motlatsi, indicated one form of labor organization required but as yet not possible in a global economy such as coal production represents:

> If you are having a dispute with Shell Oil Co., we need to know as soon as possible. . . .
>
> Because the company may, in South Africa, attempt to encourage our members to work overtime, and Saturdays and Sundays to cover their losses.

[82]United States, Government Accounting Office, *Prospects for Long-Term U.S. Steam Coal Exports to European and Pacific Rim Markets (GAO/NSIAD-83-08).*
[83]"Striking Miners Set for a 2nd Winter," *The New York Times* (October 6, 1985), p. 17.

So if we are exchanging information, we can assist you immediately. We can tell our members not to accept working overtime. And we can attempt to negotiate with that company, and teach them that we won't let them play off our members against you.

I think that would be very good solidarity.[84]

V. CONCLUSION

The efforts of miners and managers to deal with technological change in an effort to make their industry competitive holds out some fairly obvious lessons. Most importantly, changes in technology which affected the relations of miners and managers are not limited to technological change in production or even within the coal industry. Technological change in the uses of coal and other energy sources, and technological change in the production of other fuels, affected changes in the relations of miners and managers. In addition, public policy towards coal, other fuels, energy in general, labor, the environment and many other issue areas affected the relation of miners and managers.

The accord between miners and managers from 1950 to 1972 absorbs so much attention that it is too easy to overlook the important role of public policy in their relations. It is apparent that changed attitudes of the administrations after World War II made a new relationship of miners and managers necessary, but it also must be stressed that the federal government had other policies with equally significant consequences. Federal policies of land leasing also have permitted the growth of the Western surface mine industry. The acres of coal reserves on Federal lands leased for development increased almost 20 fold from 1950 to 1980, from 40 thousand to almost 800 thousand.[85] The paucity of laws, and their lax enforcement has permitted coal operators, especially of small surface mines, a relatively free hand in operation. The Coal Mining and Health and Safety Act in 1969 was the first legislation that recognized "an inability or unwillingness (of state government) to discharge their responsibility."[86]

Just as we need to recognize the influence of public policy on labor relations, we need to recognize that technological change is not the predominant causal factor in changing relations of miners and managers. The role of technological change is often portrayed inaccurately and otherwise misunderstood. A federal government study, for example, commented on the recent increase in mine ownership by oil companies and suggested that "The

---

[84]"South Africans Tell UMWA: 'Your Fight is Our Fight'", *United Mine Workers Journal* 96, no. 11 (December 1985), pp. 22–3.

[85]Seltzer, *Fire in the Hole*, p. 190.

[86]O. B. Conaway, Jr. observed that federal legislation prior to 1969 did little to "disturb the general responsibility of the states for accident prevention despite a record indicating either an inability or unwillingness to discharge their responsibility." "Coal Mining: New Efforts in an Old Field," *Annals of the Academy of Political and Social Science,* no. 400 (1972) cited in Miernyk, "Coal," p. 33.

financial, technological and managerial capabilities of the oil companies could improve productivity."[87]

This statement is remarkably short-sighted and contradicts the history of labor relations in the coal industry on several counts. First, the increased ownership of coal companies by oil companies is indicative of a much larger trend—the accumulation of capital and its use to make profits—which marks the coal industry since World War II. This trend explains the acquisition of small coal companies by large coal companies, the acquisition of large coal companies by oil companies, the acquisition of smaller oil companies by larger oil companies, the acquisition of large oil companies by conglomerates, and it will explain the acquisition of conglomerates by whatever new organization of capital is to follow. This trend in the coal industry did not end when Continental Oil bought Consolidated Coal which had acquired numerous coal companies in the 1950s and 1960s, but merely continued when DuPont bought Continental Oil.

Second, the statement is misleading because it links corporate capabilities to improved labor productivity, although corporate capabilities are first and foremost aimed at profits. Increased productivity is one obvious means to increase profits, but the surest means, which incorporates increased productivity, is to reduce production costs. Producers will use less technology and accept lower productivity if it means lower production costs. The competitive sector did this in the 1950s in the coal industry, the large producers have the means to do this through subcontracting arrangements in the recent contracts, and Exxon is employing very modest technology in its surface mine operations in Colombia. Producers will also use less technology and accept lower productivity even at higher production costs if prices rise to a level which permits profits. This was the case in the coal industry after the oil embargo.

The goal of coal corporations is not to achieve the highest productivity but to find a relative advantage over existing producers for new and existing markets. These advantages may come from substituting a lower grade product for existing products as in the mining of sub-bituminous and lignite coal in the West. They may also come from applying new technology as the large companies did in the 1950s, or in the application of existing technologies as in the Western coalfields. Relative advantage may also come from new technology in processing and transporting a commodity, which are among the advantages of South Africa and Colombia. Established producers will adjust to the relative advantage of other, new producers, perhaps by seeking improved productivity, but certainly by reducing their production costs as the competitive sector did in the 1950s and as the BCOA has done in contracts since 1978. Producers may also close existing operations and use their capital to establish new operations with improved competitive stature, as Exxon has done.

[87]U.S. Bureau of Labor Statistics, *Technology, Productivity, and Labor in the Bituminous Coal Industry, 1950–79*, p. 1.

Labor relations is one factor in establishing relative advantage. The UMWA made an effort, through the Welfare and Retirement Fund, to improve living conditions in the coalfields and to assist miners in the transitions that mechanization brought about in the 1950s. The large producers cooperated and provided royalty payments, in part to drive up the price of production, to squeeze marginal producers, and to acquire the quiescence of the UMWA in a major industry shakeout with new social costs. When the Fund became a relative disadvantage for the BCOA vis-à-vis other large producers without UMWA contracts, they first modified the Fund and then abandoned it. The ability of one set of producers to avoid or to reduce production costs related to labor and broader social conditions of the industry creates pressure for all producers to eliminate or reduce such costs as the history of the Fund makes clear.

All of which is to say the primary goal of mine managers, as capitalists, is to acquire a relative advantage over other producers by which to make profit. Other hopes for their behavior have to be related to this primary goal. This is why the government assessment is short-sighted, and why Lewis' strategy of stimulating the "social function" of capitalists was flawed. The social function of capitalists is their economic function, to pursue profit. They have no direct social function; rather their economic function has social consequences, including labor relations. These social consequences may be improved living and working conditions for some workers, as they were in the Eastern coalfields, in the 1950s, for UMWA miners left with work; for miners in the Western coalfields in the 1960s and 1970s; and for black miners in mechanized coal mines in South Africa at present.

There are other consequences for labor of the primary economic goal of profit. Structural unemployment occurs when technology is used to gain a relative advantage over other producers. This structural unemployment, in coal mining at least, created a pool of surplus labor which permitted lower standards among some coal producers and depressed the economic conditions of communities in coal mining regions. This is what makes an Appalachia possible in the United States: a region with a mechanized industry, enormous mineral wealth, and a large population in poverty and with inadequate human services. This negative flip-side to the social benefits of mechanization is occuring in South Africa as well, where fewer, better paid miners mean more, unemployed ex-miners returning to the labor reserves of the homelands.

This is not to suggest that the coal industry is solely responsible for all negative social conditions in coal mining regions.[88] But the history of miners and managers since World War II makes it amply clear that technological change is one path to profit and labor relations are a consequence of the pursuit of profits primarily, and the introduction of technology secondarily.

---

[88]For a discussion of this and a comparative analysis applicable to Wales see Raymond Williams, *The Year 2000: A Radical Look at the Future—and What We Can Do to Change It* (New York: Pantheon Books, 1983), esp. pp. 83–101.

Changes in the nature, amount, and terms of labor, in turn, are a contributing factor to the prominent inequality and human suffering of coal mining regions in several countries. These conditions are now related because of the global links of the coal economy and the international search by coal companies and their parent corporations for relative advantage over existing coal producers. Consequently, the history of miners and managers remains of great importance in understanding the continuing relation of workers and managers in an industrial, and international, economy.

10

Conflict, Cooperation, and the Global Auto Factory

Michael Indergaard and Michael Cushion

I. INTRODUCTION[1]

Since 1973, the American automobile industry has experienced a shift toward more cooperative labor relations. Many observers saw the 1984 contract between General Motors (GM) and the United Auto Workers as a pathbreaking agreement marking the beginning of a new era of cooperation. Historically, the legacy of labor relations in the auto industry has been one of conflict, from the time of bloody violence over the right to unionize in the late 1930s to the protracted standoff between workers and management over issues of workplace control at Lordstown in 1972. In contrast, since the initiation of a Quality of Worklife program at GM in 1973, there have been an increasing number of cooperative arrangements to address both new issues and reemerging issues. The central provision of the 1984 GM-UAW pact—a "job bank" providing for placement of workers displaced by new technology and other causes—is one of the most noteworthy examples. However, labor relations in the auto industry are still characterized by considerable conflict, as the 1984 pact was reached only after corporate threats and a strike by the UAW. The goal of this essay is to explain the shift toward more cooperative labor relations in the auto industry, with a special focus on the role of conflict itself. The

[1]We would like to acknowledge the work of the co-authors and faculty advisors of the GM contest paper from which this originated. We would like to give special thanks to William A. Faunce and R. C. Hill for their help and intellectual inspiration. We also wish to thank Lori Hudson and Dan Cornfield for their assistance.

Michael Indergaard and Michael Cushion • Department of Sociology, Michigan State University, East Lansing, MI 48824.

nature of this cooperation will also be examined in terms of the relative power of labor and management to pursue contradictory interests.

The coexistence of conflict and cooperation is a well established theme in social theory. Especially relevant is Simmel's observation that even the most conflict-filled relationships necessarily attain a certain amount of cooperation if only in order that the relationship may continue to exist.[2] To characterize changes in labor relations we will utilize a typology of conflict and cooperation in labor relations.[3] "Conflict" and "cooperation" can be seen as polar opposite ideal types that reflect substantively different patterns of labor relations. Under conflict relations, labor and management focus their energies on weakening each other in their struggle over control of the workplace and for a share of the wealth. Conflict fundamentally involves all-out resistance by management to the collective organization of workers, and the aggressive challenge by the workers and their organization to management's prerogatives of control. On the other end of the spectrum is cooperation, characterized by management's full acceptance of the union as an active partner in a formal plan, joint handling of both personnel and production problems, willingness to address each other's concerns, and equitable sharing of the wealth gained from cooperative efforts. The middle ground between conflict and cooperation—"adversarial relations"—involves significant quantities of each. It may range from observing legalistic minimums of cooperation while engaging in considerable conflict, to formal legalism tempered by tolerance and cooperation in practice, so as to reduce conflict.

Labor conflict is a key dynamic in changing patterns of labor relations, as union and management pursue contradictory interests. Giddens notes that one of the primary goals of workers in unionizing has been the "modification of market capacity to secure scarce economic rewards."[4] This is a strategy of "aggressive economism" in which unions stress heightened market capacity over all other concerns. A second major issue for unions has been that of control over the work process. Rather than seriously challenging the hierarchy of authority in the firm, unions have typically followed a strategy of "defensive control" whereby an effort is made by the union to make more formal the control already possessed by workers. Giddens notes that a union strategy of aggressive economism, in combination with a defensive approach to control, facilitates the institutionalization of industrial conflict. The pursuit of aggressive economism by the UAW during most of the post-war period can be seen as a factor in the auto industry's tendency during this period to stay within the bounds of adversarial labor relations.

Braverman's study of the detailed division of labor and the introduction of mechanization offers important insights into management strategies.

[2]Georg Simmel, *Conflict*, trans. Kurt Wolff (Glencoe, Illinois: The Free Press, 1955).
[3]Our discussion here borrows from the typology of managerial strategies, regarding unions, of Arthur A. Sloane, and Fred Witney, *Labor Relations* (Englewood Cliffs, NJ: Prentice-Hall, Inc., 1977). However, it bears little resemblance, analytically, to their treatment.
[4]Anthony Giddens, *The Class Structure of the Advanced Societies*, (London: Hutchinson University Library, 1973), pp. 205–206.

Through such measures management not only cheapens labor, but also increases its control over the production process.[5] It is especially important for our purpose of exploring how issues of control shape labor relations to note that there are actually different management control strategies. Friedman makes a useful distinction between "direct control" and "responsible autonomy."[6] Direct control entails making worker behavior predictable through threats, close supervision, and reduction of responsibility. The history of the auto industry suggests that this control strategy can be associated most directly with conflict labor relations. Responsible autonomy, on the other hand, attempts to realize more of the worker's inherent potential. As a strategy of control, responsible autonomy stresses winning the voluntary compliance of workers and the cooperation of their union. "Top managers try to win their loyalty, and co-opt their organizations to the firm's ideals."[7] In this light, the fundamental structures of labor–management cooperation in the auto industry, the Quality of Worklife (QWL) programs, are also structures of control over workers in which union officials actively participate. Our study suggests that QWL developed as an alternative control strategy in the face of increasing worker resistance to direct control.

In the last fifteen years developments outside the domain of labor relations have interacted with labor conflict to change the shape of labor relations. International economic change, technological change, and labor conflict are the three main causal variables of significance in this study. In the context of two major world oil crises, foreign competition and the unprecedented convergence between the U.S. and world automobile markets set in motion a general restructuring of the world automobile industry in the last decade. With corporate restructuring of production operations worldwide, management control over certain areas of decision-making assumed a significance in labor relations it had not previously had. The construction of global production networks and the sourcing of parts and vehicles from foreign suppliers has greatly increased management's leverage over workers. A global division of labor implies a global labor market. American auto workers find themselves bidding against workers who are not only outside their union, but who also live in societies with radically lower standards of living.

Technological change has also given added importance to management decision-making. The accelerated introduction of computer-based automation in the last decade facilitated the creation of global production networks. The development of this more flexible form of automation has also greatly expanded the scope of application of labor-saving technology and has resulted in a considerable reduction in the demand for labor. Management has implemented Japanese models of responsible autonomy at advanced production facilities in an attempt to reap the full potential of new technology and to approach the productivity and quality levels attained by foreign competitors.

[5]Harry Braverman, *Labor and Monopoly Capital* (New York: Monthly Review Press, 1974).
[6]Andrew L. Friedman, *Industry and Labor* (London: Macmillan, 1977).
[7]Ibid., p. 78.

Our essay addresses the interrelated effects of these three causal variables on changes in labor relations in the auto industry. We are concerned with how technological changes alter the market capacities of workers, on the one hand; yet we are also concerned with management's ability to use technology to alter its own demand for labor and undercut labor's market capacity. The decisive development underlying the shift in labor relations in the auto industry has been the companies' use of global strategies which have circumvented labor conflict and thwarted the UAW's strategy of aggressive economism. Intimately related to this shift in the balance of power has been the impact of technological change on the division of labor, as the struggle for control of the workplace has important consequences for the struggle over economic shares as well.

II. THE LEGACY OF CONFLICT AND POST-WAR LABOR RELATIONS

An analysis of transition in auto industry labor relations requires a review of the past relations from which the "new relations" have emerged. The conflictual origins of the United Automobile Workers (UAW) in the 1930s generated a legalistic structure that regularized hostilities, transforming them into adversarial relations. The union chose to relinquish shopfloor control and abandon attempts to play a part in strategic planning and decision making in return for the legitimacy and stability of the union and economic returns for the workers. The adversarial pattern survived through three decades until the 1970s when the question of its efficacy arose.

A. Origins in Conflict—Pre-1950

The UAW was born of violent and bitter conflict, unsurpassed by any subsequent labor struggle in the industry. The companies resisted worker organization, in defiance of the 1935 National Labor Relations Act, through the use of espionage, strikebreakers, and illegal company unions. Workers retaliated by seizing the means of production through the tactic of sit-down strikes. Blood was spilled and lives lost in attack and retaliation as company-hired militia fired on strikers with weapons and tear gas and workers responded with bricks, bottles, and car-door hinges.

The effectiveness of these strikes revealed the importance of technology in increasing worker leverage. The large plant, inspired by the drive for economies of scale, created a production network that was vulnerable to the stoppage of one or two key plants at the same time that it coalesced large numbers of workers who could organize and withhold their labor power. However, the larger importance of the 1930s sit-down strikes is that they not only secured the rights of the workers, but also legitimized the union.

Though conflict continued during the World War II era, a split began to occur between the workers and their leadership. The leadership sought to increase the legitimacy of the union by, in part, delivering a reliable wartime labor force.[8] This goal was exemplified by the no-strike pledge in which labor leaders agreed not to strike for the duration of the war. However, this commitment to cooperation was very much at odds with the wishes of the workers. In spite of the no-strike pledge, 1944 and 1945 saw the second and third highest number of striking auto workers involved in wildcat work stoppages. These strikes represented worker dissatisfaction with the union accommodation that sacrificed input into shop floor control for union legitimacy.

The issue of work force stability remained prominent after the war. The importance of the strike preceding the 1946 contract was its ability to channel worker discontent, which had built up during the war, away from issues of shop floor control.[9] Formal efforts were made to secure a stable labor force: Ford demanded, and received, a union responsibility clause which called for disciplinary measures for those involved in work actions that circumvented the contract. The intent of the clause was to funnel the initiative of the work force into formal channels of action and then bind it by the resulting contract agreements and the legalistic grievance procedure.

Monetary issues were in the forefront due to expectations of a post-war depression and the request for a 30% wage increase. While Ford settled in late February of 1946, Reuther was asking GM to "open up the books," supposedly to prove that it could indeed grant the proposed 30% increase without raising car prices. After a strike of nearly 6 months, the UAW settled for an 18 1/2 cent wage increase, a mere 1/2 cent more than Ford, and failed to undermine the management prerogative of setting prices.[10] This agreement set the pattern for the future; though shop floor control and economic issues were both important to workers, the union chose to press a policy of aggressive economism throughout the next decade by bargaining for large increases in economic compensation.

B. Post-War Balance of Power

The post-war period was one of growth for the auto industry and the UAW. Auto companies expanded and altered the system of production, stepping up the introduction of new technology. The post-war boom also saw the resolution of economistic and control issues in favor of an attempt to share in the new wealth.

The automakers used the end of World War II as an opportunity to engage in a giant expansion of their production facilities as they made the reconversion to civilian auto production. Between 1945 and 1955, motor vehicle and equipment companies invested $7.5 billion.[11] This massive expansion

[8]Martin Glaberman, *Wartime Strikes* (Detroit: Bewick Publishers, 1980).
[9]N. Lichtenstein, "Auto Worker Militancy and the Structure of Factory Life," *Journal of American History* **67**, no. 2 (1980), p. 342.
[10]Benjamin M. Selekman, Stephen H. Fuller, Thomas Kennedy, John M. Baitsell, *Problems in Labor Relations* (New York: McGraw-Hill Book Company, 1964).
[11]Kuniko Fujita, "Black Workers' Struggles in Detroit's Auto Industry" (Master's Thesis, Department of Sociology, Michigan State University, 1977), p. 44.

was made possible by the surprising post-war boom, fueled by pent-up consumer demand. For example, GM sales increased from $2 billion to $12.5 billion between 1946 and 1955. This boom allowed the auto industry to accelerate the introduction of new technology.

In 1946 the term automation was coined, and the technology of this era has alternately been called "Detroit automation" or "hard automation"; hard not only because it relied on gears and cams to position the part to be worked on, but because of its inflexibility. Machinery essentially had to be rearranged at model changeover time. Once laid out by the engineers, the machinery dictated the flow of work. However, although the automation was "hard" and inflexible, decentralization gave the industry flexibility through an expanded production network.

The new technology of the era placed the auto industry, according to Woodward's[12] typology, into a mixed category of large batch/mass and process technology. A large portion of the new technology was made up of automatic transfer machines. In the past, the unit to be altered was transported from one station to the next, where the operation was performed, and then moved on. The new transfer machines drove the part along a conveyor to a station, automatically positioned it, performed the operation and then automatically passed it on.

A technological advance which has especially effected the work of the skilled machinist is the numerically controlled (NC) machine tool. Likened to the assembly line in its power to revolutionize manufacturing, the numerically controlled machine tool is a method of information processing and machine control. The NC machine tool performs the same operations, using the same cutters, as a machinist.

These technological changes brought structural changes to the work tasks and the work force that in many respects continue today. One of the largest was the transformation of many semi-skilled operatives into machine tenders. With the old technology these workers had some degree of control over the work pace, which would, for instance, enable them to work ahead and use that time to rest. Now, the new machines set the pace, and the worker was forced to pay more attention to the machine in order to ensure its continued operation.

The uninterrupted operation of the transfer line increased the importance of the skilled maintenance worker, because a breakdown of one of these machines stops the entire line. Because of the large amount of capital tied into it, this machinery tended to be operated at full speed, which strained the equipment and led to frequent breakdowns.[13] Cole makes the point that management has limited flexibility in defining the tasks of skilled workers, since the content of their jobs is fixed by "custom and contract."[14] Consequently, skilled workers have the leverage to pursue issues informally.

[12]Joan Woodward, *Industrial Organization: Theory and Practice* (New York: Oxford University Press, 1980). p. 39.
[13]Harley Shaiken, *Work Transformed: Automation and Labor in the Computer Age* (New York: Holt, Rinehart and Winston, 1984), p. 67.
[14]Robert Cole, *Work, Mobility and Participation* (Berkeley: University of California Press, 1979).

"Among the skilled trades, most problems are settled on the floor and rarely go into the grievance machinery."[15] This leverage of the skilled workers, based on the power derived from traditional craft control and the increased reliance on continuously operated machinery, allows them to enjoy some tolerance from management. They would put this to use later in an effort to advance their own interests.

The semi-skilled workers, such as assemblers, stand in contrast since their job tasks can be modified by management. In the event of a dispute over the content of a job it becomes a matter of negotiation between union representatives and management. The continual rearrangement of the manufacturing process within the plants is a source of many strikes over work standards when workers and management are at odds over the combination of tasks which will be performed by workers and the numbers of workers assigned to those tasks. Because the semi-skilled workers have little autonomy and leverage in the determination of their own work roles, they resort to wildcat strikes to stop the work process when they do not receive satisfaction from the negotiation through formal channels.

In spite of occasional intra-union disputes over the designation of a particular bundle of tasks to a particular semi-skilled job classification, the union as a whole has staunchly defended the elaborate system of job titles and wage rates. Perlman's thesis explains this in terms of the historical development of organized labor in an era of labor shortage that focused labor's attention on the issue of control of job opportunities, that is, market capacity. Along with this, the presence of Tayloristic techniques of job division provided two options for the incipient unions. The first, more radical, solution would have been to enlarge jobs or insist on a voice in their design. The other solution was to ". . .accept the given framework of power and struggle to make quantitative improvements in worker rewards."[16] The latter, as aggressive economism, was the solution the UAW chose while supporting the system of job classifications and work roles.

This discussion shows that the post-war economic growth of the auto industry allowed the union to press its economic demands. As the workers' market capacity increased because of the legitimation of the union, they were able to share the economic wealth of increased productivity while the union substituted "union responsibility" for efforts to gain shop floor control. In contrast is the balance of power in the late 1970s and 1980s, in which the UAW would not only be forced to abandon its push for economic gains, but would also aid in tearing down rigid job classifications in the interests of job security.

C. Collective Bargaining Issues and Agreements

The collective bargaining table served as labor's primary arena of struggle over its interests, and the concerns that were raised in bargaining reflect

[15]Stanley Aronowitz, *False Promises: The Shaping of American Working Class Consciousness* (New York: McGraw-Hill, 1973).
[16]Cole, pp. 102–104.

priorities set by union leadership. The most prominent subject was that of monetary issues and sharing the wealth. The 1948 contract followed a pattern similar to that of 1946 with concentration on economic and union security issues and relative lack of concern over issues of control, which had been relegated to juridical grievance procedures. The economic gains were important as workers were granted a cost of living allowance (COLA) pegged to the BLS consumer price index (CPI) and an annual improvement factor based on productivity gains. The first allowed workers to keep pace with inflation, though they took three wage cuts between 1948 and 1950. The annual improvement factor derived from union acceptance of new technology and cooperative attempts to share in the wealth it produced, rather than an attempt to impede its implementation.

The most remarkable aspect of the 1950 contract was that it was scheduled to run for a five-year span unless reopened to address economic issues. Other notable economic features were the continuation of COLA and annual productivity factor increases along with a new company-financed pension and an improved insurance plan. The sacrifice of control is indicated by the union's granting to the company the right to establish and enforce production standards while the union's right to question them was restricted to reaction through the grievance procedure. Production standards were no longer a strikeable issue.

The financial largesse of the 1950 contract, "hailed . . . as the start of a new era of peaceful industrial relations,"[17] did not prevent trouble from brewing. While all auto workers were concerned with mass layoffs, skilled workers, in particular, pushed the proposal of a shortened work week.[18] All parties agreed to reopen negotiations in 1953 and among the provisions was a 10-cent differential for over 150 skilled classifications. Yet, while workers kept the issue of a shortened work week alive, Reuther's 1955 solution was for a guaranteed annual wage to augment technological productivity gains. The result was supplemental unemployment benefits (SUB) which, when combined with local unemployment compensation, entitled workers to 65% of their salary for 4 weeks and 60% for another 22 weeks. However, a study of auto workers[19] indicated that most workers still preferred a shortened work-week to avoid the layoffs that SUB was designed to alleviate.

In spite of SUB's attempt to ameliorate technological layoffs, plus an additional 8-cent wage increase for skilled workers, the skilled workers were unmoved as they walked out in protest at GM and Ford over the inadequacy of the differential. Aronowitz asserts that the annual improvement factor and escalator clause were the UAW's payoff for providing long-term freedom from strikes. Yet just months after the signing of the 1950 contract, 13,000 Chrysler workers walked off the job in a dispute over work standards. The

[17]James R. Green, *The World of the Worker: Labor in Twentieth-Century America* (New York: Hill and Wang, 1981), p. 208.

[18]Art Preis, *Labor's Giant Step: Twenty Years of the CIO* (New York: Pathfinder Press, 1964), p. 439.

[19]W. A. Faunce, "Automation and Leisure," in *Work and Leisure*, ed. Erwin O. Smigel (New Haven, CT: College and University Press, 1963).

early 1950s was a period of substantial wildcatting in disapproval of the emphasis on aggressive economism over shop floor issues such as increased line speed. Removing the issue of production standards from the strike mechanism caused frustration to mount as grievances piled up. "By 1955, the turmoil in the auto shops was so widespread that the next agreement abandoned the five-year no-strike formula. . . ."[20]

A number of non-economic measures were installed during the 1950s through the collective bargaining procedure in order to administer to the effects of technological change. While they gave no voice to workers in matters of the introduction of technology, they set guidelines for the redistribution of workers whose plants were closed or whose jobs were replaced by a machine. Among these measures were: preferential inter-plant hiring for those laid off: attrition rights giving high-seniority employees the right to be rehired at other plants before those of lower seniority at that plant; and the transfer-of-operations principle, whereby displaced workers had the opportunity to move to the plant replacing the operations of another. As the end of the 1960s approached, the question of the redistribution of jobs would become transformed into the protection of jobs.

The union's growing concern over the erosion of the bargaining unit because of technological change became a strikeable issue during the 1967 contract negotiations. The introduction of computer-operated test equipment and numerically controlled machines meant that work previously performed by union workers was being assigned to salaried personnel.[21] The union believed that old job classifications should be utilized, since the new technology did not mean that new work was being performed, but rather that the same task was being performed in a different manner. Here, the effect of technology on job and union security became formally recognized.

This issue was addressed and solved through the collective bargaining process via the establishment of a six-member National Committee on Technological Progress, made up of three representatives of management and labor. Its purpose was to settle disputes arising from the introduction of new technology, such as the "shift[ing] of work from represented to non-represented classifications, or by alleged improper assignment of work to non-represented employees."[22] Reassignment of work was one way in which management could use technology to gain greater control over the workplace. As more new technology-related jobs were introduced and assigned to non-represented employees, the proportion of union-controlled positions in the corporation would decline, and important operations such as machine tooling would be removed from union control. The newly established committee was designed to cushion the introduction of technological change by discussing its

[20]Aronowitz, p. 369.

[21]"Statement on Unit Erosion Presented by United Auto Workers to General Motors Corporation," *Daily Labor Report*, no. 230, 28 (Washington DC: Bureau of National Affairs, Nov. 1967), p. D-1.

[22]GM-UAW 1967 Contract Agreement between United Automobile Workers and General Motors Corporation, September 1967.

impact before it became problematic. Yet it also clearly reaffirmed the UAW's acceptance of the introduction of new technology as an instrument of increasing productivity.

Aside from discussing the effects of technology on the bargaining unit, the contract supplement defining the committee provided for short-range, specialized training programs for those employees qualified to perform the new or changed work. If the committee failed to resolve any dispute, the issue would enter the jurisdiction of the grievance procedure. Though the committee represented a move toward cooperative relations, the older legalistic procedures had not been abandoned.

Throughout the 30 years after the beginning of the UAW, labor relations in the auto industry moved from the conflict end of the continuum to a position of adversarial relations. Management attempts to eliminate worker organization gave way as the collective bargaining and grievance procedures took their place as the avenue of dispute. Conflict within this legalistic framework took the form of organized strikes aimed at economic goals, while workers utilized wildcat strikes to confront unaddressed problems of workplace control.

By the end of the 1960s the issue of shop floor control showed increasing strain, as indicated by the overloaded grievance system. In the next two decades, labor conflict in conjunction with major changes in technology and the international economy would erode the accommodation forged early in the post-war era.

III. CAUSES OF THE SHIFT IN LABOR RELATIONS

Technological change, major transitions in the world economy and continued labor conflict were the three factors that interacted to produce the shift toward more cooperative labor relations in the automobile industry. Labor conflict led to the establishment of an alternative model of labor relations in the form of the Quality of Worklife program and remained a central dynamic in the continued evolution of labor relations. Economic crisis created new imperatives for corporate profitability, especially as foreign competitors suddenly won a large chunk of the U.S. market. In an attempt to regain profitability, the U.S. auto makers have utilized a new generation of technology which has increased the mobility of capital on the one hand, and expanded the application of labor-saving technology on the other. Both strategic thrusts have reduced the demand for the UAW's labor, decisively tipping the balance of power against the union.

A. Technological Change

The development and introduction of new technology has been greatly shaped by the revitalization strategies of auto corporations intent on weathering economic crises by making the best of new opportunities. Shifts in market demand and wholesale downsizing of automobiles since the mid-1970s required the reorganization of production, providing auto companies with the opportunity for large-scale introduction of new, more flexible forms of automation. Flexible automation is based on the "information processing capabilities of the computer and the ability of micro-electronics to bring computer power directly to the point of production."[23] By 1983 the auto companies were buying 45% of the robots and 30% of the computer software systems sold in the United States.[24]

The ongoing development of computer-based technologies in the auto industry revolves around the twin efforts of automating specific production operations and tying together these "islands of automation" into flexible manufacturing systems. Computer-aided design (CAD) allows engineers to use computer simulations to solve problems of design and production, and is especially important in the drive to integrate design and production. Complementing CAD is CAM, or computer-aided manufacturing. CAM directs numerically controlled machines and automatically guides workpieces from machine to machine on computer-controlled material handling systems. The use of computer networks as management information systems to collect data is the central technology for management planning and the monitoring of machines, product quality, and increasingly, workers. Because of its flexibility, the robot has been applied to numerous tasks in auto production: loading and unloading machine tools, welding, painting, assembly, and inspection. The robot, more than any other technology, is directly intended to replace human workers. By 1980 the economic incentive proved critical, as the total cost of a robot was about $6 an hour while the total compensation cost for an autoworker was $20 an hour. GM plans to acquire 20,000 robots by 1990.[25]

Flexible automation portends two distinct blueprints in the corporate reorganization of automobile production. The computer chip greatly reduces the limits of time and space on corporate strategy, facilitating global strategies and the decentralized global production network which is captured in the image of the "Global Factory."[26] At the same time the computer chip promotes the integration of the various stages of auto production into the centralized manufacturing complex or "Factory of the Future." In sum, computer-based automation offers corporations expanded options for dealing with uncertain economic conditions and militant workers.

B. Economic Transition and Corporate Revitalization

The passage to a new global economic structure in the auto industry was initiated with the jolt of oil shortages in the 1970s. Oil crises in 1973 and 1979 resulted in drops in North American auto sales of over 10 and 30%, respec-

[23]Shaiken, p. 2.
[24]Richard Child Hill, "A Global Marriage of Convenience: General Motors and Toyota at Fremont," paper presented at the Annual Meeting of the Society for the Study of Social Problems, Detroit, Michigan, August 28, 1983. p. 4.
[25]Shaiken, p. 162–168.
[26]Shaiken, op. cit.

tively. GM, Ford, and Chrysler lost a record $4.2 billion in 1980 and more than $1 billion in the first 3 quarters of 1981.[27] This bath of red ink threatened the very survival of Chrysler, and to a lesser extent Ford.

The recent turnaround—record profits of $6.15 billion in 1983, and nearly $10 billion in 1984 for the Big Three—belies long-term uncertainty. World-wide, the industry faces excess capacity, stagnating market demand, and rising protectionism. Auto corporations are struggling to make the transition from a world industry characterized by corporate monopolies over national markets to a transnational industry that is global in many more dimensions.[28] Energy shortages and subsequent government regulations brought into existence a considerable U.S. market for smaller, fuel efficient cars causing the convergence of product characteristics in the American and world markets.

Accustomed to meeting and reinforcing the traditional preference of Americans for full-size automobiles, the U.S. automakers were immediately vulnerable to foreign competitors who had a well-established tradition in producing small cars. The share of foreign imports in the U.S. market rose from 5% in 1965 to nearly 25% in 1980.[29] With a cost advantage of around $2000 per car, Japanese imports have been held back for the last four years by "voluntary restraints," informal quotas which in 1985 limited the number of Japanese imports to 1.85 million units annually.[30] The near future is likely to bring even sharper foreign competition with the lifting of voluntary restraints and the continued trend toward downsizing cars. Of 9.2 million cars sold in the United States in 1983, approximately 45% were small cars and nearly half of these were of Japanese origin.[31]

The Global Factory and the Factory of the Future are useful abstractions for differentiating the immediate strategies which specific corporations have followed to meet new challenges and opportunities. Ford and GM can be said to have followed the logic of the Global Factory, responding to new global competition with global strategies: the world car, global integration, and global sourcing. The logic of these global strategies implies a new international division of labor characterized by increasing concentration of conceptual activities in advanced industrial countries, revolving around "high technology, research, design and global management while manufacturing is decentralized throughout the world."[32] The combination of computer tech-

---

[27]Lydia Fischer, "Auto Crisis and Union Response," in *Labor and Technology: Union Responses to Changing Environments,* eds. D. Kennedy, C. Craypo and M. Lehman (Penn State University: Dept. of Labor Studies, 1982).

[28]Hill, 1983a., p. 2.

[29]Richard Child Hill, "The Auto Industry in Global Transition," paper presented at the Annual Meetings of the ASA, Detroit, Michigan, September 3, 1983b.

[30]James V. Higgins, "GM Calls New Process More Important than the Car," *Detroit News,* 13 Jan 1985, 19a.

[31]Quinn Mills, and Malcolm S. Salter, "A Lot More at Stake than Money." *New York Times,* 22 July 1984.

[32]Richard Child Hill, "Transnational Capitalism and Urban Crisis: The Case of the Auto Industry and Detroit," paper presented at the Annual Meeting of the Society for Study of Social Problems, August 23, 1981, pp. 7–8.

nology and telecommunications has aided corporate efforts to reorganize production on a world scale. For example, thousands of Ford engineers and technicians throughout the world can work on the same project by plugging into a new computer center at Ford Headquarters in Dearborn, Michigan. Using this system to synthesize designs from around the world underlay the development of the Ford Escort—the first world car. In turn, a standardized product sets the stage for worldwide production.[33]

Their strategic vision having expanded to international dimensions, auto companies "produce different parts and assemble finished vehicles in different countries depending upon the advantages offered in each and integrate their operations on a global plane."[34] By designing a world car for production in all major markets, automakers attain economies of scale in product development, component design, and production. The world car and the location of production and supply sites through a global sourcing strategy greatly increases the leverage of auto companies over the work force of any one country.

Japan's Toyota has made the most of the opportunities of the new era through the use of a home-based export strategy that contrasts greatly with the logic of the Global Factory. One of the foundations of the Toyota model is the concentration and integration of various production stages through the just-in-time supplier system, an idea pioneered long ago at Ford's massive River Rouge complex. The principle of just-in-time permits a close coordination between manufacturer and suppliers that reduces inventory and storage requirements while promoting more consistent quality in parts. A second basis of the Toyota model is a system of flexible manufacturing practices through which the auto maker is able both to achieve high quality control and continually reduce the amount of human labor in each car. A final ingredient critical to Toyota's success is paternalistic labor relations epitomized by the "company town" atmosphere of the huge Toyota City complex where over 35,000 employees work and live.[35] Work relations and practices on the shop floor reflect patterns of labor–management cooperation that are the norm in the core operations of Japanese automakers. The central feature of the Japanese model of cooperative labor relations is consensual decision-making and responsible autonomy circumscribed by the structure of the small work group. The relative autonomy of Japanese auto workers is granted in the context of weak unions and management's control over the parameters of decision-making and goal-setting.[36]

Toyota City appears to be an influential model for competitors who are now devising strategies to develop international competitiveness in the long run. An American emphasis on integrating advanced forms of flexible automation into these strategies has brought forth futuristic imagery.

[33]Ibid.

[34]Hill, 1983b, p. 12.

[35]Richard Child Hill, "The Global Factory and the Company Town: The Changing Division of Labor in the International Automobile Industry," paper presented at a Conference on the Urban and Regional Impact of the New International Division of Labor. University of Hong Kong, August 14–20, 1985.

[36]Cole, 1979.

The most advanced blueprint of a Factory of the Future appeared in the aftermath of the 1984 collective bargaining between GM and the UAW in the form of GM's Saturn Project. The goal of Saturn is to put a facility into operation by the end of the decade that can produce small cars in the United States at a cost that is competitive with the Japanese. The first major feature of the Saturn model is the progressive integration of various computer-based technologies, especially the unification of design and production techniques, with the long term goal of achieving the completely computerized factory. Secondly, Saturn is to be a highly centralized manufacturing complex organized along the lines of the just-in-time system. A third component of the Saturn model is modular assembly, a manufacturing practice somewhat analogous to the way automobiles were constructed by teams of skilled craftsmen before the introduction of the assembly line. The U.S. automakers are experimenting with combining modular assembly and flexible automation at various sites such as GM's Pontiac Fiero plant. "Entire components or sections of the car are built up at stationary work sites by teams of workers and are brought to the assembly line on a computer-controlled cart."[37] Maintaining a small buffer supply of modules allows work teams to set their work pace in the assembly of items of varying complexity, maximizing quality in the process. As a result, modular assembly can make considerable inroads into traditionally labor-intensive assembly work.

At certain points the Global Factory and the Factory of the Future work as complementary strategies. Some observers speculate that eventually aspects of each will be integrated in the form of regional production networks that engage in only supplementary global sourcing. Important areas of overlap at present are appearing through intercorporate networks and cross-penetration. In the last five years American corporations have forged increasing numbers of cooperative relationships with their European and Japanese counterparts so as to minimize business risks posed by the high costs of developing new design and production technology. An especially important case is GM's joint venture with Toyota at Fremont, California to learn the fine art of designing and producing small cars. The other side of the coin is that the Japanese are engaged in cross-penetration—locating some production facilities in their major foreign markets in order to circumvent existing tariff barriers and to minimize protectionist sentiments.[38]

The establishment of auto manufacturing facilities in the United States by Japanese corporations has had profound ramifications in the struggle for control in the workplace, especially as the Japanese are held up as arch-competitors. Their presence in the United States reinforces management attempts to install the Japanese model of labor relations in American factories, particularly the advanced production facilities deemed to be progenitors of the Factory of the Future. The critical fact for American auto workers is that the Factory of the Future is unfolding in the shadow of the Global Factory.

---

[37]James V. Higgins, "Saturn: Auto Plant of the Future." *Detroit News*, 10 Jan. 1985, p., 10a.
[38]Hill, 1985.

C. The Conflict over Control

Increasing worker resistance to authoritarian controls in the workplace during the late 1960s and early 1970s turned the focus of labor relations to workplace conditions and production decisions of management. Wildcat strikes temporarily took the initiative out of the hands of union leadership and challenged the authority of the union hierarchy. By moving to address workplace issues in collective bargaining and co-sponsoring Quality of Work-life programs, the union leadership harnessed worker militance over issues of control on the one hand, and diffused worker rebellion against corporate and union authority on the other.

The latter half of the 1960s saw increasing individual and collective manifestations of worker resistance to management structures founded on the strategy of direct control. From 1965 to 1969, absenteeism increased by 50% and turnover rates by more than 70%. Grievances and disciplinary layoffs rose 38 and 40%, respectively, and seemingly indicated an escalation in shop-floor conflict.[39] Also suggestive of increasing conflict were higher numbers of strikes and striking workers from 1965 to 1969, with strikes hitting 144 in 1968 and 111 in 1969, involving 166,900 and 134,100 workers, respectively.[40]

Especially significant were a series of wildcat strikes led by militant black auto workers at Detroit plants beginning in 1968. Their protests crystallized around the view that aged, inner-city plants that had not been modernized and had large black work forces relied upon labor intensity and speed-up "as their production schedules were synchronized to conform to the output of new automated plants in the suburbs."[41] There was a continuity between these strikes over unsafe machinery and speed-up and wildcat strikes in two of the same plants in 1973. These strikes would play an important role in a historic shift in UAW strategy.

The sluggishness of the union in pursuing workplace issues contributed to worker willingness to engage in militant job actions. With the union leadership hesitant to abandon its economistic thrust, the 1970 negotiations saw another economic crusade, but the 67-day strike against GM was perhaps the last gasp of aggressive economism by the UAW.

Although the corporations were concerned about the general rise in labor unrest on the shop floor, they found it especially painful when labor conflict negated potential benefits expected from the introduction of advanced technology. For example, GM hoped to build a small car, the Vega, at a cost competitive with European imports through the use of computer-based technologies at its Lordstown, Ohio plant. In 1971 the General Motors Assembly Division (GMAD) was brought in during model changeover at Lordstown to bring the line speed up from 60 cars to its theoretical specification of 100 cars per hour. An aggressive campaign by GMAD to increase control over work

[39]Rosabeth Moss Kanter, *The Change Masters* (New York: Simon and Schuster, Inc., 1983).
[40]U.S. Bureau of Labor Statistics, "Analysis of Work Stoppages," BLS Bulletins 1302, 1339, 1381, 1420, 1460, 1525, 1573, 1611, 1646, 1687, 1727, 1777, (Washington, DC: GPO, 1960–1971).
[41]Fujita, op. cit., p. 46.

practices met with sabotage and work slowdowns. The company retaliated by sending the whole workforce home whenever repairs had reached a predetermined level and by letting grievances build up.[42] A bitter three-week strike ensued and eventually GM shifted production of the Vega to a Canadian plant, which cut costs using the old technology.[43]

In the 1973 auto talks, union leadership felt compelled by widespread worker discontent over heavy overtime to make this workplace issue their central bargaining issue. Two wildcat strikes over health and safety conditions at old Chrysler plants in Detroit during national bargaining induced the union to push for establishment of joint labor–management committees to address broader workplace issues. The GM agreement initiated the first Quality of Worklife (QWL) program in the auto industry.

The auto corporation's increasing use of new technology and global production networks heightened conflict over issues of control throughout the late 1970s and early 1980s. One of management's apparent goals in the introduction of new computer-based technology has been to gain more control over the independent-minded skilled trades. Management information systems have been applied to lessen the autonomy of skilled maintenance workers and skilled tool and die makers, as was illustrated in an attempt to rationalize diemaking through computer scheduling at Ford's River Rouge complex in 1977. Fearing an erosion of their trade, and suspicious because they had not been involved in its planning, the leaders of the tool and die making teams effectively resisted the project by refusing to provide information on the status of their groups' work during the crucial stage of fine-tuning the computer system. Another form of flexible automation, numerical control, has shown some potential for allowing automakers to bypass their traditional vulnerability to the production of dies by the tool and die makers. GM was able to send numerical control tapes for the Cadillac Seville to a nonstriking GM plant when strikes at the original plant threatened to hold back introduction of the new model.[44] By 1979, auto workers such as those at Ford Local 600 at River Rouge aggressively challenged the ways in which the auto companies were using new technology. The River Rouge local set the tone for national bargaining, proclaiming that "using technology for speed-up, breaking of work rules, union-busting, or robot-like control over workers must be prevented."[45]

Developments in technology, economic structure and labor conflict not only raised new labor relations issues, but also brought new life to old issues that had been settled by the early post-war accommodation between the union and the auto companies. The conflict over control that existed during the 1970s was reinforced by the introduction of new technology, but other

[42]B. J. Widick, "The Men Won't Tow the Vega Line," *Nation* 214 (March 27, 1972), pp. 403–474.
[43]James V. Higgins, Saturn's Revolution: How GM Set Course to Next Century" *Detroit News*, 13 Jan. 1985, p. 18a.
[44]Shaiken, op. cit.
[45]Mike Rinaldi, "New Technology—A Strikeable Issue," *Ford Facts*, Ford Local 600, 39, no. 9, 1979.

issues also became salient. Job security held center stage as outsourcing combined with new technology to threaten union jobs. Union input into strategic decision-making became an important issue as sourcing, the introduction of new technology and the location of investments combined to dramatically lower the demand for labor.

Since the unprecedented 1980–1982 economic crisis in the auto industry, management seemingly has taken the initiative in pursuing labor relations issues. The threat to the well-being of the industry provided management with the opportunity to challenge work rules and job classifications traditionally negotiated by union locals. The adverse effect of labor conflict, especially on the introduction of new technology, led the auto makers to make the very nature of labor relations an issue. Because of economic uncertainty, management was able to demand that the union cooperate in reducing fixed labor costs in order to meet foreign competition. Encouraged by the record profits of 1983 and 1984, the union attempted to regain the momentum in the 1984 GM negotiations with an aggressive challenge to the prerogatives of management control and a demand for restoration of economic concessions. However the militant bargaining posture of the UAW belied the fact that the union's leverage against the auto companies had steadily eroded with the accelerated introduction of labor-saving technology and the unfolding of global production networks.

D. The Shift in the Balance of Power

The UAW has experienced a downward swing in membership and power since 1979, finding little reprieve in the recent return to prosperity by the American auto makers. The union has failed to recover from the 1979 to 1982 crisis, when layoffs hit a record level of 254,000 and reached into the ranks of workers who had 15 and 20 years seniority.[46]

The auto corporations took immediate advantage of the fact that the auto market slump and subsequent corporate revitalization strategies resulted in a reduction in the general demand for labor. In 1981 GM Chairman Roger Smith used the leverage of the Factory of the Future against the union when he warned that for every dollar-an-hour rise in wages of a UAW worker, 1,000 more robots became economically feasible.[47] In 1982, Smith wielded the Global Factory early in contract negotiations, with the threat that "if we don't get a competitive wage rate, there are going to be a lot of plants closed."[48] The UAW was forced to give up its annual productivity raises and agreed to deferred COLA payments in a move foreshadowing a break with the postwar pattern of labor relations.

Since 1982 the industry has enjoyed a full economic recovery without a

[46]Ann M. Job, "UAW's Primary Goal is Job Security," *Detroit News*, 29 July 1984.
[47]Shaiken, p. 168.
[48]James Risen, "GM Tells UAW, It's Wage Cuts or Plant Closings," *Detroit Free Press*, 1 Jan 1982, section A, p. 1.

corresponding recovery in employment. The U.S. auto makers have used new technology in their reorganization of production in the United States to cut costs, and have increasingly turned to global sources for cheaper parts and even completed vehicles. Increases in productivity allowed a production force with 200,000 fewer workers to produce 6.8 million vehicles for record profits in 1983, whereas sales of 6.6 million in 1980 had resulted in record losses. Although 1984 saw even higher profits, the auto workforce of 565,000 was still 170,000 fewer than in 1978.[49]

The failure of the old formula linking employment stability and growth to company prosperity was one indication that crisis still threatened the survival of the union. The UAW went into the 1984 contract negotiations with the knowledge that pressure on employment was likely to intensify. Automation alone was predicted to eliminate 5% of the work force annually. The union's worst-case scenario was that one-third of the auto work force could lose their jobs by 1987.[50]

Thus, the 1984 bargaining with GM was considered to be a critical point in the union's history, with the union focusing its energy on the issue of future job security. The UAW demanded restrictions on the sourcing of parts and vehicles and the right to review potentially job-displacing technological changes. GM flatly refused to allow the union to restrict its strategic options, and instead continued the offensive against union local jurisdiction over work rules and job classifications. GM defined the modernization of work rules and job classifications as the critical intersection of union and corporate interests: "A full measure of job security . . . . can only be realized within a work environment which promotes operational effectiveness. . . . [the corporation warned that] . . . . "up to 130,000 jobs could be outsourced, or moved to nonunion and overseas plants, if GM does not get a competitive contract."[51] GM made the Saturn project a bargaining chip in the negotiations, with the GM Chairman's comment that an expensive contract would induce GM to postpone or cancel Saturn or "move it en masse to Germany or Japan."[52]

The union attempted to generate some leverage from the fact that larger, more profitable cars were in high demand and relatively low supply by launching a selective strike against key GM plants producing these lines. Despite a 13-day strike, the 1984 settlement was based on GM's definition of job security and contained no restrictions on the corporaation's strategic deci-sion-making. Although the 1984 agreement represents a landmark in a shift toward cooperative labor relations, an essential characteristic of this new era appears to be the decline in the union's power to confront the automakers.

[49]Marcia Stepanek, "Auto Imports Aided Efficiency too." *Detroit Free Press*, 15 Feb 1985, p. 6c; David Moberg, "Unions Seek Job Security, But Bosses Still Want Cutbacks." *In These Times*, 8–21 Aug. 1984, p. 10.

[50]"What the UAW will be Shooting for at GM and Ford" *Businessweek* 18 June 1984, p. 98; "Showdown in Detroit" *Businessweek* 10 Sept. 1984, p. 103.

[51]Ann Job, James Higgins, and John Nehman, "Two Views of the Auto Negotiations," *Detroit News*, 23 Sept. 1984, p. 3d.

[52]Ann Job, "GM Moves into a New Era" *Businessweek*, 16 July 1984, p. 52.

IV. THE EMERGENCE OF NEW LABOR RELATIONS

Since 1973, conflict over a new set of issues has tended to bring forth new forms of cooperation between management and the union. Initially, structures of labor management cooperation were relatively insulated from other spheres of labor relations. More recently, labor management cooperation itself has become a key issue in collective bargaining and is increasingly incorporated into the organization of production at new facilities.

A. Job Security Measures

In 1976 the heightened "technology consciousness" of the UAW led it to reopen the dialogue on the relationship between productivity and employment. In what some observers saw as a push for the four-day week, the UAW asked for, and received, more paid personal holidays in 1976 and 1979. By 1982 the threat to jobs stemmed from a market slump and resultant shifting of work overseas by the ailing auto makers. In the crisis negotiations of that year the paid personal holidays were dropped as the corporations claimed they contributed to high fixed labor costs. In return the UAW received a number of temporary job security measures such as a pledge by Ford and GM not to close plants on account of outsourcing, a Pilot Employment Guarantee program, and some funding to retrain laid-off workers.[53]

Going into the 1984 contract talks, both corporate and union representatives agreed that the negotiations should center on job security and cooperative efforts to make domestic auto production internationally competitive.[54] GM used its power advantage to link its demand for simplified job classifications and work rules to expanded job security. The central feature of the accord, a "job bank," is one of a number of unprecedented measures for union–management cooperation. Funded at $1 billion by GM, the job bank is a labor exchange network within the corporation for the training and/or placement of eligible workers (those with at least one year seniority who are displaced by new technology, consolidation of parts plants, productivity drives, or the transfer of work to other facilities). Assignments could be made to a wide range of tasks without regard to many work rules. A key aspect of the job bank is the creation of new labor–management structures at the local, regional and national levels to oversee the program. These committees will execute much of the actual reformation of work rules and job classifications, exploring ways to improve efficiencies at GM plants even if that means waiving or changing parts of the national contract. The local job bank committees will be notified of any technological change or outsourcing that would affect 25 or more workers.[55] In

[53]R. Milkman, and D. Stevens, "The Anti-Concessions Movement in the UAW," *Socialist Review*, no. 65 (1982), pp. 26–27.

[54]"What the UAW Will be Shooting for at GM and Ford," *Businessweek*, 18 June 1984, p. 95.

[55]"The Right Kind of Auto Contract," *Businessweek*, 8 Oct 1984. p. 160; Serrin, William, "Pioneer Bid to Save Jobs," *New York Times*, 22 Sept 1984, p. 1; "What New GM Pact with UAW Offers," *Detroit News*, 27 Sept 1984, p.

sum, the union is surrendering its right to shape work roles and job classifications through collective bargaining at the local level, in exchange for a consultative role and a job bank to cushion job loss. The Saturn labor agreement reached in 1985 appears to reinforce the move toward more comprehensive job security. Eighty percent of Saturn workers will be protected from layoffs "except in situations arising from unforseen or catastrophic events or severe economic conditions."[56]

B. Sharing the Wealth

UAW wage concessions to save Chrysler from bankruptcy set an industry pattern that has yet to be reversed. Since 1982, the auto corporations have striven to overturn the economic formula forged in the early post-war days that guaranteed workers raises for increases in productivity and the cost of living. In the name of reducing fixed labor costs Ford and GM forced the UAW to give up its annual productivity raises and to defer COLA in the 1982 contract in exchange for profit sharing. Despite two years of record profits, the settlement in 1984 reinforced this break with the past. GM succeeded in using performance bonuses to replace automatic productivity raises for two of the years of the contract, and maintained profit sharing. In addition a multi-tier wage structure favored by GM was established, indicating a divergence from the UAW's traditional policy of promoting equity between skill levels. This trend will be extended at the Saturn plant. A base salary at 80% of the annual pay under conventional contracts will be supplemented by a "Saturn Sharing" program linking profit sharing to the performance of work teams.

The sharing of the economic gains derived from cooperation to date appears less equitable than in the past. Cooperation that brought record profits has cost auto workers money at the same time that executive bonuses at GM alone reached $181.7 million. The first profit sharing payments at GM and Ford averaged $640 and $440 per employee, respectively, in contrast to the $3,400 given up by each worker in annual improvement factor and cost-of-living payments.[57]

C. QWL and Cooperative Work Practices

The Quality of Worklife program established a partnership between the union and management within a parallel structure relatively insulated from the formal hierarchy of the firm. The long-term significance of QWL is that it has served as an incubator for the evolution of cooperative work practices. QWL has not remained segmented from the larger realm of labor relations, and labor conflict has played an important role in its continued evolution. As the power of the union has waned, later cooperative developments more directly reflect the imprint of management in its attempt to structure responsible autonomy into new production facilities.

[56]John F. Nehman, "Saturn Pact called Peril to Unionism," *Detroit News*, 10 July 1985, p.
[57]David Bensman, "The Downslide of the GM Contract." *The Nation*, 3 Nov. 1984, p. 440; Ann M. Job, "Hefty Profits Bolster UAW Pay Hike Goals," *Detroit News* 30 July 1984, p. 7a.

QWL can be defined as "a process by which an organization attempts to unlock the creative potential of its people by involving them in decisions affecting their work lives."[58] More formally, two goals were to receive equal emphasis in QWL—improving the work experience through worker participation and improving organizational performance. As such, QWL from its very beginnings was amenable to the implementation of a "responsible autonomy" strategy of management control. Because GM associated a drop in its financial performance in the period 1965 to 1969 with increasing worker discontent, it had already conducted research on absenteeism, turnover, and participative management, which was incorporated into the early QWL program.[59]

The central structural characteristic of the QWL established in the 1973 GM agreement was that the corporation and the union would become co-equals in making decisions related to the QWL process. This principle was to rule at all levels of the program, from a national joint committee to local work groups. The concrete content of QWL programs was to be largely determined by local participants exploring their mutual concerns. Actual program developments covered a wide spectrum: health and safety, attendance, alcohol rehabilitation, product or service quality, as well as efforts to reduce scrap and costs.

Influenced by Western European conceptions of industrial democracy, union advocates of QWL such as UAW Vice-President Irving Bluestone cautioned that "unless the union is involved as an equal partner, these programs amount to paternalism. Whatever management gives, management can take."[60] In addition unionists took the firm position that QWL was to complement the adversarial collective bargaining relationship, not replace it. Among the restrictions that a wary UAW International imposed on the local QWL programs were that these programs could not result in job loss or an increase in production standards nor violate collective bargaining agreements. Union representatives were to be involved in all aspects of program development and participation by workers was to be on a strictly voluntary basis.[61]

By 1975, indications of a more unilateral push by management appeared with a mandate by GM that QWL principles be reflected in the design of all new plants. By the late 1970s, management had begun to channel QWL programs toward the more paternalistic Japanese model of labor–management cooperation.[62] These developments have contributed to the different

---

[58]Robert H. Guest, "Quality of Work Life-Learning from Tarrytown," *Harvard Business Review* (July–August, 1979), p. 76.

[59]Howard C. Carlson, "Organizational Research and Organizational Change: GM's Approach," *Personnel* (July–Aug., 1977).

[60]Kanter, op. cit., p. 334.

[61]Irving Bluestone, "Opportunities and Barriers to Union and Worker Cooperation with Management," presented at the Automobiles and the Future: Competition, Cooperation and Change—The Third U.S.–Japan Automobile Industry Conference, Ann Arbor, MI, 16 March 1983.

[62]Robert E. Cole, and Taizo Yakushiji, *American and Japanese Auto Industries in Transition* (Ann Arbor: Center for Japanese Studies, University of Michigan, 1984).

trajectory that QWL has taken in the last five years as the program has been subsumed by union–management conflict over issues of workplace control. Between the 1982 and 1984 national contracts, workers associated the changes in work practices made under the auspices of QWL with GM's drive to wrest control over work practices and job classifications from local unions. Workers at some locals complained that the changes brought through union–management cooperation had resulted in the loss of hundreds of jobs at plants where relief methods were changed, inspection responsibilities shifted, and workloads increased. There were also complaints that even at plants with high quality ratings, efforts were made to subcontract work to non-union suppliers and workers have been "asked" to accept lower wages in order to narrow the gap in labor costs with overseas GM plants. A number of union leaders proposed that support of QWL programs was a major factor in the downfall of many incumbents in the union's triennial elections held shortly before the 1984 negotiations. On the eve of the 1984 GM-UAW talks many upper level UAW officials in the GM division actively opposed QWL because they suspected that it would divide the union.[63]

Given current worker antagonism toward QWL, the formal diffusion of the program may have hit a dead end. However many of the innovations developed under QWL are being incorporated into new plants and continue to evolve. Especially with the increased influence of the Japanese model in recent years, cooperation is being structured into the shop floor through flexible work roles and practices in conjunction with management's strategic control over decision-making and the flow of information. GM's new Orion Township plant has its own closed-circuit television system that broadcasts a daily program of plant news to 76 TV sets on the production line with the feature attraction being a "Face the Nation"-style program where the plant manager will answer questions. Another feature in management's effort to win the hearts and minds of Orion workers is a rumor control hotline.[64] At the Pontiac Fiero plant, often cited as a blueprint for developing Saturn, GM workers are organized into groups of 10 to 20, for the purposes of problem-solving and goal-setting. Structuring increased responsibility into workers' tasks has resulted in a near doubling of the foreman's span of control. Lastly, Fiero has only 32 job classifications in contrast to several hundred at conventional sites.[65]

In the past, new plants achieved more innovation and worker participation, suggesting that they proved more amenable to QWL because they represented a fresh start at labor relations that bypassed established patterns of conflict. For example, in QWL programs at some new plants workers were given the responsibility to select, train, and evaluate new team members.

[63]David Moberg, "Prudent Militancy." In *These Times*, 10–16 Oct. 1984; p. 9; Dale Buss, "Many Officers at UAW Locals Voted Out, Portending Problems in GM Labor Talks," *Wall Street Journal*, 30 May 1984, p. 9; Ann Job, "Workplace Plan Splits Top UAW Unit." *Detroit News*, 19 Aug 1984, p. 3a.

[64]Colin Covert, "Jobs Don't Solve Their Fears," *Detroit Free Press*, 9 March 1984, p. 3b.

[65]H. Fogel, "Blueprint for Saturn," *Detroit Free Press*, 17 Feb. 1985, p. 18a.

Complementing such practices had been the development of assessment centers to screen both hourly and salaried employees by testing their response to a variety of real-plant situations.[66]

The culmination of the development of cooperative labor relations and the most publicized fresh start in the U.S. auto industry is the Saturn model. Although Saturn boosters use a separate and distinct imagery associated with advanced technology for the project, Saturn's proposed blueprint clearly shows the imprint of responsible autonomy as it has evolved within the QWL program. Workers will have more control over their work and will have access to production information. Structuring control over the Saturn work force begins with an extensive selection, training, and indoctrination process for new hires drawn from GM plants across the country. The union's acceptance of a simple job classification system will leave management relatively free to use workers as it sees fit. Non-skilled production workers will have a single job classification—"operating technician"—whereas there will be three to five classifications of skilled workers. Lastly, Saturn's linking of profit sharing to the performance of work teams means that some degree of labor control will be structured into the system of economic compensation.[67]

D. Strategic Planning and Decision Making

In recent years the increasing importance of sourcing, the introduction of technology, and the location of investment has elevated the issue of control to the highest levels of corporate decision-making. The UAW had half-heartedly probed the auto companies with requests for board seats in 1976. When the union chipped in $403 million in wage and benefit concessions to help Chrysler gain government loan guarantees in 1979 they were in a position to win something extraordinary in return. What the UAW received was a board seat for its president, Douglas Fraser.[68] Although it was uncertain at the time whether this was temporary compensation to the UAW, the union continued to hold the seat when Owen Bieber succeeded Fraser to the union presidency in 1983.

In the 1984 talks at GM and Ford that followed two years of robust recovery, a UAW spokesman declared that "we want veto power. We want joint determination across the board. You wanted us to be partners in adversity and we were. Now we want to be partners in success".[69] The union specifically sought a seat on the GM and Ford boards of directors as well as restrictions on corporate practices that cost jobs. The UAW was largely rebuffed in this attempt although it received some new if secondary roles in high level decision-making. Besides the somewhat controversial positions on

[66]Steven Fuller, "Corporate Approaches to the Quality of Work Life," *Personnel Journal* (August 1984), p. 637.

[67]Nehman, op. cit.

[68]"The Price of Peace at Chrysler," *Businessweek*, 29 Nov. 1979, pp.

[69]David Moberg, "Unions Seek Job Security, But Bosses Still Want Cutbacks," *In These Times*, 8–21 Aug. 1984, p. 10.

the job banks, the union won the right to have a UAW vice president discuss outsourcing decisions with the company board of directors or other executive groups. In addition, national joint business development committees are to be established that would create new ventures and jobs in the corporation.[70] The UAW leadership claimed that GM's commitment during negotiations to build the Saturn project in the United States, was an example of such a venture. In fact the union has had an unprecedented role in the Saturn project from the outset, as it engaged in secret negotiations and joint planning with GM for nearly a year before the 1984 national talks.

Although Saturn is to have union participation in decision-making at all levels, the union will have only a consultative role at the highest levels, as GM has declined to allow a union representative to sit on Saturn's board of directors. The limits of the UAW's influence in the new era were made obvious several months after the 1984 GM pact and the Saturn understanding, when the head of GM's small-car projects worldwide noted that "we are now in business to import Isuzus and Suzukis in perpetuity."[71]

V. CONCLUSION

Major structural changes in the world economy, technological change, and labor conflict are the three factors that interacted to produce the shift toward more cooperative labor relations in the automobile industry. A decisive shift in the balance of power in the early 1980s signalled both the demise of the adversarial accommodation established shortly after World War II and a move toward more cooperative labor relations. Underlying the new era of cooperation is the fact that the corporate use of global sourcing and labor-saving technology has undercut the bargaining power of the UAW. In fact, a comparison of the adversarial period and the new era shows the respective patterns of labor management cooperation to be imprinted by the relative power positions of management and union.

Our historical review has shown that the adversarial accommodation represented a movement away from all-out conflict as the union leadership attempted to steer worker militance away from challenging management's control over the shop floor in exchange for providing workers a guaranteed share of growing corporate wealth. Underlying the early post-war accommodation in labor relations was the monopoly position of the auto industry in the U.S. economy.[72] Economic upheavals of the last dozen years profoundly shook this arrangement, as the emergence of a global market and competition brought the U.S. auto companies record losses and the UAW record layoffs.

Foreign competition continues to motivate the effort by U.S. automakers to adjust to a new era. The American auto companies have been forced to

---

[70]"The GM Settlement is a Milestone for Both Sides," *Businessweek*, 8 Oct 1984, pp. 160–162.
[71]Job, op. cit., 1985.
[72]O'Connor, James, *The Fiscal Crisis of the State* (New York: St. Martin's Press, 1973).

reexamine all factors affecting product quality and productivity, especially in competing with Japanese companies in the new U.S. market for small cars. As a result, Japanese production and labor relations models have greatly influenced the revitalization strategies of the American auto companies. An especially relevant lesson from the Japanese experience is that limited worker involvement in decision-making may increase productivity, quality, and labor peace.

A new generation of technology based on the flexibility of computer-based automation, has also influenced the corporate reorganization of both production and labor relations. Flexible automation portends two distinct models in the corporate reorganization of automobile production with different implications for labor relations. The Global Factory implies a conflict strategy in that the geographical mobility of capital serves to threaten and discipline U.S. workers. The Factory of the Future strategy seems to promote cooperation, partly because management has found from past experience that labor conflict is incompatible with the effective use of the sophisticated technology that is central to this production strategy. It is in the development of this strategy that the U.S. auto companies are incorporating the lessons of Japanese labor relations and production models. Because new technology and corporate strategies have shifted the locus of strategic power in the organization of production, it is relatively painless for management to grant workers increased autonomy within the pre-set confines of advanced facilities.

It is the shift in the strategic locus of power that has seemingly outflanked the union's traditional points of leverage. The decisions of top executives on the introduction of new technology, global sourcing, and the location of investment have assumed a new significance in labor relations, culminating in a dramatic reduction in the demand for labor. The leaders of the UAW, neither figuratively nor literally the risk-taking crusaders of the 1930s, have failed to find new points of leverage for the union. The negotiations in 1982 and 1984 mark the critical turning point in the industry's labor relations as the auto corporations took full advantage of the union's quandary by imposing a new framework for labor relations.

Developments of the last dozen years illustrate a basic relationship between power and cooperation in labor relations. When an equal balance of power existed, cooperation centered on issues of mutual concern such as the increasing labor conflict of the late 1960s and early 1970s which threatened the post-war accommodation. The QWL effort developed to address this situation, mandated joint union–management decision-making at all levels of the program and, as such, represents the only cooperative effort in the auto industry in which there was a full acceptance of the union by management as an active partner. In contrast, the manner in which the specific concerns of the union and management have been addressed in the wake of the 1982 crisis has been much more one-sided. The auto companies have gained the union's compliance in lowering fixed labor costs and in simplifying job classifications and work rules. The corporations have not felt compelled to directly address the imperative issues of labor—corporate practices that threaten jobs.

Instead, the union has been given ameliorative measures, such as the job bank, that soften the dislocation and reshuffling of workers. Although the scope of cooperation has expanded beyond the terrain covered by the QWL program, corporate acceptance of the union as a full partner is more qualified, precisely at the strategic levels of decision-making. The UAW's failure to gain board seats at GM, Ford, and Saturn in 1984 suggests that the board seat won at Chrysler was a dead-end development, a premature fluke as the later tip in the balance of power set a different course for the new era.

The fact that many of the new consultative and lower level decision-making roles of the union help ease the transition to a shrinking work force leads us to another characteristic feature of the new cooperation. It is in the area of joint handling of production and personnel problems that union–management cooperation is furthest developed. There is a basic continuity between the new cooperative era and the era of adversarial accommodation in the union's role as a functionary in the production process charged with controlling the work force. However, the nature of cooperation in this realm has also changed with the undermining of the union's leverage. The development of a union role in reducing the job classifications and work rules that it once zealously guarded is an extraordinary example, especially given that the same union officials are to help operate the job banks. Finally, conspicuously absent in the new era of cooperation mandated by the auto makers is a more equitable sharing of the wealth to reward labor's cooperation.

The degree to which auto workers can be said to have grudgingly accepted the more cooperative labor relations drafted in the early post-war period related directly to their sense of gaining a fair share of the wealth and of affecting their own destiny through the union. In assessing the staying power of the new cooperative era, it is important to note that it begins from a much different starting point. The threat of foreign competition and global sourcing maintains a climate of economic uncertainty that at present is the central support of the new cooperative edifice. Since worker militance over equity is greatly affected by the economic climate, and the corporate use of global sourcing makes salient contradictory positions of interest, the present foundation of cooperation appears inherently unstable. The likelihood that the new cooperation will prevail in the long term probably depends on the diffusion of the Factory of the Future as the strategy to meet foreign competition. Even then it is still problematic in the American context as to whether a sense of "corporate community" and increased worker autonomy at a plant in the Saturn mold will substitute for a powerful union. The settlement of issues at the intersection of sharing the wealth and control over the work process will ultimately determine whether the auto industry's second movement toward cooperation proves as enduring as its first.

11

Technological Change, Market Decline, and Industrial Relations in the U.S. Steel Industry

Dennis A. Ahlburg, Ann E. Carey, Bruce A. Lundgren, Sandra L. Barrett, and Lawrence D. Anderson

I. INTRODUCTION

In the 1960s, the United States led the world in steel production: the economy was booming, the work force was young, and foreign competition was minimal. However, on closer scrutiny signs of change were evident as early as the 1950s.[1] The domestic integrated steel producers had failed to adopt new steelmaking processes as fast as their competitors and were beginning to lose their technological superiority.

In the boom period of the 1960s cooperation was forged between union leaders and top management in the steel industry. This cooperation at the top continued in the face of the decline in the integrated-steel sector, because union leaders and top management tended to blame external forces for the industry's decline and to stress the need for rationalization to ensure the long-run survival of the integrated industry. However, the decline has led to an adversarial relationship at the shop-floor level and conflict between union

---

[1]Donald F. Barnett and Louis Schorsch, *Steel: Upheaval in a Basic Industry*, (Cambridge, MA: Ballinger Publishing Company, 1983), p. 3.

Dennis A. Ahlburg, Ann E. Carey, Bruce A. Lundgren, Sandra L. Barrett, and Lawrence D. Anderson • Industrial Relations Center, University of Minnesota, 271-19th Avenue South, Minneapolis, MN 55455.

leaders and local leaders and rank and file, as the adjustments taking place in the industry involved losses in income and jobs.[2]

The purpose of this paper is to investigate recent developments in labor relations in the U.S. steel industry, especially in light of technological change. We begin with a brief portrait of the steel industry and then discuss technological changes and their impact on employee skill requirements. Finally, we examine the emergence of cooperative labor relations at the national level and adversarial relations at the local and intra-union level.

II. THE STEEL INDUSTRY: A BRIEF PORTRAIT

The U.S. steel industry consists of integrated producers, non-integrated producers, and alloy/specialty steel producers. Integrated producers, such as U.S. Steel and Bethlehem Steel, start the production process with iron ore and coal and finish it with a wide range of steel products. About twenty such firms operate an average of 2.5 plants, each producing from two to six million metric tons of steel per annum.[3]

The non-integrated producers (mini-mills) start with ferrous scrap and make a more limited range of steel products such as wire-rod and reinforcing bars. Over fifty mini-mills produce between 0.5 and 0.7 million tons per annum. Mini-mills can be built for less than 20% of the investment cost per ton of capacity of integrated mills and may require less than 50% of the labor hours per ton of finished product.[4] Although total labor compensation in some plants is the same as in integrated mills, productivity is higher, leading to lower unit labor costs.[5]

Alloy/specialty steel producers start with scrap steel and make higher priced, more technologically advanced steel products such as stainless steel and tool steels. Although these products accounted for only 2% of industry output in 1978, their share of dollar value of output was several times this level.

The integrated producers dominate the industry. The oft-cited decline in the U.S. steel industry, reflected in the data in Table I, is more accurately a decline in the fortunes of integrated producers. Indeed, non-integrated producers have increased their market share from 3% in 1968 to almost 20% in

[2]See, for example, the statements cited in "Edgy Steelworkers Set Their Goals High," *Business Week*, December 24, 1980 and Charles G. Burck, *Working Smarter*, (New York: The Viking Press, 1982).

[3]Joel S. Hirschhorn, "Troubles and Opportunities in the United States Steel Industry," in *Industrial Vitalization: Toward a National Policy*, ed. Margaret E. Dewar, (New York: Pergamon Press, 1982).

[4]Bela Gold, "Provisions for Re-Structuring the World Steel Industry in the 1980s: A Case Study in Challenges to Industrial Adaptation," *Quarterly Review of Economics and Business*, 22, (Spring 1982), pp. 45–66.

[5]Hirschhorn, p. 24.

Table 1. Descriptive Statistics for the U.S. Steel Industry,
1967–1982[a]

	1967	1972	1977	1982
Number of Companies	200	241	395	399
Number of Employees (in thousands)	533.1	469.1	441.9	297.5
Percentage of Workers who are Production Workers	81.4	80.8	79.2	72.8
Hours Worked by Production Workers	845.4	739.1	668.7	378.1
Average Hourly Wages of Production Workers	3.98	5.75	9.94	16.40
Payroll as a Percentage of Value Added	49	53	56	NA
After Tax Profit as a Percentage of Stockholders Equity	6.9	5.8	0.1	NA
Steel Profit Rate as a ratio of All Manufacturing Profit Rate	.55	.48	.01	NA

[a]Source: U.S. Bureau of the Census, *1982 U.S. Census of Manufactures, Preliminary Statistics,* Washington DC, 1984 p. 3 for the first six series. American Iron and Steel Association, *Steel at the Cross Roads: The American Steel Industry in the 1980s,* Washington DC, 1980, p. 89.

1985 and earn a considerably higher return on investments than integrated producers[6] (see Table II). Since it is the integrated sector of the industry that is most dominant and most troubled, we will focus primarily on this sector.

By any standard, the U.S. steel industry is included in the "core" of the U.S. economy. Characteristics of the core are oligopolistic structure, a high degree of unionization, high wages, capital intensive production processes, high productivity, and high profits.[7] The industry is oligopolistic with four firm concentration ratios in 1963 and 1972 of 50 and 45 respectively.[8] In 1978 United States Steel Corporation accounted for 24% of industry production capacity, Bethlehem Steel 13.6%, National Steel 8.4%, LTV 8.5%, and Re-

[6]Barnett and Schorsch, p. 93. See also "Union Positions," *Steel Labor Update,* Pittsburgh, February 1, 1985.

[7]Barry Bluestone, William M. Murphy and Mary Stevenson, "Low Wages and the Working Poor," Working paper, Institute of Labor and Industrial Relations, University of Michigan, 1973. Also see Charles Tolbert, Patrick M. Horan, and E. M. Beck, "The Structure of Economic Segmentation: A Dual Economy Approach," *American Journal of Sociology,* 85, (March, 1980), pp. 1095–1116.

[8]Frederic M. Scherer, *Industrial Market Structure and Economic Performance,* (Chicago: Rand McNally and Company, 2nd ed. 1980).

public Steel 7.1%.[9] However, Table I shows that the number of firms in the steel industry has grown significantly since 1967 although the fortunes of the industry have declined. This increase is largely attributable to the growing non-integrated sector.

The steel industry is also heavily unionized. In 1968–72, 77% of all workers and 98% of production workers were covered by a collective bargaining agreement, and in 1973–75 72% of all workers and 84% of production workers were union members.[10] Most unionized workers are employed by the integrated producers. Membership was held primarily in the United Steelworkers of America (USWA).

Steelworkers earn high wages relative to workers in other manufacturing industries and relative to foreign steelworkers. In 1982 steelworkers earned a 95% hourly wage premium over workers in other U.S. manufacturing industries. In 1982 steel worker hourly wages were $24.42 in the U.S., $11.03 in Japan, and $13.35 in West Germany.[11] While U.S. labor costs are higher than those of competitors, the gap is narrowing. Between 1969 and 1982, hourly employment costs rose 11.6% in the United States, 17.6% in Japan, and 15.4% in West Germany.[12] Nonetheless, payroll as a percentage of value added in the United States continues to rise, as shown in Table I.

Until the last decade, the U.S. steel industry enjoyed a labor productivity advantage over its competitors, as measured by hours of labor input per net ton of finished steel. However, over the decade 1969 to 1978 domestic productivity increased by 2.2 percent per annum while that in Japan increased by double this rate, closing the productivity gap.[13]

One characteristic of core firms that no longer applies to the integrated steel makers is high profits. In the late 1950s, the steel industry rate of return of 12% equaled that of all manufacturing. However, in only four of the last 25 years (1955–7 and 1974) has steel industry profitability (after tax profit as a percentage of stockholder equity) exceeded that for all other manufacturing industries. As shown in Table I, relative profits have fallen significantly since the late 1960s. From 1965 until 1978 the profit rate was below the prime rate of interest.[14] The rate of return on investment and pre-tax profit per ton of shipped product of the integrated producers is significantly lower than for non-integrated producers and alloy–specialty steel producers (Table II.). Also, unit labor costs in the integrated sector are 50% higher than that of the non-integrated sector. While growth in the alloy/specialty steel sector has not

[9]Robert W. Crandall, *The U.S. Steel Industry in Recurrent Crisis*, (Washington, DC: The Brookings Institute, 1981).

[10]Richard B. Freeman and James L. Medoff, "New Estimates of Private Sector Unionism in the United States," *Industrial and Labor Relations Review*, 32, (January, 1979), pp. 143–174.

[11]"Special Edition: Why Are America's Steel Plants Closing?", *U.S. Steel News*, Pittsburgh, PA, July, 1982.

[12]Barnett and Schorsch, p. 67.

[13]"Steel at the Crossroads: The American Steel Industry in the 1980s," *American Iron and Steel Institute*, Washington, DC, 1980, p. 11.

[14]Hirschhorn, p. 6.

Table 2. Characteristics of U.S. Steel Producers by Type, 1978[a]

	Integrated	Non-Integrated	Alloy/Specialty Steel
Percentage of shipments	85	13	2
Return on Investment	6.9	12.3	11.1
Pre-tax profit per ton shipped	$9.60	$31.60	$81.33
Employment Cost per ton shipped	$209.00	$138.00	$341.00

[a]Source: Office of Technology Assessment, *Technology and Steel Industry Competitiveness*, Washington, DC, 1980.

been as strong as in the non-integrated sector, it has been profitable and competitive with imports.[15]

The industry blamed external forces for its decline: the government, for inadequate tax law provisions for capital recovery, excessive control and regulations (pollution control), and interference in the market determination of steel prices; competitors, for "dumping" steel in the U.S. market; and suppliers of inputs (labor and energy), for rapid cost increases.[16]

Moreover, Crandall attributes the decline of the U.S. steel industry to "natural economic forces of competition in a world of declining shipping costs, mobile technology, and declining real ore prices."[17] The sharp increase in relative labor costs during the 1970s also contributed to the decline. Other commentators, such as Hirschhorn or Barnett and Schorsch, attribute the decline to steel-industry management strategy. According to Barnett and Schorsch, the oligopolistic U.S. steel industry, "mesmerized by the nostalgia for its former dominance," has adopted newer and more sophisticated technologies at a slower rate than that of its foreign competitors.[18] Moreover, the industry has sought modifications of government-mandated regulatory programs (notably environmental) and firm assurances from some foreign producers and the government that imported steels will not disrupt the domestic steel market. These actions may retard the rationalization needed in the domestic industry.

III. TECHNOLOGICAL CHANGE IN THE STEEL INDUSTRY

In the 1950s, the U.S. industry enjoyed a significant technological advantage over its competitors which, with its scale advantage and relatively strong resource base, offset its higher labor costs.[19] However, in the 1960s and 1970s, the U.S. industry lost its technological supremacy as it failed to adopt the

[15]Barnett and Schorsch, p. 93.
[16]American Iron & Steel Institute, pp. 11–12.
[17]Crandall, p. 152.
[18]Barnett and Schorsch, p. 51.
[19]Ibid.

Table 3. Adoption of New Technologies, by
Country 1960–1981[a]

	Percentage of Output Basic Oxygen Furnace and Electric Arc Furnace		
	United States	Japan	EEC
1960	11.8	32.0	11.5
1965	27.9	75.3	31.5
1970	63.5	95.9	57.7
1975	81.0	98.9	82.6
1981	88.8	100.0	98.6
	Continuous Casting		
1971	4.8	11.2	4.8
1976	10.5	35.0	20.1
1981	21.1	70.7	45.1

[a]International Iron and Steel Institute, *Steel Statistical Yearbook*,
Brussels: various years.

major steelmaking innovations of the postwar period: the basic oxygen furnace (BOF), electric arc furnace (EAF), and continuous casting. Its competitors quickly adopted these innovations as their domestic markets and trade in steel products expanded. This is clearly seen in Table III.

A. Technological Changes

1. *The Basic Oxygen Furnace*

The dominant method of steel production until the 1950s was the open hearth furnace (OHF). The typical open hearth furnace produced up to 350 tons of steel in five to eight hours.[20]

The basic oxygen furnace (BOF) was introduced in 1952 by the Austrian firm Voest-Alpine and directly competed with the open-hearth technology. Heat times in the early BOFs were roughly one-tenth those required in the average open hearth furnace and the BOF could produce up to 300 tons of steel in about 45 minutes. In addition, the BOF requires about 20 percent of the labor input of the OHF and uses mostly semi-skilled operators, while the OHF required a higher proportion of unskilled laborers.

The first BOF was introduced into the United States in 1955 by McLouth Steel, but its adoption by other steelmakers was slow, as shown in Table III. Barnett and Schorsch argue that the larger steelmakers remained sceptical of

[20]For a further discussion of the technologies of steel, see Crandall, Barnett and Schorsch, and Jack Stieber, "Steel," in *Collective Bargaining: Contemporary American Experience*, ed. Gerald Soimmers, (Madison: Industrial Relations Research Association, 1980), pp. 151–208.

the new technology because they had not developed it, were unaccustomed to BOF techniques, and had invested in 40 million tons of new open-hearth capacity.[21]

2. The Electric Arc Furnace

The electric arc furnace (EAF) uses directly reduced iron and/or scrap metal to produce steel. Whereas the BOF uses high-pressure oxygen and the open hearth uses natural gas, heat in the EAF is supplied by electricity. The adoption of EAFs was promoted by the increasing availability of steel scrap from the shredding of automobile hulks and the enforcement of pollution laws against OHFs.[22]

The adoption of the electric arc furnace was the single most important factor contributing to the improved competitive position of relatively small steel mills. The use of cold iron, the electric arc furnace, and combination mills offered high levels of productivity at roughly 75 to 80% lower investment cost per ton of capacity in relatively small capacity packages.[23] The rapid growth of mini-mills made possible by the EAF has, in turn, improved electric furnace technology through the development and adoption of water cooling of the furnace, the use of ultra-high power oxygen enrichment, and ladle metallurgy.[24]

3. Continuous Casting

The traditional route for processing molten steel was to pour it into ingot molds where it was allowed to cool and solidify. These molds were then reheated and rolled into semi-finished shapes in a primary rolling mill. The continuous casting process greatly enhances the efficiency of the industry by eliminating the extra processing steps in the production of steel slabs or billets. The process takes molten steel directly from the furnace to the continuous casting machine where it is molded into semi-finished shapes. Continuous casting yields improvements of 8 to 15 percent per net ton, energy savings of 1.5 to 2 million BTU per net ton, and labor savings of 40 to 50%.[25] Despite these estimated savings, the adoption of continuous casting by the U.S. industry has been extremely slow. In 1982 only 21% of the American industry's raw steel was continuously cast, compared to 71% in Japan (Table III).

Lagging behind in the implementation of new technology, the U.S. industry is consequently facing an "aging crisis." The very low replacement rates for steel facilities left the American industry with an average age of equipment in 1979 of 17.5 years.[26] The average life span of a steel facility is

[21]Barnett and Schorsch, p. 55.
[22]Crandall, pp. 6–7.
[23]Gold, p. 47.
[24]Barnett and Schorsch, p. 90.
[25]*American Iron and Steel Institute*, p. 21.
[26]Ibid.

considered to be 25 years. In 1979, 20% of the U.S. facilities were over 25 years old:[27] Studies by Arthur Little, Inc., suggest that 25% of American steel plants would be only marginally profitable, even if operated at 90% capacity. During 1982, production dropped to as low as 45% of capacity.[28]

B. Management's Failure to Introduce New Technologies

There are several reasons why U.S. management failed to introduce new technologies as rapidly as its competitors. These include insufficient capital, insufficient allocation of funds to research and development, and corporate structure and managerial style.

In the 1960s the U.S. industry made a commitment to modernization—particularly the basic oxygen furnace. Lacking the internal funds for this modernization program, the steel industry turned to the capital markets. The average ratio of long-term debit to equity rose from 24% in 1960 to 38% in 1970, and to over 50% in 1980.[29] External financing allowed the industry to rapidly adopt the BOF after its initial decade of delay, although it still lagged behind its chief competitors. However, by the 1970s further increases in the debt-to-equity ratio were undesirable[30] and new equity issues were no longer attractive to the market. While its competitors rapidly adopted continuous casting in the 1970s, the U.S. industry lacked the investment funds to do so. Despite the substantial investment in BOF, the competitive position of the integrated producers continued to decline, leading to meager returns on investment which further discouraged investment in new technologies such as continuous casting.

The financial position of the integrated companies has continued to weaken. In April 1985, Wheeling-Pittsburgh Steel Corporation, the seventh largest U.S. steel producer, filed for bankruptcy. A month earlier, Armco, the fifth largest steel producer, had faced an equally severe crisis but survived. The continued weakening of the financial position of the integrated industry has led some lenders to refuse to add more steel lending to their portfolios and to shift lending from integrated producers to mini-mill and specialty steel producers. These actions have, in turn, led to the use of non-conventional sources of financing by integrated producers such as Bethlehem Steel.[31]

Another reason why the U.S. steel industry has lagged behind its competitors is its failure to develop new technologies. Research and development expenditures as a percentage of revenues have declined since the early 1960s. Over the period 1975–1980 less than 0.6% of steel industry net sales revenue

[27]Ibid.
[28]"The Outlook: Givebacks Won't Spur Industrial Comeback," *Wall Street Journal,* January 31, 1983.
[29]Barnett and Schorsch, p. 83.
[30]Hirschhorn, p. 6.
[31]J. Ernest Beazley, "Banks Fret Over Exposure in Steel Industry," *Wall Street Journal,* May 2, 1985. p. 6.

was devoted to research and development. Of this, less than 20% was devoted to basic and applied research on new technologies. The majority of research and development was for product development. In contrast, over the same period the Japanese steel industry invested 1.6% of net sales revenue in research and development.[32]

However, in the early 1960s the industry began to reorganize through rationalization and diversification. Rationalization was based upon the closure of unprofitable, older facilities and the focusing of resources on newer, more profitable plants.[33] U.S. Steel announced it would concentrate "on only those things that make money."[34] As U.S. Steel President William R. Roesch stated, "there are obsolete plants and equipment that must be closed. This will then allow the channeling of available capital to those facilities which can be modernized or expanded and made profitable.[35]" Rationalization was accompanied by diversification. For example, U.S. Steel now has seven business areas of operation: steel, chemicals, resource development, fabricating. engineering, domestic transportation, and utility sales.[36] Kaiser Steel Corporation has abandoned steel production entirely and Armco planned to have 49% of its total assets diversified into non-steel operations by 1985.[37]

Despite its plan for further rationalization, the U.S. industry will probably continue to lag behind its competitors in terms of technological innovation. In 1983, the industry announced plans to invest seven billion dollars in steel mill modernization and expansion. Operating efficiencies were to accrue from an expansion of continuous casting from 21% of capacity to 45% by 1990.[38] However, high interest rates and the deteriorating financial position of the industry have disrupted the implementation of this plan. Even so, by 1990 the planned level of continuously cast output would still be below the current level of the Japanese steel industry.

IV. THE IMPACT OF TECHNOLOGICAL CHANGE ON SKILL REQUIREMENTS

The new technologies rely on more computerized instrumentation and control and require less physical contact with the process than the old technologies. They also demand more responsibility for a greater number of processes. The transition from the open-hearth furnace to the oxygen furnace has replaced unskilled workers mainly with semi-skilled workers. However, the percentage of production workers declined from 81% in 1967 to 73% in 1982

[32]Barnett and Schorsch, p. 59.

[33]"Bethlehem Tightens Up to Compete," *Iron Age*, January 12, 1983, pp. 11–12.

[34]"Big Steel's Liquidation," *Business Week*, September 17, 1979, pp. 78–96.

[35]George J. McManus, "Steel Scales Down to Drive Profits Up," *Iron Age*, May 25, 1981, p. 25.

[36]David B. Thompson, "Under New Management," *Industry Week*, December 8, 1980, pp. 61–68.

[37]David Cluttenback, "Armco Builds a Superior Company Out of Steel," *International Management*, November, 1979, pp. 41–43.

[38]*American Iron and Steel Institute*, p. 13.

(Table I), with the increased relative demand for office workers and skilled craft workers.

Changes in technology, job mix, and the introduction of new and modified jobs has increased the complexity of production job content. The average scores of steel production and maintenance jobs on the job evaluation index increased from 8.5 in 1960 to 10 in 1977.[39]

Technological change has had a similar impact on the composition of occupations in iron and steel and non-ferrous foundries. Foundry work forces consist of a growing proportion of engineers, technicians, and maintenance workers. Further decline in the proportion of manual production occupations is anticipated with the adoption of robots.[40]

V. THE EMERGENCE OF COOPERATIVE LABOR RELATIONS IN STEEL

A. Labor–Management Relations over the Last Two Decades: The Collective Bargaining Agreements

In their 1956 study of the transition from handrolling to integrated steel production in Britain, Scott *et al.* concluded that "the course of technological change . . . influences, and is influenced by, many aspects of the general situation in which it takes place. One of the most important of these is undoubtedly management–union relations."[41] According to Scott *et al.*, the formal structure of management–employee relations, supported by traditional values which promoted cooperation, effectively limited conflicts and problems arising from technological change. Such conflict was also minimized by the relatively small impact of technological change on the social structure and relative rewards of occupational groups. However, the relative growth of maintenance jobs and differentiation of managerial functions which accompanied technological change led to diverse reactions among occupational groups. Scott *et al.* found the least acceptance of technological change among workers in the lower echelon occupations. Maintenance workers and supervisory management were more approving of the technological change than production workers and junior management. What resistance there was to technological change came from craft groups that felt their pay increases were too small. Also, the crafts were excluded from the formal structure of labor–management relations and lacked the traditional shared values held by production workers. These observations of Scott *et al.* presaged developments in the U.S. steel industry.

---

[39]Stieber, p. 194.

[40]U.S. Bureau of Labor Statistics, *Technology and Labor in Four Industries,* Bulletin 2104, (Washington, DC: U.S. Government Printing Office, 1982).

[41]W. H. Scott, J. A. Banks, A. H. Halsey, and T. Lupton, *Technical Change and Industrial Relations,* (Liverpool: Liverpool University Press, 1956), p. 259.

Cooperative labor relations arrangements were first established in the steel industry after a prolonged strike in 1959. The major companies recognized the precedence of their common over their individual interests and authorized a four-member committee to negotiate on their behalf on all issues. When agreement was not reached, the union favored a return to individual bargaining, which the companies opposed.[42] As a result of the strike, the parties recognized the need for a consultative mechanism and established the Human Relations Committee to address issues such as wage and benefit adjustments as well as changes in the structure of employment, such as layoff and recall and the job classification system, that were related to declining demand and technological change within the industry. The Committee was co-chaired by the chief industry and union negotiators and the remainder of its membership was made up of the other three principal negotiators on each side. Also established were subcommittees composed of union and industry representatives charged with studying in-depth issues of particular interest to the industry.

The Human Relations Committee had already reached agreement on most issues before the collective bargaining negotiations of the early 1960s, effectively diminishing the role of district directors and local union leaders in negotiations. However, with complaints from local union officials that negotiations had been turned over to technicians (the research staffs of the Committee), the Committee was abandoned in 1965, although its essential joint study committees remained intact.[43]

Increased foreign competition and the growing urgency for technological innovation facilitated the development of national cooperative labor relations arrangements and to increased tension between union leadership and the rank and file. In the 1968 negotiations, supplemental unemployment benefits were increased and an earnings protection plan was instituted for workers subject to a wage decrease due to automation or other technological change. At the 1968 convention, the United Steelworkers of America rejected its former free trade position and joined management in calling for quotas and attacking dumping and government subsidization of foreign steel.

The 1971 contract included an agreement to establish joint productivity committees at each basic steel plant. These committees were staffed by both management and labor representatives. Their charge was to identify production problems and find solutions that would improve productivity. However, this cooperative effort was not particularly successful, largely because of the confrontational relationship of labor and management at the local level.

In May 1972 James Hodgson, Secretary of Labor, encouraged the industry to pursue productivity bargaining. This would have required the union to accept technological changes and work rule changes; and management was to apply the "attrition principle" in work force reductions, to fund retraining

---

[42]Stieber, p. 166.
[43]Ibid., p. 168.

programs, and to establish total plant incentive schemes.[44] Hodgson's advice was not taken, as evidenced by contract settlements which guaranteed narrow job classifications, preserved positions which would otherwise have been eliminated by new technologies, and contained no retraining requirements and few plant-wide incentive systems. The failure of management and labor to follow Secretary Hodgson's advice is not surprising. Despite increasing foreign competition, the industry experienced strong demand throughout this period, which peaked in 1974, enabling both management and labor to successfully pursue their interests.[45]

In 1973, labor and management adopted the radical Experimental Negotiating Agreement (ENA). The major provisions of the ENA included an agreement not to strike or lockout at the expiration of a contract and the submission of all unresolved national bargaining issues to binding impartial arbitration. Previous strikes or threat of a strike had caused buyers to stockpile steel, shift to imported steel, or use substitutes such as aluminum, plastics, and glass. Profits and work lost during a strike became permanent as buyers entered long-term contracts with foreign suppliers or continued to use steel substitutes. The ENA was designed to ensure continuity of domestic supply and thus help prevent movement of buyers from domestic steel. This agreement reflected the increasing trust and cooperation evolving between union and management leaders. Although the ENA was successful in smoothing production cycles it was allowed to expire in 1980 largely because the steel producers considered it to be too expensive.

Steel industry profitability had begun to decline before the 1977 negotiations. Both labor and management appeared to be concerned about the steady decline in profits and employment. Although the union sought lifetime job security, union president McBride did not support rank-and-file demands for restrictions on plant closings, because he recognized that the long-run survival of the industry might require the elimination of obsolete plants.[46] Instead, he supported the development of "Alert Committees," staffed by both management and labor, which would anticipate and hopefully ward off actual closings through immediate remedial actions (e.g. temporary wage cuts, limited product lines).[47] Management also espoused lifetime employment.[48]

The 1977 contract was originally rejected by the Basic Steel Industrial Conference of the USWA and was accepted only after the personal appeals of union leaders Abel and McBride.[49] Opposition to the contract was led by representatives of iron ore miners and clerical and technical workers who felt that the production and maintenance workers would benefit at their expense.

[44]James D. Hodgson. "Keep America Competitive; Productivity and the Work Force," *Fortune,* May 9, 1982, p. 14.
[45]Crandall, p. 158.
[46]*Wall Street Journal,* January 31, 1983, p. 27.
[47]*Business Week,* December 24, 1980.
[48]"A Major Steel Accord in Lifetime Security," *Business Week,* October 30, 1978, p. 35.
[49]Stieber, p. 167.

The clerical workers were also dissatisfied with the lack of protection against job loss from computerization.

The final contract settlement included the Employment and Income Security Program which guaranteed two years of full income to employees with twenty or more years of service (40% of the steel labor force) in the event of a plant shutdown. Subsequently, management quickly laid off many workers with almost 20 years of service who would have eventually benefited from the program.[50] The contract also called for the establishment of Alert Committees.

These steps toward national labor–management cooperation engendered intra-union tension over cooperation. The retirement of USWA President Abel prompted a contested election in 1977 between moderate Lloyd McBride and insurgent Edward Sadlowski. Sadlowski opposed ENA and charged that USWA leadership was ignoring local interests by becoming too close to management. McBride barely survived the challenge from Sadlowski, winning 57% of the 578,000 votes. The election underscored the severity of the rift between top union officials and the rank and file.

During the next three years, companies continued to close obsolete plants and diversified into non-steel product lines. For example, U.S. Steel intensified its efficiency drive, closed unprofitable facilities, made capital investments for production improvements, and diversified into non-steel product lines. U.S. Steel and Jones and Laughlin closed major integrated mills, eliminating 14,500 jobs.[51]

Despite the union anger which accompanied these plant closings,[52] management and the union jointly sought relief from the government. While their efforts yielded no coordinated national industrial policy, several policy initiatives were taken. A reference or "trigger" price mechanism to control import prices was enacted in 1978; the Tripartite Advisory Committee, comprising government, management, and labor representatives, was founded in 1980 to study steel industry problems and recommend legislative changes to congress; the allowable rate of depreciation of steel assets was increased; and Clean Air compliance deadlines were extended. In 1981, the specialty steel industry and the USWA jointly petitioned the U.S. International Trade Commission to curb foreign imports.

These cooperative developments have been followed by recent strains in labor–management relations. In February 1980, the employees and union officials at U.S. Steel's Youngstown plant sought legal recourse to stop the closure of the plant. A restraining order was obtained to keep the plant open temporarily, but the plant was eventually closed. The action, however, represented a new challenge to management's traditional right to follow the market wherever this might lead in terms of products and geography. Labor–

[50]Ibid.
[51]*Business Week*, December 24, 1980.
[52]"Labor's Shrinking World," *Steelabor*, June, 1978, p. 20.

management relations were further damaged by the U.S. Steel decision to purchase Marathon Oil in 1982 rather than build a new integrated mill.

Labor–management strain is also reflected in the protracted negotiations of 1983. Three contract proposals were considered before agreement could be reached. The first proposal was unanimously rejected by the USWA International Executive Board. Although the union had been willing to discuss "givebacks" on a company-by-company basis, President McBride explained that this proposal requested "too great a sacrifice for our members to make."[53] A second contract proposal was brought to the Basic Steel Industry Conference for a vote in November, 1982. President McBride supported this plan, emphasizing that it included no pension or insurance reductions and provided for a one-year moratorium on plant shutdowns. Nonetheless, local USWA Presidents voted it down. Their unwillingness to follow executive direction further underscores the split which had developed between national union officials and the rank and file.[54]

An agreement was ratified on March 2, 1983. This agreement temporarily cut wages by about 9%, reduced some benefits, included company guarantees to invest savings in steel operations, and established a one-year moratorium on plant closures.[55] The agreement demonstrated a management commitment to invest in steel production; and, according to the USWA newspaper *Steelabor*, it demonstrated the willingness of the union to "take unpopular positions, positions which may be contrary to the immediate membership attitudes."[56]

However, later that month U.S. Steel threatened the cooperative labor–management relationship when it announced plans to purchase 3.5 million tons of semi-finished steel per annum from British Steel for finishing at its Fairless Works near Philadelphia. In an angry response, President McBride stated that "it stands to reason that, had the union's U.S. Steel negotiating team been advised of these plans and their viability regardless of the outcome of a labor agreement, then their approach would have been in an entirely different light."[57]

U.S. Steel's recent actions in acquiring Marathon Oil and proposing to buy British steel have severely strained its relations with the USWA. This may hinder future labor–management cooperation, particularly if other companies follow suit. These capital investment decisions have recently become the target of rank-and-file criticism. A statement by Tom Du Bois, president of USWA Local 1014 in Gary, Indiana, illustrates rank and file criticism:

[53]"Too Great A Sacrifice for Our Members to Make," *Steelabor*, June 1982.
[54]Carol Hymowitz, "Concessions Still Splitting Steelworkers," *Wall Street Journal*, January 27, 1983, p. 31.
[55]Carol Hymowitz and Thomas O'Boyle, "USW Ratifies Contract with Paycuts and Company Promises to Invest in Steel," *Wall Street Journal*, March 2, 1983, p. 2.
[56]"McBride: First Task of the Mission is to Serve Its Members," *Steelabor*, October 1981.
[57]"Steel Confrontation: Givebacks or Layoffs? Pick One or The Other. Steelmakers Tell USW," *Wall Street Journal*, March 30, 1983, p. 1.

Steelworkers' jobs are in jeopardy now because the poor management strategies of the steel coporations allowed many manufacturing facilities to become outdated and inferior to those of foreign corporations. The companies' current emphasis on making profits rather than making steel makes the problem even worse.[58]

B. Labor's Response to Technological Change

In general, USWA leadership has accepted the inevitability of technological change but, according to newly elected USWA President Lynn Williams, "[the union] wants to make sure that the exciting promises technology offers humanity will not neglect the human needs of the individuals replaced by it."[59] The USWA view seems to prevail in other organized industries. In the United States, only 17 percent of 400 major collective bargaining agreements studied by the Bureau of National Affairs restricted management's ability to make technological changes. Of these, half required discussion and 15% contained restrictions requiring the employer to address the retraining of displaced workers.[60] McLaughlin estimated that U.S. unions accepted the new technology in over 60 percent of the cases in this study.[61] Union opposition to technological change was expressed in only 20 percent of these cases. Also, arbitrators commonly interpret management rights clauses as providing management with broad rights to introduce mechanization.[62] Moreover, unions "have conceded to management the right to effect change and to select the labor force to operate the new process."[63] This occurred in the conversion from hand-rolling to integrated production in the British steel industry studied by Scott *et al.* and also in the recent history of the U.S. steel industry.

The current USWA position on technological change was set forth in a 1983 paper prepared by the USWA International Wage Policy Committee.[64] The union adopted a two-part bargaining strategy, one for distressed industries and another for healthy industries. For distressed industries, such as the integrated steel industry, the bargaining strategy was to provide benefits for those on layoff, "stem the tide of unemployment and make jobs more secure." Recognizing the short-run nature of this strategy, the union stated that "in the long-run, changes in technology and market conditions may make some facilities obsolete."[65] Also, advance notice and alternatives to plant

[58]Bensman, p. 10.

[59]*Steelabor*, November, 1984.

[60]Cited in Hoyt Wheeler and Roger Weikle, "Technological Change and Industrial Relations in the United States" *Bulletin of Comparative Labour Relations*, 12, (Summer 1982), pp. 15–34.

[61]Ibid.

[62]F. Elkouri and E. A. Elkouri, *How Arbitration Works*, (Washington, DC: Bureau of National Affairs, 1983.

[63]Scott, p. 250.

[64]"Wage Policy Statement," International Wage Policy Committee, United Steelworkers of America, Pittsburgh, PA, adopted January 12, 1983.

[65]Ibid., p. 21.

closure, such as retraining and interplant transfers, were deemed to be necessary.

For healthy industries, the union sought "higher wages, improved benefits, and a full measure of job and income security." Its approach to technological change was reactive rather than pro-active, and thus was similar to that taken by most British and Australian unions.[66] According to the USWA: "solving the problems posed by rapidly changing technology, including robotics and other forms of automation, must be one of our highest priorities. The fundamental problem is how to minimize the shrinkage of the work force in the face of these technological changes."[67] The union demanded advance notice of plant closings *and* technological change to ensure the establishment of training and retraining programs. For example, in the 1983 contract with Northstar Steel (Minnesota), the company agreed to contribute up to $35,000 in matching funds for displaced worker training under the Federal Job Partnership Training Act. Other provisions in the 1983 contract included: (1) new job evaluations which reflect technologically induced skill changes; (2) retraining for improvements in job performance; (3) broadly defined seniority rights to allow for displaced worker transfers; and (4) increased time off (with pay), such as vacation, holidays and personal days, to permit work-sharing for workers who would otherwise be displaced.[68]

The relatively passive acceptance of technological change by the USWA is consistent with a recognition of the increasingly competitive and technological dynamic marketplace in which steel is produced and sold. One would have expected stronger opposition to technological change because of the large number of jobs lost—300,000 out of a dues-paying membership of 700,000 in 1983.[69] However, the union has joined management in blaming external forces, rather than technological change, for these job losses.[70] In accepting the long-run inevitability of technological change, the USWA seeks to minimize the short-run loss of jobs while appropriate strategies to deal with technological change are developed.

Recent technological change has also favored those found by Scott *et al.* to be least opposed to such change. Scott *et al.* found opposition to be inverse-

[66]In Australia and Britain, the debate on the impact of technological change is more widespread than in the United States. Some progress has been made at the local level in negotiations between shop stewards and managers, but in general most employers instigate change and unions react to it. (Bamber and Landsbury, "Labor–Management Relations and Technological Change: Some International Comparisons Between Australia and Britain," paper presented at Industrial Relations Research Association, Spring Meeting, 1983, University of Hawaii at Manoa). The only notable successes in labor's responding proactively to technological change in Britain are among white-collar unions, particularly the Association of Scientific, Technological and Managerial Staffs (ASTMS). The ASTMS has negotiated technological agreements that lay the consultive, evaluative, and bargaining framework for *consideration* of substantive issues of technological change. Ray Markey, "New Technology, the Economy and the Unions in Britain," *The Journal of Industrial Relations,* December, 1982, pp. 557–577.

[67]International Wage Policy Committee, USWA, p. 23.

[68]Ibid.

[69]Private letter from John D. Carney, Director, Department of Education, USWA, Pittsburgh, PA, February 22, 1983.

[70]International Wage Policy Committee, USWA, p. 31.

ly related to skill, and recent technological change in the steel industry has been associated with skill upgrading and a declining proportion of production workers.[71]

C. Rise in Cooperative Arrangements and USWA Changes

The U.S. integrated steel producers have lagged behind domestic and foreign competitors in the invention, innovation, and diffusion of new steel making technologies. This resulted, in part, from their failure to allocate sufficient funds to research and development, from the incompatibility between existing corporate structure and managerial style, on the one hand, and the emerging process technologies, on the other, and from the poor financial position of the integrated companies.

When management has adopted new technology it has done so as a management prerogative. This has been aided by the cooperation that has emerged between management and union leaders since 1960. The early establishment of the Human Relations Committee was the first sign of joint study. The 1971 Joint Productivity Committees, the 1977 Alert Committees, and the 1980 Tripartite Advisory Committee demonstrated management's willingness to consider labor's ideas. The Experimental Negotiating Agreement and labor and management's coordinated efforts to enlist U.S. government support indicate their understanding of the need for cooperation. The latest contract agreement, containing wage reductions and guarantees from management to invest any savings in modernization, further demonstrates their ability to implement long-range solutions to the industry problems.

The leaders of the United Steelworkers of America have accepted the inevitability of technological change and have striven within the framework of collective bargaining to minimize attendant short-run job loss. The cooperative relations which have emerged between top management and union officials have survived shocks from U.S. Steel's diversification policy and intention to buy British Steel and the difference with management over the responsibility for retraining displaced workers. Both management and union leaders blame adverse international market conditions for the decline of the industry and the consequent loss of jobs. This may explain labor's passive acceptance of technological change and the emergence of labor–management cooperation at the top.

Within the union, the rank-and-file have been less accepting of the impact of technological change and job loss. The rank-and-file seem to have taken a more short-run view than their leaders and have mounted challenges to the cooperative approach of the leadership. Examples are the rejection of the 1977 contract and the close election for union president in the same year. This challenge has influenced the collective bargaining stance of the union which is currently pushing for more short-run safeguards against job loss and automation. However, this has not fundamentally affected the cooperative approach adopted by the union leadership to the problems of the steel industry.

[71]Ibid.

12

Computer-Based Automation and Labor Relations in the Construction Equipment Industry

Gerald Gordon, Sally Moulton, Tom Wachtell, John Francis, and Ashraf Zahedi

I. INTRODUCTION

In the late 1970s, labor relations in construction equipment manufacturing became increasingly conflict-ridden. Record-length strikes over job security, wage and benefit concessions, and the handling of grievances from 1979 into the early 1980s ended two decades of relative industrial peace in this industry. We focus on this shift in labor relations which occurred as automation, foreign competition, and other factors changed the nature and organization of work in the industry during the years 1960–1984. In doing so, we apply the social contract model as a means of analyzing the changing labor relations in this industry.

The social contract model is helpful because it focuses attention on both formal and informal factors that influence labor-management interactions. Formal factors include labor agreements, personnel policies, and official job descriptions. Informal factors are the unwritten rules and informal groups which spring up in the interstices of the formal organization.[1] They result in the exercise of "social controls via informal norms."[2] A social contract is a set

[1]Charles Perrow, *Complex Organizations*, 2nd ed. (Glenview: Scott, Foresman, 1979), p. 82.
[2]James D. Thompson, *Organizations in Action* (New York: McGraw-Hill, 1967), p. 7.

Gerald Gordon, Sally Moulton, Tom Wachtell, John Francis and Ashraf Zahedi • Center for Technology and Policy and Department of Sociology, Boston University, 197 Bay State Rd. Boston, MA 02215.

of informal, often implicit understandings between labor and management concerning the rights, responsibilities, and expectations of each group with regard to the other. The nature of these understandings and expectations is derived from the historical relationship between labor and management within a given firm, as well as the broader social and economic context within which the firm and the industry operate. Some elements of the social contract may also be dealt with formally through collective bargaining.

The social contract promotes relatively smooth relations between labor and management so long as both parties remain in agreement about, and by their actions do not violate, what is considered acceptable behavior between them. Breakdown of the social contract leads to resentment and, if the problem is not resolved, to conflict. In his discussion of the "indulgency pattern," for example, Gouldner noted that worker resentment which arises from management's failure to respect established, informal expectations may be displaced onto collective bargaining issues such as wage demands.[3]

Bluestone and Harrison specifically refer to the social contract in their analysis of post-World War II labor relations in the United States.[4] For these authors, the social contract develops out of phenomena which cut across different industries, whereas in our definition it also derives from events and conditions which are unique to individual companies. In their view, this industry-wide social contract grew out of two important developments in the period between 1945 and 1971. First, organized labor became increasingly powerful in its dealings with management, in part because of the passage of legislation favorable to labor. Second, this also was an enormously profitable time for American industry. However, in order to make the most of these advantageous market conditions, management first had to cope with the extensive labor unrest that occurred immediately after World War II.

In the pursuit of economic advantages and a stable relationship, each side made concessions to the other. Management recognized the unions, met wage demands, and supported certain union interests, while labor engaged in self-disciplinary activities, accepted longer contracts, and left to management the control of production. Metzgar calls this form of social contract a system of "negotiated class struggle" and noted that its outcome until the 1970s was a steady rise in real wages, increased security, and greater social autonomy.[5] The construction equipment industry, with a history of economic growth and rising wages, is a case in point. Furthermore, the recent history of this industry shows that violation of social contract norms can result in bitter confrontation between labor and management.

---

[3]Alvin Gouldner, *Wildcat Strike* (Yellow Springs, OH: The Antioch Press, 1954), pp. 17–26.

[4]Barry Bluestone and Bennett Harrison, *The Deindustrialization of America: Plant Closings, Community Abandonment, and the Dismantling of Basic Industry* (New York: Basic Books, 1982), pp. 15–19; 133–139; 164–171.

[5]Jack Metzgar, "Plant Shutdowns and Worker Response: The Case of Johnstown, PA," *The Socialist Review* 53 (September–October 1980), p. 38.

II. CHANGES IN PRODUCT DEMAND AND EMPLOYMENT

Construction equipment manufacturing has been classified as a "core" industry. Core (as opposed to peripheral) industries control vast economic resources and typically exhibit high levels of concentration, profits, capital utilization, productivity, and unionization.[6] Core industry workers generally enjoy higher wages, greater benefits, and more desirable working conditions than workers in peripheral industries. This, in fact, was the case for workers in the construction equipment industry throughout the 1960s and '70s. Hourly earnings tended to be well above the manufacturing average, exceeding it by 30%, for example, in 1978. Labor turnover, on the other hand, was below average.[7]

The construction equipment industry manufactures a wide range of heavy machinery including bulldozers, backhoes, road graders, scrapers, power shovels, and crawler tractors. Though referred to as *construction* equipment, it is purchased for a wide variety of uses including surface mining, logging, work in oilfields, atomic energy, the U.S. military, agriculture, irrigation and land reclamation projects, municipalities, power, communications and transportation systems, as well as industrial and residential construction. Percent distribution by end use in recent years has been: building construction, 20%; surface mining, 20%; public works, 20%–25%; and exports, 35%–40%.[8]

Over the last 25 years, this industry has been dominated by the Caterpillar Tractor Company, whose share of the U.S. market has been approximately 50%. The next largest producers, Deere, Allis-Chalmers, and J. I. Case, accounted for another 20%–25% of shipments, with the remainder being split among numerous firms including General Motors and International Harvester.[9] Market concentration, therefore, has been characteristic of this industry.

The United States has always dominated the world market for construction machinery, although its hold has been gradually weakening. Paradoxically, as the export market grew in importance to the industry, the U.S. share of the Free World market fell. In the late 1950s, when the U.S. exported about 22% of domestic production, it supplied 96% of the free world demand for

[6]Charles Tolbert, Patrick M. Horan, and E. M. Beck, "The Structure of Economic Segmentation: A Dual Economy Approach," *American Journal of Sociology* 85 (March 1980), pp. 1095–1116.

[7]John Duke, "Construction Machinery Industry Posts Slow Rise in Productivity," *Monthly Labor Review* 103 (1980), pp. 34–35. Duke also notes that the higher wages in construction equipment manufacturing reflect the industry's geographical concentration and its high levels of skill and unionization.

[8]United States, Executive Office of the President, Office of Management and Budget, *Standard Industrial Classification Manual* (Washington, DC: U.S. Government Printing Office, 1972), pp. 169–70; Duke p. 33; U.S. Department of Commerce, *U.S. Industrial Outlook* (Washington, DC: U.S. Government Printing Office). See editions for 1982, p. 192, and 1984, p. 22-2.

[9]N. R. Kleinfield, "Advising Caterpillar's New President," *New York Times*, 3 February 1985, p. F15; Bernard Krisher, "Komatsu on the Track of the Cat," *Fortune*, 20 April 1981, pp. 164–174.

construction equipment.[10] However, by the mid-1970s, when exports accounted for some 40% of domestic production, the United States held approximately 70% of the world market.[11] Until recently, imports supplied a negligible part of the U.S. market, accounting for less than one percent of annual domestic consumption in 1960, about 5% in 1975, and 13% in early 1982.[12] U.S. companies faced little foreign competition until the 1970s, when European and Japanese companies became more active.[13]

The construction equipment industry experienced major growth from 1960 until 1978. The value of shipments, measured in constant (1972) dollars, more than doubled from $3.6 to $8.4 billion, while employment increased by 56%, reaching a peak of 175,000 in 1979.[14]

Productivity growth, however, has tended to be slower than average for manufacturing. For a period of 20 years, from 1958 to 1978, American manufacturing productivity rose 2.6% a year, against 2% in the construction equipment industry. While it would be useful to know whether productivity in the construction equipment industry prior to 1958 was below average, average, or above average for manufacturing, these data are not available. In any case, throughout most of the 1958–78 period, productivity growth and capital expenditures per employee in the construction equipment industry were below average for manufacturing. Perhaps the industry's overwhelming success in the world market during most of the 1960s and '70s accounts for its relative inattention to productivity-enhancing investments during this period. Beginning in the mid-1970s, however, plant efficiency clearly became a high priority. Investment in new equipment increased substantially, rising above the manufacturing average, and productivity showed strong gains in 1977 and 1978.[15]

Until the recession of the early 1980s, the diversity of its customers had largely buffered the industry from a downturn in any one of its markets, providing some job stability for labor and predictability for management. This recession, however, seriously affected the industry. Industry shipments, which had risen 30% between 1972 and 1978 to a high of $8.4 billion, fell 58% between 1978 and 1983 (measured in constant 1972 dollars).[16] The value of exports, which had risen 293% between 1972 and 1981 to $6.3 billion (measured in current dollars), fell an estimated 58% between 1981 and 1983. Imports had risen 349% between 1972 and 1981 to $887 million (measured in current dollars) but then declined by 35% between 1981 and 1983. By the

[10]U.S. Department of Commerce, *U.S. Industrial Outlook*, 1961, pp. 159–160.
[11]U.S. Department of Commerce, 1974, pp. 303–306; 1975, pp. 328–331.
[12]U.S. Department of Commerce, 1961, pp. 159–160; 1976, pp. 342–345; 1983, pp. 22-1–22-3.
[13]U.S. Department of Commerce, 1970, pp. 244–245; 1980, pp. 207–209.
[14]U.S. Department of Commerce, 1982, pp. 192–194; 1984, pp. 22-1–22-4.
[15]Duke, pp. 33–36; Carol J. Loomis, "The Cat Fight," *Fortune*, 2 May 1983, p. 68; Deere & Company, 1983 Annual Report, p. 7.
[16]U.S. Department of Commerce, 1982, pp. 192–194; 1984, pp. 22-1–22-4.

mid-1980s, the industry's share of the world market (once 96%) had declined to an all-time low of 55%.[17]

The adverse market conditions of the early 1980s jeopardized the financial viability of the industry. Many companies were operating at less than half of their manufacturing capacity and suffering large losses. Standard and Poor began its 1983 review of the industry with the headline "Sales Paralysis to Continue," and a Wall Street source quoted in *Fortune* said, "Everybody in the industry is in the hospital now, and in the intensive care unit at that."[18]

Annual reports for this period show that one firm after another began streamlining production, closing older, less efficient plants and shifting operations overseas. Clark Equipment, for example, began what it called an "intensive revitalization program" in 1982, to "ensure the company's survival in each of its primary business lines."[19] Caterpillar closed five of its U.S. plants and reduced personnel and consolidated operations at other plants to "lower costs and improve efficiency." Plant consolidation was a means of furthering "a broad technology modernization program being developed for all manufacturing facilities." Caterpillar also searched for cheaper sources of materials and products that it needed to buy, in many cases looking overseas.[20]

The depth of the problem facing American construction equipment companies is evident in the market performances of Caterpillar and its major foreign competitor, Komatsu. Hit hard by the worldwide economic recession and a seven-month strike in 1982–83, Caterpillar's sales declined by 29% from 1981 to 1982 (from $9.2 billion to $6.5 billion) and by another 16% in 1983. The company reported losses of $180 million for 1982, $345 million in 1983 and $428 million in 1984. Komatsu sales increased by 15% to $3.4 million between 1981 and 1982 and the company reported 1982 profits of $139 million (down just 2% from 1981). Moreover, Komatsu's share of worldwide sales had increased from virtually nothing in 1962 to more than 50% of Caterpillar's by 1982.[21] In the U.S., Caterpillar's market share dropped from 50% to 44% between 1975 and 1984, while by 1984 Komatsu's share rose to about 10%.[22] Thus the severe decline at Caterpillar in the early 1980s was not attributable solely to the worldwide recession and the strike. The changing position of

[17]U.S. Department of Commerce, 1984, pp. 22-1–22-4; Steven Greenhouse, "A Grim Era for Heavy Equipment," *New York Times,* 22 September 1985, p. 4F.

[18]*Standard & Poor's Industry Surveys,* January 1983. M–Z, Vol. 2; David B. Tinnin, "The Bargain Hunter Nibbling at Harvester," *Fortune,* 23 August 1982, pp. 174–179.

[19]American Hoist and Derrick Corporation, 1983 Annual Report, pp. 3–4; Clark Equipment Company, 1983 Annual Report, p. 2; Harnischfeger Corporation, 1983 Annual Report, pp. 4–5, 25.

[20]Kleinfield, p. F15; Caterpillar Tractor Corporation, 1983 Annual Report, pp. 4–5.

[21]Loomis, pp. 67–68, 70.

[22]Kleinfield, p. F15; Alex Kotlowitz, "Caterpillar's 4th-Period Deficit Grew; 1st Quarter Loss, 'Uncertain' Year Seen," *Wall Street Journal,* 21 January 1985, p. 4; Alex Kotlowitz, "Komatsu Plan to Open U.S. Plant Seen Leading to More Industry Consolidation," *Wall Street Journal,* 13 February 1985, p. 6; Loomis, p. 72.

these firms relative to one another was also the outcome of long-term changes in the industry.

Komatsu's growing market share resulted in part from its lower prices. For example, in the early 1980s, the Komatsu D155A bulldozer listed for $243,000, while the comparable Caterpillar D8L listed for $276,000. By 1983, Caterpillar's prices were 10% to 15% above those of foreign companies for comparable units. The factors which contributed to this gap included Japan's lower manufacturing costs (Komatsu's labor costs were roughly half of Caterpillar's in 1982) and the value of the yen in comparison to the dollar.[23] The difference in manufacturing costs was underscored further when, in 1983, Caterpillar entered into agreements with companies in Korea and West Germany to manufacture some of its machinery at what Caterpillar called "acceptable prices."[24] Similar agreements were made by other companies in the industry, for example, between Clark Equipment and Volvo; Harnischfeger and Kobe Steel; and Deere and Hitachi.[25]

The labor force also suffered from the recession and the companywide reorganizations that followed. Total employment, which had risen by 31% during the 1972–79 period, was reduced by more than half between 1979 and 1983. Not only did total employment decline during the early 1980s recession, but the occupational mix changed as well. Production workers had accounted for a steady 72% of total employment throughout the 1970s but then fell to 62% by 1982. They consequently bore a disproportionate amount of the work force reductions in the industry at this time.[26]

While initial layoffs were a means of temporarily adjusting to plummeting sales, the subsequent, permanent labor force reductions which occurred were seen as a necessary response to long-term changes in the industry's environment. The recession, the strength of the U.S. dollar during the early 1980s and, perhaps, the industry's long record of lagging productivity strengthened the position of some foreign competitors. So severe were the economic pressures of this period that they caused an industry shakeout. Firms responded by instituting stream-lining strategies among which was the increased introduction of new, more efficient, less labor-intensive technologies. Analysis of these technological innovations demonstrates their role in labor force reduction in this industry.

In light of the changes occurring in production technology, it was inevitable that the relative size of the different occupational categories in the industry would change and that, even holding demand constant, the size of the work force would have been reduced. The recession served to increase both the extent and the rapidity of labor force reductions.

---

[23]Jerry Flint, "Cat Claws for Life," *Forbes*, 22 November 1982, pp. 39–40; Loomis, p. 74.

[24]Caterpillar Tractor Company, 1983 Annual Report, p. 6.

[25]Clark Equipment Company, 1984 Annual Report, pp. 10–11; Harnischfeger Corporation, 1983 Annual Report, pp. 4–5, 25; "Casstevens Says Deere–Hitachi Deal Will Take Work Away From U.S.," *News From the UAW*, 22 July 1983.

[26]U.S. Department of Commerce, 1982, pp. 192–194; 1984, pp. 22-1–22-4.

III. TECHNOLOGICAL CHANGE AND EMPLOYMENT TRENDS

The basic production processes used by this industry did not change radically during the 1960s and 70s.[27] Manufacturing equipment became faster and more powerful but, for the most part, the worker's relationship to the task of production remained much the same. This relationship was typified by the operation of the stand-alone machine tools used in parts fabrication. Under the continual control of an operator, each machine performed one or a few steps in the metal cutting process. The operator managed the selection of cutting tools, guided the machine through each task and used hand tools to check his work for accuracy. Although the final shape of a part was dictated by engineering blueprints (over which the operator had little or no control), the operator possessed the requisite skills and knowledge for making the part. Welders and assembly workers also had close contact with the product during its manufacture. Welders had considerable control over the tasks associated with their jobs. Assembly workers used simpler tools, needed less skill and experience to perform their work, and had much less control over the performance of their jobs.

Although much of the production technology in use during this period did not change greatly, new technologies were being developed, especially computer-based automation, which had the potential for substantially reducing human intervention in the production process. The shift to computer-based automation produced changes which can be described using Perrow's classification of technology. His classification rests on two criteria: the number of exceptions encountered in the work process and the ease or difficulty of dealing with those exceptions. The resulting typology casts technology on a continuum from the routine (only a few exceptions occur and these are easily solved) to the non-routine (many exceptions occur and their solution is hard to determine). From the worker's point of view, the introduction of computer-based automation increased the routineness of the work process.[28]

Innovations in parts fabrication technology progressed from the development of numerical control in the 1950s (i.e., using instructions stored on tape to control the operations of a single stand-alone machine tool) to computer numerical control (having one computer control one machine), and then direct computer control (having one computer control many machines).[29] These, in turn, led to the development of the flexible manufacturing system

[27]Duke, p. 35. See also Lloyd T. O'Carroll, "Technology and Manpower in Nonelectrical Machinery," *Monthly Labor Review* 94 (June 1971), pp. 56–62. O'Carroll discusses SIC industry 35, nonelectrical machinery, which includes construction equipment manufacturing. He notes that, "although less than 1% of all machine tools in the [nonelectrical machinery] industry in 1968 had numerical control, they represented a larger proportion of the industry's capacity," (p. 58).

[28]Charles Perrow, "A Framework for the Comparative Analysis of Organizations," *American Sociological Review* 32 (April 1967), pp. 194–208.

[29]Mikell P. Groover, *Automation, Production Systems, and Computer-Aided Manufacturing* (Englewood Cliffs: Prentice-Hall, 1980); Duke, p. 35.

(FMS) during the 1970s. The FMS greatly reduced direct human involvement in and control over the parts fabrication process. A computer controlled not only the machining operations at each station of the FMS, but also the movement and sequencing of parts from one station to another. A single operator could oversee production activities which previously were performed by from five to 30 workers.[30]

The degree of technological innovation in other areas related to production varied. Assembly techniques remained much the same.[31] On the other hand, improved welding methods and materials and, more recently, the introduction of welding robots, resulted in substantial labor-saving. The introduction of computer control to inventory management significantly reduced both the amount of labor involved and the quantity of raw materials and finished goods kept on hand.[32]

The exact proportion of production that has been shifted to numerically controlled and computer-automated equipment in the construction equipment industry is not known. However, investment in such equipment has increased significantly in the last 10 to 15 years. Major companies such as Deere and Caterpillar invested heavily in automated equipment in the mid and late '70s. Deere noted, for instance, that its innovations at this time resulted in "highly efficient manufacturing facilities." During this period, computer-based technologies were introduced in piecemeal fashion and they never accounted for a majority of production. Indeed, in the 1970s and early '80s, fully automated factories were still only a prospect on the horizon. However, automation spread sufficiently for workers to gain some knowledge of its potential technological and human impacts.[33]

Technological innovations substantially changed the content of jobs, the number of jobs, and the occupational distribution of employment. Machining, for example, is a skilled occupation requiring years of training and involving a wide range of knowledge. Where automation has been introduced, the majority of the machinist's tasks can be performed by computer-controlled machining equipment monitored by a less-skilled machine tender. This not only removes the worker from hands-on contact with the production task, isolating him from the end product, but also lowers the skill requirements of the job. These factors partly explain the helplessness and estrangement expressed by some workers who have encountered the new technology as well as their concern with job security.[34]

---

[30]Roland W. Schmitt, "Technological Trends: 'The Long-Term Impact of Technology on Employment and Unemployment.'" *National Academy of Engineering Symposium 30 June 1983* (Washington, DC: National Academy Press, 1982–3).

[31]O'Carroll noted that, because of the difficulty of mechanizing most aspects of assembly in the nonelectrical machinery industry (which includes construction equipment), little in the way of automatic assembly had appeared during the 1960s (p. 59).

[32]Duke, p. 35.

[33]Duke, pp. 33–35; Winston Williams, "Ailing Harvester's Grueling Battle," *New York Times*, 21 July 1981, pp. D1, D20; Deere and Company 1983 Annual Report, p. 7; Loomis, p. 68.

[34]Clinton S. Stanovsky, "Automation and Internal Labor Market Structure: A Study of the Caterpillar Tractor Company," Master's Thesis, MIT, 1981, p. 60.

IV. LABOR RELATIONS

A. Labor Relations History, 1960–1984

Construction equipment manufacturers have had a long relationship with organized labor. All of the principal companies which were active during our focal period, 1960–1984, were organized by the industry's major union, the United Auto Workers (UAW), by the mid-1940s.[35]

For most of the 1960–1984 period, labor relations can be characterized as relatively predictable, ritualistic struggles between a powerful union and powerful companies over increasingly generous wage and benefit packages. The two sides understood and agreed upon the rules of the game and managed to achieve many of their goals. Although in collective bargaining, the wage and benefit package usually took center stage, job security repeatedly surfaced as a UAW concern. Layoffs, plant closings and the subcontracting of work as well as technological innovation created job insecurity. The union addressed these causes through collective bargaining and, in some cases, by supporting legislation.[36]

Among the major goals adopted at the 1964 UAW constitutional convention were the creation of job opportunities and protection from automation. In 1970, UAW contract goals included using normal attrition rather than layoffs to implement technologically induced workforce reductions and the establishment of training programs to prepare displaced workers for other jobs in the company.[37] At its 1980 convention, the UAW resolved that collective bargaining agreements should be strengthened "to protect workers against the loss of skills and jobs." The union suggested reduced work time as a mechanism for creating more jobs and spreading available work, and supported legislation aimed at controlling plant closings.[38]

The UAW position on job security and technology has been that technological innovation is essential to increasing productivity and the standard of living, but that it also threatens both the availability and content of jobs. While the UAW stresses the necessity of technological progress, it also has

[35]Walter F. Peterson and C. Edward Weber, *An Industrial Heritage: Allis Chalmers Corporation* (Milwaukee: Milwaukee County Historical Society, 1978), p. 322; U.S. Department of Labor, Bureau of Labor Statistics, "Collective Bargaining in the Farm Machinery and Equipment Industry," Report 523, (Washington, DC: U.S. Government Printing Office, April 1978).

[36]Larry T. Adams, "Auto Workers Seek Government Aid for Laid-off Workers, Ailing Industry," *Monthly Labor Review* 103 (September 1980), pp. 41–43; Sheldon M. Kline, "United Auto Workers' 23D Constitutional Convention," *Monthly Labor Review* 95 (July 1972), pp. 32–34; Linda H. LeGrande, "UAW Elects its Last Reuther-Generation President," *Monthly Labor Review* 100 (August 1977), pp. 36–37; "Casstevens Comments on Caterpillar's Announced Plans to Cut Back Certain U.S. Operations," *News From the UAW*, 30 November 1984; "Casstevens Says Deere-Hitachi Deal Will Take Work Away From U.S.," *News From the UAW*, 22 July 1983.

[37]L. A. O'Donnell, "The UAW's 19th Constitutional Convention, *Monthly Labor Review* 87 (June 1964), pp. 654–656; "UAW Board Offers Suggestions for 1970 Contract Goals," News Release, (Detroit: United Auto Workers), 16 February 1970.

[38]Adams, pp. 41–43; "Working on Two Fronts," *New Technology, UAW Publication for Skilled Tradesmen, Technicians, and Engineers* 14.1 (1980), pp. 3–4.

been described as the "American union that has gone farthest in attempting to protect its members from the negative impacts of new technology." Even so, it has achieved only limited success in this area. In 1983, UAW Vice President Donald Ephlin called for " 'a national commitment to employment security' . . . to cope with job losses related to new manufacturing technology."[39] Given increasing levels of automation in the industry and the history of union concern, the impact of new technology on job security may have played a role in the major strikes which the industry experienced from 1979 to 1983.

Concern over job security in the construction equipment industry, for most of the period under consideration, was stimulated primarily by the cyclical layoffs to which the industry was prone. Collective bargaining remedies therefore tended to focus on strengthening supplemental unemployment benefit funds. Both the problem and its remedy were short-term in nature since, as shown earlier, employment in the industry recovered from each cyclical downturn and then grew to new record levels until the recession of the early 1980s. Furthermore, although most of the productivity growth in the industry from the 1960s to the 1980s stemmed from improvements in production technology, employment levels continued to grow until 1979. As long as employment grew, technological change presented a less immediate threat to job security. In the early 1980s, however, the industry faced devastating economic conditions in all its markets, as a result of which management undertook a substantial restructuring of operations. Restructuring led to large, permanent reductions in the labor force. At this time, job security, threatened by increasing technological change, plant closings, and movement of production overseas, became a prominent issue. These conditions also threatened to end the long upward trend of economic gains for labor. In this context, the established basis for labor–management relations broke down, as evidenced by the longest and most bitter strikes in the history of the industry.

Labor relations at Caterpillar, from the 1950s until 1979, essentially followed the industry pattern. Although the UAW went out on strike at all but two contract negotiation periods (1970 and 1976), most strikes lasted only a few days to a month.[40] Lengthier strikes occurred in 1958 and later in 1979 and 1982–83, preceded in the first and third cases by unusually adverse market conditions and large layoffs.[41]

---

[39]*New Technology,* Spring, 1980, p. 3; Robert Howard, "Brave New Workplace," in Jerome H. Skolnick and Elliot Currie (eds.) *Crisis in American Institutions,* 6th ed. (Boston: Little, Brown, 1985), pp. 362–363; "UAW's Ephlin Calls for Political Solutions to Technological Displacement," *News From the UAW,* 27 May 1983.

[40]*The New York Times Index,* The New York Times Company, New York, NY, 1960–1984; *The Wall Street Journal Index,* Dow Jones Books, Princeton NJ, 1960–1984. Note that this pattern was not unique to Caterpillar. At J. I. Case, for example, strikes were a typical feature of the bargaining process. For information, see "J. I. Case Co. Workers Ratify New Contract," *News From the UAW,* 30 June 1980.

[41]"2,100 Are Laid Off by Tractor Plant," *New York Times,* 9 April 1958, p. 36; "Caterpillar Pact Ratified by UAW," *New York Times,* 1 December 1958, p. 29; "Caterpillar Net Drops; Pay Cuts, Layoffs Ordered," *Wall Street Journal,* 12 July 1982, p. 7.

Despite these occasional downturns, employment at Caterpillar (and in the industry as a whole) rose during the 1960s and 1970s, always recovering from temporary layoffs and going on to reach new highs. The period was thus one of basic job stability at Caterpillar as employment grew almost steadily and more than doubled betweeen 1960 and 1979.[42] Layoffs were few and the company was far and away first in its industry, factors which would allow a sense of job security and continuity to develop. Furthermore, by the early 1980s, workers at Caterpillar enjoyed a wage and benefit package averaging $20 an hour, one of the highest in any industry. For a time, compensation rose even faster at Caterpillar than in the auto industry.[43]

In 1979, companies throughout the industry negotiated new bargaining agreements. As part of its overall negotiating strategy, the UAW intended to strike Deere and Company and to use the settlement reached there as a pattern for agreements with other firms in the industry. (The UAW has used pattern bargaining for a number of years.) While the union did strike Deere, some UAW members at Caterpillar refused to follow this plan and struck without authorization, thereby foregoing strike benefits. The strike spread throughout Caterpillar and, after a month, was authorized by the UAW national organization. It lasted approximately three months and was then the longest in the company's history.[44]

The most important union issue in the 1979 Caterpillar strike was the "number of full-time employer-paid union representatives to facilitate the handling of grievances."[45] Final resolution of this point was based on compromise, with the UAW winning fewer additional representatives than it had sought. Other key issues included forced overtime, time off, seniority, and subcontracting. Job security concerns were demonstrated further because the UAW also made technological innovation a bargaining item. It wanted to establish conditions for the introduction of new technology including advance notice to the union, implementing technological change at a pace which would allow employment reductions to occur via attrition, company training for workers to operate the new technology, and work sharing. In the end, however, the bargaining agreement included no provisions regarding the introduction of new technology.[46]

In 1982–83, the UAW struck Caterpillar for seven months in response to company demands for union givebacks. This was the longest national strike in the history of both the company and the union. The savings which management hoped to gain from these concessions were intended to offset the strains caused by the worldwide economic recession and increasing foreign

[42]Caterpillar Annual Report, 1982, p. 45; Stanovsky, p. 35.

[43]Loomis, pp. 68, 70.

[44]Stanovsky, p. 35; "Caterpillar Faces Strike at Peoria-Area Plants by UAW's Local 974," *Wall Street Journal*, 1 October 1979, p. 7; "Caterpillar, UAW Set Tentative Agreement on 3-Year Contract," *Wall Street Journal*, 17 December 1979, p. 18.

[45]Stanovsky, pp. 35–36.

[46]Stanovsky, pp. 14, 36. Note also that the 1976 UAW-Caterpillar contract included no language specifically pertaining to technology. See: "Central Agreement Between Caterpillar Tractor Co. and the UAW, December 17, 1976."

competition.[47] Caterpillar's chief negotiator, James Ward, justified this demand, saying, "We're not trying to get down to the Japanese level. We're trying to contain costs . . . to compete" in the world market.[48] Indeed, at this time, the company was taking a number of cost-cutting steps. It cut capital spending, reduced its dividend by almost half, and announced a 10% pay cut for top-level managers and lower cuts for thousands of other salaried workers.[49]

Pointing to Caterpillar's substantial profits through 1981, and having made concessions to other firms over the last several years (including Allis-Chalmers and Harvester), the UAW refused to grant concessions to Caterpillar. Instead the union began by requesting an improved wage and benefit package. Later it withdrew most of its demands and offered simply to renew the existing contract.[50] Caterpillar rejected this offer as well because, as the company President and Chairman explained, "it failed to recognize the new competitive factors in our industry."[51]

The labor upheavals at Caterpillar were by no means unique. The UAW struck International Harvester for six months in 1979–1980 (then the longest strike in the UAW's entire history), over company demands for givebacks and compulsory overtime. The settlement on these issues as well as job security and new technology favored the union.[52] The union struck Fiat-Allis in 1983, when that company demanded givebacks. Stephen Yokich, UAW Vice President in charge of the union's Agricultural Implement Department, explained that the Fiat-Allis strike was "yet another example of a corporation attempting to punish workers for depressed sales in a depressed economy."[53]

The 1983 settlement which ended the seven-month strike at Caterpillar may have pointed to the development of a new labor relations trend in the industry. As it had elsewhere, the union accepted reductions in some economic benefits. For example, workers gave up the 3% automatic annual wage increase which had been the industry norm since 1954 and took cuts in the amount of paid time-off. On the other hand, the union won an increase for the supplemental unemployment benefits (SUB) fund, broader job security provisions (which related entirely to plant shutdowns and outsourcing) and,

[47]"UAW-Caterpillar Workers Vote Overwhelmingly in Favor of Strike Authorization," *News from the UAW*, 14 September 1982; "UAW Members at Caterpillar Solidly United Against Takeaways on 111th Day of Strike," *News from the UAW*, 19 January 1983.

[48]Flint, pp. 39–40.

[49]"Caterpillar Net Drops; Pay Cuts, Layoffs Ordered," *Wall Street Journal*, 12 July 1982, p. 7; Flint, pp. 39–40.

[50]*News from the UAW*, 1 October 1982, untitled statement by UAW Vice President Stephen P. Yokich concerning breakdown of negotiations at Caterpillar Tractor Company; Loomis, p. 67.

[51]Caterpillar 1982 Annual Report.

[52]"International Harvester Fights for Survival," *International Management*, (December 1982), pp. 51–52; "UAW–Harvester Contract: Major Improvements and Changes—1979–1982," UAW Public Relations and Publications Department (75M/4-80), pp. 2, 5–6.

[53]"Unilaterial Company Action Forces UAW Strike at Fiat-Allis," *News from the UAW*, 1 March 1983. The UAW Agricultural Implement department covers the construction equipment industry as well as farm equipment manufacturers.

for the first time, an annual profit-sharing plan. (Harvester workers had won their first profit-sharing plan a year earlier.) The new profit-sharing plan guaranteed a minimum first payment of 31 cents per hour for every hour worked in 1984. Beginning in 1985, distributions would be tied to Caterpillar's worldwide performance, with payment provided if the company exceeded a "4.5% return on its average worldwide sales and beginning-of-the-year net assets."[54] In summary, provisions in this contract dealt with the problems caused by prolonged economic crisis; there was no specific language pertaining to automation.

In its 1983 Annual Report, Caterpillar emphasized its desire to encourage "a climate of improved cooperation" and its belief that having employees participate in "matters which affect them . . . will have a positive impact on the . . . company's . . . competitive strength."[55] Along with the 1983 profit-sharing plan, this suggests the possible emergence of cooperative labor relations arrangements out of the recent labor–management strife in this industry.

B. Analysis of Changes in Labor Relations

Although the demand for union givebacks was the overt cause of the 1982–83 strike at Caterpillar, givebacks may not have been the only critical issue. While Caterpillar was asking for concessions described as crucial in order to respond effectively to foreign competition, it also had reduced employment levels and the percentage of production workers substantially. In light of the two decades of considerable job stability experienced at Caterpillar, and the company's official commitment to maintaining it, it may be that at the heart of the 1982–83 strike was not only an economic issue (though that clearly was important) but also a violation of job security expectations that formed the core of the social contract.

Caterpillar had had a history of few long-term layoffs and a reputation for generous wage and benefit settlements. Furthermore, the company had an officially expressed and generally adhered to policy of maintaining employment stability and working "to build a company–union relationship based upon mutual respect and trust."[56] However, during the 1970s, Caterpillar had gradually introduced computer-based automation throughout its plants and in 1982 its Chairman and CEO, Lee Morgan, emphasized the company's continuing, strong commitment to major plant modernization and cost-cutting programs.[57] During the latter part of this period, because of

---

[54]Caterpillar 1983 Annual Report, p. 6; U.S. Department of Labor, Bureau of Labor Statistics, "Current Wage Developments," 35.6 (June 1983), p. 1; "UAW Members Ratify Agreement With International Harvester," *News From the UAW*, 3 May 1982; "UAW Members Ratify Three-Year Pact With Caterpillar, End Historic Strike," *News From the UAW*, 23 April 1983.

[55]Caterpillar 1983 Annual Report, p. 6.

[56]Caterpillar Tractor Company, "A Code of Worldwide Business Conduct and Operating Principles," (Peoria: 1982); Loomis, p. 68.

[57]"Caterpillar Expects to Trim 1982 Outlays $100 Million or More," *The Wall Street Journal*, 30 March 1982, p. 15.

extremely negative market conditions, the company implemented large, permanent labor force reductions and placed many other workers on indefinite layoff. Consequently, worker concerns about the impact of automation and their suspicion about the corporation's concern for their welfare escalated, perhaps further strengthened by the fate of the union's 1979 contract demands relating to the introduction of new technology.

Under these conditions, workers could no longer take at face value statements from the company such as "Your job is important . . . to Caterpillar. It takes the efforts of all of us to . . . manufacture products of the highest quality. *Your future and Caterpillar's depend on this accomplishment.*"[58] Nothing over the previous 20 years had prepared them for the massive layoffs and concession demands from the company in the early 1980s. The depth of workers' feelings concerning their long held and usually fulfilled (but now unmet) expectations came through in statements such as "the company went on strike against us."[59] Stephen Yokich of the UAW concluded that company concession demands concerning "wages, benefits and contract provisions would set the employees at Caterpillar back thirty years" and that the company was "using an unfortunate economic situation . . . to deprive their workers of their just due."[60]

In the early 1980s, managers contended first with sharply falling sales and then substantial losses. Management reacted by deciding that givebacks, major layoffs, and finally permanent labor force reductions were necessary. At the time, the news media were reporting severe financial conditions and unprecedented hardship throughout this and other industries, lending apparent support to cost-cutting decisions. Meanwhile, labor perceived and experienced rapidly declining job security. Deeply entrenched in their opposing perspectives, labor and management lost the consensus which had supported their long-standing social contract.

V. CONCLUSION

Historical developments in the labor relations of construction equipment manufacturing correspond to the post-World War II pattern identified by Bluestone and Harrison. The handful of powerful companies that dominated the industry in this period experienced substantial growth. In part, the success of these companies was made possible by their ability to purchase relative labor peace by agreeing to increasingly generous wage and benefit packages. External market conditions thus enabled construction equipment manufacturers to pursue a course of repeated economic accommodation. This in turn helped shape both those features of the social contract which were

---

[58]"Welcome to Caterpillar," Caterpillar Tractor Company, 1977 (italics added).
[59]Norman Peagam and Harlan S. Byrne, "Caterpillar Workers Gird for Long Strike as Talks With UAW Seem Unlikely Soon," *The Wall Street Journal*, 4 October 1982, p. 6.
[60]*News from the UAW*, 1 October 1982.

typical of the industry as a whole and those which were unique to specific companies.

Just as external market conditions help to create a social contract, so they also help to break it. This clearly happened in several ways in the construction equipment industry. After two decades of rising wages and relative job stability, workers in this economically powerful industry faced an abrupt and permanent change in the conditions which had favored them for so long.[61] During the early 1980s, changes in the business environment forced increased attention to productivity and thus to innovation in manufacturing processes. In the long run, productivity-enhancing innovations might increase job security for the remaining work force. In the short run, technological change (and automation, in particular) further reduced the number of available jobs at a time when major labor force reductions were occurring for other reasons as well.

It should be emphasized that concern for the impacts of technological change on job content and security was simply one aspect of the overall labor relations picture in this period. Other factors affected job security as much or more and the UAW continued to focus heavily on maintaining and, where possible, improving the economic position of its members.

In responding to the newly-emerging business environment of the 1980s, companies and their workers were caught in a double bind. On the one hand, job security was a central element of the social contract and long-established precedent underlay worker expectations that such security would continue. Abrupt challenges to these expectations were likely to, and did in fact, engender conflict. On the other hand, changes in the external environment seriously threatened company viability, and demanded response. In meeting these demands, however, management created conditions which violated the social contract.

Harnischfeger's 1983 Annual Report, stating the problem for labor in words which recall Bluestone and Harrison's analysis, referred to the "inevitable clash between increasing employee expectations and decreasing company economics."[62] This clash occurred in the context of enormous layoffs, disastrous sales and profits records, concession demands, plant closings, and large, permanent labor force reductions. It marked a wrenching transition from decades of prosperity and job security to a new era of retrenchment in which the restructuring of the industry involved substantially reducing manufacturing capacity in the United States and transferring more production overseas. William Mulligan, president of the Construction Equipment Manufacturers Association, summed up the changes, saying "We don't expect to see the industry getting back to the levels where it once was."[63]

As part of its strategy for recovery, management also showed signs of seeking new, more cooperative labor relations. In one sense it had come full

[61]Greenhouse, p. 4F.
[62]Bluestone and Harrison, p. 14.
[63]Greenhouse, p. 4F.

circle from the years immediately after World War II when the desire to capitalize on favorable market conditions had led to an accommodation with labor. In another sense, however, management and labor found themselves in a new and, for this industry, perhaps unprecedented position. Once again accommodation was essential but it appeared to labor and management alike that new forms of cooperation would be necessary. This would explain, for example, the introduction of profit-sharing plans at Caterpillar and International Harvester in return for the economic concessions made by the union.

Social contracts such as the one between labor and management at Caterpillar reflect a history of confrontation and mutual accommodation. The cooperative element of the contract results from the shared benefits made possible by the stability of the labor force and growing profits. When, as in the case of Caterpillar, external pressures force a rupture in the social contract, confrontation and distrust are the results. Often the labor–management relationship deteriorates at a time when both labor and management are at their weakest. The strategies developed by Caterpillar and other companies in the industry in the early 1980s show that some degree of internal cooperation, trust, and predictability must be re-established if external threats are to be met effectively. Achieving these internal goals is also necessary for creating that degree of labor–management consensus which is a prerequisite for the renewal of the social contract. As demonstrated by the history of labor–management relations immediately after World War II, the evolution of a broad social contract aided both labor and management in obtaining their goals. Re-establishing a social contract now will be an important step for companies and workers in the construction equipment industry as they respond to the recent major changes which have occurred in their business environment.

ACKNOWLEDGMENTS

The authors are grateful for the assistance of Joan Biddle.

13

The Impact of Technological Change on Labor Relations in the Commercial Aircraft Industry

Arthur R. Schwartz, James D. Abrams, Adria M. Anuzis, John P. Byrne, Tracy Elsperman, Allison Haines, and Christopher D. Liguori

INTRODUCTION[1]

The commercial aircraft industry has always been prone to sales and employment volatility. Aircraft sales nearly doubled in the period 1964–68, before falling off by one-third in the next three years. Business success depends upon federal government contracts as well as unpredictable commercial airline demand. New production designs and production techniques are constantly being introduced in the industry, as the aircraft firms must make billion-dollar investments, hoping to produce the jet that will adhere to the demands of domestic and foreign markets.

The heavy reliance on new technology has a direct impact on labor relations in the aircraft industry. The workers and their unions are concerned about job security because the introduction of new production technology threatens to reduce the level of employment. However, management has insisted on maintaining its flexibility in introducing new technology. These divergent interests provide the basic framework for understanding labor rela-

[1]This chapter was originally written in 1983 as part of the General Motors Business Understanding Program under the auspices of the Program in American Institutions at the University of Michigan. The authors would like to thank the staff of the American Institutions Program and especially Gerry Ross, Katherine Kurtz, and John Jackson for their help. The authors bear all responsibility for error.

Arthur R. Schwartz, James D. Abrams, Adria M. Anuzis, John P. Byrne, Tracy Elsperman, Allison Haines, and Christopher D. Liguori • Institute of Industrial and Labor Relations, University of Michigan, 111 East Catherine, Ann Arbor, MI 48109-2054.

tions in the aircraft industry. Yet, despite their virtual deadlock on these issues, labor and management have begun to establish cooperative labor relations arrangements in the last two years. It is this movement toward labor–management cooperation that will serve as the overall theme of this paper.

Since 1960, the International Association of Machinists and Aerospace Workers (IAM), the dominant blue-collar union in the industry, has been asking for contract language concerning technological change.[2] However, the employers refused to bargain on the issue, and until recently the union has been unable to compel the employers to accept contract language on technological change.

From the union's point of view, the threat of new technology coupled with the overall volatility of the industry makes cooperation with management on job security a necessity. Only since the early 1980s, has management been predisposed to cooperate on this issue. International competition coupled with declining government purchases and support for research and development have put additional pressure on the major aircraft manufacturers, making them more labor-cost conscious and increasing their desire for wage concessions from the union. In the past, as in many manufacturing industries protected from competition, high profits led the aircraft companies to make large wage concessions to labor. These concessions partly compensated for the employment volatility in the industry. By 1984 the average wage in the aircraft industry was over $13 per hour and average total labor cost was over $21 per hour.[3] With increased foreign competition and the general slump in aircraft sales, concessions and cooperation are increasingly discussed in aircraft negotiations, as they are in other manufacturing industries such as auto and steel.

The aircraft industry is often thought of as an oligopoly because of the relatively small number of large firms. However, many smaller businesses manufacture parts, repair aircraft, and perform ancillary production tasks. Yet, with a high level of unionization, higher than average foreign involvement and assets, and very high profit rates, the industry may be classified as a "core" industry.[4]

The major domestic firms involved in the industry are Boeing, Lockheed, McDonnell Douglas, General Dynamics, United Technologies, and General Electric. Table 1 presents sales and profit figures for those firms. Lockheed left the commercial transport field for the military field in the early 1980s. United Technologies, General Dynamics, and General Electric serve mainly as suppliers. United Technologies provides engines and builds helicopters and some military aircraft. General Dynamics builds military aircraft and supplies

[2] "IAM Bargaining Program on Technological Change", *Collective Bargaining Negotiations and Contracts*, Bureau of National Affairs, 12 June 1980, pp. 39–42.

[3] "The Bargaining in Aerospace Goes Down to Earth," *Businessweek*, 26 September 1983, pp. 38–39 and "Wage Patterns in Aerospace," *Collective Bargaining Negotiations and Contracts*, Bureau of National Affairs, 1984, pp. 18:13–18:17.

[4] Hodson, Randy, *Workers' Earnings and Corporate Economic Structure* (New York: Academic Press, 1983), pp. 79–83.

Table 1. Financial Data for Major Aircraft Industry Firms (millions of dollars)[a]

Firm	1977	1978	1979	1980	1981	1982	1983	1984
Boeing								
Sales	4019	5463	8131	9426	9788	9035	11129	10354
Profits	180	323	505	600	473	292	355	787
General Dynamics								
Sales	2762	3205	4060	4645	5063	6352	7146	7839
Profits	103	(48)	185	195	124	133	287	382
Lockheed								
Sales	3348	3496	4058	5396	6232	5613	6490	8113
Profits	55	65	37	28	(289)	207	263	344
McDonnell Douglas								
Sales	3545	4130	5279	6066	7385	7331	8111	9662
Profits	123	161	199	145	177	214	275	325
United Technologies								
Sales	5550	6265	9053	12324	13677	13577	14669	16332
Profits	196	234	326	393	458	534	509	645
General Electric								
Sales	17519	19564	22463	24959	27240	26500	26800	27950
Profits	1088	1230	1408	1514	1652	1817	2024	2280

[a]Source: *Moody's Industrial Manual* and *Fortune 500*, various years.

parts for commercial aircraft. In 1984, 13 percent of GE's total revenues came from the production of aircraft engines.[5] Boeing and McDonnell Douglas are the chief rivals in the design and assembly of commercial aircraft. Although their revenues were nearly identical in 1984, McDonnell Douglas derived only 22 percent of its revenue from transport aircraft production, whereas Boeing earned 52 percent of its revenue in transport aircraft.[6] In addition, neither company made much profit from commercial aircraft production, implying that military aircraft production is much more profitable.

II. TECHNOLOGICAL CHANGE IN AIRCRAFT PRODUCTION

Recent technological innovations in aircraft production have been promoted by three factors: airline deregulation, increasing foreign competition, and a growing shortage of skilled blue-collar labor. Soon after the deregulation of airlines in 1978, price competition among airlines led to an increase in air transportation traffic, creating a derived demand for aircraft and parts.[7] The increased traffic proved to be temporary. However, the increased competition compelled the airlines, the chief customers of the aircraft industry, to

[5]"Survey—Aircraft Industry," *The Economist,* June 1, 1985, p. 10.
[6]Ibid. p. 10.
[7]Bluestone, Barry, Peter Jordan and Mark Sullivan, *Aircraft Industry Dynamics: An Analysis of Competition, Capital and Labor* (Boston: Auburn House Publishing Company, 1981), p. 166.

become more cost-conscious. The airlines had to keep their prices low in order to remain competitive despite losing money. Increased competition has led to a more price-conscious airline industry, which has forced the aircraft industry to become more cost-conscious.

Airbus Consortium, which is a firm jointly owned by the governments of France, Great Britain, West Germany, and Spain, has recently begun to compete with the American firms on the world market. The future market over which they will compete is large. Between 1958 and 1984, 8,443 deliveries were made to the airlines. Boeing estimates that from 1984 to 1995 there will be a total of 4,000 deliveries to airlines worth $135 billion (1985 dollars), while Airbus estimates that between 1985 and 2005, 9,125 airliners will be sold on the world market at a value of $471 billion (1985 dollars).[8] This increased demand will lead to increased competition for sales and further efforts to maintain low costs.

According to many aircraft manufacturers, the industry faces a severe shortage of experienced, blue-collar, skilled labor. The industry has relied almost exclusively on workers trained during World War II and the Korean War at the expense of the federal government. Even during the Vietnam expansion it was possible for both prime contractors and subcontractors to draw on the World War II labor force. Manufacturers complain that the training of a new generation of engineers has been insufficient to meet the demands of the industry.[9]

In order to reduce costs and address the shortage of skilled blue-collar labor, the U.S. aircraft industry has recently made five major technological changes in aircraft production.[10] First, the industry has increasingly used light-weight materials of comparable strength, thereby improving fuel economy. Second, a new bulge-forming technique has been introduced in the assembly process which has eliminated welding after forming and improved the efficiency of die-making. Third, with electrochemical machining, large jet parts are manufactured from refractory alloys, decreasing much of the labor cost in production. Fourth, computer-aided design has been incorporated into aircraft production. Finally, the most important change has been the introduction of numerical control. In 1973, 4.3% of all machine tools in the aircraft industry were numerically controlled as compared to 1.1 percent in 1968. By 1976, almost 25% of the new machine tools purchased by the aircraft industry were numerically controlled.[11] Despite these changes, aircraft production technology may be classified, according to Woodward's typology, as batch production, as the products continue to be produced on a one-unit basis.[12]

---

[8]*The Economist*, June 1, 1985, p. 8, 10.

[9]Bluestone, p. 14.

[10]U.S. Bureau of Labor Statistics, *Technological Change and Manpower Trends in Five Industries*, Bulletin 1856 (Washington, D.C., 1975).

[11]Bluestone, p. 116.

[12]Woodward, Joan, *Industrial Organization: Theory and Practice*, 2nd ed. (Oxford: Oxford University Press, 1980), pp. 40–47.

III. THE ISSUE OF JOB SECURITY

Even without the problem of technological change, the issue of job security would be important because of the volatility of the industry. This volatility is due to the many re-equipment cycles in the industry. Hundreds of thousands of jobs can disappear in months. During World War II, twenty-three aircraft firms employed 1.46 million workers. By 1946, employment bottomed, with 219,000 workers employed at five firms.[13] Table 2 presents employment trends in aircraft manufacturing (SIC 372), manufacturing, and the entire economy. Employment in aircraft production is more volatile than employment in manufacturing and the economy.

Recent labor adjustments by aircraft firms also illustrate the employment volatility in the industry. For example, with over 50% of the world market, Boeing nearly folded in 1970–71, despite the sales growth of the 747 and 727 over the preceding four years. In retreat, the company slashed its expenses, reducing its workforce from approximately 100,000 to 37,000 workers in the Seattle area within a three-year period.[14]

Foreign competition and co-production with foreign companies are causing unions to worry about a reduction in domestic aircraft jobs. Co-production is the fastest growing production arrangement in the international aircraft market. The necessity of large investments coupled with declining support by the government have led many U.S. producers to seek development and production partners among foreign aircraft companies. Such arrangements include partial financing by foreign governments as well as guaranteed markets among state-owned foreign airlines. Foreign governments are demanding that a share of production take place within their own borders. Since most foreign air carriers are government-owned, policy considerations such as the balance of payments or potential job creation enter into the awarding of contracts of both commercial and military aircraft.

The foreign demand for co-production and offset agreements became much more pronounced during the 1970s after many European manufacturers were given subsidies or were nationalized. European private enterprise was unable to compete with American firms, but their governments were unwilling to sacrifice the export revenue or the jobs. Airbus Consortium was developed explicitly to alleviate the heavy investment burden and the attendant risk among several firms, thereby reducing their competitive disadvantage.[15]

Recent declines in U.S. government support of the aircraft industry have also stimulated co-production. With few exeptions, national policy has encouraged growth and development in the aircraft industry through direct purchases, subsidies, and shelters. A shelter is a market entry barrier that

---

[13]Roe, John B., *Climb to Greatness: The American Aircraft Industry, 1920–1960* (Cambridge: MIT Press, 1968), p. 173.
[14]Bluestone, p. 2.
[15]Bluestone, p. 161.

Table 2. Employment Trends in Selected Industries[a]

Year	Total		Manufacturing		SIC 372		SIC 372 Production Workers	
	Employment (000)	Index 1972=100	Employment (000)	Index 1972=100	Employment (000)	Index 1972=100	Employment (000)	Index 1972=100
1966	63901.	86.7	19214.	100.3	753.	147.4	446.	161.6
1967	65803.	89.3	19447.	101.5	834.	163.2	502.	181.9
1968	67897.	92.2	19781.	103.3	852.	166.7	506.	183.3
1969	70384.	95.5	20167.	105.3	804.	157.3	464.	168.1
1970	70880.	96.2	19367.	101.1	669.	130.9	364.	131.9
1971	71214.	96.7	18623.	97.2	533.	104.3	286.	103.6
1972	73675.	100.0	19151.	100.0	511.	100.0	276.	100.0
1973	76790.	104.2	20154.	105.2	533.	104.3	290.	105.1
1974	78265.	106.2	20077.	104.8	543.	106.3	296.	107.2
1975	76945.	104.4	18323.	95.7	514.	100.6	273.	98.9
1976	79382.	107.7	18997.	99.2	485.	94.9	250.	90.6
1977	82471.	111.9	19682.	102.8	482.	94.3	247.	89.5
1978	86697.	117.7	20505.	107.1	527.	103.1	275.	99.6
1979	89823.	121.9	21040.	109.9	611.	119.6	332.	120.3
1980	90406.	122.7	20285.	105.9	652.	127.6	355.	128.6
1981	91156.	123.7	20170.	105.3	649.	127.0	345.	125.0
1982	89566.	121.6	18781.	98.1	612.	119.8	310.	112.3
1983	90138.	122.3	18497.	96.6	580.	113.5	283.	102.5
1984	94156.	127.8	19590.	102.3	602.	117.8	288.	104.3

[a]Source: U.S. Bureau of Labor Statistics, *Employment and Earnings*.

Table 3. Aerospace Industry R & D
as a Percentage of Gross Revenues
(Millions of 1967 dollars)[a]

Year	R&D funds	Percentage of Total Sales
1960	3687	20.3
1961	4039	21.3
1962	4263	21.1
1963	4975	23.4
1964	5334	24.6
1965	5340	24.9
1966	5610	22.4
1967	5669	20.8
1968	5635	19.9
1969	5574	22.6
1970	4768	21.0
1971	4304	22.2
1972	4234	21.9
1973	4038	20.5
1974	3457	20.1
1975	3330	20.1
1976	3351	20.4
1977	3641	21.3
1978	3749	20.3

[a]Source: Aerospace Industries Association, *Aerospace Facts and Figures, 1980/81.*

insulates an industry or firm from normal competitive pressures.[16] Over the years the aircraft industry has enjoyed benefits from a number of shelters, including cost-plus contracts guaranteeing a profit, government subsidized plants and equipment, and research and development (R&D) funding.

Shelters have also affected labor relations. The protection from shelters gave the union added bargaining power because the company (and the government) would be unwilling to tolerate a strike. With limited competition, wage increases were passed on to the consumer (or the government for defense contracts) in the form of higher prices. This led to high wages in the industry. For the companies, the higher wages were traded for a relatively free hand in running the business.

At the present time R&D funding is a key part of government involvement in the aerospace industry. Aerospace firms conduct over 20% of all industrial research and development, much of which is supported by the federal government.[17] The government has become a guarantor of continued product improvement and profits. Table 3 reveals the importance that R&D carries in the industry. Historically the largest amount of industry funds for

[16]Bluestone, p. 157.
[17]Aerospace Industries Association, *Aerospace Facts and Figures 1978–1979.*

Table 4. Aerospace Industry R & D Effort by Source of Funds: All Industries and the Aerospace Industry (Millions of 1967 dollars)[a]

Year	Total R&D for all Industries	Total Aerospace	Percentage of total	Government Funded	Privately Funded	Percentage Privately finances
1960	11027	3687	33.4	3305	381	10.3
1961	11506	4039	35.1	2626	413	10.2
1962	12092	4263	35.2	3784	478	11.2
1963	13336	4975	37.3	4499	477	9.5
1964	14193	5334	37.6	4853	480	8.9
1965	14714	5340	36.3	4667	673	12.6
1966	15784	5610	35.5	4795	814	14.5
1967	16385	5669	34.6	4531	1138	20.0
1968	17003	5635	33.1	4433	1201	21.3
1969	17271	5574	32.3	4296	1278	22.9
1970	16420	4768	29.0	3665	1102	23.1
1971	16048	4304	26.8	3418	886	20.5
1972	16440	4234	25.7	3429	804	18.9
1973	16617	4038	24.3	3173	864	21.4
1974	14563	3457	23.7	2691	765	22.1
1975	14050	3330	23.7	2585	744	22.3
1976	14593	3351	23.0	2589	762	22.7
1977	15340	3641	23.7	2840	801	22.0
1978	15950	3749	23.5	2842	907	24.2

[a]Source: Aerospace Industries Association, *Aerospace Facts and Figures, 1980/81.*

research and development has been provided by the federal government. Table 4 shows this in detail.

However, since 1964 the government-financed share of total R&D has declined, while the amount which is privately funded has increased. Multinational development of aircraft first became commonplace during the late 1960s, shortly after the government reduced its amount of R&D funds. After losing U.S. government research development and funds, the U.S. aircraft industry turned overseas for capital.[18] This has also meant more financial uncertainty for the firms involved in the aircraft industry and a loss of U.S. production jobs.

Cost-plus contracts are another form of shelter which has recently begun to erode. With the unforeseen technical difficulties which may arise at any point during the development of a product, estimates of cost in advance of production are difficult to calculate, making cost-plus contracts the rule in the industry. This arrangement gave firms no incentive to maintain low costs, but these contracts have come under fire recently, leading firms to be more cost conscious.[19]

[18]Bluestone, p. 160.
[19]"General Dynamics under Fire," *Businessweek*, March 25, 1985, p. 70–76.

Table 5. Aircraft, Engine, and Parts Sales by Customer 1966–81 (millions of dollars)[a]

Year	Total	U.S. Government	Other	Percentage of Total Sales to U.S. Government
1966	8725	5458	3267	62.6
1967	11894	7141	4753	60.0
1968	13850	7411	6439	53.5
1969	12764	7161	5603	56.1
1970	13466	7586	5880	56.3
1971	11392	6313	5079	55.4
1972	10153	4954	5199	48.8
1973	12278	5539	6739	45.1
1974	13542	5982	7560	44.2
1975	14656	6859	7797	46.8
1976	15936	8314	7622	52.2
1977	16378	8848	7530	54.0
1978	19305	8724	10581	45.2
1979	24501	8868	15633	36.2
1980	26292	10359	15933	39.4
1981	30114	12075	18039	40.1

[a]Source: Aerospace Industries Association, *Aerospace Facts and Figures, 1980/81.*

Furthermore, since 1967 the share of U.S. government purchases has diminished. Following the end of the Vietnam War, defense purchases fell below 50% and remained at that level, with the exception of 1976 and 1977. Then, in 1979 the proportion dropped substantially due to a tremendous increase in commercial sales, as shown in Table 5.

As government shelters, R&D funding, and purchases have diminished, the industry has been forced to become more labor-cost conscious and to seek financing abroad. Although this might have occurred even without the decrease in government spending, it seems likely that this reduction has given greater urgency to joint ventures. The growth of the multinational in the industry can be traced, at least partially, to changes in government policy.[20]

Technological change has caused additional job security problems. The introduction of new technology has affected the occupational distribution of employment in the industry. The 1960–80 employment distributions by major occupational group for aircraft manufacturing (SIC 372) and for manufacturing in 1980 are shown in Table 6.[21] The most striking difference between aircraft manufacturing and total manufacturing is the heavy use of professional and technical personnel in aircraft production. Among blue-collar oc-

[20]Bluestone, p. 161.
[21]Data on occupation by industry are from the Decennial Census. In each year the appropriate report is Subject Report 7C. The totals for the 1980 Census were regrouped to conform with earlier totals. There is always the danger when comparing Censuses that some of the occupational definitions have changed.

Table 6. Distribution of Employment by Major
Occupational Class[a]

	Percentage of total employment in the industry of each class			
	Manufacturing	Aircraft (SIC 372)		
Occupations	1980	1980	1970	1960
Professional and Technical	9.9	22.3	25.9	22.2
Managers	7.7	7.3	4.6	2.9
Sales	3.1	0.6	0.4	0.4
Clerical	12.5	15.3	15.6	16.9
Craft	18.8	26.7	24.0	25.9
Operatives	39.1	24.6	26.2	27.2
Service	2.2	1.8	1.9	1.6
Laborers	6.0	1.4	0.9	0.8

[a]Source: *Census of the United States,* subject report 7C, 1960, 1970, 1980.

cupations, there is a higher percentage of skilled craft workers and a much lower percentage of unskilled and semi-skilled operatives and laborers in aircraft manufacturing. Technological change has caused changes in the occupational distribution of employment in the industry. The new bulge-forming technique and the use of electrochemical machining has led to a reduction in the number of tool and die makers. The use of computer-aided design has increased the use of computer personnel and decreased the use of design personnel. The most drastic change has been caused by the increased use of numerical control which has reduced the overall need for skilled blue-collar workers.[22]

The change in distribution between 1960 and 1980 in aircraft manufacturing is also shown in Table 6. The percentage of professional and technical personnel increased between 1960 and 1970, but fell back to the 1960 level by 1980. The percentage of managers steadily increased between 1960 to 1980, while the percentage of craft workers declined slightly in the 1960s and increased in the 1970s. The percentage of operatives declined between 1960 and 1980, while the percentage of laborers increased but remained low. Managers were the chief gainers between 1960 and 1980, while the losers were clericals and operatives.

Table 7 presents a more detailed view of some of the important occupations in aircraft manufacturing between 1960 and 1980. The percentage of some of the skilled blue-collar occupations, such as machinists, sheet-metal workers, tool and die makers, and aircraft mechanics declined as did the percentage of certain semi-skilled workers such as assemblers.

In sum, with technological change, employment shifted away from the

[22]U.S. Bureau of Labor Statistics, *Technological Change and Manpower Trends in Five Industries.*

Table 7. Detailed Occupational Distribution[a]

Occupation	Percentage of industry employment in each occupation from the Census of:		
	1980	1970	1960
Engineers	12.1	14.3	12.6
Technicians	5.4	4.3	3.3
Computer programmers and analysts	0.7	1.2	*
Electricians	0.9	1.5	1.6
Blue-collar worker supervisors	5.9	4.8	4.4
Machinists	4.2	3.1	4.8
Sheet-metal workers	1.8	1.9	2.1
Tool and die makers	1.7	2.1	2.1
Aircraft mechanics	3.6	5.5	5.6
Inspectors	4.0	4.2	4.5
Grinding and abrading machine operators, metal	1.8	1.2	*
Lathe and milling machine operators, metal combination	1.5	1.6	*
Welders and flame-cutters	1.3	1.3	1.2
Assemblers	6.1	6.6	6.6

[a]Source: *Census of the United States,* subject report 7C, 1960, 1970, 1980.
*Not available

unskilled toward the skilled, especially with the increased employment of technicians and managers. The ratio of production workers to non-production workers declined continuously after the mid-1960s.[23]

IV. UNIONS IN THE AIRCRAFT INDUSTRY

A variety of unions represent workers in the highly-unionized aircraft industry. The dominant union is the IAM. The IAM was founded in 1885 and has been affiliated with the American Federation of Labor (AFL) since 1895. Initially, IAM membership comprised only skilled workers, but it now includes a wide range of skilled, semi-skilled, and unskilled workers. It is the tenth largest union in the country with a membership of 655,000 as of 1982. Like many of the unions in heavy industry in the United States, IAM mem-

[23]Bluestone, p. 14.

Table 8. Membership in the International Association of
Machinists (thousands)[a]

1962	1966	1970	1974	1978	1980	1982
868	836	865	943	921	754	655

[a]Source: Gifford, Courtney, ed., *Directory of U.S. Labor Organizations 1982–83*
(Washington, DC: Bureau of National Affairs, 1982).

bership has been reduced by foreign competition, technological change, and
the recessions of 1980–82. The IAM membership data in Table 8 document
this decline. The other major blue-collar union in the industry is the United
Auto Workers (UAW). A number of employee associations represent white-
collar and professional employees. For example, the Seattle Professional Engineering Employees Association represents 20,000 Boeing engineers and
technical employees.

The AFL granted the IAM exclusive jurisdiction over "aircraft mechanics" in 1934. In 1936, the union reached agreement on a first contract with
Boeing and in 1937 with Lockhead. The early history of the industry was
marked by rivalry between the IAM and the UAW. The raiding stopped in
1949, and since 1953 the two unions have tried to co-ordinate bargaining.[24]

The degree of unionization in aircraft manufacturing is higher than that
of the U.S. work force as a whole. The percent unionized of wage and salary
workers in aircraft production has been estimated at 40%. The percentage of
workers covered by a collective bargaining agreement is higher because some
workers in bargaining units do not belong to the union. In May 1977, 34.5% of
employees were in unions, while 41.5% were covered by a collective bargaining agreement. In May 1980, 42.4% of employees were in unions and 50.4%
were covered by collective bargaining. It has been estimated that 60% of
production workers in the industry belong to a union.[25]

V. COLLECTIVE BARGAINING IN AIRCRAFT PRODUCTION:
RECENT TRENDS

The industry has been characterized by relatively high wages. Average
earnings in aircraft manufacturing and all manufacturing are presented in
Table 9. Wages rose quite rapidly in the 1977–82 period, as was common in
the unionized manufacturing sector, and then slowed down in 1983 and 1984,

---

[24]U.S. Bureau of Labor Statistics, *Wage Chronology: Lockheed and Machinists Union*, bulletin 1904
(Washington, DC, 1976), p. 1.

[25]U.S. Bureau of Labor Statistics, *Earnings and Other Characteristics of Organized Workers*, report 556
and bulletin 2105, (Washington, D.C., 1978 and 1981) and Freeman, Richard, and James
Medoff, "New Estimates of Private Sector Unionism in the United States," *Industrial and Labor
Relations Review* 32 (January 1979), pp. 143–174.

Table 9. Hourly Earnings in Manufacturing and Aircraft Production[a]

Year	Manufacturing		Aircraft production (SIC 372)	
	Hourly earnings	Percentage change	Hourly earnings	Percentage change
1970	$3.35	5.0	$ 4.11	6.5
1971	3.57	6.6	4.36	6.1
1972	3.82	7.0	4.74	8.7
1973	4.09	7.1	5.02	5.9
1974	4.42	8.1	5.40	7.6
1975	4.83	9.3	5.99	10.9
1976	5.22	8.1	6.45	7.7
1977	5.68	8.8	6.92	7.3
1978	6.17	8.6	7.54	9.0
1979	6.70	8.6	8.26	9.5
1980	7.27	8.5	9.28	12.3
1981	7.99	9.9	10.31	11.1
1982	8.49	6.3	11.25	9.1
1983	8.83	4.0	11.84	5.2
1984	9.17	3.9	12.38	4.6
Average increase 1970–84		7.5		8.2

[a]Source: Bureau of Labor Statistics, *Employment and Earnings.*

when the recession and increased foreign competition led to some concessions in bargaining.[26]

The aircraft industry has generally not been strike-prone. The 1968–80 strike trend in aircraft manufacturing is shown in Table 10. In 1969 there was a major strike that caused a total shutdown of General Electric for 122 days. In 1975 there was a 93-day strike against McDonnell Douglas by the IAM, involving almost 19,000 workers. Since 1977–78, strike levels have been low. There were no major strikes in 1981 and 1982. In October 1983, the UAW struck three McDonnell Douglas plants with 6,200 workers.

The major issue in the 1977–78 strikes was job security. In 1977, the IAM struck both Boeing (45 days) and Lockheed (83 days), and in 1978 the UAW struck McDonnell Douglas for almost 11 weeks. The apparent cause of these strikes was the attempt by the companies to loosen seniority rules during layoffs. According to Gordon Fleming, Assistant Director, Aerospace Division of the UAW, the union recognized its limited capacity for preventing technological displacement of workers and layoffs induced by declining product demand. Yet, the UAW made job security a primary concern in negotiations for its skilled and unskilled workers, in an attempt to win important job guarantees for those who remained employed.[27]

[26]Bureau of Labor Statistics, *Employment and Earnings.*
[27]Interview with Gordon Fleming, Associate Director, UAW Aerospace Division, 9 March 1983.

Table 10. Strike Activity in Industry 372[a]

Year	Number of strikes	Mean duration days	Workers involved	Days lost (thousands)
1968	46	—	45500	594.3
1969	26	25.8	76400	1564.6
1970	12	104.6	6800	552.5
1971	24	66.8	17200	465.5
1972	18	58.1	2800	148.1
1973	13	30.5	4500	99.1
1974	27	29.4	16800	370.0
1975	20	70.0	22800	1245.6
1976	21	37.7	13000	330.5
1977	21	57.7	46700	1832.2
1978	17	78.8	12600	741.2
1979	12	22.4	6600	103.4
1980	17	25.5	4400	92.9

[a]Source: Bureau of Labor Statistics, *Analysis of Work Stoppage.*

This key issue of job security has long been an important one for the IAM. In 1960, the IAM Executive Council recommended an eight-point program to deal with labor and technological change. It called for: (1) advance notice of technological change; (2) a joint union–management committee to study problems arising from technological change; (3) preference for senior workers in new work assignments deriving from technological change; (4) the use of attrition in work force reduction due to technological change; (5) the right of current employees to be trained at company expense for new jobs created by technological change; (6) no loss of pay for any employee whose assignment to a lower job classification resulted from technological change; (7) no loss of jobs from the bargaining unit due to technological change; and (8) preference in hiring for employees who were laid off due to technological change.[28]

The major bargaining in the industry has taken place every three years. The industry pattern is usually set by the negotiations between the IAM and Boeing. Although technological change has been an issue in most contract negotiations, the IAM, until 1983, was unable to institute any of its 1960 program.

In 1977, a strike was called on October 4 at Boeing due to dissatisfaction with the company wage offer. Six days later, the workers at Lockheed rejected the company demand that it be allowed to change the seniority system to give it more flexibility in layoff, recall, and work assignment. Lockheed wanted to restrict the amount of bumping that could be done and exempt a certain percentage of workers from the seniority list. The company proposed

[28]"IAM Bargaining Program on Technological Change", pp. 39–42.

this major change in job security to lower its labor costs. The IAM opposed any tampering with the seniority system.[29]

The strike at Boeing was settled in November. At Lockheed, the strike dragged on even with the intervention of a federal mediator. Finally, on January 2, 1978, a settlement was ratified. It provided a 6.1% pay increase (versus an initial offer of 3.5%) in the first year and 3 percent in 1978 and 1979. A compromise was reached on seniority that essentially preserved bumping rights for current employees, but eliminated them for future hires. In this compromise, the company had acquired some additional flexibility in that new hires would no longer have the right to bump, but the union had protected the principle of seniority.

Although the 1980 contract round yielded no contract language on technological change, the 1982 contract between General Electric and the 13-union Coordinated Bargaining Committee contained new language on job security and technological change. Two major contract provisions pertained to technological change: first, unions would be provided with a 60-day advance warning of the installation of robots or other automated machinery; second, a worker compelled by the transfer of work to another plant or the introduction of robotics or other new technology to take a lower-paying job would receive the original higher wage rate for up to 26 weeks. Other clauses provided severance pay to certain workers and payments of up to $1,800 for job retraining for workers with more than two years of seniority.[30]

In 1982, the Electronics and New Technology Conference, an ongoing committee of the IAM, held its annual meeting in Seattle. One of the products of this meeting was a Technology Bill of Rights. This document differed from the 1960 bargaining program in its greater theoretical emphasis on principles regarding the problems of technological change. This initiated a new union drive in the aircraft industry to include language on technology in the new labor contract.[31]

The purpose of the Technology Bill of Rights was to amend the National Labor Relations Act, the Railway Labor Act, and any other appropriate acts in order to set a national policy on technology. There were ten major points in the Bill of Rights: (1) technology should be used in a way that does not decrease jobs, but creates jobs; (2) labor productivity gains resulting from new technology should be shared with production workers, and any increased leisure due to new technology should not result in loss of income; (3) a tax should be placed on all machinery and equipment that displaces workers; (4) displaced workers should suffer no loss of income and are entitled to retraining; (5) new technology must be used to develop the U.S. industrial base

[29]U.S. Bureau of Labor Statistics, *Wage Chronology: Lockheed and Machinists Union*, bulletin 1904—supplement (Washington, D.C., 1979), p. 2. Bumping is the displacement of a worker by a more senior worker in a parallel or lower-rated job.

[30]*The Machinist*, August 1982, p. 1.

[31]Newell, Reginald, Research Director, IAM, "New Technology, Collective Bargaining, and Organizing: An IAM Perspective," January 1983.

before it can be licensed or exported abroad; (6) new technology should not be destructive of the workplace or the community's natural environment; (7) workers, through their unions, should participate in all aspects of the decision to introduce new technology; (8) new technology should not be used to monitor, measure, or control work practices of individual workers; (9) storage of an individual worker's personal data and information file should be tightly controlled and the individual worker should have the right to inspect his or her data file at all times; and (10) when new technology is adapted for military use, the workers, through their unions, should have the right to bargain over the establishment of committees to adapt that technology to socially useful production in the civilian sector of the economy.[32]

Although these are general statements, some specific contract demands were generated from them. These included the creation of technology stewards to monitor the impact of technological change at the workplace and a proposal for a 30-hour week to spread the declining number of jobs among more workers.[33]

In 1983, the IAM brought to Boeing proposed contract language on the effects of new technology. These proposals were also backed by the Professional Engineering Employees Association. The IAM proposed retraining programs, advance notice on technological change, and job loss by attrition only. Also, the union wanted to limit the amount of co-production with foreign firms. Given the proposed defense buildup, the IAM also sought high wage increases.[34] The new technology proposals were derived from both the bargaining agenda on technological change and the Technology Bill of Rights.

Initially Boeing rejected all of the IAM technology proposals. However, the firm was very concerned with maintaining low labor costs and avoiding a strike, and thus was willing to discuss some of the technology issues. On October 4, a significant agreement was reached which established many new contract provisions in the aircraft industry. The agreement provided for a two-tier wage structure in which new employees would be paid on a lower pay scale than existing employees. Therefore, as new employees replaced existing employees, the average pay rate at Boeing would decline. In addition, current workers in the highest pay grades received higher increases than workers in lower pay grades. This was an attempt to attract and retain highly skilled labor. Since raises in 1984 and 1985 would be lump sum productivity bonuses equal to 3% of annual earnings, wage rates would not rise during the life of the contract.

Later in October, the IAM negotiated a contract with Lockheed that did not include as many economic concessions as the Boeing contract. The IAM settled with McDonnell Douglas, over the objections of the union's lead-

---

[32]*Let's Rebuild America,* a publication of the International Association of Machinists and Aerospace Workers, 1984, pp. 202–204.

[33]*The Machinist,* November 1982, p. 3.

[34]*Businessweek,* Sept, 26, 1983, "The Bargaining in Aerospace Goes Down to Earth" and "Machinists Will Resist Concessions, Seek Language on Technology in Negotiations with Aerospace Firms," Daily Labor Report, May 6, 1983, Bureau of National Affairs, p. A-5.

ership, gaining terms similar to those in the Boeing agreement. The Professional Engineering Employees Association settled with Boeing without any technology references in the contract. The UAW workers at McDonnell Douglas rejected the two-tier wage concept and struck the company in October. The strike lasted until February 1984, when the union returned to work on the company's terms.

The major difference between the Boeing contract and all other contracts in the industry was the creation at Boeing of a labor–management technology committee. The 1983 Boeing–IAM joint advisory committee was to be concerned with the impact of new technology on the workplace. It was funded by the company to serve as the coordinator of the effects of technology on labor. The committee selected skills that would be required in the future, set up a training program, and developed ways to refer laid-off workers to the program. Section 20.1 of the new contract summarizes the thinking of the two parties:

> The Company and the Union agree that it is to their mutual benefit and a sound economic and social goal to utilize the most efficient machines, processes, methods, and/or materials. In this way the Company will be able to compete effectively in the marketplace and, thereby, provide economically secure jobs for its employees. It is the Company's policy to assure that training is available for its employees so that they may have the opportunity to acquire the knowledge and skills required by the introduction of new technology.[35]

The contract language is regarded by the IAM as a first step in limiting the impact of technological change on workers. However, the union gave many concessions to gain this language. Nonetheless, one of the clauses from the 1960 bargaining agenda on technology was incorporated in the 1983 contract.[36]

VI. CONCLUSIONS

The aircraft industry illustrates the beginning of labor–management cooperation on issues which accompany technological change. The industry is heavily unionized, and like so many other unionized manufacturing industries, has been weakened recently by increased foreign competition. In addition, airline deregulation and reduced government protection and support of aircraft manufacturing have introduced more competition into the aircraft production industry.

Although the unions in the industry, most notably the IAM, have for twenty-five years proposed arrangements to protect technologically displaced workers, it was not until the early 1980s that language on technological change was incorporated into a contract. Increased foreign competition and job loss during the 1982 recession appear to have increased union resolve to

[35]Collective bargaining agreement between the Boeing Company and the International Association of Machinists, 3 October 1983, section 20.1.
[36]*The Machinist*, July 1985, p. 3.

include, as well as managerial acceptance of, contract language on technological change in the 1983 contract. In order to demonstrate their resolve on the subject, a Technology Bill of Rights was drawn up by the IAM in 1982. The 1983 IAM–Boeing contract established the first joint labor–management advisory committee in the industry to address the impact of technological change on workers.

The experience in the aircraft industry is typical of many unionized industries. Cooperation between labor and management comes grudgingly and only when the firms are in jeopardy. In other industries, such as autos, steel, airlines, and trucking, cooperation has been caused by increased foreign competition, a deep recession, or deregulation. The domestic aircraft industry has suffered from all three catalysts: foreign competition, recession, and deregulation. In the past, the companies would have been cushioned by earnings from their military production, but now the overall profitability of the industry is threatened. That problem is of mutual concern to both labor and management, thus opening up the possibility of increased cooperation.

While only the 1983 Boeing contract included language on technological change, the next round of negotiations in the industry may lead to similar changes in the labor agreements with other manufacturers. Yet, the parties may decide the worst is over and not move forward on cooperation. Or they may decide that the Boeing–IAM technology committee has helped the industry and build it into the next contract. In collective bargaining, the contract following a major change is often a guide to the future. This may be the case in the aircraft industry.

14

Technological Change in the Public Sector

The Case of Sanitation Service

David Lewin

How does technological change affect the social organization of the workplace and, in particular, labor–management relations? This question is now being widely addressed by researchers, who are studying a variety of workplace contexts.[1] Most of this research deals with the private sector of the American economy, however the same question may be posed about the public sector generally and specific services within it.

The present paper examines recent technological changes in local sanitation service and their effects on the process and outcomes of labor-management relations. The paper begins with a description of the organizational, employment, and labor relations characteristics of local sanitation departments in United States (U.S.) cities. Then a conceptual model of the public sector labor relations process is presented together with a discussion of technological change as one of the variables operating within this model. Next, several quantitative assessments of the effects of technological change on sanitation employment and unionization are offered. This is followed by a combined quantitative and qualitative examination of the effects of technological change on labor relations in municipal sanitation departments. Finally, the analysis and findings about sanitation service are assessed in terms

---

[1]See, for example, Daniel B. Cornfield, "Workers, Managers and Technological Change," in Cornfield, ed., *Workers, Managers, and Technological Change: Emerging Patterns of Labor Relations* (New York: Plenum, 1987), pp. 3–26.

David Lewin • Professor of Business, Graduate School of Business, Columbia University, 708 Uris Hall, New York, NY 10027.

of their larger significance for technological change and labor relations in the public and private sectors.

I. CHARACTERISTICS OF SANITATION SERVICE

Sanitation service is popularly thought to be provided to service recipients by municipal governments, but most cities have two or more types of service providers. Moreover, the mix and proportional distribution of service providers vary by category of service recipient.[2] Municipal governments provide the bulk of sanitation service for streets and other open or public spaces, while private firms provide the largest share of sanitation service to institutional, commercial, and industrial recipients. In the case of residential recipients, the distribution of service providers varies by detailed category of recipient, but clearly municipalities, private firms, and self-service all have important places in this "market." Note that the use of special districts or authorities to provide sanitation service (which are the main components of the "other" column in Table 1) is substantial in the cases of streets, parks, and litter baskets and, to a lesser extent, for institutional recipients.

On average, there were 46 full-time paid personnel per municipal sanitation department in the United States in the 1983, or 0.70 per 1,000 population.[3] More notable, however, are recent changes in municipal sanitation employment.[4] Between 1975 and 1983, proportional sanitation employment in U.S. cities declined by fully half, from 1.41 to 0.70 full-time paid employees per 1,000 population. This was, by far, the sharpest proportional decline among the three major categories of uniformed service personnel—police, firefighters and sanitation workers—employed by municipal governments.

Data concerning the unionization of publicly-employed sanitation personnel are given in Table 1. In 1980, approximately 40% of all full-time sanitation employees of local governments belonged to labor organizations (unions and associations). However, less than two-thirds of all organized sanitation employees are actually represented by their labor ogranizations for purposes of collective bargaining. The difference between organization and representation reflects (1) the failure of certain labor organizations to attain the status of certified bargaining agents in local governments, (2) the prevalence of public sector bargaining laws in certain states that do not require or otherwise provide for the certification of bargaining agents, and (3) the failure of some labor organizations to negotiate first or successor contracts with local government employers. Despite these factors, the difference between sanitation employee membership in labor organizations and employee representation in collective

[2]See E. S. Savas and Christopher Niemczewski, "Who Collects Solid Waste?," in *The Municipal Yearbook—1976* (Washington, DC: International City Management Association, 1976), p. 18.
[3]See Gerard J. Hoetmer, "Police, Fire, and Refuse Collection and Disposal Departments: Personnel, Compensation, and Expenditures," in *The Municipal Yearbook—1984* (Washington, DC: International City Management Association, 1984), p. 146.
[4]*Ibid.*, p. 145.

Table 1. Sanitation Employment, Unionization, Bargaining Units, and Representation, 1980[a]

	Local Governments				
Labor Relations Characteristics	Total	County	Municipal	Township	Special District
Total Full-Time Employment	119,274	10,802	102,746	5,322	404
Full-Time Employees who belong to a Labor Organization	47,981	1,612	43,003	3,271	95
% of Full-Time Employees who belong to a Labor Organization	40.2	14.9	41.9	61.5	23.5
Number of Bargaining Units	475	NA[b]	NA	NA	NA
Number of Employees Represented	31,492	NA	NA	NA	NA
Number Represented as a Proportion of Employees Belonging to Labor Organizations (%)	65.5	NA	NA	NA	NA

[a]U.S. Bureau of the Census, *Labor-Management Relations in State and Local Governments: 1980*, State and Local Government Special Studies No. 102. Washington, DC: G.P.O., 1981, pp. 7 and 155.
[b]NA = not available.

bargaining declined by more than nine percentage points between 1972 and 1980.[5]

How has sanitation employee membership in labor organization changed over time, and how does it compare with the incidence of labor organization in local government generally? Figure 1 contains data relevant to these questions. In essence, unionization among full-time sanitation employees declined by 10% between 1972 and 1980, compared to a one and one-half percent decline among full-time local government employees as a whole. For both sanitation employees and local government employees, almost all of the decline in the incidence of unionism took place between 1976 and 1980. Moreover, compared with other specific local government services, the incidence of unionism among sanitation employees is relatively low, as the following data (percentage of full-time employees who belong to a labor organization) indicate:[6]

Education	61.3%
Instructional staff	67.9
Other	44.4

[5]For further analysis of the differences between union membership and union representation in the public sector generally, see John F. Burton, Jr., "The Extent of Collective Bargaining in the Public Sector," in Benjamin Aaron, Joseph R. Grodin, and James L. Stern, eds., *Public-Sector Bargaining* (Washington,DC: Bureau of National Affairs, 1979), pp. 1–43.
[6]U.S. Bureau of the Census, *Labor-Management Relations in State and Local Governments: 1980*, Special Study no. 102 (Washington, DC: 1981), p. 7.

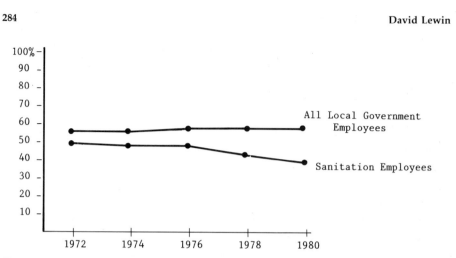

Figure 1. Local government and sanitation employee union rates, 1972–1980. Data are for paid full-time personnel. From U.S. Bureau of the Census, *Labor-Management Relations in State and Local Governments: 1974, 1976, 1978 and 1980,* State and Local Government Special Studies, Nos. 75, 88, 95 and 102. Washington, D.C.: G.P.O., 1976, 1978, 1980, and 1981, various pages.

Highways	37.6
Public welfare	42.4
Hospitals	29.4
Police protection	52.8
Local fire protection	70.6
Sanitation (other than sewage)	40.2
All other	38.3

Particularly notable is the considerably higher incidence of unionism among police and firefighters than among sanitation personnel; these three employee groups are often lumped under the heading of "uniformed services." Additionally, the (proportional) decline in the unionization of sanitation employees between 1972 and 1980 was larger, by far, than for any other functional employee group listed above.

II. CONCEPTUALIZING TECHNOLOGICAL CHANGE AND PUBLIC SECTOR LABOR RELATIONS

What factors can explain the recent decline of employment *and* unionism in public sanitation service in the U.S.? In particular, what role does technological change play in these respects? In considering these questions, we must first recognize the significant advances that have been made in the modeling and empirical study of public sector labor relations. Drawing on this research, Figure 2 presents a model of the public sector labor relations process. While, as shown, the model assumes that public employees are organized (into unions and associations) and negotiate written agreements with

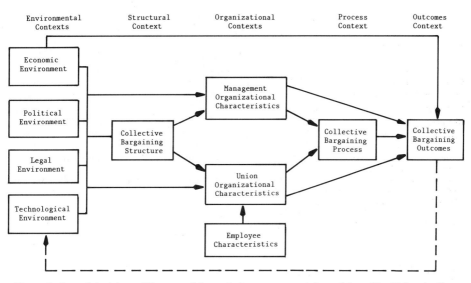

Figure 2. A model of the public sector labor relations process. Adapted from David Lewin, Peter Feuille, and Thomas A. Kochan, *Public Sector Labor Relations: Analysis and Readings,* Second Edition. Sun Lakes, Ariz.: Horton and Daughters, 1981, p. 3.

public employers concerning terms and conditions of employment, it can easily be generalized to include unorganized employees and management-determined terms and conditions of employment.

The "economic context" is especially important to the analysis of public sector sanitation service employment and unionism. First, the mid-1970s marked the end of a quarter century in which local government was the fastest growing "industry" in the United States. Public and managerial attention began to focus heavily on the costs of government services and the potential for improving governmental efficiency and productivity.[7] Previously, attention had been directed primarily toward expanding the role of government services in the economy, and local (as well as state and some federal) taxes were raised to finance these services. By the late 1970s and early 1980s, citizen tax "revolts" became prominent, if not commonplace.[8]

Second, and specific to sanitation service, evidence began to be produced in the mid-1970s that showed publicly provided sanitation service to be significantly more costly than privately provided sanitation service. For example, a

[7]See David Lewin, "Collective Bargaining and the Right to Strike in the Public Sector," in A. Lawrence Chickering, ed., *Public Employee Unions: A Study of the Crisis in Public Sector Labor Relations* (San Francisco: Institute for Contemporary Studies, 1976), pp. 145–163.

[8]David Lewin, Peter Feuille, and Thomas A. Kochan, *Public Sector Labor Relations: Analysis and Readings,* 2nd ed. (Sun Lakes, AZ: Horton and Daughters, 1981), pp. 17–24. Note that during the 1960s and early 1970s the major environmental influence on public sector labor relations was the "legal context," as numerous states enacted legislation supporting unionization and collective bargaining rights for public employees in state and local governments.

Table 2. Average Annual Cost per Household[a] for Once-a-Week Curbside Collection, by Collection Arrangement and City Size[b]

Collection arrangement	When population held constant at				
	3,000	15,000	30,000	60,000	90,000
Contract	$23.25	$17.77	$17.30	$18.40[c]	$18.26[c]
Municipal	25.51	19.51	19.95	23.77[d]	23.59[d]
Private	29.49[d]	22.55[d]	25.10[d]	24.10[d]	23.92[d]

[a]Note: Annual cost was estimated holding wage rate, refuse per household, density, service level, and temperature variation constant.
[b]Source: Barbara J. Stevens and E. S. Savas, "The Cost of Residential Refuse Collection and the Effect on Service Arrangement," in *The Municipal Yearbook—1977*. Washington, DC: International City Management Association, 1977, p. 204.
[c]Significantly different from the cost of municipal collection at the 0.5% level.
[d]Significantly different from the cost of contract collection at the 0.5% level.

1975 study of 315 municipalities found that "the average city with a population of more than 50,000 [which was] served by a municipal [sanitation] agency had costs which are [sic] from 29 to 35 percent more than the costs of an average city of the same size served by a private [sanitation] firm with an exclusive territory."[9] In the same study, similar, if smaller, cost differentials between privately and publicly provided sanitation service were found to exist in smaller cities.

Third, and in light of the two aforementioned points, government officials and managers undertook initiatives to reduce the cost and improve the productivity of sanitation service. One initiative was to expand the use of private sanitation service, typically on an exclusive franchise (contract) basis.[10] The data in Table 2 provide one rationale for this behavior. They show that the average cost per household for weekly curbside refuse collection is consistently and, in some cases statistically, significantly lower under a contract arrangement than under municipal and private (competitive bidding) arrangements.

What accounts for these cost differences? Table 3, which compares municipal and contract collection arrangements, provides some clues. Private contractors use larger trucks and proportionately fewer rear-loading vehicles than municipal sanitation agencies. However, the most significant differences have to do with labor utilization. Private contractors employ smaller crews, have less absenteeism, and operate under incentive systems more frequently than municipal sanitation agencies, and the differences are statistically significant in most cases. Hence, operating costs appear to be significantly lower and productivity significantly higher in contract than in municipal sanitation

[9]Barbara J. Stevens, "How Management Decisions Explain Cost Differences Between City Pickup Systems," *Solid Wastes Management* 20 (September 1977), p. 32.
[10]See Eileen Brettler Berenyi, "Union Opposition Could Not Overcome Movement Toward Contract Collection," *Solid Wastes Management* 23 (October 1980), pp. 14–16 and 105–106, and Savas and Niemczewski, pp. 167–172.

Table 3. Management Practices in Sanitation Service, by Collection Arrangement and City Size[a]

Management Practice	Population				Cities having backyard collection location	
	50,000 and under		Over 50,000			
	Municipal	Contract	Municipal	Contract	Municipal	Contract
Mean crew size	3.08	2.06	3.26	2.15	3.04	1.98
Mean truck capacity (cubic yards)	19.04	22.21	20.63	27.14	19.90	23.50
Mean absentee rate	12%	6%	12%	6.5%	12%	4%
Mean % of vehicles loading at front and side	26%[b]	23%[b]	13%	44%	16%	30%
Mean % of cities with incentive system	57%	80%	80%[b]	86%[b]	73%	87%[b]

[a]Source: Barbara J. Stevens and E. S. Savas, "The Cost of Residential Refuse Collection and the Effect on Service Arrangement," in *The Municipal Yearbook—1977*. Washington, DC: International City Management Association, 1977, p. 204.
[b]No significant difference at the .05% level.

collection arrangements.[11] This provides a clear incentive for financially strapped municipalities to adopt contracting arrangements, which is consistent with the observed proportional growth of private contracting and decline of municipality-provided sanitation service since the mid-1970s.

Another recent initiative undertaken by local government officials and managers has been to alter the technology of sanitation collection (and disposal). What are these changes? Probably the most important has been the introduction and expanded use of semi-automated and automated collection systems.[12] Whereas conventional refuse collections featured a rear-loading vehicle with a three-person crew, modern refuse collection features semi-automated and fully automated vehicles that load from the side or front and that operate with two and sometimes one-person crews. Put differently, municipal refuse collection increasingly favors continuous process type tech-

[11]Barbara J. Stevens and E. S. Savas, "The Cost of Residential Refuse Collection and the Effect on Service Arrangement," in *The Municipal Yearbook 1977*, (Washington, DC: International City Management Association, 1977), pp. 200–205. Here and in the remainder of this paper, the emphasis is on residential refuse collection rather than on commercial and industrial refuse collection, street and park maintenance, or litter basket collection.

[12]See Stevens, pp. 32, 36, 72, 98, 100, and 102–105, and Berenyi, pp. 14–16 and 105–106. Other examples of technological change in sanitation service discussed in this section were drawn from accounts contained in various issues of *American City and County, Public Works, Solid Wastes Management, Waste Age*, and *World Wastes* published beteen 1971 and 1984.

nology over batch type technology. This means, in essence, that refuse is loaded onto a truck's waste bin by the truck's automated equipment rather than by manual labor. Recall that private sanitation collection differs from public sanitation collection primarily in terms of the types of vehicles used and in crew size. Within the public sector, municipal sanitation agencies appear to be adopting "private-like" sanitation collection policies and practices.

Accompanying the use of semi-automated and fully automated refuse collection systems in some cities is the use of standardized carts, typically of 82–90 gallon capacity, which are issued to residents by the municipality. The carts provide a uniform size container which permits the use (and purchase by the municipality) of a single type automated vehicle designed specifically to lift and unload the standardized container. A preceding—and, in some cases, accompanying—"technological" change was the conversion from metal cans to plastic bags for the containment of refuse. Such bags are lighter than cans, more easily (and economically) lifted, are disposable (whereas cans must be reused), and, most important, are relatively more consistent with automated technology. Note, further, that conversion from metal cans to plastic bags for residential *and* commercial refuse collection is associated with a significant reduction in sanitation worker injuries irrespective of whether a municipality adopts an automated refuse collection system.[13]

Just as a municipal refuse collection system incorporates managerial and worker behavior, it also encompasses consumer-resident behavior, and the introduction of automated equipment significantly affects consumer behavior. Specifically, automated refuse collection systems operate on the principle of curbside collection rather than backyard collection. Thus, in altering its refuse collection system to emphasize automated collection, a municipality must convince its residents to agree to curbside collection. Put differently, a municipality must get its citizens to agree to use their own labor, rather than municipal employees' labor, to haul refuse to the curb (and not leave it in the backyard).

While most municipalities that have adopted curbside collection have been able to convince residents of the net advantages of such an arrangement, the "convincing" comes at a cost (of advertising, promotion, trial periods, noncompliance, etc.) and reflects a new social organization with respect to a particular public service.[14] The extensive literature on resistance to change in the workplace[15] can be generalized to the "consumption context," and this

[13]See "Refuse Pickup Personnel Injuries are Nine Times National Industry Average," *Solid Wastes Management* 19 (January, 1975), pp. 10–11, 44 and 48, Ralph Stone, "Survey Reveals Trends in the Use of Disposable Refuse Bags," *Public Works* 101 (September 1970), pp. 86–87, and Don Campbell, "One City's Analysis of Accidents," *Waste Age* 15 (May, 1984), pp. 75–77.

[14]See, for example, "Atlanta: The Biggest Municipal Collection System to Adopt Cart Service," *Solid Wastes Management* 19 (February 1976), pp. 24–25, 28 and 52.

[15]As examples, see Lester Coch and John R. P. French, Jr., "Overcoming Resistance to Change," *Human Relations* 1 (July 1948), pp. 512–532, and R. M. Steers, "Antecedents and Outcomes of Organizational Commitment," *Administrative Science Quarterly* 22 (March 1977), pp. 46–56.

literature helps us understand why community residents do not necessarily or immediately make a favorable response to a major alteration in the arrangements for providing a traditional public service. Consumer behavior may arguably be considered a component of "technological" change in the provision of sanitation service, but it is unarguable that such behavior must be carefully considered in adopting—and can significantly affect the success of—new refuse collection arrangements.

In the same vein, many cities that have adopted automated refuse collection and curbside pickups have also altered—which is to say reduced—their collection schedules. Specifically, residential refuse collection has been reduced from twice a week to once a week in perhaps 30 percent of U.S. cities that feature automated refuse collection and curbside pickup.[16] As with curbside pickup itself, alteration of refuse collection schedules affects the social organization of the local community, requires an investment by the municipality to obtain customer-resident acceptance of the change, and must be taken account of in planning and implementing change if the putative net benefits of the change are, in fact, to be realized.

Numerous other changes in the technology of sanitation service have occurred in recent years and can be mentioned here only briefly. These include the use of trucks with longer life diesel-type engines, longer-life radial tires for sanitation vehicles, and roll-off and tilt type truck frame beds; more efficient and longer-life trash compactors; computer-controlled refuse collection and compaction equipment; two-way truck radio systems for crew assignment and response to refuse collection "problem" situations; three-wheel scooters for certain types of lighter trash collection; and supercarts for high density refuse generation and collection locations.

How have these and other changes in the technology of local government refuse collection affected sanitation employment and sanitation employee unionization? This question is addressed quantitatively in the next section.

III. QUANTITATIVE ANALYSIS OF TECHNOLOGICAL CHANGE, SANITATION EMPLOYMENT, AND UNIONIZATION

To examine the effects of technological change on employment and unionism in municipal sanitation service, we must first consider the determinants of technological change itself. The reason for this is that as with employment, unionism, pay, and bargaining outcomes, technological change may be endogenously determined, that is, determined within the "system" represented by local government. Previous research has shown that measures of unionism and union effects on wages and other terms and conditions of

---

[16]Robert J. Bartollatta, "Several Strategies to Improve Collection Systems," *Solid Wastes Management* 19 (September 1976), pp. 54, 74, 78, and 84, and Jim Talebreza, "Overhaul of Collection System Produces Dramatic Results," *Public Works* 114 (April, 1983), pp. 44–45.

employment vary substantially when such phenomena are treated as endogenously rather than exogenously determined.[17]

To conduct this analysis, data were obtained on technological change in
the municipal sanitation service of 147 cities. This "convenience sample" was
drawn from published accounts of technological change that occurred in
these cities between 1975 and 1983.[18] Hence, cities for which no technological
changes were reported and cities that had no public sanitation service (between 1975 and 1983) are not included in the data base. Further, data on the
independent variables included in the analysis, which are discussed below,
are cross-sectional data where the point of observation is any single year
between 1975 and 1983. The data tend to cluster around 1980, but the reader
should be aware of the different points (years) of observation included in the
analysis and of the need to pool the cross-sectional data over several years.

In order to subject the data to quantitative examination, a rating scale
reflecting the extent and type of technological change was developed. The
scale ranges between zero and 100 points, and weights a "major" technological change, such as adoption of fully automated equipment, more heavily than a "minor" technological change, such as conversion from cans to
bags for refuse storage and pickup. Further, changes in consumer-resident
behavior, such as acceptance of curbside rather than backyard collection and
the instigation of reduced collection schedules, were included in the idea of
technological change.[19]

What factors determine technological change in municipal sanitation service? The following variables are included in the analysis:[20]

Es = the ratio of municipal sanitation employment to municipal population

[17]See, for example, Ann Bartel and David Lewin, "Wages and Unionism in the Public Sector: The
Case of Police," *The Review of Economics and Statistics* 63 (February 1981), pp. 53–59. For a
specific application to sanitation service, see Linda N. Edwards and Franklin R. Edwards, "The
Effects of Unionism on the Money and Fringe Compensation of Public Employees: The Case of
Municipal Sanitation Workers," Working Paper, Queens College, City University of New York,
1979.

[18]Specifically, these sources include those given in footnote no. 9 above, articles and data contained in *The Municipal Yearbook* annual volumes published between 1975 and 1983, and data
supplied by E. S. Savas from his study, *The Organization and Efficiency of Solid Waste Collection*
(Lexington, MA: Lexington Book, 1977 (see Appendices A, B, and C of this work for a detailed
description of the data collection methods used in the study of 315 municipalities).

[19]For guidance in constructing this index, we relied on J. Guilford *Psychometric Methods*, 2nd ed.
(New York: McGraw-Hill, 1954), Fred N. Kerlinger, *Foundations of Behavioral Research*, 2nd ed.
(New York: Holt, Rinehart and Winston, 1973), and Lawrence R. James, Stanley A. Mulaik, and
Jeanne M. Brett, *Causal Analysis: Assumptions Models, and Data* (Beverly Hills, Calif.: Sage Publications, 1982). The index was also discussed with two managers of municipal sanitation
departments, who made several recommendations for revision, and with three academics who
were asked to rate technological change in a subset of 30 cities, using the index. The resultant
inter-rater reliability of .74 (significant at p = < .05) provided additional support for use of the
index in the present analysis.

[20]The model year of the data for the variables listed below was 1980 in five cases, 1976 in two
cases, and one case each in 1977, 1979 and 1982.

Ps = the ratio of privately provided sanitation service to publicly provided sanitation service, measured by tons of refuse collected

Fs = the fiscal stress experienced by a municipality, measured by the difference between the actual and the legal maximum tax rate per $100 of assessed property value

A = Age of the municipal government, measured in years

R = Ratio of payroll costs to total costs of municipal sanitation service

U = Extent of unionization of municipal sanitation employees, measured by percent organized

S = The log of the size of city, measured by population per square mile

L = Location of city, represented by a discrete variable where Northeast = 3, Midwest = 2, South = 1, and West = 0

G = Form of government, where council-manager = 1, all other forms = 0.

The estimating equation thus takes the following functional form:

$$TC_r = TC \ (Es, \ Ps, \ Fs, \ A, \ R, \ U, \ S, \ L, \ G, \ \text{and} \ e) \tag{1}$$

where TC_r = rate of technological change in local government sanitation service, measured by an index of technological change e = an error term, and all other variables are as previously defined.[21]

Of the continuous variables included in the analysis, Es and R are expected to be positively related to TC_r. The rationale for these hypotheses is that the more labor intensive the sanitation service provided by the municipality, the greater the incentive to make technological changes in sanitation collection. The other continuous variables, namely, Ps, Fs, A, U and S, appear at first glance to be indeterminate, *a priori*. For example, a city with a relatively high Ps might have less incentive to change the technology of municipal sanitation collection than a city with a relatively low Ps on the ground that, in the former, a substantial portion of the community receives relatively efficient (or relatively cheap) sanitation service. Alternatively, the presence of a relatively large (and more efficient) private sanitation sector may spur a city to adopt technological changes in order to improve municipally provided sanitation service and, hopefully, reduce the private sector-public sector efficiency (or cost) differential.

Fiscal stress (Fs) may, on the one hand, negatively affect technological change because financial resources are not available to fund such change. On the other hand, Fs may motivate city officials to improve service efficiency and/or reduce service cost, and thus lead to a positive effect on TC_r. The age of a municipality (A) may have negative or positive effects on TC_r, depending

---

[21]The variables included in equation (1) and in other equations to follow were drawn from careful reviews of the relevant literature and considerations of the particular characteristics of sanitation service. Equation (1) is, in essence, a reduced form of a larger set of equations specifying determinants of the demand for and supply of public sanitation service. Recall that annual data for 1975–83 are pooled to derive cross-section estimates of the independent variables.

on whether it generates a preference for or dissatisfaction with the provision of public services in traditional, well-known ways.

Employee unionization (U) may have a negative effect on TC_r if, out of concern for possible threats to their livelihood, union members and officials oppose new technology and structure their bargaining agreements with local government employers accordingly. Alternatively and given that unionization brings about higher pay and benefits for public employees,[22] such higher costs may provide an incentive for government employers to invest in technological change. Moreover, most unions, whether in the public or private sector, have sought to bargain over the effects of technological change, notably in the area of job security, rather than to oppose technological change, *per se*.[23] City size (S) may be negatively related to TC_r if city officials judge the scope and diversity of residential housing and sanitation arrangements to mitigate effective implementation of technological change. However, S may be positively related to TC_r if it is perceived by city officials to provide returns to scale from investment in new technology. On balance and taking account of plausible arguments to the contrary, we expect Ps, Fs, U and S to be positively related to TC_r, and A to be negatively related to TC_r.

With respect to the discrete variables, L and G, we expect to find that location in the South and West and a council-manager form of government are positively related to TC_r. The former hypothesis stems from the fact of relatively rapid population growth in the Southern and Western regions of the U.S. in recent years, and an associated belief that such growth generates relatively high demand for more efficient public service delivery, including sanitation service. The latter hypothesis rests on conceptual arguments in the public administration and management literature that city-manager operated governments are relatively more efficient than other types of governments because the city-manager form of government affords relatively greater centralization and control of management decision-making.[24]

Ordinary least squares (OLS) estimates of the coefficients on the variables in equation (1) are shown in Table 4. As predicted, Es, Fs, U, and S are significantly positively associated with technological change in the sanitation services of local governments over the 1975–1983 period. These findings mean that a city is more likely to make technological changes in refuse collection the more labor intensive its sanitation service, the more it experiences

[22]See David Lewin, "Public Sector Labor Relations: A Review Essay," *Labor History* 18 (Winter, 1978), pp. 133–144.

[23]See, for example, Jack Barbash, "The Impact of Technological Change on Labor–Management Relations," in Gerald G. Somers, Edward L. Cushman, and Nat Weinberg, eds., *Adjusting to Technological Change* (New York: Harper and Row, 1963), pp. 44–60, and Harold Levinson, Charles R. Rehmus, Joseph P. Goldberg, and Mark L. Kahn, *Collective Bargaining and Technological Change in American Transportation* (Evanston, IL: The Transportation Center, Northwestern University, 1971).

[24]See, for example, O. Glenn Stahl, *Public Personnel Administration*, 8th ed. (New York: Harper and Row, 1983), and Thomas P. Murphy and Charles R. Warren, *Organizing Public Services in Metropolitan America* (Lexington, MA: Lexington Books, 1974).

Table 4. OLS Estimates of Coefficients on Variables
from the Technological Change Equation
(t-values in parentheses)

Independent Variable	Dependent Variable
	Index of Technological Change (TR_c)
Es	+4.22**
	(2.62)
Ps	−2.88
	(−1.54)
Fs	+5.61**
	(3.04)
A	+1.72
	(1.04)
R	+2.67
	(1.38)
U	+3.74*
	(2.09)
S	+3.47*
	(2.03)
L	−1.62
	(−1.02)
G	+1.04
	(0.64)
N	147
R^2	.43

*Significant at the .05 level in a two-tailed test.
**Significant at the .01 level in a two-tailed test.

fiscal stress, the more unionized its sanitation workforce, and the greater its population density. The signs of the coefficients on variables Ps, A and L were opposite of those predicted, but the coefficients were not statistically significant. Nevertheless, the results suggest that older cities and those located in the Northeast and Midwest are *more* likely to make technological changes in sanitation service than younger cities and cities located in the South and West, respectively.

Having identified some of the determinants of technological change in local government sanitation service, we proceed next to specify a sanitation employment equation which includes the following variables:

$$Ps, Fs, A, U, S, L. G, TC_r$$
$$Ma = \text{the proportion of 18–35}$$
$$\text{year old males in a city's}$$
$$\text{population}$$

The estimating equation thus takes on the following functional form:

$$Es = Es \ (Ps, Fs, A, U, S, L, G, TC_r, Ma \text{ and } e) \tag{2}$$

Table 5. OLS Estimates of Coefficients on Variables
from the Employment Equation
(t-values in parentheses)

	Dependent Variable
Independent Variable	Sanitation Employment Ratio (Es)
Ps	−4.27**
	(−2.43)
Fs	−3.31
	(−2.17)*
A	+1.04
	(0.62)
U	−1.37
	(−0.82)
S	+3.14
	(2.09)*
L	+2.97
	(2.01)*
G	+1.25
	(0.77)
TC_r	−4.14**
	(−2.39)
Ma	+1.19
	(0.73)
N	147
R^2	.59

*Significant at the .05 level in a two-tailed test.
**Significant at the .01 level in a two-tailed test.

where Es = as previously defined, e = an error term, and all other variables are as defined above.

The variables Ps, Fs, and U are predicted to be negatively related to Es, while positive relationships are expected between A and Es and S and Es. Cities located in the Northeast and Midwest are expected to have higher ratios of municipal sanitation employment to municipal population than cities located elsewhere.[25] Because it is often thought to be a less efficient or more patronage conscious form of government than other types of governments, a mayor-council form of government is expected to be positively related to sanitation employment (for this purpose, the variable G was coded as mayor-council = 1, all other forms = 0). The variable Ma, which represents the potential labor supply available to municipal sanitation departments, is also expected to be positively related to Es.

Table 5 presents the results of OLS tests of equation (2). As expected, Ps

[25]Recognize that, in most Northeastern and Midwestern cities, sanitation personnel also perform snow removal service. This "larger" set of job duties is expected to translate into higher sanitation employment/municipal population ratios in the colder regions of the United States.

and *Fs* are significantly negatively associated with *Es*, thereby demonstrating that the extent of private sanitation service and fiscal stress reduce municipal sanitation employment, other things being equal. As predicted, the size (*S*) of a municipality is positively related to municipal sanitation employment, and such employment is significantly higher in Northeastern and Midwestern cities than in Southern and Western cities. Perhaps most important for the present analysis, technological change has a significant negative effect on municipal sanitation employment. Specifically, the results for this variable suggest that a one percent increase in (the rate of) technological change in municipal sanitation service is associated with a four-tenths of one percent reduction in municipal sanitation employment. Note that the variables *U, A, G,* and *M* are not significantly associated with *Es*.

To this point, the empirical results indicate that both technological change and employment in municipal sanitation departments are systematically determined (by exogenous variables). However, decisions about technological change and employment are made by local officials within the context of municipal government. Thus, these variables appear to be endogenous to the "system" of municipal government and should be modeled accordingly. Indeed, if this is not done, then there is a substantial probability that the *OLS* estimates previously derived are biased. To deal with this problem, we specify and subsequently test a simultaneous equation system in which *TC*_r and *ES* serve as the dependent variables, respectively, and in which the equations take the following functional forms:

$$TC_r = TC_r(Es, Ps, Fs, A, R, U, S, L, G, \text{ and } e) \tag{3}$$

$$Es = Es(Ps, Fs, A, U, S, L, G, Tc_{r*}, Ma, \text{ and } e) \tag{4}$$

Note that the value of TC_{r*} is that estimated from the TC_r equation.[26] Table 6 presents the results of two-stage least squares (TSLS) estimates of the *Es* equation within this simultaneous system. The coefficients (and associated *t*-values) indicated that TC_{r*} and *Ps* are significantly negatively associated with municipal sanitation employment ($p = < .01$). Further, *U* and *Fs* are also significantly negatively associated with *Es*, while *S* is significantly positively associated with *Es*. To summarize, the level of municipal sanitation employment in U.S. cities declines with the size of the private sanitation market, the extent of fiscal stress, the degree of employee unionization, and the rate (index) of technological change, and increases with city size. Moreover, there is a tendency (though not a statistically significant one) for Northeastern and Midwestern cities to have reduced municipal sanitation employment more

[26]The rationale and specific techniques for estimating simultaneous equation systems are more fully discussed in Peter Schmidt, "Estimation of a Simultaneous Equations Model with Jointly Determined Continuous and Qualitative Variables: The Union-Earnings Equation Revisited," *International Economic Review* 19 (June 1978), pp. 453–465. Note that to satisfy the estimating conditions of simultaneous equation testing, at least one independent variable must be exclusive to each equation.

Table 6. TSLS Estimates of Coefficients on Variables
from the Employment Equation Simultaneously
Determined with the Technological Change Equation
(t-values in parentheses)

Independent Variable	Dependent Variable
	Sanitation Employment Ratio (Es)
Ps	−4.65**
	(−2.61)
Fs	−3.47*
	(−2.30)
A	+1.41
	(0.75)
U	−2.90*
	(−1.95)
S	+2.99*
	(2.02)
L	+2.81
	(1.89)
G	+1.31
	(0.79)
TC_{r^*}	−5.06**
	(−2.71)
Ma	+1.10
	(0.66)
N	147

*Significant at the .05 level in a two-tailed test.
**Significant at the .01 level in a two-tailed test.

than Southern and Western cities over the 1975–83 period. These findings are
believed to be the first to be produced via systematic empirical testing using a
large cross-sectional and longitudinal data base.

If technological change and employment are endogenous to the system
of local government, cannot the same be said about unionization? While
scholars disagree over the proper treatment of unionization in this regard,
there is no denying that quantitative estimates of the effects of unions, especially public sector unions and specifically unions of sanitation workers,[27]
change substantially when unionism is treated as an endogenous variable and
modeled within a simultaneous equation system.[28] Further, we also wish to

[27]See, for example, Daniel J. B. Mitchell, *Unions, Wages, and Inflation* (Washington, DC: Brook-
ings, 1980), pp. 104–111, and Linda N. Edwards and Franklin R. Edwards, "Wellington-Winter
Revisited: The Case of Municipal Sanitation Collection," *Industrial and Labor Relations Review* 35
(April 1982), p. 313.

[28]Bartel and Lewin, pp. 57–58, and David Lewin and Harry C. Katz, "Payment Determination in
Municipal Building Departments Under Unionism and Civil Service," in Werner Z. Hirsch, ed.,
The Economics of Municipal Labor Markets (Los Angeles: Institute of Industrial Relations, Univer-
sity of California, 1983), pp. 90–121.

know what role, if any, technological change has played in the recent decline of public sector sanitation unionism.

In light of these considerations, a sanitation unionization equation can be formed with includes the following variables:

$Ps, Fs, A, R, S, L, G, TCr$
PS_u = the rate of unionization
of private sector employees
for the state in which
a city is located[29]

The estimating equation is

$$U = U(Ps, Fs, A, R, S, L, G, TC_r, PS_u, \text{ and } e) \tag{5}$$

where U = previously defined, e = an error term, and all other variables are as defined above.

The variables A, R, S and PS_u are expected to be positively related to U, whereas Ps and Fs are predicted to be negatively related to U. Cities located in the Northeast and Midwest are expected to have higher levels of sanitation employee unionism than cities located in the South and Midwest, and such unionism is also expected to be relatively higher in municipalities with a mayor-council form of government (compared to other forms of municipal government). These predicted relationships are based on recent theoretical and empirical research which emphasizes the determinants of the demand for and supply of union services.[30] The main independent variable of interest, TC_r, cannot be predicted, a priori, in terms of its effects on U. While as noted (and as found) previously, TC_r can be expected to be negatively related to Es, there is no theoretical or empirical justification for predicting such a relationship or, alternatively, a positive relationship between TC_r and U. Because of the aforementioned concern about simultaneity bias, we estimate the U equation simultaneously with the TC_r equation (equation 3) and limit the discussion to the results of the TSLS estimates. As before, the value of TC_{r*} is that estimated from the TC_r equation.

Table 7 shows that, in all cases, the signs of the coefficients on the

[29]This variable is commonly used in modeling the determinants of public employee unionism. See, for example, David Lewin, "The Effects of Civil Service Systems and Unionism on Pay Outcomes in the Public Sector," in David B. Lipsky, ed., *Advances in Industrial and Labor Relations*, vol. 1 (Greenwich, Conn.: JAI Press, 1983), pp. 150–151. Inclusion of the PSu variable in equation (5) also allows us to satisfy the aforementioned condition of one exclusive variable per each equation in a simultaneous system.

[30]See, for example, Lewin, Feuille, and Kochan, chapter 1, David Lewin, "The Effects of Regulation on Public Sector Labor Relations: Theory and Evidence," *Journal of Labor Research* 6 (Winter 1985), pp. 77–95, Richard B. Freeman and James L. Medoff, *What do Unions Do?* (New York: Basic Books, 1984), chapters 1 and 3, and William T. Dickens and Jonathan S. Leonard, "Accounting for the Decline in Union Membership, 1950–1980," *Industrial and Labor Relations Review*, 38 (April, 1985), pp. 323–334.

Table 7. TSLS Estimates of Coefficients on
Variables from the Unionization Equation
Simultaneously Determined with the
Technological Change Equation
(t-values in parentheses)

Independent Variable	Dependent Variable
	% of Sanitation Employees Unionized (U)
Ps	−3.64*
	(−2.17)
Fs	−2.43
	(−1.58)
A	2.73
	(1.68)
R	3.11*
	(2.02)
S	3.69*
	(2.20)
L	3.42*
	(2.06)
G	1.09
	(0.37)
TC_{r^*}	−1.82
	(−1.03)
PS_u	3.21**
	(2.09)
N	147

*Significant at the .05 level in a two-tailed test.
**Significant at the .01 level in a two-tailed test.

independent variables are in the predicted directions. However, significant coefficients were attained only for the variables $Ps(-)$, $R(+)$, $S(+)$, $L(+)$, and $PS_u(+)$. Fiscal stress (Fs) is negatively but not significantly associated with sanitation employee unionism (U), while age of a city (A) is positively but not significantly associated with U. The incidence of sanitation unionization does not vary significantly by form of government (G). Most important, technological change is not significantly associated with U (although TC_{r^*} is negatively related to U).

To test further for the effects of technological change on sanitation unionization, equation (3) was rerun using the rate of change in sanitation unionism (Ur) over the 1975–83 period as the dependent variable. The results of this test (not reproduced in detail here) show the following for the TC_{r^*} variable with respect to U:

$$-3.34*$$
$$(2.12)$$

*Significant at the 5.0 level in a two-tailed test.

Hence, in this specification, the rate of technological change in sanitation departments of U.S. cities during the latter 1970s and early 1980s is shown to be significantly negatively associated with the unionization of sanitation employees during roughly the same period.[31]

En toto, the empirical findings of this section indicate that certain factors systematically determine the rate of technological change in public sanitation service in U.S. cities. Such change, in turn, is significantly negatively associated with levels of sanitation employment and sanitation unionization, especially in older cities located in the Northeastern and Midwestern regions of the country.

These conclusions have been reached through quantitative analyses, and perhaps because of this, pertain to the most "obvious" (or the most quantifiable) aspects of labor relations, namely, employment and the incidence of unionism. But how has technological change affected the labor relations process in public sanitation departments, particularly the responses of labor and management officials to such change? This question is taken up and explored for the most part qualitatively in the next section.

IV. TECHNOLOGICAL CHANGE AND THE SANITATION LABOR RELATIONS PROCESS

In the U.S. system of industrial relations, adversarial relationships predominate, and this is no less true of the public than the private sector.[32] How have recent technological changes in sanitation service affected sanitation labor relations? Basically, there have been two contrasting effects.

On the one hand, technological change seems to have exacerbated adversarial labor relations in certain sanitation departments, contributing to labor–management conflict and, in some cases, producing work stoppages. On the other hand, technological change appears to have spurred labor–management cooperation in some sanitation departments, producing or contributing to integrative bargaining and bringing about creative efforts to deal with such change.

To gain perspective on and understanding of this issue consider the data in Table 8. They show the proportion of all organized local government employees, by function, who engaged in work stoppages in 1974 and 1980. Clearly, by this measure, sanitation is the most "strike-prone" public service. This fact is consistent with the related fact that the demand for public sanita-

---

[31]Other TSLS analyses were conducted in which equations (3), (4), *and* (5) were simultaneously estimated. The results of these analyses were not significantly different from those presented in the text. Note that we also chose not to include an employment variable in the unionization equation because there is no theoretical or empirical justification for such inclusion—that is, employment, per se, is not conceived to be a determinant of unionism.

[32]See, for example, Lewin, Feuille, and Kochan, Chapter 4, and Gordon F. Bloom and Herbert R. Northrup, *Economics of Labor Relations*, 8th ed. (Homewood, IL: Irwin, 1981), Chapters 1, 4 and 6.

Table 8. Proportion of Full-Time Organized
Local Government Employees Involved in Strike
Activity by Functional Service Category,
1974 and 1980[a]

Functional Service Category	Proportion %	
	1974	1980
All Functions	3.8	5.6
Education	3.4	5.0
Instructional Staff	3.2	5.0
Others	4.2	5.0
Highways	4.8	2.9
Public Welfare	0.7	3.9
Hospitals	1.2	4.5
Police Protection	0.5	1.7
Fire Protection	1.4	3.6
Sanitation other than Sewerage	10.4	8.3
All Other	7.9	10.5

[a]Source: Derived from U.S. Bureau of the Census, *Labor–Management Relations in State and Local Governments: 1974 and 1980*, State and Local Government Special Studies, Nos. 75 and 102. Washington, DC: G.P.O., 1976 and 1981, pp. 9 and 87 (1976) and 7 and 112 (1981).

tion service is relatively inelastic compared to the demand for other public services,[33] and with the further related fact that unions representing organized sanitation employees—for example, the Teamsters, the Communications Workers of America (CWA), the International Laborers' Union (ILU), the Service Employees International Union (SEIU), and the American Federation of State, County and Municipal Employees (AFSCME)—are well established organizations that have used the strike, albeit selectively, to achieve bargaining ends.[34]

The introduction of technological change into an adversarial labor relationship with a relatively high "militancy content" could plausibly be expected to make the relationship even more adversarial, especially if the change portends employment (and union membership) reductions. This is, in fact, what has occurred in some cities that have initiated technological change in sanitation service. For example, between 1978 and 1982, the city of Tampa, Florida instituted equipment changes, route adjustments, and reduced crew sizes for residential refuse collection, with the principal technological change being the (gradual) replacement of rear-loading with side-loading vehicles.[35]

[33]Orley Ashenfelter and Ronald G. Ehrenberg, "The Demand for Labor in the Public Sector," in Lewin, Feuille, and Kochan, pp. 33–39.

[34]See Leo Troy and Neil Sheflin, *Union Sourcebook: Membership, Structure, Finance, Directory*, 1984 ed. (West Orange, NJ: Industrial Relations Data and Information Service, 1985).

[35]Pamela K. Day and Robert D. Fiero, "When Should Refuse Collection Change?," *American City and County* 97 (April 1982), pp. 51–55.

These actions precipitated a one-day employee walkout in mid-1979 and a four-day wildcat strike in early 1980, despite the presence of a no-strike clause in the union's labor agreement with the city. Striking employees were suspended and those who did not return to work within 48 hours were discharged. Subsequently, the city's mayor contracted out one-quarter of the refuse collection service to a private hauler.

Similar events occurred in Salt Lake City, Utah in 1980.[36] The city's replacement of rear-loading with side-loading vehicles for refuse collection and the planned reduction of three-person to one-person crews, with the intermediate use of two-person crews, was met by an employee walkout which resulted in a reversion to the use of three-person crews. Subsequently and as in the Tampa case, management officials of the Salt Lake City government contracted out one-quarter of the municipality's refuse collection and, one year later, successfully instituted the one-person crew arrangement.

These examples of militant sanitation employee responses to technological change are paralleled by other examples of response to the contracting out of sanitation service. In Camden, New Jersey, where the city adopted a plan in 1979 to contract out sanitation service, a fledging union instigated a short work stoppage which was followed by a two-week work slowdown, demonstrations before the City Council, and the initiation of a lawsuit to prevent the city from implementing its plan.[37] The lawsuit was withdrawn when the city agreed to a no-layoff provision for sanitation employees.

At about the same time, the city of Berwyn, Illinois, whose governing Council had voted to contract out sanitation service, was confronted with sustained employee picketing of Council offices and a union-initiated lawsuit to countermand the vote.[38] Further, refuse collection trucks were damaged and a fire bomb was hurled at an alderman's house. A judicial order ended the picketing and resulted in employees returning to work, but contract collection was eventually implemented in Berwyn. In Covington, Kentucky and Middletown, Ohio, unionized sanitation employees conducted "sick-outs," filed grievances, and undertook lawsuits to prevent contracting-out plans from being implemented in 1980 (and, in Covington specifically, to prevent the city from selling its refuse vehicles).[39] These actions delayed the contracting arrangements, but, as in Berwyn, did not prevent their eventual implementation.

But if technological change has contributed to the adversarial nature of certain municipal sanitation labor relationships, in other cases it has provided opportunities for instituting or enhancing labor–management cooperation. For example, in Rochester, New York, where in 1980 new refuse collection vehicles with high-speed trash compaction capability were adopted, crew size

[36]"Cities Contract Out Collection to Save Money and Avoid Headaches," *Solid Wastes Management* 23 (August 1980), pp. 40–45.

[37]Berenyi, p. 15.

[38]"Cities Contract Out . . . ," pp. 42–43.

[39]Berenyi, p. 105.

was reduced, and the method of financing refuse collection was changed from general taxation to user fees, an agreement was reached with the sanitationmen's union that provided for reductions in force via attrition and monetary incentives for remaining employees.[40] The city further agreed not to contract out sanitation service to private haulers. City officials and union representatives jointly conducted communication and training sessions with employees to explain the new refuse collection arrangements and to ensure the smooth implementation of these arrangements.

In Clinton, Oklahoma in 1982, the conversion from rear-loading to fully automated side loading refuse collection vehicles and the replacement of trash cans with standardized carts were achieved with the full cooperation of the sanitationmen's union.[41] Work force reductions were achieved via attrition, jobs were redesigned to raise skills and pay, and sanitation employees, who became drivers and equipment operators where they had once been laborers, experienced statistically significant increases in morale and job satisfaction (as determined through the analysis of responses to mail questionnaires). A similar experience took place in Kingsville, Texas in 1982, where technological changes of the type undertaken in Clinton were coupled with skill upgrading for sanitation employees, who were converted from truck drivers to route managers responsible for the physical condition of alleyways and the relay of street maintenance orders to the City's Street Department.[42]

In Atlanta, Tulsa, Detroit, Washington, DC, Erie, St. Louis, Fort Lauderdale, Phoenix, Chicago, and several other cities, technological changes in municipal sanitation service—changes of the type noted above—were instituted in the late 1970s and early 1980s with the explicit cooperation of sanitation employee unions.[43] In some cases, displaced employees were transferred to jobs in other city agencies and departments, but more common were plans for phased attrition, skill upgrading, and periodic communications to employees informing them of the details of and schedules for implementing the changes in technology. A few of these cities developed videotapes showing the reduced physical effort and work injuries as well as the productivity improvements associated with the new technology of refuse collection. Perhaps most important under the new refuse collection arrangements, employees who remained in sanitation service typically received a five to fifteen percent pay increment due to the combination of skill upgrading and productivity improvement.

[40]"We Cut Collection Cost, Not Service," *American City and County* 96 (March 1981), pp. 39–43.
[41]Carl Sidney, "System Solves Labor Cost Problem," *Solid Wastes Management* 25 (August 1982), pp. 38–40.
[42]"News and Views," *American City and County* 97 (March 1982), p. 12.
[43]See, for example, John O'Connor, "Refuse Collection Practices 1980: An Exclusive National Survey," *American City and County* 95 (April 1980), pp. 34–38, "Atlanta: The Biggest Municipal Collection System to Adopt Cart Service," *Solid Wastes Management* 19 (February 1976), pp. 24–25, 28 and 52, "Team of City Officials Modernizes Collection System," *Solid Wastes Management*, 20 (February 1977), pp. 36–37, Paul Baker and John Albert, "Automated Refuse Collection Stresses Cycle Time," *World Wastes* 26 (July 1983), pp. 41–43, Larry Roth, "Chicago—Home of the World's Largest Cart System," *World Wastes*, 27 (May, 1984), pp. 66–70, and "Mechanized Collections for Big City Neighborhoods," *Waste Age* 14 (September 1983), pp. 47–50.

Indeed, what may (because of its size) be the most notable example of union–management cooperation in municipal sanitation service under the impetus of technological change occurred in New York City during the early 1980s.[44] There, city officials and the Sanitation Workers' Union (a Teamsters affiliate) engaged in productivity bargaining and, under the aegis of an arbitration award, agreed to replace smaller, less efficient refuse collection vehicles operated by three-person crews with larger, more efficient semi-automated vehicles using two-person crews. The 1981 agreement, which covered selected rather than all routes, contained a no-layoff provision, and work force reductions were to be achieved (and, in fact, were achieved) through attrition. Additionally, each employee member of a two-person crew received an eleven dollar per shift bonus, and an experiment in contracting-out was postponed for two years. In light of the city's frustrating and ineffectual record of productivity bargaining with municipal unions during the 1970s and the frequency of sanitation employee strikes and work slowdowns during the same period,[45] the parties were probably correct in describing their agreement as "historic." From an analytical perspective, this agreement, along with other sanitation labor agreements that have been reached in certain U.S. cities, demonstrate that technological change can bring about union–management cooperation even where adversarial labor relations have predominated.

Referring once again to the model of public sector labor relations presented in Figure 2, this section has emphasized the effects of technological change on the labor relations (or collective bargaining) process in municipal sanitation departments. As shown in the model, other variables besides technological change affect the bargaining process, and in certain instances the direction and magnitude of the effects of such other variables may run counter to or override the effects of technological change. Lacking a comprehensive data base, we are not able to conduct multivariate analyses that would permit us to separate the effects of technological change from the effects of other variables on the bargaining process in municipal sanitation departments. Nevertheless, the qualitative analysis undertaken here illustrates that the parties to labor–management relations in municipal sanitation departments respond to technological change in one of two fundamental ways.

One type of response to technological change in public sanitation service is characterized by distributive bargaining in which each party, labor and management, attempts to minimize its own and maximize its "opponent's" losses.[46] The issues that arise in conjunction with technological change are

[44]This account draws liberally from Lewin, Feuille, and Kochan, pp. 177–178. For additional background, see Mary McCormick, "Labor Relations," and James M. Hartman assisted by Linda Mitchell, "Sanitation," in Charles Brecher and Raymond D. Horton, eds., Setting Municipal Priorities, 1982 (New York: Russell Sage, 1981), chapters 7 and 10, respectively.

[45]See, for example, "Strike Chokes New York City," Solid Wastes Management 18 (July 1975), p. 76, "Rear Loaders Preferred in New York City," Solid Wastes Management 20 (October 1977), pp. 14–15, McCormick, pp. 199–214, and David Lewin and Mary McCormick, "Coalition Bargaining in Municipal Government: New York City in the 1970s," Industrial and Labor Relations Review 34 (January 1981), pp. 175–190.

[46]The term "distributive bargaining" was coined by Richard E. Walton and Robert B. McKersie, A Behavioral Theory of Labor Negotiations (New York: McGraw-Hill, 1965), chapter 1.

perceived as areas or arenas of conflict, and each party seeks to gain an advantage over or impose a cost on the other. In sanitation labor relations characterized by this type of response to technological change, opposition to the change prevails, as does an authoritarian mode of implementing the change; strikes and work slowdowns occur, and workers are suspended and discharged; management threatens or proceeds to carry out subcontracting, and minimal investments are made in communicating and explaining the changes to employees; militant employee actions often delay and sometimes prevent the changes from taking place; and, occasionally, violence accompanies opposition to the change.

In a second and far different type of response to technological change in public sanitation service, labor and management perceive such change as an opportunity and the parties engage (or continue to engage) in integrative bargaining.[47] Issues associated with technological change are treated as problems to be solved and the parties seek to obtain net benefits for both sides; the change is accepted and provisions are made for skill upgrading and work force reductions (where they occur) through attrition; management invests in programs to communicate and explain the changes to employees, and union officials cooperate with and often join management in carrying out such programs; emphasis is placed on the reduced physical effort and work injuries associated with the new technology; joint labor–management productivity improvement and technological change monitoring committees are sometimes established, and revisions in the implementation of technological change are made periodically, with the intent of improving the change process.

Recognizing the limitations on the analysis of sanitation labor relations presented above, it may nevertheless be suggested that integrative bargaining seems to have become more prominent, and distributive bargaining less prominent, in public sanitation service. The reduced incidence of municipal sanitation strikes, the case examples of sanitation bargaining in certain municipalities described earlier, and especially the changing patterns of labor relations in other sectors of the U.S. economy which have experienced severe competitive stress, shrinking unionization, and major bargaining concessions, support this observation.[48] Such a conversion from predominantly

[47]Ibid. It should be recognized that "cooperative" labor–management efforts to deal with technological changes are more likely to be reported in the type of industry and trade publications cited above than "adversarial" or "uncooperative" efforts. Thus, in the account presented in this section, we may have underrepresented the incidence of adversarial bargaining over technological change in public sanitation service.

[48]See, for example, David Lewin, "Public Sector Concession Bargaining: Lessons for the Private Sector," *Proceedings of the Thirty-Fifth Annual Meeting of the Industrial Relations Research Association.* (Madison, Wis.: IRRA, 1983), pp. 383–393, and David Lewin, *Opening the Books: Corporate Information-Sharing with Employees.* (New York: The Conference Board, 1984). Unfortunately, the present study does not allow us to test for the effects of intercity variation in political party affiliation or variation in local union structure, centralization and affiliation (with a regional or national union) on variation in integrative bargaining among municipal sanitation departments.

distributive to predominantly integrative bargaining is perhaps particularly characteristic of U.S. labor relations, in which the parties to bargaining apparently come to recognize opportunities for joint or mutual gain only under extremely threatening environmental conditions—including rapid technological change.

Note, however, that whether integrative or distributive bargaining and labor–management relations prevail in response to technological change in municipal sanitation service, certain outcomes are common or similar. Typically, indeed almost without exception, employment is reduced, pay is increased, subcontracting is undertaken, contemplated, or discussed, work injuries decline, productivity improves (though with considerable variation), and bargaining agreements are in fact reached. But the emphasis in this section is on process, specifically the labor relations and bargaining process, not outcomes, and the recent experience of U.S. cities in responding to technological change in sanitation service shows that such change produces a diversity rather than a uniformity of reactions on the part of labor and management. The intriguing question, one which remains unanswered and which therefore provides an opportunity for further research, is "what factors determine how the parties to a particular labor–management relationship respond to technological change in public sanitation service?"

V. THE SANITATION LABOR RELATIONS EXPERIENCE IN LARGER CONTEXT

Placed in larger context, the record of labor–management responses to technological change in public sanitation service during the 1970s and early 1980s accords closely with the broader public and private sector industrial relations experience of the United States. The major elements of this accordance are as follows.

First, changes in one or more environmental contexts cause the parties to rethink service (or goods) "production," technology, and labor relations. In public sanitation service, the major recent environmental changes have been financial and economic. The reduced rate of growth of the U.S. public sector, which emerged in the mid-1970s following a sustained 25-year expansion of that sector, and the development and increased recognition of private markets for sanitation service, combined to stimulate discussion, debate, and analysis of local government arrangements for sanitation service. Mayors, city councils, city managers, town commissions and, more basically, citizens of local communities became more aware of the relatively greater efficiencies and lower costs of privately provided compared to publicly provided sanitation service. In some communities, this recognition was translated into specific decisions to contract with private firms for some or all sanitation service, either on a single franchise or competitive basis.

Second, with growth of and changes in the demand for sanitation service, expansion of the supply of privately provided sanitation service, and increased competition between the private and public sectors for sanitation service, strong incentives emerged for the development of new refuse collection (and disposal) technology. The advent of new equipment, indeed of whole new systems, for refuse collection, provided local government officials with an alternative to private contracting, namely, the retention and modernization of publicly provided sanitation service via the adoption of new technology. And, as we have seen, many governments availed themselves of this option during the 1970s and early 1980s.

Third, the new sanitation technology is fundamentally labor-saving (rather than labor neutral) technology, and its adoption by local governments translated into major sanitation work force reductions. In fact, virtually every recent change in the technology of publicly provided sanitation service (for which documentation exists) has been accompanied by a permanent work force reduction and a decline in the rate of sanitation unionization.[49]

Fourth, and in light of this, it is hardly surprising that sanitation union officials and members have evidenced great concern about the consequences of technological change. But concern does not necessarily translate into opposition, and what is probably most notable about sanitation labor relations in an era of rapid technological change is that the dominant response of managers and organized workers to such changes has been to pursue more integrative and less distributive bargaining. Unionists have basically sought to bargain over technological change and to cushion the workers they represent from the effects of technological change, though even then the cushioning rarely takes the form of outright job or income guarantees. To the contrary, sanitation unions have in the main focused on improving the terms and conditions of employment for those who remain employed in public sanitation service following the implementation of technological change. Typically the improvements are in the form of skill upgrading, higher pay and benefits, and productivity improvement incentives and rewards.

If this predominant union response to technological change has come as a surprise to local government officials and sanitation department managers, it should not be surprising to students of industrial relations. From longshoring and maritime to automobile and steel manufacturing, from printing and publishing to pulp and paper manufacturing, from railroads and airlines to oil and chemical manufacturing, unions, when faced with technological change, have attempted to mitigate its effects on their members rather than to oppose

---

[49]As determined by the author's assessment of written accounts of technological change in public sanitation service published between 1971 and 1984 in *American City and County, Public Works, Solid Wastes Management, Waste Age,* and *World Wastes.* Some 161 accounts of technological change in municipal sanitation departments were published in these journals between 1971 and 1984, of which 135 reported employment data. In 127 cases, sanitation department employment declined after the technological change, and in eight cases no employment change occurred. Not a single case of employment expansion following technological change in sanitation departments was reported during these years. Note also that for cities reporting precise post-technological change employment data, the average decline in sanitation employment during the first two years following technological change was 21 percent.

or prevent it.[50] This is not to deny that some unions—and some unorganized workers—have on occasion successfully warded off technological change through distributive bargaining and related tactics; that militant action, including violence, has accompanied certain instances of technological change; or that unions generally raise the cost to management of adopting and implementing technological change.[51] Rather, it is to support the premise that the dominant response of private sector unionists to technological change—and also of public sector unionists in education, social welfare, health care, police and fire protection, and other services—is to bargain or seek to bargain integratively over the effects of change on union members. The recent experience in public sanitation service is fully in keeping with this historical tradition.

Fifth, managerial approaches to labor relations in public sanitation service in the context of rapid technological change also appear to accord closely with history and experience in the private sector as well as in other public services. Recall that, in recent years, management officials in numerous cities decided to contract out sanitation services to the private sector, and that such action was motivated in large part by a desire to reduce labor costs and avoid work stoppages. Precisely the same rationale has motivated private managers to subcontract work previously performed by union members, and subcontracting has mushroomed in the private sector since about 1970.[52]

In undertaking technological change in sanitation service, public managers have focused the bulk of their attention on the decision to adopt such change, and only later have they addressed the implementation of change. In other words, public managers have rarely permitted or invited organized (and, for that matter, unorganized) sanitation employees to exercise joint authority in decisions to adopt technological change—and unions have rarely pressed for such joint authority. Similarily, it is the rare private company management that seeks or is willing to share decision-making authority with unionized workers over planned technological change. In general, private

[50]See, for example, Barbash, chapter 1, Levinson, Rehmus, Goldberg, and Kahn, chapter 11, Neil W. Chamberlain and James W. Kuhn, *Collective Bargaining*, 3rd ed. (New York: McGraw-Hill, 1986) chapters 9–11, Sumner H. Slichter, James J. Healy, and E. Robert Livernash, *The Impact of Collective Bargaining on Management* (Washington, DC: Brookings, 1960), chapters 24–27, James J. Healy, *Creative Collective Bargaining* (Englewood Cliffs, NJ: Prentice-Hall, 1965), Paul T. Hartman, *Collective Bargaining and Productivity: The Longshore Mechanization Agreement* (Berkeley: University of California Press, 1969), Robert B. McKersie and L. C. Hunter, *Pay, Productivity and Collective Bargaining* (New York: St. Martin's, 1973), and Gerald Somers, Arvid Anderson, Malcolm Denise, and Leonard Sayles, *Collective Bargaining and Productivity* (Madison, WI: Industrial Relations Research Association, 1975). On the public sector, see Chester A. Newland, ed., *MBO and Productivity Bargaining in the Public Sector* (Chicago: International Personnel Management Association, 1974), and Melvin H. Osterman, "Productivity Bargaining in New York—What Went Wrong?," in Lewin, Feuille, and Kochan, pp. 162–174.

[51]Albert Rees, *The Economics of Trade Unions*, revised ed. (Chicago: University of Chicago Press, 1977), chapters 7–9, and Paul A. Weinstein, ed., *Featherbedding and Technological Change* (Lexington MA: Heath, 1965).

[52]U.S. Bureau of Labor Statistics, *Subcontracting*, Bulletin No. 1425-8 (Washington, DC: GPO., 1969), and U.S. Bureau of Labor Statistics, *Characteristics of Major Collective Bargaining Agreements—January 1, 1980*, Bulletin No. 2095 (Washington, DC: GPO., 1981).

and public managers regard decision-making about technological change as the exclusive prerogative of management.[53] Consequently, integrative bargaining (whether in sanitation service or elsewhere) may emerge during an early stage of technological change, but may develop more fully only if such change persists or, indeed, quickens.

The doctrine of reserved management rights perforce limits employee involvement and participation to matters of implementing management-initiated changes, and it is in the implementation process that one observes major variation in management approaches to labor relations. We have seen that, in some sanitation departments, management has involved organized employees closely in the implementation of technological change, and has undertaken policies and programs to make union and worker participation a reality in this regard. In other sanitation departments, however, management has implemented technological change more or less unilaterally, and has kept union and worker participation to a minimum. In still other sanitation departments, management has encouraged limited union and worker participation in implementing technological change, often focusing such participation on a single dimension of change, for example, training in the use of new sanitation equipment and collection procedures.

In the private sector and in other public services, the recent emphasis on concession bargaining and two-tier labor agreements and the enhanced use of worker participation schemes, such as joint productivity and quality of work life committees, profit-sharing and employee stock ownership (in the private sector), and even occasionally membership on boards of directors (in the private sector),[54] may seem to imply that labor relations in the United States have become more cooperative and less adversarial. But it has yet to be shown that these are more than short-term or cyclical changes—there is some truth to the assertion that when it can't give money to workers management gives participation—and during this same recent period other private managements have filed for bankruptcy to overturn labor agreements, used consultants to ward off unionization, and refined various techniques, such as shifting production to offshore locations, to limit union participation in the enterprise.[55]

---

[53]See, for example, Chamberlain and Kuhn, Chapter 5, and Paul Prasow and Edward Peters, "New Perspectives on Management's Reserved Rights," *Labor Law Journal* 18 (January 1967), pp. 3–14.

[54]See D. Quinn Mills, "When Employees Make Concessions," *Harvard Business Review* 61 (May–June 1983), pp. 103–113, Peter Cappelli, "Concession Bargaining and the National Economy," *Proceedings of the 35th Annual Meeting of the Industrial Relations Research Association* (Madison, WI: IRRA, 1983), pp. 362–371, Allen M. Ponak and C. R. P. Frasor, "Union Members Support for Joint Programs," *Industrial Relations* 18 (May 1979), pp. 197–209, and Michael Beer, Bert Spector, Paul R. Lawrence, D. Quinn Mills and Richard E. Walton, eds., *Human Resource Management: Text and Cases* (New York: Free Press, 1985), chapter 5.

[55]See for example, John J. Lawler and Robin West, "Attorneys, Consultants, and Union-Avoidance Strategies in Representation Elections," paper presented to the Berkeley Conference on Industrial Relations, February, 1985, and Robert J. Flanagan, "Compliance and Enforcement Decisions Under the National Labor Relations Act," paper presented to the Berkeley Conference on Industrial Relations, February, 1985.

Whether managers of local government sanitation departments are, on average, more or less inclined than their private or other public sector counterparts to encourage union participation in implementing technological change is uncertain, and the "average" managerial posture toward this matter may not be relevant in any case. Rather, and has been shown here, sanitation labor relations tend toward distinctive patterns, with cooperative integrative relations on the one hand, and adversarial, distributive relations, on the other hand, as the dominant types.

The irony in all of this—and it is an irony characteristic of labor relations more broadly—is that technological change improves the position and conditions (that is, the "outcomes") of workers *who remain employed*. In public service, and irrespective of whether a particular labor relationship is predominantly cooperative or adversarial, recent technological changes have raised employee pay and benefits, generated skill upgrading, reduced work injuries, and enhanced employee autonomy and control over the work process. These beneficial effects of the new economic and social organization of the public sanitation workplace must be given considerable weight in any assessment of technological change in sanitation service. However, the costs attending such change cannot be overlooked, and these costs primarily take the form of worker displacement which, as earlier analysis showed, was substantial during the 1970s and early 1980s.

In the American system of decentralized industrial relations, management and union officials who are party to a specific labor relationship are not well equipped or positioned to deal with the specific worker displacement effects of technological change. This is perhaps especially true for the union which, as Dunlop has shown, must choose between maximizing membership and maximizing "benefits" per member.[56] In public sanitation service, union leaders have given more emphasis to the latter objective, though not entirely ignoring the former. In this, they mirror the "objective function" of the public managers with whom they deal, and reflect the dominant, if not singular, behavior of union leaders in the private sector and in other public services in the United States.

ACKNOWLEDGMENTS

The research assistance of Nancy Lewis in the preparation of this paper is gratefully acknowledged.

[56]John T. Dunlop, *Wage Determination Under Trade Unions*, rev. ed. (New York: MacMillan, 1950). While Dunlop offers an economic analysis of this tradeoff, others emphasize the political dynamics of unions in deciding the tradeoff. See, for example, Arthur Ross, *Trade Union Wage Policy* (Berkeley: University of California Press, 1948). Whether viewed from an economic or political perspective, union behavior and the effects of technological change on unions can be distinguished from individual employee behavior and the effects of technological change on employees. In the context of public sanitation service, some unions that have seen their membership reduced by private contracting and technological change have organized private sanitation workers. Thus, on balance, sanitation union membership may be reconstituted rather than reduced by technological in public sanitation service. Note, further, that if integrative bargaining is sustained or spreads more widely through municipal sanitation service, it may permit the parties to achieve new and different "membership-wage" combinations than are obtainable via distributive bargaining.

15

Deregulation, Technological Change, and Labor Relations in Telecommunications

Dick Batten and Sara Schoonmaker

Technological change and industry deregulation have promoted the development of cooperative labor relations arrangements in U.S. telecommunications. With the entry of non-union competitors and the continuous adoption of labor-saving technology in the industry, union membership and AT&T's market share have been jeopardized, compelling labor and management to resolve their divergent interests and address their mutual concerns.

In order to analyze this shift in labor–management relations in the telecommunications industry, we view the relationship between changes in technology, industrial organization, and labor relations in a socio-economic framework. From this perspective, technological innovations are developed, supported, and modified by social groups with divergent interests. Technological change, along with the political organization of an industry, facilitates changes in the balance of power between labor and management, leading them to institutionalize new labor relations arrangements. Using the telecommunications industry as an example, this chapter addresses the interdependency of regulatory politics, technological changes, and their impact on industrial organization and labor relations. We begin by describing technological and regulatory changes in the industry. Then, we discuss the effects of these trends on the reorganization of telecommunications and the institutionalization of cooperative labor relations.

Dick Batten and Sara Schoonmaker • Department of Sociology, Boston College, Chestnut Hill, MA 02167.

I. TECHNOLOGICAL CHANGE IN TELECOMMUNICATIONS

In the past decade, improvements in computerized information storage, retrieval, and data-processing technologies have led to the adoption of multi-purpose telecommunications transmission equipment. Electro-mechanical and other non-electronic technologies are being replaced by computerized technologies.

Computer applications in telecommunications include telematics and fiber-optic cables. Telematics is the computerized transmission of information over microwave, satellite telecommunications links. Satellite transmission costs have fallen rapidly in the last decade due to steady advances in technology. Cellular radio innovations will make mobile, wireless phone transmission available in the next several years.[1] Fiber-optic or light-wave communications cables are rapidly replacing conventional coaxial cable phone wires and are supplanting radio transmission as well. In 1982, Bell companies had invested over $200 million in the construction of new Bell fiber-optic systems. Presently, there are more than 60 fiber-optic systems in operation.[2]

Fiber-optic technology has facilitated the shift from conventional analog transmission to microelectronic digital mode of transmission. In the traditional system of wires and radio links, sound waves are carried as continuous signals by analog transmission. While suitable for voice transmission, this method is inefficient and expensive for data or visual-image transmission. All sound, data, and visual image telecommunications are gradually being transferred to digital modes. Today, more than half of all metropolitan trunk lines between central offices are digital. The percentage of digital transmissions is expected to exceed 90% by 1990.[3] Moreover, digital transmissions increasingly rely on microelectronic technology and computerization as the basis for telecommunications. In the near future, microwave, radio, and satellite transmission will all be in digital mode, and fiber-optics will replace most long distance wires.[4]

These data technologies are facilitating the automation of traditional information processing functions. Directory assistance, switching of calls, phone-book production, toll-call rate information, circuit-networks testing, as well as clerical work and record-keeping are all being rapidly computerized.[5] Advanced computers are now being developed which can recognize and synthesize human voice and language. When implemented, perhaps within ten years, these talking and listening devices will virtually supplant operators.[6]

[1]Interview with Robert Luckey, Executive Director of Research Communications, Science Division, Bell Laboratories, Morristown, NJ, 19 February 1983.
[2]*A.T.&T. Annual Report*, 1982, p. 14.
[3]Ibid.
[4]Interview with Robert Luckey.
[5]*The 1979 Conference: A Final Report, Technology—Its Impact on CWA* (Washington, DC: C.W.A., 1979), p. 16.
[6]Interview with Robert Luckey.

Microelectronic data technologies also allow for the creation of a wide array of new products and services. Many of these new products, such as a phone with a built-in memory for storage of telephone numbers, automatic dialing, wireless operation and ports for computer hook-ups, are traditional telecommunication products enhanced by microelectronic technology. Centrally located computer software makes the new products compatible with newly created services such as call-waiting and call-forwarding. Many businesses are installing inter-office teleconferencing, private voice, facsimile and data systems, international telex data transmission, and private branch switching equipment which automatically selects the most efficient phone routings and coordinates internal and external phone traffic. Some large companies such as Atlantic Richfield have installed comprehensive, multi-million dollar private computer-communications systems that fulfill almost all their diverse communications needs, including global voice, high-speed data, and full-motion color video-teleconferencing facilities.[7]

II. THE POLITICAL ECONOMY OF TELECOMMUNICATIONS REGULATION

In the early years of the telephone industry, patents were used to establish formal conditions for access to the newly developed technology and for entry into the industry. Gardiner G. Hubbard and Thomas Sanders bought a large share in the patent rights to Alexander Graham Bell's invention of the telephone in 1875. They claimed that their ownership of these rights justified their exclusive position in the industry. Hubbard and Sanders sued Western Union for infringement of patent rights after the telegraph company sought to enter the telephone business in 1878 and founded the American Bell Company in 1879.[8] The case was eventually settled when Western Union withdrew from the telephone market in exchange for a 20% share of American Bell's patents royalties.[9] Through the early twentieth century, patents continued to be deployed in order to minimize competition.[10]

Despite the eventual surge in competition that accompanied the expiration of Bell's patents in 1893 and 1894, Bell's extensive network and possession of major patents on long distance technology were important advantages that limited business opportunities for competitors. The first long distance line was opened between Boston and Providence in 1882 and American Bell formed the American Telephone and Telegraph Company (AT&T) as a new subsidiary to manage the long lines business in 1885. Although three thou-

[7]Frederick R. Feldman, "Avoiding Obsolescence in Telecommunications," *The Office* (November 1982), p. 66.

[8]Gerard W. Brock, *The Telecommunications Industry: The Dynamics of Market Structure* (Cambridge: Harvard University Press, 1981), p. 94.

[9]Paul R. Lawrence and Davis Dyer, *Renewing American Industry* (New York: The Free Press, 1983), p. 209.

[10]Brock, pp. 102–106.

sand non-Bell commercial telephone systems had been formed between 1895 and 1902, Bell merged with many of these competitors, increasing its market share from 58% in 1912 to 78% by 1932.[11]

The dominance of the Bell long distance division was institutionalized in 1899 when AT&T became the holding company of the Bell System. AT&T gained controlling interests in Western Electric, the manufacturing subsidiary; the Bell Telephone Laboratories, the research and development facility; the AT&T Long Lines division, which provided long distance services between the regional operating companies; and the operating companies themselves.[12] This vertically integrated industrial enterprise would dominate the telecommunications industry for the next eighty years.

Regulatory reforms of the 1930s further established the monopoly of AT&T. As part of its economic recovery effort during the Great Depression, the New Deal Administration established government regulatory agencies to monitor the development and operation of industries which were considered to be vital for economic recovery. The general approach that prevailed during this period was an attempt to regulate prices, capital investment, and the volume of production. The Communications Act of 1934 applied this general strategy to telecommunications, establishing the Federal Communications Commission (FCC) and charging it with regulating the telephone industry.[13] The regulation also granted "natural monopoly" status to the telephone industry which was now dominated by AT&T. The FCC reinforced AT&T's dominance because the government agency was authorized to require independent telephone companies to employ AT&T's communications network for their long distance transmissions. Because the FCC was empowered to allocate frequencies, determine tariff rates, and approve new communications facilities and services, other companies could not use competitive strategies to increase their share of the market.[14]

Beginning in the late 1960s, the FCC made a series of decisions that modified the AT&T monopoly and the impact of technological change in the industry. The Carterphone decision of 1968 authorized private parties to connect their own equipment to Bell's lines. The decision was motivated by a lobby of petroleum companies and other major telecommunications users who had already established extensive private communications networks. These users argued that linking their private networks into the general exchange network of the common carriers was vital to their business operations. For example, oil companies contended that their inability to connect these private systems with the public network slowed communication between remote drilling sites and central offices and hindered the coordination of production activities. However, AT&T vigorously opposed the Carterphone

[11]Brock, pp. 112, 151, 157; Lawrence and Dyer, pp. 212–213.
[12]Lawrence and Dyer, pp. 210–214.
[13]Brock, p. 178.
[14]Brock, pp. 176–179; Stanley Aronowitz, *False Promises: The Shaping of American Working Class Consciousness* (New York: McGraw-Hill Book Company, 1973), pp. 267–268.

decision and lobbied successfully to delay interconnection until the late 1970s.[15]

The 1968 FCC decision on Computer Inquiry I established distinct markets for the data processing and communications industries. Data processing services were declared unregulated, leaving business users with substantial freedom to employ sophisticated systems at their own discretion and to function in the expanding telematics markets without competition from AT&T.[16] The telecommunications industry retained its regulated status. AT&T was effectively confined to this industry and banned from providing data processing services. Thus business users had won a significant victory by gaining access to the public communications network for the implementation of telematics.[17]

During the 1970s, corporate users increasingly exerted pressure to mold the public communications network to their requirements for advanced computer-communications systems. Although these users were urging AT&T to loosen its traditional control over the telecommunications market, they also relied on its network. Therefore, corporate users lobbied for modernization of AT&T's system and for the provision of cost efficient data communications services and equipment.[18]

AT&T resisted limitations on its control over its telecommunications network and made no immediate efforts to diversify into non-voice services. In 1976, Bell tried to limit the growing competition and the expansion of the telecommunications market into telematics by supporting the Consumer Communications Reform Act. Referred to as the "Bell Bill," the Consumer Communications Reform Act was a last attempt to return monopoly control to the AT&T system. The bill prohibited the authorization of private lines, facilities, and services of specialized carriers that duplicated those of other telecommunications carriers.[19] State commissions, which were less supportive than the FCC of the pro-competition policy, were to be given exclusive jurisdiction over terminal equipment manufacturing.[20]

---

[15]William H. Melody, "Interconnection: Impact on Competition, Carriers and Regulation," in U.S. Senate, Hearings Before The Subcommittee on Antitrust And Monopoly of the Committee of the Judiciary, The Industrial Reorganization Act, Part 2: The Communications Industry (Washington, DC: GPO, 30, 31 July; 1, 2 August 1973), pp. 1260–1271; Dan Schiller, Telematics and Government (Norwood, New Jersey: Ablex Publishing Corporation, 1982), pp. 15–21); U.S. Federal Communications Committee, "In the Matter of the Use of the Carterphone Device in the Message Toll Telephone Service, F.C.C. Docket No. 16942, Notice of Inquiry (Washington, DC: GPO, 21 October 1966).

[16]U.S. Federal Communications Committee, "In the Matter of Regulatory and Policy Problems presented by the Interdependence of Computers and Communications Services and Facilities," F.C.C. Docket No. 16979, Notice of Inquiry (Washington, DC: GPO, 10 November 1966).

[17]Ibid.

[18]Schiller, p. 60.

[19]Richard E. Wiley, "The Consumer Communications Reform Act: The F.C.C. Position on the Proposed Legislation," Telecommunications Policy (March 1977), pp. 109–110.

[20]Brock, pp. 289–290.

Despite their traditionally adversarial relationship, the communications unions and Bell management joined forces in support of the bill but were unsuccessful in securing the legislation. The Bell Bill was defeated through the efforts of an alliance of corporate telecommunications users who sought greater access to the communications network. As Schiller put it, this struggle was a "war for position," in which each alliance attempted to gain control over the development of the telecommunications infrastructure and the expanding markets.[21]

The conflict between the two alliances was also reflected in the 1980 FCC Computer Inquiry II decision. Under pressure from the alliance of corporate telecommunications users, the FCC established a distinction in data processing between "basic" services that transfer data and "enhanced" services that restructure or add data. The decision allowed AT&T to provide "basic" services, enter the data processing sector, upgrade its telecommunications network and expand its operations into telematics.[22] Thus, corporate users gained an improved network for data communications but with the prospect of competing with AT&T in the information industry.[23]

Recognizing AT&T's potential strength as a competitor, the users formed a broad coalition in order to protect their common interest in shaping a competitive market for the new information industry. Called the Telecommunications Competitive Alternatives for Users Services and Equipment, or Tele-Cause, the coalition united over 5,000 equipment manufacturers, service suppliers, and business users. Tele-Cause membership included: the major trade association of the computer services industry, ADAPSO; TCA, the largest business user group; the Independent Data Communications Manufacturers Association, a group of equipment manufacturers; Control Data Corporation; International Telephone and Telegraph Corporation; Satellite Business Systems, which includes IBM, Comsat and Aetna Life and Casualty; General Telephone and Electronics Corporation; the National Retail Merchants Association, with 4,000 members; and the Tele-Communications Association. With the overarching goal of securing a competitive market in the context of the FCC decision, Tele-Cause continued to lobby for favorable consequences of Computer Inquiry II.[24]

The 1982 settlement proposed in an antitrust suit filed by the U.S. government against AT&T formalized new legal conditions for the next phase in the "war for position" between AT&T and the large telecommunications users. By breaking up the Bell System under a divestiture plan, the court decision provided the legal grounds for the expansion of AT&T into telematics. At the same time, the legislation mandated that AT&T divest itself of

[21]Schiller, p. 61.

[22]"In the Matter of Amendment of Section 64.702 of the Commission's Rules and Regulations (Second Computer Inquiry)," *Final Decision,* Released 2 May 1980, cited by Schiller, p. 85.

[23]Brock, pp. 273–274; Schiller, pp. 87–89.

[24]"Mike Woody and Dan Grove Tell of TCA Plans and Progress," *Telecommunications News,* September 1981, pp. 52–57; "Coalition of Communications Users Groups Forms Tele-Cause," *Telecommunications News,* November 1981, pp. 78–79.

its 22 General Operating Companies. These companies were charged with the provision of local telephone service and restricted from providing long distance or interexchange telecommunications services, customer equipment, and unregulated or value-added information services.[25] AT&T retained control over Western Electric, Bell Labs, the highly lucrative Yellow Pages, and intra-state long distance telephone service. In addition, Bell was allowed to enter new markets for enhanced services and equipment through "Baby Bell" unregulated subsidiaries.

III. THE CHANGING INDUSTRIAL ORGANIZATION OF TELECOMMUNICATIONS

The markets for local and long distance telephone service had been closely linked in the monopoly era of telecommunications. Separations formulas had been used customarily to transfer some of the costs of local telephone service to long distance companies. During the last twenty years, the cost of providing long distance services declined with the advent of satellites and other new technologies. In this same period, local service costs increased. In spite of the growing cost disparity between the two services, the proportion of long distance revenues paid to local companies under the separations formulas was increased in order to subsidize local service. As long as the monopoly existed, this transfer remained a formality that reinforced the overall linkage between the local and long distance sectors. However, the 1982 antitrust suit broke the linkage between these markets. The costs of local service were now borne solely by the General Operating Companies, while AT&T was allowed to develop its operations in new arenas.

The break in the linkage between the local and long distance markets created different investment climates in the two sectors and fostered the development of an uneven pattern in the organization of the telecommunications industry. In the late 1970s, long distance revenues increased in relation to local service revenues. Long distance revenues comprised 49% of the total operating revenues in 1976 and increased to 51% in 1982. Local revenues constituted a 45% share in 1982, a decline from the 47% in 1976.[26] As indicated in table 1, there was no significant new investment by local telephone service companies after the passage of the antitrust legislation. The lower revenues of the non-Bell companies on the local market suggest that new competitors were discouraged from investing in local services, even though formal legal conditions for such investment had been established by the antitrust suit. Bell operating companies retained 94% to 97% of the local telephone service market between 1949 and 1983, thereby maintaining a set of regional near-monopolies in local telephone service.

---

[25]Schiller, p. 91–92.

[26]*Moody's Public Utility Manual, Volume 1* (New York: Moody's Investors Service, Inc., 1983), p. 136.

Table 1. Operating Revenues of Class A Telephone Carriers*[a]

	1949	1960	1970	1982	1983
Local Telephone Service					
Bell Companies	$1,697	4,665	8,685	29,632	31,008
	(94%)	(97%)	(95%)	(94%)	(96%)
Non-Bell Companies	104	158	430	1,852	1,198
	(6%)	(3%)	(5%)	(6%)	(4%)
Toll Telephone Service					
Bell Companies	$1,072	3,058	8,042	33,909	30,214
	(95%)	(97%)	(95%)	(92%)	(78%)
Non-Bell Companies	54	90	403	3,039	8,575
	(5%)	(3%)	(5%)	(8%)	(22%)

*Revenues in millions of dollars
[a]Source: U.S. Federal Communications Commission, *Statistics of Communications Common Carriers*, (Washington, DC: GPO, 1950–1983).

However, the post-divestiture climate in the more lucrative long distance market was fertile ground for the entry of new competitors. Table 1 shows that Bell's share of toll telephone service dropped from 92% to 78% between 1982 and 1983 after hovering between 92% and 97% in the 1949–1982 period. In the wake of the antitrust decision, new long distance carriers such as MCI and Sprint began to compete with AT&T, transforming the long distance monopoly into an oligopoly.

IV. CHANGES IN THE WORKPLACE AND LABOR RELATIONS

Deregulation and technological change have jeopardized not only AT&T's market share but job security and the quality of working life as well. These changes, in turn, have led to the institutionalization of new labor relations in the industry.

A. Job Security

The most prevalent staffing reductions have arisen from the automation of information-handling skills. Such reductions have become fairly common among semi-skilled and craft workers in telecommunications equipment manufacturing, local telephone operating companies, and in Bell's Long Lines division. It has been estimated that staffing requirements in switching offices decline by 50% when "analog-stored program" devices replace "step-by-step" methods and that further labor savings of 40% are achieved when the newest digital switching technologies are introduced.[27]

[27]*The 1979 Conference: A Final Report*, p. 18.

Substantial layoffs have occurred among local and long distance operators, whose functions have been progressively automated by computerized directory information and direct overseas dialing. The percentage of operators in the telecommunications work force declined from 44% to 13% between 1950 and 1982, a loss of 140,000 operator positions, while the telecommunications workforce increased from 560,750 to 912,000.[28] The Michigan Bell work force declined by about 5,000 employees over the past two years without layoffs, and in February 1983, 350 long distance and directory assistance operators were laid off.[29] The operator work force has also declined at Bell's International Operating Centers (IOC's). Bell closed the White Plains, N.Y. IOC in 1976 and the Denver IOC in 1979. In August 1982, Bell announced the closing of the New York City IOC, a loss of over 800 positions which accounted for one half of all long lines operators.[30]

Traditional craft workers such as switching technicians, repair personnel, linestaff, and installers have been made redundant by developments such as computerized switching, testing, and repair and replacement of phone lines by satellites, radio links, and fiber-optics.[31] As a result of more intensive utilization of electronic components, the need for workers involved in the traditional craft activities of trouble shooting maintenance, repair, and installation has declined at AT&T's manufacturing and service departments.[32] Additional job losses may result from the implementation of robotics in the manufacturing of electronic components.[33] At New England Telephone, 3,000 craft workers were laid off in 1974, 1975, and 1977 due to technological changes.[34] In addition, 50 of 180 clerical jobs were eliminated with the computerization of white- and yellow-pages production.[35] According to the Communications Workers of America (CWA), almost 2,000 installers were laid off nationwide in 1982 and forced permanent transfers had become commonplace.[36] Recently, AT&T announced that an additional 24,000 workers would be laid off in its Information Systems Division within a year.[37]

Employment growth is expected in such expanded product-lines as sophisticated private branch telephone exchanges (PBX) which are able to con-

---

[28]U.S. Federal Communications Commission, *Statistics of Communications Common Carriers* (Washington, DC: GPO, 1950), p. 22; F.C.C., *Statistics of Communications Common Carriers* (Washington, DC: GPO, 1982), p. 19.

[29]C.W.A., District 1, *Hot Line*, 10, no. 2 (February 1983).

[30]AT&T Newsletter, *Northeast Connection* (28 February 1983); C.W.A., *Local 1150 Newsletter* (November-December, 1982); C.W.A. America, *Philadelphia Local Newsletter* (November 1982).

[31]*The 1979 Conference: A Final Report*, p. 20.

[32]George Kohl, "Changing Competitive and Technology Environments in Telecommunications", in: *Labor and Technology: Union Response to Changing Environments*, eds, Donald Kennedy *et al.* (Pennsylvania State University: Department of Labor Studies, 1982), pp. 67–68.

[33]*A.T.&T. Annual Report*, p. 6.

[34]Interview with New England Telephone Representative of Labor–Management Relations, (prefers to remain anonymous). Boston, Massachusetts, 15 February 1983.

[35]Interview with C.W.A. Local President, (prefers to remain anonymous) 9 March 1983.

[36]*Hot Line*.

[37]Dick Batten et al., *What Ever Happened to Job Security: The 1985 Slowdown in Massachusetts Electronics* (Watertown, MA: The High Tech Research Group, 1986), p. 54.

trol telephone traffic and electronic mail, teleconferencing, and data process-ing functions.[38] The widespread implementation of microelectronic technol-ogy creates new employment opportunities for skilled technicians, program-mers, and engineers.[39] Their scientific and technical knowledge is replacing manual skill in the operation of the telecommunications system.

B. Quality of Working Life

Computerization has lowered worker morale and job satisfaction in three significant ways.[40] First, computerization has led to closer monitoring and supervision of workers. For example, the volume of operator calls is automati-cally monitored at short intervals which increases operator accountability to the supervisor. A detailed computer-generated printout of each operator's daily call-handling activities enhances centralized long-term supervision.[41] Second, the use of video display terminals (VDT) isolates workers and re-duces on-the-job social interaction. Stored computer programs route the in-coming operator or directory assistance requests continuously to the VDT workers and assign work breaks automatically according to business needs.[42] Third, project fragmentation has increased boredom. For example, before computerization, each local phone book in New England was produced by a team of one to six people who coordinated the project from beginning to end. In this "one book-one person" system, each job allowed for significant re-sponsibility, variety, and interpersonal interaction, regardless of skill level. However, some of these tasks are now contracted out and the remaining work is divided into numerous repetitive, semi-skilled jobs which are per-formed at computer terminals. In some heavily computerized directory as-sistance operations, operators take incoming calls and only key in the name of the party. The computer not only finds the number but automatically reports it in voice form to the customer while the operator deals with the next re-quest.[43]

C. Changing Labor Relations

The regulated economic environment had created the conditions for the development of a stable system of industrial relations. The monopoly struc-ture fostered planned and consistent growth in the Bell System, enabling the

[38]Oswald Harold Ganley and Gladys D. Ganley, *To Inform or to Control?: The New Communications Networks* (New York: McGraw-Hill, 1982), p. 30; Robert William Haigh and George Gerbner, *Communications in the Twenty-first Century* (New York: Wiley, 1981), pp. 138–153.

[39]Michael Dymmel, "Technology and Labor in Telephone Communications," U.S. Bureau of Labor Statistics, *Technology and Labor in Five Industries*, Bulletin 2033 (Washington, DC: GPO, 1979), pp. 28–40.

[40]Interview with C.W.A. Local President, (prefers to remain anonymous) 24 February 1983.

[41]Ibid.

[42]Kohl, p. 66.

[43]AT&T Annual Report, p. 15.

company and its highly unionized work force to maintain generally harmonious relations. AT&T's monopoly position allowed it to offer relatively high wages and benefits to its employees, encouraging stability of employment and mitigating conflict.

The first successful efforts to organize telephone workers were promoted by the National Industrial Recovery Act of 1933 which institutionalized the right of workers to organize and bargain collectively through representatives of their own choosing. The unionization of telephone workers was also stimulated by the passage of the Wagner Act in 1935 which limited employer interference in union organizing.[44]

The National Federation of Telephone Workers (NFTW), the first national labor organization in the telephone industry, was a federation of some 50 autonomous telephone unions and represented 92,000 members in 1939.[45] In addition to raising wages, the NFTW lobbied in Washington, D.C. for the creation of a governing body for the entire industry. The National Telephone Commission (NTC) was established in 1945 and held final authority over all disputes or voluntary cases in its jurisdiction and was empowered to address labor issues for the entire industry. Composed of representatives from labor and management, the NTC applied national wage stabilization policies and promoted labor peace in the telephone industry.

The formation of the NTC was followed by a period of rising company unionism, union organizing in the Southeast, the Southwest and West Coast, and an increased number of strikes for wage increases in 1946 and 1947. AT & T had successfully resisted unionization until 1946, when the Bell System and organized labor signed their first national agreement. In that year, after the NFTW had organized several local strikes, labor perceived a need for greater national unity. A loose coalition of 50 autonomous unions that could drop out of the federation at any time proved ineffective in bargaining with large corporations. This led to the formation of the Communications Workers of America (CWA) in June 1947, when 200 delegates representing 161,669 members met at the first CWA convention.

In the following years, the CWA competed with the International Brotherhood of Electrical Workers (IBEW) in organizing the telecommunications industry. By 1952, CWA membership exceeded 300,000, while the IBEW had organized about 25,000 telephone workers. The CWA has continued to represent a growing percentage of the telecommunications work force, as shown in table 2.

During the era of the AT&T monopoly, the unions and government worked in tandem to sustain steady growth in productivity, profits, and em-

[44]Janice R. Bellace, "Regulating the Telecommuter Workforce: Implications for Employment Law in the 90's," (paper presented at the "Employment Problems in the Information Age" conference, Columbia University, 12 June 1985).

[45]Jack Barbash, Unions and Telephones: The Story of the Communications Workers of America (New York: Harper and Brothers, 1952), pp. 20–42, 79, 93.

Table 2. Employment in Telecommunications and CWA
Unionization[a]

	Employment	CWA Membership	% in CWA
1950	560,752	300,370	54%
1958	609,237	357,605	59%
1966	692,000	407,272	59%
1974	866,000	574,418	66%
1982	912,000	675,980	74%
1983	n.a.	531,000	—
1984	n.a.	511,000	—

[a]Employment figures exclude managers and managerial assistants *Source:* U.S. Federal Communications Commission, *Statistics of Communications Common Carriers*, (Washington, DC: GPO, 1950–1982); Letter from Lisa Williamson, C.W.A. Research Economist, Washington, DC, 23 July 1985.

ployment.[46] Bell profits increased and the percentage of labor costs of overall operating expenses declined over the post-World War II era, as shown in table 3. Union leaders enjoyed longevity in office as their constituency was virtually guaranteed life-long employment and occupational mobility through a regimented job classification system that rewarded seniority in employment. These harmonious relations were facilitated by the fact that labor costs became embedded in the basic rate structure from which the company derived its revenues. These stable labor costs also facilitated a harmonious relationship between labor and management at the bargaining table. At the 1974 talks, the company and the union agreed for the first time to settle such issues as basic wages, pensions, health insurance, and the length of contract on a national basis.[47]

Monopoly-era collective bargaining was characterized by: (1) prevailing wages comparable to the leading industries in the economy, such as auto, trucking, steel, and rubber; (2) multi-year contracts; and (3) pattern bargaining which evolved to a point where in 1977 the CWA and AT&T negotiated one national agreement covering all workers. Management's bargaining goals were strongly influenced by its perceptions of FCC demands for high quality and stable products. These outweighed imperatives to contain labor costs. Management actually had little incentive to reduce labor costs since they became a part of the rate base from which revenues were derived. The major objectives of management during this period were to maintain labor peace and secure a continuous supply of skilled labor. Through the mid-1970s,

[46]Dymmel, pp. 28–40; U.S. Bureau of Labor Statistics, *Productivity Measures for Selected Industries: 1954–1982*, Bulletin no. 2189 (Washington, D.C.: GPO, 1983), p. 7; "Labor Productivity Increases in Telecommunications Industry Exceeded National Average in Period Covered in Study by Diebold Group for C.W.A.," *Telecommunications Reports* 43, no. 25 (27 June 1977), p. 18.

[47]"Bargaining Goals in General Telephone Contract Talks Announced by C.W.A.," *Telecommunications Reports* 39, no. 50 (17 February 1973), p. 31.

Table 3. Bell System Net Income and Labor Cost
as Percentage of Operating Expenses[a]

	Net Income in millions	Labor Cost/Expenses (%)
1950	353	63%
1954	480	62%
1958	744	57%
1962	1,027	52%
1966	1,443	48%
1970	1,792	47%
1974	3,211	47%
1978	5,476	44%
1982	6,621	43%

[a]Source: U.S. Federal Communications Commission, *Statistics of Communications Common Carriers*, (Washington, DC: GPO, 1950–1982).

union demands routinely called for substantially higher wages, extended benefits, and better worker conditions. These bargaining efforts remained successful through the seventies and the early 1980s. For example, the average hourly wage increased from $5.35 in 1973 to $11.47 in 1982.[48]

The 1980 negotiations constituted a turning point in the collective bargaining process. Technological change and deregulation had begun to undermine the conditions which had allowed for labor–management accomodation and "regulated" prosperity in the post-World War II monopoly era. Technological change jeopardized union membership, increased managerial control on the shop floor and diluted the craft skills in the industry.[49] Deregulation facilitated the entry of non-union competitors who not only threatened CWA bargaining strength but also lowered AT&T's market share. These firms could operate with lower labor costs than AT&T, as shown in table 4. For the union, the 1980 negotiations marked the advent of national concern about automation and its effects on employment in the industry. The conditions which promoted high wages, a high market share and secure profits—a high level of unionization and the monopoly structure of the industry—had begun to erode. This erosion has compelled the unions and AT&T to address their respective concerns by institutionalizing new labor relations arrangements in the most recent, post-monopoly era.

[48]U.S. Federal Communications Commission, *Statistics of Communications Common Carriers* (Washington, DC: GPO, 1973), p. 19; FCC, *Statistics of Communications Common Carriers* (Washington, DC: GPO, 1982), p. 19.

[49]*Committee on the Future Report* (Washington, DC: C.W.A., March 1983), pp. 61–75; "C.W.A. Placing Emphasis on 'Job Security' in 1977 Contract Negotiations in Bell System; Points to 100,000 Reduction in Work Force Since 1973; Improved Payments to Pensioners Will Also Be Key Demand in Discussions," *Telecommunications Reports* 43, no. 7 (22 February 1977); Dymmel, 1979, pp. 13–17).

Table 4. Average Hourly Wages in Telecommunications, by Occupation and Carrier, 1981[a]

	Carrier	
Occupation	Bell System	Non-Bell Companies
All full-time employees	$11.63	$ 9.33
Clerical supervisors	14.68	11.23
Non-supervisory clerical workers	9.54	6.89
Chief telephone operators	13.94	10.77
Telephone operators	8.65	6.29
Installation, exchange supervisors	15.03	12.88
Installation, exchange personnel	11.76	10.01

[a]Source: U.S. Bureau of Labor Statistics, *Industry Wage Survey: Communications, October–December 1981*, Bulletin no. 2188 (Washington, DC: GPO, 1983).

For the CWA, job security and protection of the quality of work life became the major issues in the negotiations. This concern is indicated by the CWA emphasis on developing new retraining and educational programs to adapt the skills of its members to new job requirements.[50] According to the CWA, "the key to employment security is through training and retraining, so that we can ride the crest of the wave of technological change."[51] William Claxton, Assistant Vice-President for Labor Relations at AT&T, summarized some of the managerial concerns: "We will need additional flexibility and ability to assign our forces as they are needed without restrictive and costly contractual restrictions."[52]

In 1980, a formal effort was made to redefine and extend the boundaries of the traditional labor relations arrangements. The 1980 contract between AT&T and the two major unions (CWA and IBEW) called for the establishment of Joint Labor/Management Committees. These committees were composed of equal numbers of labor and management representatives, and consisted of three programs.[53] First, a joint national Working Conditions and Service Quality Improvement Committee was formed to address issues of the quality of work life (QWL) in the industry and to devise methods for implementing these principles at the shop floor level. Second, a committee was established to formulate a job evaluation process. This involved evaluating the appropriateness of job definitions and job classifications in light of technological changes which demanded new job specifications, lines of responsibility and compensation rates.

[50]*Committee on the Future Report*, pp. 7–14, 67–83; *Recommendations for 1983 Negotiations* (Washington, DC: C.W.A., 1983); Ronnie J. Straw, Patrick J. Hunt, *C.W.A. Strategies for Dealing With New Technology in the Communications Industry* (Washington, DC: C.W.A., 28 April 1982).
[51]*Committee on the Future Report*, p. 7.
[52]Interview with William H. Claxton, Assistant Vice-President, AT&T, Basking Ridge, NJ, 5 April 1983.
[53]"A.T.&T. and the Communication Workers of America," *Q.W.L. Resource Bulletin* 2, no. 1 (January 1983); Kohl, pp. 72–76.

The third program established Technological Change Committees in each of the Bell Operating Companies, Western Electric, the Bell Labs, and the Long Lines Division. These joint labor–management groups focus on employment issues of workers affected by technological change and provide instructional materials, teachers, and apprentice training at the local level through the National Training Fund.[54] Also, they channel information about technological change in equipment, organization, and methods of operation to the rank-and-file.

In order to improve worker understanding of technological change, the CWA has argued for the development of a data steward system. CWA data stewards would inform the union members about the overall organization of the company and industry and the planning, design, and implementation of technological change. The data steward would have expertise in the following five areas: (1) the social choices involved in making technological changes; (2) the nature and history of technology; (3) job design and work organization; (4) the social implications of technology; and (5) electronics and computer theory. The data steward system is a new proposal which reflects the union stance on increased worker participation and, ultimately, co-determination in the implementation of new technology.

The demise of the regulated environment in the telecommunications industry and the adoption of labor saving technology forced both labor and management to reevaluate their positions in the existing labor relations arrangements. Joint labor–management programs have been implemented in an effort to reconcile the union concern with employment protection and the managerial desire for greater flexibility.

V. CONCLUSION

Technological change and the political economy of deregulation have facilitated qualitative changes in the industrial organization and labor relations in the U.S. telecommunications industry. Changes in the balance of power between labor and management and increased industry competition have led to the institutionalization of labor relations based on participatory cooperation between labor and management rather than the stable, though adversarial, negotiations of the past.

The development of new communication technologies such as fiber-optic cables and satellite transmissions challenged the hegemony of AT&T which had been based on its control over the network of conventional telephone cables and the ownership of patents on long distance technology. Over the past 25 years, a series of FCC regulatory decisions has permitted increased competition in the industry and signalled the end of the era of AT&T's dominance.

The actual divestiture of AT&T and deregulation of telecommunications

---

[54]*Committee on the Future Report*, pp. 71–72.

had significant consequences for job security, quality of working life and labor relations in the industry. Because of increased competition by non-unionized enterprises, traditional labor arrangements in the monopoly era, based on narrowly defined job classifications and hierarchical career ladders, are being replaced by more cooperative arrangements between labor and AT&T.

Joint labor–management programs have been developed in an attempt to reconcile the union concern with employment security but still enable AT&T to circumvent limitations imposed by negotiated worker rights. Under the guidelines of cooperation, workers have made concessions to save jobs by relaxing job classifications and seniority rules, thus allowing management greater flexibility in production and recruitment. Although such programs could weaken the institution of collective bargaining, telecommunications workers and their unions support this qualitative shift in labor relations and the new technological applications in the hope that these will increase AT&T's competitiveness in the industry. They hope their concessions will generate new jobs for them and improve their quality of working life.

The new labor relations are based on the premise that the expected growth in the sales and service sectors of the industry will mitigate job displacement. The upgrading of jobs through automation, participatory decision making, retraining of displaced employees, and work force reduction by attrition are expected to limit losses in the quality and quantity of employment. However, the evidence shows that even the sectors characterized by the highest growth rates are expected to experience significant displacement of workers in the traditional job categories.

The implementation of new technology and deregulation reflect the shift in the balance of power between labor and management, changes in the organization of the industry, a decrease of autonomy in computer-mediated work, and a growing inequity in labor relations. Technological change and the politics of deregulation are facilitating factors in the transformation of industrial relations within a socio-economic framework, mediated by the social choices that lie behind adoption of technological innovations and policy changes. The shift in labor relations from arrangements based on adversarial negotiated rights to cooperative labor–management relations may provide insufficient compensation for workers' loss of job security. Technological change, deregulation and cooperative arrangements in labor relations bring into question whether the unionized rank-and-file in the telecommunications industry will continue to "ride the crest of the wave of technological change."

ACKNOWLEDGMENTS

The authors would like to thank Helen Levine Batten and Daniel Cornfield for helpful comments and encouragement on earlier drafts of this chapter. Our initial interest in deregulation, technological change, and labor relations in the telecommunications industry was sparked by the "1983 General Motors Business Understanding Program: The Impact on the Roles and Responsibilities of Labor and Management." We would like to express our appreciation to Russ Eckel, William Schwartz, Larry Snyder, and Betsy Wright who conducted the interviews and with whom we co-authored for this program the paper "Industrial Relations and High Technology: The Transformation of Telecommunications." We also wish to thank Severyn Bruyn, Charles Derber and Paul Gray for their assistance and comments.

IV
CONCLUSION

16

Labor–Management Cooperation or Managerial Control?
Emerging Patterns of Labor Relations in the United States

Daniel B. Cornfield

I. INTRODUCTION

Throughout the twentieth century in the United States, managements have deployed new production technologies in order to maintain enterprise profitability, while workers have attempted to protect their job security. Technological change has not only raised these divergent issues for labor and management, but also compelled them to establish procedures for ensuring that technological change fulfills their interests. Technological change has been accompanied by a continuous struggle over controlling its implementation and outcomes.[1]

The analyses of the 14 industries in this book suggest the emergence of two broad patterns of labor relations arrangements in response to tech-

[1]See, for example, chapter 1 of this book; International Labour Office, *Technological Change: The Tripartite Response, 1982–85* (Geneva: International Labour Office, 1985); Donald Kennedy, Charles Craypo, and Mary Lehman, eds., *Labor and Technology: Union Response to Changing Environments* (Department of Labor Studies, Pennsylvania State University, 1982); Doris McLaughlin, *The Impact of Labor Unions on the Rate and Direction of Technological Innovation*, PB 295084 (Springfield, VA: National Technical Information Service, 1979); Sumner Slichter, James Healy, and E. Robert Livernash, *The Impact of Collective Bargaining on Management* (Washington, DC: The Brookings Institution, 1960); Melvyn Dubofsky, ed., *Technological Change and Workers' Movements* (Beverly Hills: Sage, 1985).

Daniel B. Cornfield • Department of Sociology, Vanderbilt University, Nashville, TN 37235.

nological change during the post-World War II era. The first and more prevalent pattern in the United States is increasing unilateral, managerial control of
labor in the shop or office. Managerial control strategies have taken diverse
forms, including job deskilling, technical control, and/or bureaucratic control
in internal labor markets.

The second pattern is an increase in formal, labor–management cooperation at the company- and industry-wide management decision making levels.
Recent developments in formal cooperation include such voluntarily established measures as joint labor–management productivity, technology-
monitoring, research, and long-term industry development committees, joint
lobbying efforts for the enactment of protective legislation and government
policies, and union representation on company boards. These changes at the
company- and industry-wide decision-making levels are often accompanied
by, if not partly motivated by, the implementation of managerial control
strategies in the shop or office.

This divergence in labor relations trends has resulted from the uneven
development of unionization and uneven occurrence of adverse macroeconomic conditions among U.S. industries during the post-World War II era.
Increasing unilateral managerial control in the shop or office—without formal
cooperation—has accompanied technological change in industries with little
unionization and/or with favorable macroeconomic conditions. In these industries, management encounters little organized worker resistance to technological innovation, either because, in the absence of unionization, workers
have low attachment to their employers and lack sufficient bargaining
strength to demand participation in managerial decision making; or because
favorable macroeconomic conditions lessen the threat of technological displacement for workers.

In contrast, formal cooperation has emerged in the highly unionized
industries which have faced macroeconomic adversity during the post-World
War II era. Formal cooperation was institutionalized only after collective bargaining and unionization were legitimized in the 1930s and had become widespread in the mass production industries during World War II. Along with
the related development of internal labor markets, unionization served to
stabilize employment in the mass production industries, vesting worker interests in the survival of their employers and giving workers the bargaining
strength to demand participation in managerial decision making, especially
under conditions of macroeconomic adversity.

The entry of new producers, foreign and domestic, in these "core" industries, especially during the 1970s and early 1980s, has jeopardized management's interest in profit-maximization and labor's interest in job security,
compelling them to reconcile their differences by institutionalizing cooperative decision making. Some of these core industries, such as autos, steel,
construction equipment, aircraft and coal mining, have been jeopardized by
their declining position in the world market, as other nations industrialized
and began exporting their products to the United States and other markets.

Selected acts of U.S. government disinvolvement in some industries also have jeopardized labor and management interests, leading them to establish formal cooperation measures. These acts of disinvolvement include the deregulation of entry into an industry and the "privatization" of government services, as in the telecommunications and sanitation; and they include declining government purchases and withdrawal of support for research and development, as in aircraft manufacturing.

In sum, formal labor–management cooperation has emerged as a bargaining outcome in industries in which both labor and management perceive a necessity for technological innovation; profits and job security are jeopardized by foreign competition or government disinvolvement; worker interests are vested in the survival of their employers; and workers have the bargaining strength to demand participation in managerial decision making.

The uneven development of formal labor–management cooperation constitutes a redistribution of workplace authority that has entailed, in some industries, increased labor participation in managerial decision making. Yet, theories of workplace control tend to focus on trends in shop- or office-floor decision making, neglecting these developments in company-wide and industry-wide decision making. Therefore, I turn now to a discussion of these theories and then to an analysis of the development of labor–management cooperation in the United States.

II. THEORIES OF WORK PLACE CONTROL

Three social science theories have been recently formulated in order to account for changes in workplace control relationships that have accompanied technological change during the post-World War II era. First, according to Braverman's neo-Marxian theory, management has adopted new technologies in order to deskill jobs and thereby gain greater control over work in the shop or office. For Braverman, post-World War II deskilling of white-collar work is the latest phase of workplace rationalization that has accompanied capital centralization, beginning in the early twentieth century.[2] Second, and in a similar vein, Edwards argues that bureaucratic control strategies are supplanting technical control strategies in the current era. Technical control, a managerial strategy which wrests discretion about the determination of work methods and pace from workers through the adoption of technologies such as the assembly line, was implemented widely during the 1920s in order to quell labor unrest and increase efficiency. Edwards maintains that technical control actually proved to be counterproductive for management because it linked all workers in the plant, allowing them to disrupt production, as in the sit-down strikes of the 1930s. Bureaucratic control, whereby management gains worker loyalty and compliance through the creation of seniority-based labor allocation and compensation procedures in internal labor markets and through the provision of fringe benefits, according to Edwards, has been

[2]Harry Braverman, *Labor and Monopoly Capital* (New York: Monthly Review Press, 1974).

increasingly adopted during the post-World War II era, especially among higher-skill jobs in large corporations, in order to compensate for the deficiencies in technical control.[3]

Third, while Braverman and Edwards imply an increase in managerial control, Bell's post-industrial thesis suggests a shift of workplace authority away from owners and managers and toward a salaried, professional elite. With technological change and the separation of ownership from control, according to Bell, the significance of ownership as a source of workplace authority has declined in comparison to that associated with the possession of specialized technical knowledge.[4]

Their differences notwithstanding, these theories may be viewed as complementary parts. That is, while the neo-Marxian theories address managerial control of labor in the shop or office, Bell implies a growing importance of salaried professionals in company-wide management planning. Indeed, workplace rationalization through job deskilling, technical control, or bureaucratic control often requires engineering, personnel, and legal expertise in the design and implementation of these strategies. Management's growing reliance on professional expertise at the company-wide level of decision making, then, may derive in part from a continuous effort to rationalize work and thereby control it.

However, the neo-Marxian and post-industrial theories fail to consider formal cooperation in capitalist societies during the post-World War II era. With the rebuilding of Western European economies shortly after World War II, many Western European nations enacted national legislation requiring worker representation on the boards or work councils of business enterprises. During the 1970s, these nations amended the legislation in order to increase worker involvement in company-, industry-, or nation-wide managerial decision making, while others enacted such legislation for the first time, in response to deteriorating macroeconomic conditions and technological change. The types of Western European "industrial democracy" vary between the British system of joint consultation, in which workers are given the right to express opinions on a limited range of issues, to the West German system of codetermination, in which workers participate in decision making on a broad range of issues. Despite empirical evidence which suggests that managers and skilled workers often dominate the deliberations of these joint bodies in Western Europe, the redistribution of formal authority toward labor in these industrial democracy systems implies a more complex view of the changing employment relationship than the virtual, unilateral managerial and professional control depicted by the neo-Marxian and post-industrial theories.[5]

---

[3]Richard Edwards, *Contested Terrain* (New York: Basic, 1979).

[4]Daniel Bell, *The Coming of Post-Industrial Society* (New York: Basic, 1973).

[5]Charles King and Mark van de Vall, *Models of Industrial Democracy* (New York: Mouton, 1978); Nancy Lieber, ed., *Eurosocialism and America* (Philadelphia: Temple University Press, 1982); Peter Brannen, *Authority and Participation in Industry* (New York: St. Martin's Press, 1983); Ronald Mason, *Participatory and Workplace Democracy* (Carbondale: Southern Illinois University Press, 1982), pp. 159–160; Industrial Democracy in Europe International Research Group, *Industrial Democracy in Europe* (Oxford: Clarendon Press, 1981).

Although industrial democracy legislation has not been enacted in the United States, beginning in the late 1950s, diverse forms of voluntary, formal labor–management cooperation have emerged in a minority of business establishments. Fearing "excessive management . . . control, . . . as well as a very real possibility of economic growth occurring [sic] in the face of growing unemployment" and technological change, the AFL–CIO has recently sent delegations to Western Europe to study systems of industrial democracy.[6] Some of these cooperative developments are addressed above in chapters 9–15. Others include the establishment of the 1959 Armour Automation Committee, in which union and management representatives at the Armour meat-packing company met to study and devise solutions to adverse effects of plant closings on workers; the 1968 Railroad Labor–Management Committee, which was charged with studying and devising solutions to such industry-wide issues as service reliability, production bottlenecks, job security, safety, creation of new business and management planning techniques; the 1974 Joint Labor–Management Committee of the Retail Food Industry, which has addressed industry problems such as work practices, technological change, and productivity; the 1972 Jamestown Area Labor–Management Committee, a community-wide effort in Jamestown, NY which proposes solutions to the problems of plant shutdowns and community economic decline; and the naming a union representative to the board of Pan American World Airways in 1982.[7]

Further, the preceding chapters show that changes in managerial control strategies—deskilling, technical control, and bureaucratic control, as well as the transfer of production knowledge from workers toward management or a professional elite, may or may not be accompanied simultaneously by company- and industry-wide, formal cooperation. This suggests that the arrangements—whether individual or collective bargaining, or formal cooperation—which are developed by labor and management to reconcile their divergent interests in technological change derive from forces other than capital centralization and technological change.

III. DEVELOPMENTS IN LABOR–MANAGEMENT COOPERATION

What accounts for the rise of labor–management cooperation? The sporadic experiences with labor–management cooperation in the United States and the advent of Western European industrial democracy have led scholars

[6]Dennis Chamot and Michael Dymmel, *Cooperation or Conflict: European Experiences with Technological Change at the Workplace* (Washington, DC: Department for Professional Employees, AFL-CIO, 1981), p. 2.

[7]U.S. Bureau of Labor Statistics, *Plant Movement, Transfer, and Relocation Allowances*, Bulletin no. 1425-10 (Washington, DC: GPO, 1969), pp. 1–2; Edgar Weinberg, "Labor–Management Cooperation: A Report on Recent Initiatives," in *Labor–Management Cooperation: Recent Efforts and Results*, ed. U.S. Labor–Management Services Administration and Bureau of Labor Statistics, LMSA Publication 6 and BLS Bulletin no. 2153 (Washington, DC: GPO, 1982), pp. 30–39; John Williams, "Pan Am to Name Unions' Choice, A Pilot, to Board." *Wall Street Journal*, 5 March 1982, p. 4.

to ask this question at various times during the twentieth century.[8] I will attempt to answer it in two ways. First, I compare the cooperative institutions and conditions leading to their establishment in four periods of U.S. history: World War I, 1920s, World War II, and 1970s–present. Second, I compare the 14 industries covered in this book in order to discern which conditions have promoted labor–management cooperation in the United States during the latter period.

This analysis of labor–management cooperation differs in two ways from much of the research on cooperation. First, I distinguish between labor–management consensus on employment issues and formal labor–management cooperation. Formal cooperation, the object of analysis in this chapter, refers to committees or other joint bodies which are composed of labor and management representatives who participate in advisory or binding, enterprise- or industry-level decision making on management issues. Formal cooperation entails institutionalized labor participation in managerial decision making beyond the issues that pertain directly to the employment relationship. Hence, while the "opposite" of labor–management consensus, or informal cooperation, is conflict, the opposite of formal cooperation—or, more appropriately, the historical and empirical alternative to formal cooperation—has been bargaining in an adversarial labor–management relationship.[9] Indeed, formal cooperation has been the exception in the United States, where the adversarial relationship based in individual or collective bargaining has predominated. In no period of U.S. history have more than a

---

[8]A. B. Wolfe, *Works Committees and Joint Industrial Councils* (Philadelphia: United States Shipping Board, Emergency Fleet Corporation, Industrial Relations Division, 1919); Carrol French, *The Shop Committee in the United States*, Johns Hopkins University Studies in Historical and Political Science, Series 41, no. 2 (Baltimore: Johns Hopkins Press, 1923); Sumner Slichter, *Union Policies and Industrial Management* (Washington, DC: The Brookings Institution, 1941); Carol Riegelman, *Labour–Management Co-operation in United States War Production* (Montreal: International Labour Office, 1948); Dorothea de Schweinitz, *Labor and Management in a Common Enterprise* (Cambridge: Harvard University Press, 1949); Clinton Golden and Virginia Parker, eds., *Causes of Industrial Peace under Collective Bargaining* (New York: Harper & Brothers, 1955); Milton Derber, *The American Idea of Industrial Democracy, 1865–1965* (Urbana: University of Illinois Press, 1970); H. M. Douty, *Labor–Management Productivity Committees in American Industry* (Washington,DC: National Commission on Productivity and Work Quality, 1975); King and van de Vall; U.S. Bureau of International Labor Affairs, *Industrial Democracy in 12 Nations*, Monograph No. 2 (Washington, DC: GPO, 1979); William Moye, "Presidential Labor–Management Committees: Productive Failures," *Industrial and Labor Relations Review* 34 (October 1980), pp. 51–66; U.S. Labor–Management Services Administration and Bureau of Labor Statistics, *Labor–Management Cooperation: Recent Efforts and Results*, LMSA Publication 6 and BLS Bulletin no. 2153 (Washington, DC: GPO, 1982); Sanford Jacoby, "Union–Management Cooperation in the United States: Lessons from the 1920s," *Industrial and Labor Relations Review* 37 (October 1983), pp. 18–33; Michael Schuster, "The Impact of Union–Management Cooperation on Productivity and Employment," *Industrial and Labor Relations Review* 36 (April 1983), pp. 415–430 and "Models of Cooperation and Change in Union Settings," *Industrial Relations* 24 (Fall 1985), pp. 382–394.

[9]For a discussion of cooperation which illustrates the informal meaning, see Richard Walton and Robert McKersie, *A Behavioral Theory of Labor Negotiations* (New York: McGraw-Hill, 1965), pp. 184–221; on the formal meaning of cooperation, see Carole Pateman, *Participation and Democratic Theory* (Cambridge: Cambridge University Press, 1970), pp. 70–71.

tiny fraction of business establishments institutionalized cooperative decision making.[10]

The second way in which my analysis differs from other research on cooperation concerns the relationship between collective bargaining and formal cooperation. Collective bargaining and formal cooperation are often regarded as alternatives to one another or as opposites. This conception derives from the tendency of research on formal cooperation to focus solely on unionized settings.[11] However, as I argue below, one of the major differences between formal cooperation and the adversarial relationship is that the former has almost never been found in non-union settings, where individual bargaining between labor and management prevails. Empirically, collective bargaining appears to be a prerequisite for formal cooperation, rather than a mutually exclusive alternative.

Collective bargaining is enmeshed in a set of three factors which have contributed to the development of formal cooperation. First, cooperation assumes a long-term vested *interest* of labor in the survival of a particular business enterprise. The advent of internal labor markets with seniority-based rules for allocating and compensating labor, rules which have been often advocated by the labor movement in collective bargaining, has stabilized employment, tying the interests of workers to continuous service with one employer and, therefore, to the financial viability of the enterprise itself. Similarly, the shift from craft to industrial unionism, in which the local union membership is largely defined by a shop-specific work force rather than a location- and craft-specific group of casual laborers, has made local union survival directly dependent on that of a specific employer.[12]

Second, in a society where the adversarial relationship has prevailed and preceded the development of formal cooperation, labor's main source of influence at the workplace has been the threat of withholding labor from the employer. Under individual bargaining, the most prevalent variant of the adversarial relationship, the individual employee has little capacity for disrupting production and, therefore, for gaining a say in management, which is otherwise reserved for the enterprise owner or his/her managerial surrogates. With the power of the union largely based on its capacity for disrupting

[10]Derber; Philip Selznick, *Law, Society, and Industrial Justice* (New York: Russell Sage, 1969).

[11]See, for example, Schuster, "The Impact of Union–Management Cooperation" and "Models of Cooperation"; Thomas Kochan and Lee Dyer, "A Model of Organizational Change in the Context of Union–Management Relations," *Journal of Applied Behavioral Science* 12 (January-February-March 1976), pp. 59–78; Lee Dyer, David Lipsky and Thomas Kochan, "Union Attitudes toward Management Cooperation," *Industrial Relations* 16 (May 1977), pp. 163–172; Robert Thomas, "Quality and Quantity? Worker Participation in the U.S. and Japanese Automobile Industries," in *Technological Change and Workers' Movements,* ed. Melvyn Dubofsky (Beverly Hills: Sage, 1985), pp. 162–188.

[12]Slichter *et al., The Impact of Collective Bargaining,* p. 841; Daniel Cornfield, "Declining Union Membership in the Post-World War II Era: The United Furniture Workers of America, 1939–1982," *American Journal of Sociology* 91 (March 1986), pp. 1112–1153.

production by striking,[13] collective bargaining has provided some workers with the *power* to demand participation in management.

Third, an *external threat* to the viability of the business enterprise has to be present in order to motivate both labor and management to perceive any value in cooperation.[14] In the twentieth century, unionization and collective bargaining have been concentrated in metal working and mass production industries that were prone to major external threats—wartime labor shortages, foreign competition and government deregulation. Therefore, the motivation to institutionalize cooperation has often occurred in industries that were already engaged in collective bargaining.

However, the effect of these three forces on the development of formal, labor–management cooperation partly rested on organized labor's acceptance of the adversarial employment relationship and the wage system. It also rested on the spreading of unionization into the mass production industries.

As used in the nineteenth century, the term "cooperation" mainly referred to joint business ventures among self-employed manual workers or producer cooperatives. Producer cooperatives, which were espoused by the Knights of Labor in the late nineteenth century, originated in the romantic rejections of urban factory life and the wage-system during the 1830s and were promoted by such reformers as Robert Owen, Albert Brisbane, and Horace Greeley.[15]

By the early twentieth century, "cooperation" referred to both parties of the labor–management relationship. The late nineteenth century, when the American Federation of Labor (AFL) supplanted the Knights as the major U.S. labor organization, constituted a turning point in organized labor's attitude toward the wage system. By rejecting the earlier ideas of reform and accepting the wage system, the AFL effectively developed an ideological foundation for adversarial collective bargaining as well as for labor–management cooperation.[16]

During the twentieth century, the meaning of "cooperation" shifted from labor–management consensus toward formal cooperation. This shift in meaning is evident in the four major periods in which different types of labor–management committees flourished. The World War I and 1920s periods reflect an emphasis on consensus, while the World War II and 1970s–present periods suggest an emergence of the formal meaning.

A. World War I: Legitimizing Collective Representation

The establishment of labor–management committees during World War I was not only novel, it also constituted a first effort at legitimizing the collec-

---

[13]Daniel Cornfield, "Economic Segmentation and Expression of Labor Unrest: Striking versus Quitting in the Manufacturing Sector," *Social Science Quarterly* 66 (June 1985), pp. 247–265.

[14]Kochan and Dyer; Schuster, "Models of Cooperation."

[15]John Commons, David Saposs, Helen Sumner, E. B. Mittelman, H. E. Hoagland, John Andrews, and Selig Perlman, *History of Labour in the United States* (New York: Macmillan, 1918), vol. 1, pp. 493–521 and vol. 2, pp. 430–438.

[16]Ibid., volume II, pp. 430–438, 519–520; Daniel Rodgers, *The Work Ethic in Industrial America 1850–1920* (Chicago: University of Chicago Press, 1974).

tive representation of employees in specific shops or establishments. In order to ensure industrial peace and productivity in the war industries, President Wilson declared in 1918 that during the War workers were to have the right to unionize and to engage in collective bargaining; strikes and lockouts were prohibited; and, existing union shop and open shop agreements were to be honored. The AFL and the National Industrial Conference Board (NICB), representing employers, agreed to these principles.[17]

Collective representation, in the form of labor–management commitees, was effectively implemented in the war production industries by the National War Labor Board, U.S. Fuel Administration, U.S. Railroad Administration, and the Shipbuilding Labor Adjustment Board. These government agencies attempted to forestall or settle labor disputes by establishing joint labor–management committees in specific private business enterprises. On the eve of the War, some 20 committees had already been established at employer initiative in the United States. According to a 1919 NICB survey, the War spawned 225 committees, 53% of which had been established by the government agencies and the remainder at the initiative of employers. Over 80% of the committees were established in war industries: metal trades, shipbuilding, and coal and iron mining.[18]

Collective representation during World War I was not synonymous with unionization and collective bargaining. About half of the committees were established in unionized shops. Nonetheless, most of the committees consisted of equal numbers of worker and management representatives who dealt mainly with wage and hour adjustments and other issues that pertained directly to the employment relationship. Few committees addressed production issues.[19]

In sum, the labor–management committees of the World War I era constituted a commitment to informal cooperation. The committees served as a forum for bargaining over employment issues, rather than worker participation in managerial decision making. Through collective representation—with or without a union—labor and management were to achieve consensus on employment conditions and get on with the business of war production.

B. 1920s: Collective Bargaining or Employee Representation?

While the War Administration had given some legitimacy to collective representation, it did not mandate which form of collective representation, if any, was to prevail. The major labor relations issue after the war concerned the legitimacy of unionization. The chief contenders in the controversy were the AFL and the open-shop movement, led by anti-union employer groups such as the National Association of Manufacturers (NAM). Each espoused a model of collective representation.

---

[17]Valerie Conner, *The National War Labor Board* (Chapel Hill: University of North Carolina Press, 1983); W. Jett Lauck, *Political and Industrial Democracy 1776–1926* (New York: Funk & Wagnalls, 1926), pp. 12–16.

[18]French, pp. 17, 26; National Industrial Conference Board, *Works Councils in the United States*, Research Report no. 21 (Boston: National Industrial Conference Board, 1919), pp. 13–14.

[19]Ibid., pp. 69, 117.

The AFL espoused craft unionism and collective bargaining. However, several. factors, according to Wolman, led to an absolute decline in union membership during the 1920s, including: post-war demobilization of such unionized war production industries as metals, machinery, and shipbuilding; post-war disappearance of government support of collective bargaining; the growing incompatibility between AFL craft jurisdictions and mass-production factory work; aggressive employer resistance to unionization; technological unemployment of potentially organizable workers and union members; and the shift of such industries as clothing, textiles and coal mining to the non-union South. The percentage unionized of the U.S. work force declined from 17.5% to 9.3% between 1920 and 1930.[20]

Employee representation plans, the model advocated by the open-shop movement, flourished during the 1920s. Berated by the AFL as company unions, these plans were labor-management committees which were established at the initiative of the employer and were virtually identical in structure and function to those of the World War I era.

Following the endorsements of employee representation plans by the U.S. Chamber of Commerce in 1919 and the NAM in 1921, the number of plans grew rapidly through the mid-1920s. Most of the committees which were initiated by the government agencies during the war had disappeared by 1922. However, only about one-third of those initiated by employers had been discontinued by 1922. Moreover, NICB surveys identified 725 employer-initiated "works councils" in 1922 and 814 in 1924, almost a fourfold increase over the total number which were established during World War I.[21]

Employee representation plans predominated in non-union enterprises. A 1933 NICB survey of these plans showed that many had been established during the 1920s in non-union shops. Moreover, employee representation plans and unionization tended to develop in different industries. The 1933 NICB survey showed that almost three-fourths of unionized shops were found in coal mining, food products, metal working, clothing, and textiles; for employee representation plans, almost three-fourths were found in metal working, textiles, printing and publishing, wood and wood products, and paper and paper products. In the two industries in which both types of collective representation were found—metal working and textiles—establishments with employee representation plans outnumbered unionized shops by at least a twofold margin.[22]

---

[20]Leo Wolman, *Ebb and Flow in Trade Unionism* (New York: National Bureau of Economic Research, 1936), pp. 29–42, 116.

[21]National Industrial Conference Board, *Experience with Works Councils in the United States*, Research Report no. 50 (New York: National Industrial Conference Board, 1922), pp. 1, 4, 25, 34, and *The Growth of Works Councils in the United States*, Special Report Number 32 (New York: National Industrial Conference Board, 1925), p. 5; Ernest Burton, *Employee Representation* (Baltimore: Williams & Wilkins, 1926); French, p. 30.

[22]National Industrial Conference Board, *Individual and Collective Bargaining under the N.I.R.A.* (New York: National Industrial Conference Board, 1933), pp. 16, 22, 24 and *Individual and Collective Bargaining in May, 1934* (New York: National Industrial Conference Board, 1934).

Amidst the collective representation controversy and union decline of the 1920s, a handful of companies in the railroad, clothing, and textile industries established *union*–management committees. According to Jacoby, these committees were established "under dire economic circumstances," such as competition from non-union competitors and declining industry growth rates.[23] The committees operated alongside of collective bargaining and dealt with such management decisions as setting production standards, conducting market studies, and determining production methods, in addition to resolving employment-related issues. As such, these committees constituted the first effort in the United States at formal cooperation, but they were a small exception in an era which was characterized otherwise by the controversy over which form, if any, of collective representation was to prevail.[24]

In sum, the employee representation plans of the 1920s were an outcome of the broader labor relations controversy concerning the type of collective representation in the shop. Like the World War I committees, they served as forums for bargaining over employment conditions, rather than labor participation in managerial decision making. To this extent, they constituted an effort on the part of employers to generate informal cooperation without collective bargaining.

Although the employee representation plan emerged victorious in the contest between types of collective representation during the 1920s, the outcome of the contest was reversed by the New Deal Administration during the Great Depression of the 1930s. The National Industrial Recovery Act of 1933 and the National Labor Relations Act of 1935 effectively prohibited company unions and employer interference in union organizing and allowed workers of a specific shop to choose unionization through a representation election. However, most of the union–management cooperation arrangements did not survive the Depression, as the issue of job security assumed a greater importance than cooperation. Employee representation plans met their official demise in 1937 when the Supreme Court prohibited company unions by upholding the National Labor Relations Act. Moreover, the percentage unionized in manufacturing increased from 9% to 34% between 1930 and 1940.[25]

C. World War II: Limited Formal Cooperation

The labor–management committees which were established during World War II constituted a limited effort at formal cooperation. The effort was limited with respect to the prevalence and scope of the committees. Although over 5,000 establishments set up committees during the war, far exceeding the numbers of committees in the previous eras, they accounted for a minority of war-goods-producing establishments. The committees were limited in

---

[23]Jacoby, "Union–Management Cooperation," pp. 27–29.
[24]Ibid.
[25]Derber, pp. 299–301.

their scope in that a minority addressed production problems. Furthermore, those committees which addressed production problems did so mainly at the intra-plant and shop floor decision making levels. Committee involvement in long-range planning decisions about engineering, plant organization, marketing, and finance was relatively rare.[26] Indeed, the issue about the type of management decisions in which labor was to participate partly shaped the functions of labor–management committees in this era.

Labor shortages and partial utilization of plant capacity were two problems in production that were identified by the government. In 1942, the U.S. Bureau of Labor Statistics (BLS) estimated that the President's $50 billion war production program would require 10 million more workers than were already employed in the war industries in December 1941. Other reports held that 2 million workers would be withdrawn from the labor force by the Armed Services in 1942. Furthermore, in the Spring of 1942, the War Production Board received reports from an increasing number of war goods producers that labor shortages were interfering with maximum plant utilization.[27]

Announced in March 1942, the War Production Drive was one of many steps taken by the War Production Board to address the labor shortage and plant utilization problems in civilian war production. The purpose of the Drive was "to encourage the voluntary establishment of joint labor–management plant committees as incentives to increased plant output."[28]

Organized labor gave its support to the War Production Drive. Three unions affiliated with the Congress of Industrial Organizations (CIO)—Steel Workers, Automobile Workers and the Electrical Workers—and the AFL-affiliated Machinists had begun to urge the establishment of factory committees before the initiation of the War Production Drive.[29] Although many trade unionists "feared that management might use the committees to dominate labor and thwart unionism,"[30] both the CIO and the AFL announced their support of the War Production Drive in 1942.

The issue about labor participation in management decision making was especially reflected in employer reactions to the announcement of the Drive. According to de Schweinitz, "management feared that labor might take over its prerogatives."[31] Riegelman claims, for example, that "the National Association of Manufacturers initially received the proposal with some skepticism, asking first whether it was not, in fact, an acceptance of labour's desire to enter the field of management's prerogatives."[32] Nonetheless, both the NAM and the United States Chamber of Commerce endorsed the Drive in 1942.

---

[26]Riegelman, pp. 184, 223; de Schweinitz, p. 70.
[27]U.S. Bureau of Demobilization, *Industrial Mobilization for War: History of the War Production Board and Predecessor Agencies 1940–1945*, vol. 1, General Study no. 1 (Washington, DC: GPO, 1947), pp. 411, 416.
[28]Ibid., p. 423. Also, see Riegelman, p. 186.
[29]Riegelman, p. 185; de Schweinitz, p. 13; Sanford Jacoby, "Union–Management Cooperation in the United States during the Second World War," in *Technological Change and Workers' Movements*, ed. Melvyn Dubofsky (Beverly Hills: Sage, 1985), pp. 100–129.
[30]De Schweinitz, p. 35. Also, see Reigelman, pp. 186–187.
[31]De Schweinitz, p. 35.
[32]Riegelman, p. 187.

Although some 20,000 war contractors were approached by the War Production Board to establish labor–management committees, only 5,000 reported that committees had been organized. The number of committees increased by a fivefold margin between 1942 and 1944, from 932 to 4,835. Committees were established mainly in war production industries. Almost two-thirds of the committees in operation during 1944 were in the ordnance, iron and steel, coal and iron mining, machinery, synthetic products, textiles, communications equipment, and non-ferrous metals industries. Furthermore, given the rapid and widespread unionization of mass production industries during the 1930s and World War II, over three-fourths of the committees were established in unionized shops.[33]

The committees, typically comprising equal numbers of worker and management representatives, often received and considered suggestions from rank and file workers through a suggestion system which had already been established in the plant before the War. Many companies awarded individual workers for meritorious suggestions and the War Production Board awarded civilian workers whose suggestions had industry- and nation-wide applicability.[34]

Few committees addressed production issues. According to de Schweinitz, 10% to 20% of the 5,000 committees which operated during the war dealt with such intra-plant production issues as improving production methods and work quality, conservation of materials, care of tools and equipment, and discussion of production schedules.[35] The remainder conducted war activities such as rallies, handled employee transportation, and addressed absenteeism and safety. Several hundred committees either "registered but never functioned," or conducted "one patriotic rally."[36]

The relegation of committee decision making to intraplant production issues, rather than to long-range, managerial planning, resulted from efforts taken by the War Production Drive, management, and organized labor. In order to gain the support of employers, the War Production Drive emphasized that committees were not to be designed "to conform to any plan that contemplates a measure of control of management by labour."[37] Indeed, organized labor accepted this ground rule and most of the committees which addressed production problems were chaired by the top operating official of the plant. Among the many intra-plant production problems recommended by the Drive for committee action were quality of work, improvements in the use of tools, elimination of bottlenecks, conservation and salvage of materials, and preventing absenteeism. Also, some committees were prevented from discussing technical production issues by Government departments which required military secrecy.[38]

Management attempted to confine committee deliberations to intra-plant

[33]De Schweinitz, pp. 18–23.
[34]Riegelman, pp. 226, 230.
[35]Ibid., pp. 231–237; De Schweinitz, pp. 19, 36.
[36]De Schweinitz, p. 19. Also, see Riegelman, pp. 238–249.
[37]Riegelman, p. 199.
[38]Ibid., pp. 199–200, 224; De Schweinitz, p. 94.

production issues for two reasons. The first was company competitiveness in the market. Fearing the disclosure of trade secrets and plant inefficiency, top management was often unwilling to share information about production plans and processes with the committee. Second, management argued frequently that committee members lacked sufficient technical knowledge for making production decisions, an argument which often received support from the engineering department of a company. In many instances, the committees lacked competent technical representation.[39]

The impact of organized labor on limited committee involvement in managerial decision making stemmed from labor's commitment to union organizing and collective bargaining during the War. The rate of union membership growth in the United States exceeded 50% during the War. For unions which participated in many of the labor–management committees, such as the Automobile Workers, Steel Workers, Machinists, Carpenters, Rubber Workers, Boilermakers, and the International Brotherhood of Electrical Workers, the rates of membership growth between 1940 and 1945 varied from 100% to 263%.[40] Between 1940 and 1947, the percentage unionized increased from 30.5% to 40.5% in manufacturing; 72.1% to 83.1% in mining; and 47.3% to 67.0% in transportation. Furthermore, it was estimated that over 1,000 new or renewed labor agreements were signed every week during the war.[41]

The worker representatives on committees in unionized plants were often those who actively participated in collective bargaining and union organizing—union officers, shop stewards, business agents, and organizers. Given the high volume of organizing and bargaining activity during the War, "most of the trade union organizations . . . were overworked and understaffed, and therefore in many instances relegated to a position of secondary importance the promotion of joint committees in the plants."[42] According to de Schweinitz, organizing and collective bargaining detracted from the time available to both unions and employers for participation on joint committees.[43]

The rapid increase of unionization in the mass production industries during the 1930s and the war years facilitated formal cooperation in the latter period in three ways. First, seniority rules for allocating and compensating labor proliferated with unionization, giving workers a long-term vested interest in their employers. The rate of quitting had declined since the 1910s as employers increasingly adopted seniority rules.[44] According to Jacoby, the percentage of all industrial firms using seniority rules increased from 50% in 1939–40 to 83% in 1946–48; and, the percentage in which layoffs resulted in

[39]Riegelman, pp. 205, 223–224; De Schweinitz, p. 70.

[40]De Schweinitz, pp. 24–25, 29; Leo Troy and Neil Sheflin, *Union Sourcebook* (West Orange, NJ: Industrial Relations Data and Information Services, 1985), Appendix B, pp. 1–20.

[41]De Schweinitz, p. 29; Troy and Sheflin, Chapter 3, p. 15.

[42]Riegelman, p. 196.

[43]De Schweinitz, p. 29. Also, see Reigelman, p. 207.

[44]Sanford Jacoby, "Industrial Labor Mobility in Historical Perspective," *Industrial Relations* 22 (Spring 1983), pp. 268, 276.

the loss of all seniority declined from 3% in 1935–36 to 1% in 1946–48.[45] Second, unionization had spread in the mass-production industries, providing workers not only with the collective strength which derived from unionization itself, but also with experienced leaders who could serve effectively on committees. Third, war production problems—labor shortages and plant under-utilization—occurred in the highly unionized war production industries, compelling labor and management, with the urging of the War Production Board, to develop forums for cooperative decision making.

Nonetheless, the newness of both unionization and formal cooperation limited the prevalence and scope of labor participation in managerial decision making. Despite their support and involvement in the War Production Drive, unions concentrated their efforts on organizing and bargaining, giving less attention to participation in committees. Cautiously guarding their managerial prerogatives, employers were typically unwilling to share information that pertained to long-run production, engineering, marketing, and finance issues. In an effort to gain employer support, the War Production Board promoted cooperative decision making on intra-plant issues.

By 1947, approximately 70% of the committees which were established during the war had been dissolved.[46] The post-war dissolution of the committees partly reflects their limited decision making scope and attention to war-related activities as well as the end of war production problems. As de Schweinitz put it, "the activities for which committees were especially responsible—bond drives, car-pooling, blood bank, Army-Navy E celebrations, patriotic rallies—became less important or ceased entirely."[47] According to a BLS study on the discontinuation of labor–management committees, 62% of the establishments surveyed reported "end of war" or "lack of interest" as the reason for discontinuation.[48]

After the war, the compulsion for labor and management to engage in cooperative decision making dissipated in the growth economy of the 1950s. Collective bargaining entered its so-called "Golden Age," when labor and management established the basic package of employer-provided fringe benefits—retirement pensions and health and life insurance plans—cost of living allowances, and periodic wage increases.[49] The question of labor–management cooperation was not to return until the 1970s.

D. 1970s–Present: Labor–Management Cooperation or Managerial Control?

Recent developments in formal cooperation, described earlier in this chapter and chapters 9–15, are unique in comparison to those of the 1920s

---

[45]Sanford Jacoby, "The Development of Internal Labor Markets in American Manufacturing Firms," in *Internal Labor Markets,* ed. Paul Osterman (Cambridge: MIT Press, 1984), p. 48.

[46]De Schweinitz, p. 32.

[47]Ibid., p. 33.

[48]Ibid., p. 34.

[49]Jack Stieber, Robert McKersie, and D. Quinn Mills, eds., *U.S. Industrial Relations 1950–1980: A Critical Assessment* (Madison: WI: Industrial Relations Research Association, 1981), p. iv.

and World War II eras because they entail labor participation in company- and, in some cases, industry-wide decision making. Like the experiments in union–management cooperation during the 1920s, formal cooperation is now occurring in industries which are experiencing macroeconomic adversity from such causes as foreign competition and government deregulation. Also, like the earlier efforts at formal cooperation, the recent ones are found in only a small proportion of business establishments. According to BLS surveys of labor agreements covering 1,000 or more workers, less than 5% had provisions for joint labor–management productivity committees in 1963–64 and 1980.[50] Nevertheless, many of the recent developments, including some described in chapters 9–15, have occurred alongside of collective bargaining and are not reflected in the BLS statistics.

Formal cooperation is one of a set of labor relations arrangements (others include individual and collective bargaining) that management and labor have devised for reconciling their divergent interests in, and controlling the implementation and outcomes of, technological change during the 1970s and 1980s. The following comparison of the 14 industries covered in this book shows how industry and product market characteristics have shaped the diverse ways in which labor and management have attempted to control technological change during the 1970s and 1980s.

The industries covered in Part II of this book—agriculture, newspaper printing, longshoring, the Postal Service, insurance, public school education, and air traffic control—show no signs of cooperative developments. Instead, managements have adopted control strategies of the types described by Braverman and Edwards. The trends in increased managerial control in these industries, analyzed in Chapters 2–8, are summarized here. In agriculture, management has adopted technical control when the supply of politically vulnerable non-citizen labor was scarce, and direct personal supervision of workers, what Edwards refers to as "simple control," when the supply of such labor was more abundant; among newspaper printers, the advent of computerized printing has deskilled the work force and facilitated the implementation of technical control; with computerized containerization, longshoremen increasingly work under technical control and, with the employment decasualization accompanying the advent of full-time "steady men," management has begun to implement bureaucratic control; in the Postal Service, automation has led to deskilling and technical control, while labor arbitrations have upheld management's right to define new positions with the adoption of new technology; in insurance, management has gained technical control through office automation and deskilling and has adopted bureaucratic control of clerical workers by implementing a paternalistic managerial philosophy; the traditional professional autonomy of school teachers has been jeopardized by the implementation of computerized educational tech-

---

[50]U.S. Bureau of Labor Statistics, *Management Rights and Union–Management Cooperation*, Bulletin no. 1425-5 (Washington, DC: GPO, 1966), p. 25 and *Characteristics of Major Collective Bargaining Agreements, January 1, 1980*, Bulletin no. 2095 (Washington, DC: GPO, 1981), p. 32.

nologies, allowing principals and school boards to exercise greater technical and bureaucratic control; with the demise of PATCO and the adoption of more automated air traffic control technology, management has deskilled air controllers, implemented technical control, and adopted centralized bureaucratic control of the air controllers.

In contrast, the industries covered in Part III of this book—coal mining, automobiles, steel, construction equipment, commercial aircraft, public sanitation and telecommunications—have developed formal labor–management cooperation. The developments in formal cooperation in these industries are analyzed in chapters 9–15 and are summarized here. In 1978, the coal mining industry established the UMWA Industry Development Committee (renamed the UMWA-BCOA Joint Interests Committee in 1984), in order to study and resolve issues pertaining to job security, technological change, industry competitiveness, productivity, and labor relations. In automobile manufacturing, the United Auto Workers (UAW) and General Motors (GM) developed a national quality of work life program in 1973; the UAW gained a seat on the Chrysler board in 1979 and the right to discuss outsourcing problems with auto executives in 1984; at GM, the UAW helped to establish and has participated in the operation of a job bank since 1984, as well as in the planning of the new Saturn plant and in national, long-term development committees. In the steel industry, the United Steelworkers and company representatives lobbied jointly in support of import quotas in 1968 and 1978; joint productivity committees were established in 1971 and Alert Committees were established in 1977 to ward off plant closings; and, in 1980, the Tripartite Advisory Committee, comprised of union, steel company and government representatives, was established to study steel industry problems and to propose legislative changes. Although no measures of formal cooperation have been developed in construction equipment manufacturing, the UAW and Caterpillar have begun to discuss possible worker participation in company decision making. In aircraft manufacturing, the Machinists and Boeing established a labor–management technology committee in 1983 which identifies new skills that accompany technological change and refers laid off workers to a training program. In public sanitation, "integrative bargaining," coupled with joint labor–management committees that address issues associated with productivity and technological change, has become increasingly prevalent since the 1970s. In 1976, the Communication Workers of America (CWA) and AT&T lobbied unsuccessfully for the Consumer Communications Reform Act, which would have prohibited the duplication of AT&T services by other telecommunications carriers; in 1980, the CWA, International Brotherhood of Electrical Workers and AT&T established joint labor–management committees for monitoring and addressing issues pertaining to quality of work life, job evaluation, technological change, and training.

The industries which have developed measures of formal cooperation share three features which distinguish them from the other industries, as shown in Table 1. The first feature is long employee tenure on the job. Comparable job tenure data for all industries are unavailable. However, the BLS

Table 1. Selected Characteristics of 14 Industries[a]

Industry or Occupation	(1) 1970–78 mean quit rate[b]	(2) 1981 median years on job	(3) (4) Percentage unionized in:		(5) Presence and type of external threat[c]
			1974	1980	
Industries with formal cooperation					
Coal mining	0.8	n.a.	72.7	66.4	1,2,3
Automobiles	1.0	9.8	·71.9	66.0	1
Steel	0.6	n.a.	73.0	69.2	1,2
Construction Equipment	1.2	n.a.	47.4	43.8	1
Aircraft	0.7	n.a.	41.6	43.5	1,4
Public Sanitation	n.a.	n.a.	50.1[d]	43.8[d]	2,4
Telecommunications	0.7	n.a.	60.5	64.2	2,4
Industries without formal cooperation					
Farm Laborers	n.a.	2.7[e]	3.0	2.2	None
Newspaper Printing	2.2	n.a.	19.2	19.2	None
Longshoremen	n.a.	n.a.	76.5	71.2	None
Postal Service	n.a.	9.3	65.2	75.0	None
Insurance	n.a.	3.0[f]	4.3	4.4	None
Public School Teachers	n.a.	5.9[g]	73.7[d]	64.3[d]	None
Air Controllers	n.a.	n.a.	29.1	59.8	None
All Industries	2.0[h]	3.4	24.5	20.9	

[a]Source: For column 1, U.S. Bureau of Labor Statistics, *Employment and Earnings, United States, 1908–78*, Bulletin no. 1312–11 (Washington, DC: GPO, 1979); for column 2, U.S. Bureau of Labor Statistics, *Job Tenure and Occupational Change, 1981*, Bulletin no. 2162 (Washington, DC: GPO, 1983); for columns 3 and 4, Edward Kokkelenberg and Donna Sockell, "Union Membership in the United States, 1973–1981," *Industrial and Labor Relations Review* 38 (July 1985), pp. 497–543 and U.S. Bureau of the Census, *1982 Census of Governments, Labor–Management Relations in State and Local Governments*, GC82(3)-3 (Washington, DC: GPO, 1985), pp. vi, 2.
[b]Average annual number of monthly quits per 100 full-time employees.
[c]Key for external threat codes: 1 = foreign competition; 2 = domestic, non-union competition; 3 = declining product demand from increasing product substitution; 4 = declining government purchases or support.
[d]1972 and 1982 data.
[e]Includes supervisors.
[f]Finance, insurance and real estate.
[g]Includes private school teachers
[h]All manufacturing industries.

publishes quit rate data for some industries and/or tenure data for others, shown in columns 1 and 2, respectively, in Table 1. All of the industries with formal cooperation, shown in the upper panel of Table 1, have either below-average quit rates and/or above-average, employee, on-the-job tenure. Most of the industries which lack formal cooperation have either high quit rates or below average job tenure. Exceptions are the Postal Service and public school teachers. Data on quit rates and job tenure are unavailable for longshoring and air controllers. In the case of longshoring, in which the system of casual employment, whereby contractors hire workers through the union hiring hall, has only recently begun to be replaced by the employment of full-time "steady men," job tenure with specific employers is likely to be very low. With the replacement of the PATCO strikers by non-union air controllers after the demise of PATCO in 1981, it is likely that air controller job tenure has since declined.

Second, the industries with formal cooperation are distinguished by their uniformly high percentages of unionized workers, shown in columns 3 and 4 of Table 1. The percentages of unionized workers in all of these industries exceeded the national average in 1974 and 1980. Moreover, these industries have been widely unionized for approximately 40 to 50 years. In contrast, most of the industries which lack formal cooperation have relatively low unionization. In the case of air controllers, unionization grew rapidly during the 1970s and then disappeared after the decertification of PATCO in 1981. Exceptions are longshoring, public school teachers, and the Postal Service.

The third distinguishing feature of the industries with formal cooperation is the presence of an external threat to the industry which jeopardizes both job security and profits, as shown in column 5 of Table 1. These external threats are analyzed in greater detail in the preceding chapters and are summarized here. Eastern coal mining companies are threatened by foreign coal imports, the substitution of oil and gas for coal, the rise of Western coal mining, and domestic, non-union competition. In the steel industry, unionized, integrated producers are threatened by foreign imports and the growth of non-union, domestic "mini-mills" and other non-integrated producers. U.S. automobile manufacturing and construction equipment manufacturing are threatened by foreign imports. Similarly, aircraft manufacturing has been threatened by foreign imports, declining government support of research and development, and declining government purchases. With recent government deregulation, the Bell System is threatened by the entry of non-union, long-distance telephone and other telecommunications carriers. The citizen tax revolts during the 1970s led many municipal sanitation departments to "privatize" sanitation collection by contracting with non-union providers. The industries which lack formal cooperation are characterized not only by the absence of external threats, but also by favorable macroeconomic conditions.

In sum, the industries with formal cooperation are characterized simultaneously by the three conditions which were mentioned earlier and hypothesized to motivate and facilitate formal cooperation: worker interest vested in the employer, high unionization and bargaining strength, *and* the presence of an external threat to the viability of the industry. In contrast, the industries which lack formal cooperation are characterized by no more than two of these three conditions and all have experienced favorable macroeconomic conditions in recent years.

Unionization is associated in three ways with the recent developments in formal cooperation. First, as a force in promoting the use of seniority rules, the labor movement has helped to build internal labor markets and thereby to stabilize employment. By subsequently vesting the long-term interests of workers in their employers, unions contributed to the establishment of bureaucratic control. However, such bureaucratic control in the shop or office has contributed to the establishment of formal cooperation, with union involvement in company- and industry-wide managerial decision making. Workers and their unions gained a vested interest in the survival of their employers and hence a desire for representation in management, especially during periods of adverse market conditions.

Second, unionization has given those workers who are motivated to establish formal cooperation the bargaining strength to request or demand cooperation. Indeed, the establishment of formal cooperation has often occurred in the wake of bitter strikes or under a strike threat, as shown in Chapters 9–15. Cases in point include the beginning of discussions on cooperation between the United Automobile Workers and Caterpillar after a 7-month strike in 1982–83; in coal mining, the UMWA Industry Development Committee was established after a 111-day strike, the longest strike in the history of the United Mine Workers; and, the 1973 quality of work life program at General Motors (GM) followed numerous strikes in the auto industry during the late 1960s and early 1970s, including a 67-day strike at GM in 1970.

Third, the external threats which have recently motivated formal cooperation have tended to occur in the oligopolistic, mass production industries which have been widely unionized since the late 1930s. As other industrialized and industrializing nations increase their exports to the United States and other nations, the dominant position of U.S. producers in the world market, along with U.S. union memberships and job security, are jeopardized. Similarly, declining government support of unionized, oligopolistic industries, whether through decreasing government purchases, privatization, or deregulation of entry, have jeopardized the formerly protected and stable financial status of these industries, motivating management and labor to engage in cooperative decision making. In these respects, the entry of foreign and domestic non-union producers into a unionized, oligopolistic industry, has contributed to the development of formal cooperation in the unionized sectors of some mass production industries.

In sum, this comparison of 14 industries suggests that the institutionalized responses of an industry to technological change—increasing unilateral managerial control or increasing formal, labor–management cooperation—are shaped by both the legacy of labor relations and the macroeconomic conditions in an industry. The comparison implies that management has been able to exert greater technical or bureaucratic control over the work force in less unionized, high-growth industries. In unionized, low-growth industries, management may have exerted greater technical and bureaucratic control in the shop or office, but labor has increased its control over company- and industry-wide managerial decision making during the 1970s and early 1980s.

The comparison of the 14 industries also suggests that forces external to the firm, especially the labor movement and product market conditions, have motivated and facilitated the efforts taken by labor and management to redistribute work place authority. However, the neo-Marxian and post-industrial theories have emphasized the impact of such intra-firm forces as technological change, capital accumulation and work place rationalization on the capacity of management to control work. Missing from these theories are those external forces which have affected the motivation and capacity of both labor and management to institutionalize cooperative or adversarial relationships. As such, these theories account for a process—increased unilateral managerial control—which has mainly occurred in high-growth, less unionized industries, where the adversarial relationship based in individual bargaining prevails; where labor has little capacity for gaining a say in managerial decision making; and where management has not been motivated to share decision making with labor.

Unevenness in unionization and product market conditions has generated diverse trends in labor relations arrangements among U.S. industries during the post-World War II era. This suggests that the likelihood of labor participation in managerial decision making varies directly with the extent of unionization and the adversity of product market conditions in an industry.

The foregoing also suggests that three forces could unravel cooperative, labor–management arrangements. First, the return of favorable macroeconomic conditions to an industry may reduce the compulsion for the two parties to cooperate and motivate them to pursue their divergent interests in an adversarial relationship.

Second, the price of formal cooperation for labor, as shown in chapters 9– 15, often includes layoffs, union membership losses, wage concessions, and two-tier wage structures, in which new employees are hired in at a wage scale which is lower than that which is applied to the extant work force. This price for cooperation may erode the bargaining strength of the unionized work force if it results in significant losses in union membership dues and in the percentage of unionized workers in the industry. Furthermore, as shown by the cases of the steel and auto industries, the price of cooperation, especially wage concessions, may engender widespread rank-and-file unrest and possibly motivate the union to abandon its cooperative venture with management.

Third, the price of formal cooperation for management, namely, decreased control of decision making, may motivate management to seek alternative methods for overcoming the external threat to the industry. For example, in industries faced with foreign competition, such as automobiles, aircraft, construction equipment, steel, and coal mining, managements have established "coproduction" ventures with their foreign competitors—essentially developing cooperative relationships with other managements in addition to, or instead of, formal labor–management cooperation. Coproduction may not only reduce the external threat to the industry, but also lead to declines in both U.S. employment and union memberships. Therefore, coproduction may reduce the incentive for management to cooperate with labor, as well as labor's capacity to demand cooperation with management.

In short, just as collective bargaining has served as a prerequisite for the establishment of formal cooperation, it may also contribute to the dismantling of cooperative arrangements. The price paid by both adversaries for cooperation may generate labor–management tension and, thereby, return them to a more adversarial relationship.

IV. EMERGING PATTERNS OF LABOR RELATIONS IN THE UNITED STATES

How workers and managers advance their interests in technological change, and how they control the implementation and outcomes of technological change, have been affected by the legacy of labor relations in their industries and by the security of their industries in the market. The future course of unionization and industry security are likely to affect developments in labor relations—toward unilateral managerial control or labor–management cooperation—as workers and managers attempt to control technological change. The post-World War II decline in the percentage of unionized U.S. workers does not bode well for further diffusion of labor–management cooperation. By 1984, the percentage unionized of U.S. workers had declined to 19%, a comparable magnitude to that of the early 1920s; in manufacturing, the percentage unionized declined from 42% to 25% between 1953 and 1984.[51] This implies an erosion of the bargaining strength and capacity of labor for gaining participation in managerial decision making.

However, national political conditions are likely to affect the course of U.S. unionization, and therefore the likelihood of increased formal labor–management cooperation. Union membership has increased at its highest rates in eras when the Federal government supported unionization. These are the World War I and 1935–1947 eras.[52] During these eras, the government either condoned unionization and/or enacted pro-labor legislation (i.e., the 1935 Wagner Act) which limited employer interference in union organizing campaigns. Union membership growth rates declined after the passage of the 1947 Taft-Hartley Act which restricted the organizing capacity of unions in many ways.[53] This suggests that a return of pro-labor political conditions and the enactment of legislation which facilitates unionization could contribute to a reversal of the present trend of union decline and to further institutionalization of labor participation in managerial decision making. However, union membership growth depends not only on the capacity of unions to organize, but also on their ability to retain existing members. The absence of national legislation which regulates capital mobility within and out of the United States has led to plant shutdowns and union membership losses.[54] Therefore, the enactment of such legislation would be expected to slow the rate of union membership losses, if not reverse the decline.

National political conditions are likely to affect product market conditions

---

[51]Troy and Sheflin, chapter 3, p. 15. For analyses of declining union membership, see chapter 1 and Cornfield, "Declining Union Membership."

[52]Ibid.; also, see Wolman, *Ebb and Flow.*

[53]For a discussion of the effect of the Taft-Hartley Act on union organizing, see Cornfield, "Declining Union Membership."

[54]For discussions of capital mobility and its impact on labor and communities see Barry Bluestone and Bennett Harrison, *The Deindustrialization of America* (New York: Basic Books, 1982) and Warner Woodworth, Christopher Meek and William Foote Whyte, eds., *Industrial Democracy* (Beverly Hills: Sage, 1985).

and, therefore, labor–management motivation to institutionalize cooperative relationships. The current government emphasis on deregulating entry and facilitating the importation of foreign products into formerly protected industries and product markets has threatened labor and management alike, forging cooperative decision making between them. A shift toward a more protectionist international trade policy, and to the regulation of entry into product markets, could stabilize product markets and return labor and management to a more adversarial relationship.

In conclusion, how workers and managers control the implementation and outcomes of technological change, whether with increased managerial control or labor participation in managerial decision making, will depend on their capacities and motivation to redistribute authority in the work place. The continuation of political conditions which further the decline in unionization is likely to facilitate increased, unilateral managerial control of the workplace. However, a return of political conditions which favor unionization will not necessarily realize greater participation of labor in managerial decision making. Labor–management cooperation has flourished under adverse product market conditions; the adversarial employment relationship, based in individual or collective bargaining, has prevailed in periods of prosperity.

ACKNOWLEDGMENTS

I am gratefully indebted to Kenneth Betsalel, William Form and Randy Hodson for their helpful comments on earlier drafts, to Doris Davis and Mamie Padgett for typing the manuscript and to the AFL-CIO Department for Professional Employees for providing me with materials.

Index